Society and the Individual

Frank O. Taylor, Ph. D. | Lawrence J. Mencotti, Ph. D.

CENGAGE
Learning™

Australia • Brazil • Japan • Korea • Mexico • Singapore • Spain • United Kingdom • United States

CENGAGE
Learning™

Society and the Individual
Frank O. Taylor, Ph. D.
Lawrence J. Mencotti, Ph. D.

Executive Editors:
 Maureen Staudt
 Michael Stranz

Senior Project Development Manager:
 Linda deStefano

Marketing Specialist:
 Courtney Sheldon

Senior Production/Manufacturing Manager:
 Donna M. Brown

PreMedia Manager:
 Joel Brennecke

Sr. Rights Acquisition Account Manager:
 Todd Osborne

Cover Image:
Getty Images*

For product information and technology assistance, contact us at
Cengage Learning Customer & Sales Support, 1-800-354-9706

For permission to use material from this text or product,
submit all requests online at **cengage.com/permissions**
Further permissions questions can be emailed to
permissionrequest@cengage.com

Compilation © 2008 Cengage Learning

ISBN-13: 978-1-4266-2608-1

ISBN-10: 1-4266-2608-8

Cengage Learning
5191 Natorp Boulevard
Mason, Ohio 45040
USA

Cengage Learning is a leading provider of customized learning solutions with
office locations around the globe, including Singapore, the United Kingdom,
Australia, Mexico, Brazil, and Japan. Locate your local office at:
international.cengage.com/region.
Cengage Learning products are represented in Canada by Nelson Education, Ltd.
For your lifelong learning solutions, visit **custom.cengage.com.**
Visit our corporate website at **cengage.com.**

Printed in the United States of America

CONTENTS

BIOGRAPHIES

I received a Ph.D. in sociology from the University of Nebraska-Lincoln. I have taught in community colleges, private religious schools, and large state universities. Fourteen years into my career, I currently am a tenured Associate Professor of Sociology and serve as the chair of the Sociology Department at Edinboro University of Pennsylvania. I have also served as the President and Vice President of the Pennsylvania Sociological Society. I have taught most courses in sociology. My research interests include social psychology, the sociology of inequality, and gender. I have taught in high schools, prisons, trailers, by television, and the internet. I have taught in large lecture halls and broom closets, I'm sure. I am a very proud veteran of the United States Navy, and an avid sailor to this day! I dedicate this book to my daughter Karen, and my sons Daniel, Zachary, and Marshall, and to my parents, Frank and Margaret, and lastly, but not in the least, to my ever-supportive wife, Kathy. To my comrade-in-guitars, Mike, I say, "Thanks for being a friend." For those of you who know – *oooh rah!*

Frank Taylor

Let me introduce my coauthors.

Lawrence Mencotti is a distinguished professor of Sociology that, to the relief of many, has officially retired. Born in 1942, he acquired various degrees of literacy in several languages, with a special emphasis on vulgar phrases, before learning English through his family of origin and the Detroit Public School System. He grasped Sociology first in cooperation with Wayne State University [B.A. 1965] and Northwestern University [Ph.D. 1976], and later in occasionally obstinate disputes with these and other august educational institutions. For more than three decades Professor Mencotti taught at Edinboro University of Pennsylvania, influencing both the learning and lives of many future leaders, government officials, incarcerated felons, and others who have followed his teachings.

Alex Rice received his bachelor's degree in Sociology in December 2005 from Edinboro University of Pennsylvania, graduating Summa Cum Laude. He is currently pursuing a master's degree in social science with a concentration in Sociology at Edinboro. Recently, he helped co-author an introduction to sociology textbook titled Read This Book: Sociology Not for Dummies, with Frank Taylor, Lawrence Mencotti, and Ivan Chompalov as well as conducting a study on gender traits and human behavior published in Sociological Viewpoints. He plans to pursue his Ph.D. in Sociology in the spring of 2008. Alex would like to thank his wife Denise and daughter

Jessica for tolerating his abnormal behavior while assisting with this book. He would also like to thank the professors at Edinboro University for all of their assistance throughout his collegiate career, especially Dr. Frank Taylor, who has guided him into the wonderful world of academia. Without the support of these fine people, my accomplishments would not be possible.

Valerie R. Matteson is currently a graduate student about to finish her Master's degree at Edinboro University of Pennsylvania, where she also received her BA in Sociology and a minor in Psychology. She is a single mother residing with her daughter, Chelsea and their two cats. Facing many struggles and adversity throughout her life has given her the drive to succeed. She is succeeding with great support, compassion, and empathy from her family, her friends, and her professors, to them she says Thank You.☺

Reneé L. Pistory is currently the secretary for the Foreign Languages, Philosophy, and Sociology Departments at Edinboro University of Pennsylvania, and has been employed at Edinboro University since 1990. She is a Certified Professional Secretary® (CPS®) and a member of the International Association of Administrative Professionals® (IAAP®). In the past, she assisted Drs. Frank Taylor, Lawrence Mencotti, and Ivan Chompalov in editing *Read This Book: Sociology Not for Dummies*.

ഈ ഗ ഈ ൙

PREFACE

I have taught social psychology to students for a good many years. However, I have never really encountered a textbook I have been completely happy with. There are really two social psychologies – one leans more toward sociology and the other toward psychology. As a sociologist, I am, of course, more interested in sociological social psychology than the psychological branch. Thus, the main goal of this text is to focus on the *sociological* side of social psychology.

A second complaint I've had, over the years, is that most social psychology textbooks review thousands of experiments, individually. This has become overwhelming to read, both for me and my students, particularly since something about the research hypothesis and research methodology must be reviewed in each and every example. Is it necessary, for example, to cite and review two or three experiments for each and every point you want to make in reference to one concept or another? I have begun to feel that my fellow academics are more concerned about referring to everyone under the sun than they are with telling students what we think we know on the subjects of social psychology. In this textbook I am taking a different approach. I have written in a non-academic fashion, more like an essay or conversation, in which I summarize for the reader what I think sociologists agree on. Thus, the in-text citations are sparse. In spite of the non-academic style of the writing, nevertheless, all of the appropriate reference material to support the claims I make are provided at the end of each chapter.

The book is divided into two parts. In the first part, the emphasis is on Symbolic Interaction, which is but one of many perspectives in social psychology. In this section we review the basic concepts related to the self, self presentation, and interaction. In the second part of the book we take a micro-sociological approach. Here, the emphasis is on real lived human experiences in the institutions where we live out our lives, such as the family, religion, peer groups, and personal relationships.

80 CB 80 CB

PART ONE: SYMBOLIC INTERACTION

1 | SOME PRINCIPLES OF SYMBOLIC INTERACTION
by Lawrence J. Mencotti, Ph.D.

THE THREE PRINCIPLES OF SYMBOLIC INTERACTIONISM

This textbook uses as its general orientation the symbolic interactionist perspective. We will spend some time unpacking this term [and its basic principles] as a background for showing how useful it is in understanding the chapters of this book and also showing its utility in everyday life as well.

Let's begin by looking at the term itself: Symbolic Interactionism. The term is simple and you don't need a Ph.D. to figure it out. "Interactionism" can be split into "interaction" and "-ism." Interaction is pretty straightforward: it's describes social encounters between people. You walk into class and sit down next to a student and ask how he/she is doing. The student replies and asks you the same. An interaction has just taken place and if stop and think about it what I've just described [and you've experienced countless times] is fairly typical of ALL social encounters.

The term "symbolic" focuses on the quality of what has been exchanged and how it has been exchanged. Well, what was exchanged? In a word, a social pleasantry. Asking someone how they are is an extension of acquaintanceship [and maybe friendship] communicates that you are at least minimally interested in the well-being of the other. It's done through language which is the bedrock communication system of humans and, of course, language is a complex system of symbols.

So putting the two together we're simply saying that the most fundamental way in which humans interact with each other is through symbols with language being the usual medium.

Finally, the suffix "-ism" simply calls your attention to the idea that sociologists who use this perspective are using a perspective [which is one of the many meanings of the suffix -ism.] It is the conviction of these sociologists that symbolic interactionism is the most powerful, straightforward account to describe and explain what they think are the most important features of social life.

There you have it: symbolic interactionism in its simplest form. Well, that's not quite all there is to it; but we won't get too technical and too carried away in presenting the rest of the essentials.

The term symbolic interactionism was coined by Herbert Blumer—an All-American football player who earned his way through graduate school by playing professional football with the Chicago Cardinals. Blumer played several more years of pro ball while on the faculty of the University of Chicago. After finally trading in his bandages and liniment for books he became the mentor of many of who were to solidify the symbolic interactionist perspective. Blumer argued that this approach to everyday life could be organized around three principles.

Principle 1: People Act On The Basis Of Meanings

Breaking down this sentence looks straightforward enough. However, it contains a sneaky element or two. If we act because of meanings then where does that leave human instinct? Nowhere since instincts are pre-programmed genetically transmitted bases for action which require neither thought nor meaning but only the correct instructions. In a similar fashion, where does that leave us with culture as an explanatory variable? Not much better off since people may share the same culture but have widely differing patterns of acting. Obviously, culture sets the stage but the actual drama of social life itself and how the participants play their parts will vary significantly. Consequently, we can conclude that the symbolic interactionist perspective relies neither on biology [a deep-down and inside-out perspective] nor culture [an overarching outside-in point of view] to explain behavior. No, symbolic interactionists look at the social world as individuals coming together and all active participants in a social setting will act according to the meanings the situation has for them.

Let's take an example with which we are all very familiar: a classroom. Let's pretend that we have a bird's-eye view from just outside the window. In this classroom [let's make it a 5th grade class] there are the usuals: students, teacher, desks, chalkboard, etc. In the corner is a flag of the country. The teacher stands in front of the pupils who are reciting in unison. There is nothing really strange about this except to some readers an entire class reciting aloud might seem a bit old-fashioned. Be that as it may, let's look beyond the teacher and above the chalkboard where is affixed to the wall just under the clock: a crucifix [or a Christian cross if you prefer.] Noting this perhaps we can surmise that the recitation is from a catechism which might lead some of you to say that religious indoctrination is taking place in a parochial school.

Let's whisk ourselves to another time and place. Here we have a comparable classroom with a flag in the corner but no cross hangs over the blackboard. Instead the teacher is again leading a class in recitation but here everyone is pledging allegiance to the flag while giving a stiff-armed salute. The flag has a red background with a white circle in the center and within that: a black swastika. This is a German school in the

1930s and the children are indeed being indoctrinated in the conduct of being good citizens of the Master Race.

Let's bring ourselves back to the United States and this time there is an American flag in the corner of the 5th grade classroom and the teacher is leading the children who have their hands placed over their hearts in the Pledge of Allegiance: "....one nation, under God, indivisible...." Some readers might argue that this is also a case of indoctrination all the more egregious since it unites rather than separates religious belief from political allegiance. Others would argue vigorously against that interpretation.

What these three examples have in common besides the obvious: classroom, students, teacher, flag, recitation is that in each case the meaning of the behavior is **not** immediately obvious nor can we predict how observers might interpret the behavior and evaluate it. We can agree however, that both for the participants and for the observers "people act on the basis of meanings."

Principle 2: Meaning Arises From Interaction

This sentence seems simple enough but is often overlooked by students. Let's return to those two potent symbols: the cross and the swastika. The meanings of these artifacts are NOT inherent to them. That is, the meanings don't "live in" the objects themselves; rather, the meanings come about because of the way humans act toward the objects. Put another way, the meaning of the cross or the swastika isn't determined by examining the cross and the swastika but by examining how people act in relation to the cross and the swastika. Put still another way, the meaning is not "in the thing." The meaning lies with the interactions of people in relation to the thing.

Demonstrating this is simple. What is the inherent, unchanging meaning of the Christian cross? It doesn't have one. Before there was Jesus and before there was the crucifixion of Jesus there were countless others who were crucified and the dominant meaning of a crucifixion was that of a horrible and humiliating death. In fact, the earliest followers of Jesus themselves were humiliated that their spiritual leader was executed the way political prisoners were dispatched. These earliest Christians did not have the crucifix as their rallying symbol; rather, theirs was that of a fish. In fact, the cross does not begin to appear in Christian religious art until several hundred years after Jesus' death.

The swastika has been around in various forms and in sundry cultures for thousands of years and often has connoted the notions of peace, goodwill, and other smiley face ideas; certainly not those associated with the barbaric Nazis. The lesson to be drawn here is clear: the meanings of these potent symbolic artifacts have changed and

3

changed drastically. Why? Because groups of people have adopted different meanings than those that were previously associated with these symbols. Thus, meaning of anything and everything ultimately comes from how people act toward social objects: things, ideas, emotions, etc. Indeed, an object to symbolic interactionists is anything toward which people can act.

This does not mean that if people don't act toward an object it necessarily disappears. That if people don't attend to an object it ceases to exist. Symbolic interactionists believes that if a tree falls in the forest and there is no one around to hear that the important point is that the tree is real and it fell. However, symbolic interactionists also believe that if no human is impacted then the human significance for that tree falling is nil.

Another more pertinent example would be that at the end of the day when the teacher and students leave the classroom and the custodian turns out the light in the rooms. The flag remains there. It has a physical, empirical reality independent of people. Its meaning however is totally dependent upon how people choose to act toward it. Here is another example. Anthropologists digging in East Africa may turn up a hominid fossil that has been buried for several hundred thousand years. This physical object was not wished into existence. Its empirical existence is a stubborn fact of what we call physical reality. So we can assume that objects which are **discovered** have an existence independent of the wishes, fears, knowledge of, longing for, disgust by humans. However, the meanings of these objects have a distinctly social dimension as well and these meanings are in a very real sense, **invented**. Seen another way, the meanings can change, be modified, revert, be discarded, and so on. And just who are these agents of meaning-change? Why people are [in the course of their interactions, of course].

Let's look at some other examples that illustrate this principle. One of the most important applications of the symbolic interactionist perspective is in the area of deviance and social control and the important terms to know are: **labeling** and **stigma**.

Just as the meanings of objects are not inherent to the objects and so are not self-evident the symbolic interactionist approach to deviance will emphasize the same interpretative process to the issue as to what constitutes deviance.

The first point to note is that deviance, like any other kind of meaning, does not reside in act itself but rather in the interpretation that people give to the act. In other words, deviance is relative because the same act can be and is interpreted in alternative ways. Let's look at several examples. One way examining how the same act might be interpreted in different ways is to ask, WHO commits the act? In a classic study

Chambliss has shown that two groups of high school boys—the Saints and the Roughnecks—did not differ so much as to the kinds and frequency of their mischief but were, in fact, reacted to quite differently by the authorities depending in no small part on their reputations which in turn was correlated with their social class. A variation of this example can be seen by who organizes a particular activity. If a daily state lottery is held and the winning numbers are broadcast daily this type of gambling is fine as the proceeds go to help [in Pennsylvania] "senior citizens." If in Philadelphia or Pittsburgh people decide to play "the numbers" with some gentlemen with "interesting" pasts then that form of lottery is taboo and thus illegal. So it isn't the act itself—betting on numbers that is deviant/criminal/immoral/fattening; it is who sponsors it and when the government sponsors it everything is just hunky-dory.

Another question we might ask is WHERE is an act committed? Briefly [and modestly] it makes a world of difference to most of us if a sexually intimate act between consenting adults is performed behind closed doors as opposed to on the front lawn in front of a dormitory. They may both be examples of sexual intimacy but the latter acknowledges the meaning of the norm: discretion and adheres to it while the latter either ignores that same norm or involves a deliberate flouting of it.

As long as we've noted sexuality on that theme another question that could be asked is HOW is an act performed? Under what we would in the West consider traditional courtship patterns the male is suppose to pursue the female who, in turn, is supposed to play hard to get [but not too hard is she's really interested in the male.] Nevertheless, in traditional courtship rituals the male is supposed to be the more aggressive one [in a respectful and courteous manner, of course.] Now consider the Gusii, a sub-Saharan African culture in which the man is expected to inflict much sexual pain in his rape of his bride on their wedding night while she is expected try and delay the consummation by whatever means at her disposal including tying tightly her pubic hairs to prevent/delay penetration. So exactly what is sexual assertiveness and when is it deviant and by which culture's standards?

Another variable would be WHICH CONTEXT? Depending on the context the very same act could be seen as instance of heroism and bravery or that of madness. For example, an American soldier might kill three dozen of the enemy in the War on Terror and earn the undying gratitude of patriots on the home front as well as the admiration of his peers whereas a disgruntled and obviously very disturbed student will kill nearly three dozen students and professors and be seen as a homicidal maniac.

One last example should suffice. Here we may inquire about deviance not as act but as a state. For a Caucasian to acquire and display a deep rich tan procured over spring break is a mark of elevated status to many as it shows not just "tan-ability" but also the wherewithal to fly to and loll around on a spot devoted strictly to leisure. However, people of color who come equipped with darker skin tones are, in America, rarely accorded equal racial status let alone superior socio-economic standing. In other words, in America to this present day if dark skin is standard equipment you are placed by the dominant majority into an inferior status but if a darker skin is optional NOT having a tan could deem you unfortunate [but not inferior.] Indeed, in a later chapter it will be argued that simply being a person of color is a deviant status in America.

Deviance then refers to an act the meaning of which is problematic. Deviant refers to a person who commits an act which violates some standard. Which standard? Well, it might be a violation of a folkway such as going to a nice restaurant and eating mashed potatoes with your knife and not your fork. That kind of infraction may not get you arrested but will get you tagged as a boor and probably save you from being arrested from a dormitory front lawn infraction [see above] which WOULD get you arrested, if caught, for violating a law. In both cases the person is has deviated but does that make him a deviant? Well, we're getting ahead of ourselves a bit since we must first look at some implications of our discussion.

At this point we need to look at a derivation from symbolic interactionism: labeling theory, which has informed much of the discussion on deviance up to this point and deserves some "face time" on its own. In a nutshell labeling theory directs our attention to the stubborn social fact that deviant acts [deviance] and actors [deviants] aren't born; they're made. In its most fundamental sense, labeling theory argues that no act is deviant unless powerful people/groups [whom Howard Becker termed **moral entrepreneurs**] assert that it is and that no person is a deviant unless so labeled [usually by the same groups or their representatives—see police, prosecutors, legislators, judges, social workers, and all other social control agents].

To elaborate a bit, labeling some act or person or group of people as deviant requires that some other group creates a negative moral evaluation of some behavior/status seen to be morally inferior. To be effective the moral evaluation must be institutionalized [i.e. made into law, custom, etc.] and then it must then be applied to some number of miscreants.

So then **labeling as a process** is the creation of moral rules that govern behavior: what to do and what not to do; implying how to do it; when and where; with whom, and so on. It should be remembered that not all the do's and don'ts of a society are due to a conscious labeling process; much of it comes from custom

On the other hand, **labeling as a product** results in a negative moral tag put on a person or more likely a category of people. Labeling as a product results in a public identity with which the labeled must somehow deal. This public identity involves a **stigma** which comes from allegedly possessing a "flawed character" and/or membership in a discredited group. In fact, it's hard to see the relevance of labeling as a significant social process *unless* its product is a severe downgrading of one's being: i.e. a stigma. [Note: one can also suffer from the fallout of being seen as possessing a disability—physical or mental without being morally condemned. In place of moral condemnation self-righteous others extend pity rather than openly casting blame.]

Nothing we discussed to this point should lead us to think that there is not a logic behind the process of labeling and the assigning of social stigmas. For example, to ascribe a label to a member of a social category that you suspect of being morally dubious you are engaged in deductive "reasoning"—arguing from the general to the specific. Here, mere membership in an "inferior" group [e.g. a subordinate racial/ethnic/religious group is enough to take an otherwise upright and innocent person and make him/her suspect. Whereas, to take a person who has allegedly transgressed many times and place him/her into a category of other similar deviants/criminals is to argue inductively. It is important to keep these distinctions in mind: while the logical process may be valid the premises may be invalid and end result may be unjust.

It is beyond the scope of this chapter to detail all of the ways people might manage the stigmas with which they are labeled. It is impossible to assign a percentage breakdown as to how many persons labeled "fight back"; how many hide their shame and/or pass as "normal"; or how many passively accept their label and thus internalize the stigma making it part of their identity. In no small part the quantification of stigmatization is misleading since the same person at different times may indeed passively accept the label; hide their shame; fight back by joining a movement that celebrates the stigma: etc.

Suffice to say, internalizing the stigma others thrust on you implies acceptance of a dominant viewpoint in which you are a living, breathing example of social, personal, and moral inferiority. Further, given that fact then *successful labeling is, at bottom, about power: who has it and who doesn't*. Thus, the rejection of the stigma might be delusional while fighting the legitimacy of those who stigmatize could be futile. It is sobering to think that some will be stigmatized through no necessarily wrongdoing of their own—but rather just for being who they are and that by itself is sufficient to guarantee their status of inferiority. For many it is even more difficult to contemplate the idea that functioning groups often need scapegoats whereby various intra-group tensions can be discharged via scapegoating unto powerless "others." Put still another way, it may well be that for most to feel good about themselves a few are sacrificed: their reputations; their identities; and perhaps their lives.

With all of that said, we can come to this general conclusion applicable to both deviant and non-deviant phenomena alike: *the meaning of acts and the attributes of people are the result not from some inherent trait of either act or person but rather the result of a social construction arising from interaction.*

Principle 3: Meanings Are Handled In, and Modified Through, an Interpretive Process

Now this principle is the least obvious of the three. What is meant by this is that meanings are not just automatically given to us or that meanings are not just unquestionably accepted by us. Rather, we work at interpret meaning especially when the situation is important and/or ambiguous.

In many ways this principle is the closest Blumer gets to talking about what is often called motivation. Let's elaborate a bit on this while consciously acknowledging that not all symbolic interactionists will agree with this interpretation.

Value, sacrifice, and meaning. Let's start with the idea that something has value for you and you are in a situation where the value is relevant. Assume that the value is the desire to attain a good college education so as to get a well-paying career. To the extent that you value that desire then you would expect to invest a good deal of your time, energy, and money in its pursuit. One marker of getting a solid education would be achieving good grades and so you sacrifice much to your studies. This, in turn, means that the support network of family, friends, professors, and such will be salient **reference others** for you while you pursue your education. It also means that part of your sacrifices will be to forgo many parties and other leisure time activities to get those good grades. This whole situation becomes even more complicated if you have to juggle one or more jobs, extra-curricular activities and the like.

Suppose in this example that your first two years in college has been worth your investments. That is, your desire to get good grades has been achieved through many sacrifices. Now you see yourself as well as being defined by others as being a good student. At this point, the value/goal has been *attained* but now it must be *maintained* which entails, guess what? More sacrifices. So, in a linear fashion we can say that initial sacrifices led to initial attainment and now attainment switches to maintenance which requires further sacrifices. Interestingly, with sufficient reinforcements such as good grades, praise, respect from family and peers the idea of putting in all of this work for the great paying career may wane just a bit while getting good grades for their own sake may become an end in itself. Of course, you can perform your own thought experiments and come up with other applications of how meaning is massaged and the flux of your life brings you to different points. The point to remember is that while value and sacrifice are inextricably woven together in so much of our lives they are also attached to those emotions that can play such a huge role for us as well. For example, during your fourth semester you receive for your final grades all As and one B and you are crestfallen. You wanted that perfect semester. Meanwhile, your study partner received all Cs and one B [in the same course where you received a B] and quite frankly thinks you are off-kilter and lacking in perspective. Your study partner has defined and interpreted the very same result [a B grade] differently and that is the point of Blumer's principle 3.

To sum up, value and sacrifice are major inputs into how we handle meaning and define situations and our place in them. Value and sacrifice are bound together [it is difficult to think of one without the other] and both impact how we interpret meaning and definitions of the situation while the interpretation of meaning and our definitions of the situation in turn affect our assessment of the values and sacrifices that define so much of our lives. Suffice to say we are dealing with many feedback loops rather than a set of strict linear cause-effect relationships.

The value-sacrifice conceptual tandem points to a very important reality in everyone's life: it is the nexus of meaningful emotions. Emotions so full of meaning that we should really refer to them as our passions. When you feel passionately about some one or some thing [and the list of possible candidates is theoretically endless: lover, spouse, child, parent, friend, sports, reading, hunting, writing, rock climbing, surfing, gardening, skydiving, pet breeding, protecting nature, motorcycling, to name just a few] you are living and breathing this value-sacrifice connection. It seems that no sacrifice is too great because what you value IS so great. While this great sacrifice for an intensely held value makes much sense to describe our positive affections it can also be used to explain negative ones as well. The great love of your life that is the reason why you feel you are alive has, metaphorically speaking, the same infrastructure as those who feel so passionately about some worthy cause: banning abortion, banning hunting, maintaining gun rights, saving wild species, and so on all of which are personified by evildoers who must be stopped and defeated! Seen another way, moral entrepreneurs feel as passionately about their particular cause as you do about your beloved love object. No sacrifice is too great if the value is worthy—and if they are willing to sacrifice much on behalf of their sacred mission they usually have no compunctions about demanding great sacrifices from their enemies, either. Perhaps we might conclude that a true moral entrepreneur is in love—not with Mr. or Ms. Right—but with Righteousness itself.

So, to review: **People act on the basis of meanings.** On your first day of class your instructor gives you an assignment: purchase this book and read this chapter. You do so. You act on the basis of meanings and what could be more meaningful for doing well in this course then to listen and follow the directions and suggestions of the professor. Whether it is, for student A, to please the professor; or as is the case for student B to suck up to the professor: or for student C just to do as good a job with the course as you can to elicit some good old self-satisfaction the initial motive makes little difference since the result is the same—reading this chapter. Next, we have argued that **meaning arises from interaction** and that is illustrated simply enough when all three students form a study group and between them [mostly A and C] work toward a consensus on what are the major points of this chapter. Finally, we posited that **meanings are handled in, and modified through, an interpretive process**. However, our three intrepid students have some unanswered questions and make an appointment to see the professor. After some discussion the professor determines that these unanswered questions are basically due to the students holding overly individualistic ideas of human behavior—ideas that are precluding a full absorption of these three principles. The professor tries to rectify this with some on the spot examples and eventually the students undergo a symbolic interactionist epiphany. This awakening restores their self-concept as well as boosting in their minds what they thing the professor now thinks of them and it is with the concept of self that we turn to the next section.

BLUMER'S THREE PRINCIPLES APPLIED TO SOCIAL INTERACTION

Blumer's 1ˢᵗ Principle: Meaning and Action

With social interaction we find the applicability of Blumer's three principles of symbolic interactionism in still another way. To begin, W. I. Thomas' famous assertion that "if we define a situation as real it is real in its consequences" is the cornerstone of Blumer's first principle. For example, unicorns and mermaids are concepts with particular meanings but few truly believe that they exist independent of our imaginations. Another, more dramatic example which is hotly debated by some would be the idea of Satan and it is here that Thomas' idea comes into its own. If some people believe that Satan really does exist then for the purposes of their actions and the meaning it infuses into their lives then Satan exists. Whether Satan exists independently of the group's belief system is an issue that won't detain us except for us to note that an interesting exercise would be for the reader to list prominent examples in which some people guide their lives by certain ideas which others find to be ludicrous. Of these ideas which political or religious mermaids and unicorns are believed in so fervently that some are willing to die for [or to kill for] those beliefs?

While it is true that we act on the basis of meaning as Blumer's first principle reminds us and that if we think something is real we'll act as if it is [which is Thomas' theorem] we find that these same ideas apply not just to extreme examples but rather Blumer and Thomas' notions apply to our everyday mundane lives as well. To pursue this a bit, role-taking and role-making are complementary concepts which are important in understanding everyday life. Role-taking refers to understanding the world from the viewpoint of another and we've touched upon how Mead thought that mind and self can only adequately develop if the child is able to grasp a whole situation and not just remain egocentrically mired in one's own narrow perspective. Role-making points to how we play a role in a concrete situation.

There are many interpretations of these ideas but perhaps the most famous [and interesting] is that of Erving Goffman and his dramaturgical model of society. Goffman argued that the real "action" of social life is found in **encounters**—structured situations that have their own rules, normative expectations, and the like regardless of who engages in them. Encounters are social frames where social reality is defined in a particular way and the behavior of the participants is directly constrained. An obvious example of an encounter is the college classroom. Without the ability to take the role of the other both professors and students would be completely ignorant of each others' intentions, motives, perspectives, and the like with the depressing consequence that knowledge would neither be generated nor transmitted.

When someone is playing a role [cf the theater allusion in his dramaturgical model] one plays a role with a certain style, confidence, and effectiveness. One makes [i.e. performs] a role but not all role performances are equally effective or persuasive either in the theater proper or in our own everyday lives. Put simply, performances differ. The classroom is a theater of sorts and teaching is a performance art. Whether it is done artfully is a separate issue. In an encounter role-taking cannot occur without role-making occurring simultaneously. That is, role-taking and role-making, as are the I and the me, coincident and co-emergent. The I must know of something [the me] and for A to role-take B must role-make.

However, this doesn't mean that role-taking is either completely accurate or uniform and this brings us to one of Goffman's important insights. Very often we cannot discern whether the performance on the part of our interactional partner is sincere or just cynical. The issue is not just reducible to intention either as Goffman notes since intention does not capture fully the state of the person making the role performance. What Goffman does is alert us to the level at which we recognize our role-making behavior. When we are fully aware of what we are saying and doing and the planning that goes into our performance Goffman calls that **cynical behavior**. However, if you are totally immersed in the role and don't even realize that it is a role then this is an instance of **sincere behavior**. It is not an issue of whether or not you perform in a role but it is an issue of whether or not you are aware, self-consciously, of your performing the role. At the minimum, if you are an active participant in an encounter then since all encounters have pre-existing roles, expectations, norms, and the like you WILL perform

some role. The question is at any given moment at what level will you be conscious of
your performance.

Here is an example to which you will relate. You are taking a course and the professor
is not just boring but also a boor. You receive a poor grade on a paper and you think
the prof has been unfair as well as obtuse. You talk with the professor. You begin by
feigning interest in the intellectual merit of your argument because you feel that might
get you somewhere. In fact, you have even rehearsed what you will say to the prof. In
other words, you start out the encounter with the professor in a cynical manner that you
don't maintain since you become increasingly [and authentically] peeved with the
professor's obstinance. At that point where you "lose it" and noticeably seethe at the
professor's obvious stupidity you are performing sincerely: you are angry; you know
you are angry; and you are showing anger. You also begin to realize that being sincere
will get you nowhere on this paper and might put you in danger on future assignments
so you wrap up your encounter with your favorite professor by feigning agreement with
his point of view and acting like you really want to do better in the course for the greater
good of humankind. At that point you've returned to cynicism.

What we're dealing with is to what extent is the true inner state of a person transparent
or opaque and to whom?—the other or one's self? This becomes much more
interesting when either a person's everyday identity is hidden or when the encounter
transforms one's everyday identity. Briefly, here are two famous case studies to
illustrate these points.

Stanley Milgram's research was a landmark in social science. His subjects were
ordinary people who were duped into thinking that they were engaged in research on
learning when in fact they were engaged in research on obedience to authority. When
the "learners" [actors] in the research made a mistake the structure of the experiment
was such that the "teachers" [the actual subjects] were to deliver what they thought
were electric shocks increasing the amount of charge as the "mistakes" increased.
Milgram found that the proportion of ordinary Americans who would deliver the
maximum electric shock was, well, shocking—far in excess of the estimates made by
psychiatrists prior to the inception of the research. As Milgram varied some of the
conditions of the experiment he found that the further removed and more impersonal the
relationship between teachers and learners the greater the likelihood that the learners
would deliver maximum shocks.

It is evident that the teachers [the subjects] were duped as they acted on a false
meaning of the experiment. They actually thought that they were delivering electrical
shocks when in fact there was no [literal] connection between the console where the
teachers flipped the switches and the learners who were strapped into chairs and who

were allegedly being shocked. Certainly the meaning of Milgram's research may vary but perhaps of greatest value for those who demand a payoff for this kind of research would the conclusion that ordinary Americans put in the wrong situation could make very good order-following, brutalizing Nazis. That being the case, one would wonder that if this is the case in a sanitized laboratory situation why travesties such as My Lai and Abu Ghraib are met with such widespread disbelief or horror by such large sections of the military and American citizenry.

Another instance of famous social science research is the Rosenhan experiment. Here it was not everyday Americans that were duped but professionals themselves; psychiatrists to be precise. Rosenhan was able to get eight "pseudo-patients" admitted to a variety of mental hospitals by faking symptoms. Each of the 8 was admitted as a psychotic when in fact they were psychiatrically normal. During their stay each of the fake patients acted all of the time in a way that you and I would call "normal." After an average stay of 19 days each of the 8 were eventually discharged as psychotic "in remission." No psychiatric professional in any of the 8 different cases ever caught on to the ruse and Rosenhan commented that once someone is diagnosed that the label [and stigma] serves as a filter whereby others evaluate the patients' behavior.

In retrospect that's not surprising. Blumer's first principle tells us that people act on the basis of meaning and that once the in-take psychiatrists misread the symptoms [they had no reason to think the patients weren't genuine] then subsequent psychiatric professionals continued the misinterpretations and thus perpetuated the original errors.

After initially reporting his results some West Coast psychiatrists thought that they were too savvy to be duped so Rosenhan bet them that he would try and sneak some pseudopatients past them. Over a period of three months 193 patients were admitted and 23 were thought to be fake patients. In fact, none were pseudo patients so these psychiatrists made the opposite error. Whereas in the main experiment psychiatrists saw illness where there wasn't' "really" anyone mentally ill in the subexperiment psychiatrists saw much fakery when there wasn't any. In two very important senses the subexperiment is actually more important in its implicative meanings. First, when on the alert psychiatrists still committed a significant proportion [.125] of diagnostic errors. Second, and generalizing a bit, one can't help but wonder how many people are misdiagnosed and inappropriately treated for conditions they don't have.

Indeed, people do act based upon meaning/their definition of the situation but not all meanings are equally valid [nor are they equal in their effects.]

Blumer's 2nd Principle: Meaning and Interaction

His second principle reminds us that meaning arises through social interaction. Let's return to the idea of role-making but here offer what would be a symbolic interactionist reinterpretation of personality. To most persons [given the obsession Americans have with the idea of individuality it's not surprising] personality is something that people carry around with them as they move from encounter to encounter. Well, here's another way of viewing it. If meaning arises through social interaction then in no small part someone's personality is not so much independent of situations but is grounded in and is a function of particular encounters.

Sasha Weitman's argued that every act of inclusion is simultaneously an act of exclusion. To be an object of love is to simultaneously exclude everyone else [excepting instances of ménage a trois] from participating in it. Less controversially, a simple hug or kind word directed to another is by its nature not directed toward anyone else. To include is to simultaneously exclude. By my including X I exclude Y and if Y is observing this then very often Y cannot help but be negatively affected. If our personalities are in no small part built and re-built on interactions then the same act has different effects depending on how the encounter is constructed and interpreted.

Let's take another example. Davis and Schmidt analyzed the obnoxious and the nice. While most people would say "isn't he obnoxious" or "isn't she nice" in this particular role-complement Davis and Schmidt call our attention to how the obnoxious and the nice are not only made for one another but they also how in a real sense make and re-make each other. Think about it this way. Assume for the moment that you can be quite obnoxious. To be obnoxious is possible only in the presence of others. Do you stand in your bathroom and taunt yourself in the mirror with obscenities or boorish behavior. I would hope not. One NEEDS others so as asinine behavior might be engaged.

Now who will put up with the inanities? Enter someone whom people think is nice. How do we know this person is nice? Are they nice because they stand in front of their bathroom mirror and are nice to themselves? No, they are nice by the way they act with others and if their self-concept is in no small part to be "really nice" then they will either actively seek out [or at least not excuse themselves] from situations in which the obnoxious will be present and accounted for.

We are not denying psychological traits. We are denying that one's personality is reducible to those traits. Put another way, these traits will not manifest themselves except in social encounters. Let's look at still another example to give a somewhat nuanced look at this topic. Drawing inspiration from the Davis and Schmidt piece Mencotti argued that a similar role-complement exists between the shy and the graceful.

14

In several ways the graceful person is the mirror opposite of the obnoxious type. While the graceful person is highly sensitized to the preferences of others the obnoxious is self-centered. While the graceful steers conversation to include others the obnoxious tends toward monopolizing attention toward him/herself. The conversational partners relish the graceful person and feel honored to be included while the conversational attendees to an obnoxious person will look for the first feasible exit strategy.

With all of that said what would be the role-complement of the graceful? I think it's defensible that the shy might be one possibility. A person who is shy in one particular situation may be shy because they are a complete stranger in a rather formidable social gathering. The graceful can sense this and take the initiative by including the shy in a conversational group or two. In turn, the shy person reciprocates by being an attentive listener for whomever might be holding forth which makes the shy an excellent audience for a variety of social performers [e.g. the life-of-the-party; the story-teller; and so forth.] The shy person in situation A could be the nice person in situation B while the graceful person in situation A could also be the [merely] nice in situation C when coupled with [ugh] still another obnoxious type.

Again, we are not saying that people do not possess what have been called personality traits. However, we are arguing that we are not reducible to these putative traits; these traits are expressed in social encounters; and we may express different personality types depending on several factors not the least of which would be the particular situation in which we might find ourselves.

Further, we are saying that by implication what we feel and how we should express such feelings is a function of the interplay between specific social encounters, self-concept, inner states, and the roles we are expected to play in such encounters. Some reflection on this topic leads us to the rather obvious conclusion that we are such emotionally-laden creatures that much effort is invested in making sure that we feel what we are supposed to feel. Arlie Hochschild has referred to this as **emotion work**.

There are innumerable instances of this but here are a few:

- Getting yourself psyched for a party
- Trying to remain calm during a stressful situation
- Showing some enthusiasm for a parental visit

Far from being strictly internal and purely personal emotions are thoroughly social and as such are not innate but learned. We need to learn what to feel, when to feel, how to feel, and why to feel and all of this comes from socialization starting early on and continuing for the rest of our lives. Note too that emotion work is also a subcategory of the larger instance of what we might call "meaning work." How do we know what to feel and how to express it without doing some meaning work in the process?

One last example should suffice in our assertion that meaning is possible only through social interaction. If you think deeply enough about the implications of this example it will undoubtedly lead to some emotionally disquieting thoughts. This case is in many ways one of the most [in-] famous in all of social science; even more notorious than the Milgram experiment. It has come to be called the Stanford Prison Experiment led by Philip Zimbardo. The subjects were Stanford undergraduates, volunteers who were to be paid for their efforts. They were pre-screened to exclude those with obvious emotional problems. They were then, and this is important, *randomly* assigned to play a role of either guard or prisoner. The experiment which was to last two weeks lasted just six days. Zimbardo called it to a halt as the subjects' student selves became submerged in their guard or prisoner roles. For example, after being denied "parole" one of the student/prisoners docilely returned to his cell. In less than a week he no longer thought of himself as a student volunteer in an oppressive experiment. If he had, he would have told Zimbardo to take his money and insert it "where the sun don't shine" and would have walked into the California sunshine a free young man. Rather, he now saw himself as a prisoner. Such was the redefinition of self-concept in such a short period of time; a redefinition that derived from a radical reconstitution of the volunteers' social environment. To those who are shocked by the abuses by American guards on Abu Ghraib prisoners it is all too predictable. Again, given the *wrong* set of circumstances seemingly normal, decent service men and women may commit brutal acts of dehumanization.

Taken together, the Milgram, Rosenhan, and [especially] Zimbardo experiments are chilling in their implications. We may think long and hard on these experiments but they do not bolster confidence in authority figures or the belief that character alone will some how save us from the power of brutalizing situations.

Blumer's 3rd Principle: Meaning and Interpretation

Thinking is intra-individual communication and in some ways thinking is a dialogue between the I and the me. In another and very important way thinking doesn't just take place within people but also between people. If meaning can be modified through an interpretive process and that process involves others then much conversation between people is "collective thinking."

You talk through a problem with a friend, parent, sibling, or lover and in the talking through as each person in the exchange gets a clearer idea of what the other[s] as well as themselves "really" mean Blumer's third principle is illustrated: meanings are handled and modified through an interpretive process. Meanings become more clear as we work through and match up what is intended with what was misinterpreted; what is possible from what is not. Whatever else communication might be it is, at bottom, "meaning work."

To update this idea just a bit email, chat groups, web browsing, text messaging, blogging, YouTubing, videoconferencing; to many, all of the preceding merely involve new technological formats for communication—old wine in new bottles. Even if true there are several effects of these new communication modes not the least of which is the unprecedented degree to which people are interconnected because of the unprecedented number of ways of interconnectedness. Twenty years ago [during the late 1980s] personal computers were a relative novelty, cell phones were in their infancy, and the World Wide Web was non-existent. Today, if you have a friend in San Francisco and you reside in the Eastern Time Zone you may talk cheaply [and directly] with your friend via your cell phone, or perhaps send a text message. You might take a picture with your cell phone and send that relatively instantaneously. All of this is possible between [never during] your classes. Upon returning to your room you check your email and dash off an idea or just a hello to another friend. Later, you join a favorite chat group and converse with several people you have never met face-to-face but nevertheless feel that you know quite well. After that [and instead of doing some reading for that exam in the morning] you cruise the web to check the latest incredibility posted on YouTube, submit an entry on your blog, then thanks to the built-in camera on your laptop engage in a "videoconference" with your California buddy [or maybe a friend in Munich or Hong Kong, or Buenos Aires.] All of this is possible to do within a couple of hours and makes our lives denser, richer, and much more quickly experienced.

Alternatively, the near-instantaneous nature of our high-tech gadgetry renders us much less patient while waiting for the "other" to respond to our needs/demands and thus, in the process, making us all that much more ego-centric. What is gained in technological wonderment might be lost in civility. In addition, our lives have also become much less private and much more prone to electronic snooping by anonymous others. These developments vindicate Simmel's prescient writings on the inherent ambivalence of modern culture because of the division of labor where "the production of the product is attained at the cost of the development of the producer." In our age, we post, we blog, we text message, we email, we produce via electronic expression all sorts of communications without knowing [or seemingly caring] about their ultimate fate [and consequence.] All the while, the potential for commercial and political entities to know more and more "facts" about more and more people increasingly shrinks the boundaries of privacy. All the while the areas of our lives that we can call truly personal shrink apace. While the revolutionary technical marvels increase one's sense of "I" the "me" becomes more and more accessible, commoditized, and publicized.

Be that as it may, the fundamental point remains: however we communicate, Blumer's same three principles apply. Even web-browsing, ordinarily a solitary activity, constantly involves intra-individual communication: i.e. meaning-making; that is, thinking.

Motives and Motivation

Unlike most approaches to human behavior that emphasize the personal and the individual and indeed see motivation as something discoverable our symbolic interactionist perspective will emphasize, in keeping with text, that motivation is undiscoverable but motives—the reasons we give for why we act as we do—are very discernible. Indeed, even if Freud and his followers were correct: that the real "action" of people is below the surface of consciousness, we would still have to find ways of penetrating all of the defense mechanisms to get at one's "true" motivation and that always involves dealing in some serious capacity with people's motives: the reasons they give for why they do what they do. Whether psychoanalysis is ultimately compatible with symbolic interactionism is beside the point. Rather, the symbolic interactionist stress on motives is an emphasis that reflects the reality of everyday life which is: we live with others.

Now, what are motives? Motives are the reasons we give for why we do what we do. As such, we tell ourselves and we tell others reasons for our behavior that will generally coincide with our values which, in turn, are generally shared with others. In fact, group boundaries are in no small part signified by acceptable and unacceptable motives. For example, if you belong to a religion then the chances are good that the values of the group will determine which motives are acceptable to explain behavior. Motives for treating people compassionately often involves "citing" Jesus. This can be seen when, in the middle of a sermon, a clergy cites sayings of Jesus referring to chapter and verse the way many an academic does when delivering a scholarly paper. In turn, compassion in a Judaic or Islamic context would be somewhat less likely to be justified by references to Jesus.

So motives are grounded in group membership and are given by group members often as a way of justifying their behavior to other group members. Some readers may still be bothered by a lack of concern over why people *really* do the things they do. Such readers are welcome to take psychology courses that offer a rather bewildering array of theories of motivation that come packaged in a variety of shapes, sizes, colors and flavors to satisfy just about anyone's taste. For symbolic interactionists it is just this plurality of competing speculations that points to the conclusion that to no small extent motivation is in the eyes of the theoretical speculator. In fact, the Dark Swamp of Motivation offers an opportunity to apply the concept of motive. When students are asked why they would be interested in studying human motivation various responses are possible: "I want to know about people"; it's important to know why people behave the way they do;" "it just interests me"; etc. All of these responses are examples of motives and they function to justify the interest in the topic of motivation. They are expressions of values and preferences and despite all of the scholars and students of the topic of motivation it is still a field dominated by perspective and opinion and not one of empirically derived definitive answers.

Given that as an accurate description symbolic interactionists sort of shrug their shoulders and say "people act and what we CAN study directly are the reasons that they give for why they do what they do. Hence our skepticism of motivation and our preference for motives.

The study of motives is one way that self and interaction can be brought together and, in turn, motives themselves can be fruitfully studied in terms of Blumer's three principles. Recall the first principle: "people act on the basis of meanings." So a student is interested in "why do people do the things they do?" This is a legitimate interest. It is also a motive and it connects to behavior: enrolling in a course in the psychology of motivation.

Blumer's second principle alerts us to the fact that "meaning arises through interaction." The student attends the course and learns about the major psychological theories [past and present] which purport to explain why people act the way they do. The student also reads about research that supports each of these theories as well as investigating the shortcomings of each theory. The student may have a favorite theory that emerges from the course but also realizes that his/her enthusiasm is dampened by class discussion in which the professor and other students lodge some valid criticisms.

As the course winds down Blumer's third principle, "meanings are handled and modified through an interpretive process" is highlighted. The course professor gives a take-home final exam in which the sole question asks for the student to construct a synthetic motivation model which incorporates the best of each of the theories. Of course, our fictional student realizes right away that it is an impossible task since if such a synthetic theory was truly possible the experts in the field would have already constructed it and that, in turn, would be what they would have been studying all semester long. Nevertheless, an assignment is an assignment and so our student bravely tackles it but finds that it is daunting and so calls some friends in the class and they are able to hammer out some ideas that they all can use. Several students express dismay at the difficulty of the assignment and in a somewhat ironical way exchange motives for taking the course: "it's required"; "it's an elective for me—I must have been out of my mind;" "it was the only elective open that fit into my schedule;" and so forth and so on. In so doing and by working together the students find, create, and modify meaningful ideas for the assignment and as well as rationales for why they find themselves in this particular predicament.

๛ ๙ ๛ ๙

REFERENCES

Becker, H. S. (1973). *Outsiders: Studies in the sociology of deviance*. New York: Free Press.
Blumer, H. (1969). *Symbolic interactionism*. Englewood-Cliffs, NJ: Prentice-Hall.
Davis, M., & Schmidt, C. (1977). *The Obnoxious and the nice. Sociometry, 40*, 201-213.
Goffman, E. (1959). *The presentation of self in everyday life*. Garden City, NY: Doubleday.
Goffman, E. (1961). *Encounters*. Indianapolis, IN: Bobbs-Merrill.
Goffman, E. (1963). *Stigma*. Englewood-Cliffs, NJ: Prentice-Hall.
Goffman, E. (1971). *Relations in public*. New York: Basic Books.
Goffman, E. (1974). *Frame analysis*. New York: Harper and Row.
Hochschild, A. (1983). *The managed heart*. Berkeley CA: University of California Press.
Mencotti, L. (1986). A common malady. *Contemporary Psychiatry, 5*, 268-269.
Milgram, S. (1974). *Obedience to authority*. New York: Harper and Row.
Rosenhan, D. (1973). On being sane in insane places. *Science, 179*, 250-258.
Simmel, G. (1971). *Georg Simmel: On individuality and social forms*. Donald Levine (Ed.). Chicago: University of Chicago Press.
Weitman, S. (1970). Intimacies: Notes toward a theory of inclusion and exclusion. *European Journal of Sociology, 11*, 348-367.
Zimbardo, P. (2007). *The Lucifer effect: Understanding how good people turn evil*. New York: Random-House.

2 | THE SELF AND SELF DEVELOPMENT
by Frank O. Taylor, Ph.D. and Lawrence J. Mencotti, Ph.D.

What is this concept we refer to as **self**? When you think about your "self," you are likely to think about a variety of things. You may begin to think about the social categories you belong to. Social categories include many things, such as sex and gender, religious affiliations, social class, level of education, occupation, and the like. Or you may begin to think about how you are different from others. Differences may include likes and dislikes, talents, abilities, aptitudes, attitudes, and even behaviors. The self is a collection of beliefs we hold about ourselves, regarding talents, abilities, and attitudes.

One way to think about self is to refer to **self-concept**. Self concept includes our likes and dislikes, hobbies, and things we are good at. It also includes are statues and roles. For example, you can find out a lot about yourself by simply answering the question: "Who am I?" With a little reflection you may come up with answers like these:

- I am a woman (or a man)

- I am a mother (or a father)

- I am a sister (or a brother)

- I am a friend

- I am a good listener

- I am an artist

- I am a wife (or husband)

Some of these answers refer to statuses, such as woman, mother, or sister. Some of the answers refer to behaviors, such as being a good listener or friend. Other answers refer to talent or ability, such as being an artist.

Self-esteem is also usually part of you self-concept. Self-esteem refers to an overall evaluation we make of ourselves – either high or low. People with high self-esteem generally have a clear sense of their personal qualities. Personal qualities include things like being an introvert or extrovert, ambitious, motivated, and so on. People with high self-esteem also think reasonably well of themselves. They have attainable goals, rather than unrealistic goals. In difficult situations, people with high self-esteem have good coping skills.

People with low self-esteem have less clear conceptions about themselves. They tend to have low evaluations of their personal qualities, desirability, and talents and skills. Sometimes they have very few goals in life or none at all. Other people with low self-esteem have set goals for themselves that are unachievable and unrealistic. They tend to be pessimistic about the future. In stressful situations they do not have good coping skills. People with low self-esteem do not respond well to criticism or negative reflected appraisals.

An important point to make is that the self is **emergent**. This means that the self emerges from social interactions with others. At first, these others are significant others, such as mothers, fathers, siblings, and others in the home with the child. As children get older they begin to interact with others in church, the neighborhood, and school. The point is that the self does not exist without two other related concepts, mind and culture. **Mind** refers to the ability to think, particularly about the self. Mind depends upon language and symbols, in turn generated by culture. It is the capacity to think about ourselves and others, through the use of language and symbols that gives rise to self.

STAGES OF SELF DEVELOPMENT

Imagine yourself sitting before class and wondering about yourself as a college student: why me? Why here? Why am I taking this course? Why am I majoring in that major? and so on. Perhaps your ruminations are a symptom of discontent or perhaps just a series of associations to kill time before the class starts. Whatever. The particular topic of your imaginings—your internal conversation with yourself—is not as important as the fact that you are talking *to* yourself, *with* yourself, and *about* yourself [and hopefully the conversation is taking place *inside* your head.] This "**self-talk**" is one particular example of what is usually called thinking. In any case, such self-talk is at the heart of our lives and symbolic interactionists put it front and center in our development and flourishing as human beings. Indeed, self-talk is an important indicator of being fully human.

So how did we get this way? How do we become human? One approach to this problem is to argue that humans possess *instincts:* pre-programmed genetically transmitted instructions that govern behavior. This inside-out approach is easily called into question by looking at the exceptions to those instincts humans might conceivably possess. For example, a survival instinct is questioned by suicide [the conscious decision to end one's own life.] Similarly, a supposed "killer instinct" is questioned by pacifism. The question is begged: if instincts can be overcome by choice then how powerful are the instincts? So the instinctual approach founders on the reality of behavioral variation: human behavior that *varies between cultures as well as within a culture.*

Which brings us to culture [the outside migrating to the inside approach.] The cultural perspective is used in explaining human behavior is to look at those behaviors we perform and argue that we are who we are and we are what we are due to the culture in which we are raised. Certainly distinctively different behavior and values are instilled in members depending upon the culture in which they grow up. There is no doubt that culture can explain much but while it is *necessary* to explaining us it is definitely *not sufficient* in explaining our behavior, our selves, or our lives. This is easily demonstrated by the following question. If we grow up in the same culture why might there be such differences in values, behavior, and self-concepts between the culture's members? Put another way, culture may explain similarities among members but for different reasons than the instinctive approach it too can't explain behavioral or cognitive differences between members of the same culture. For example, while you and the student sitting next to you might exhibit identical behavior in your role as student the reasons why you behave identically may be radically different: you are in the class and want to do well because the course genuinely interests you while the student next to you is there because it is a required course. Both of you may study hard for this course but for different reasons: you because it is a matter of pride while the other student does so because they want to keep on track and not have to repeat the course.

Well, if it's not instincts and it's not simply culture then what makes us human? For the symbolic interactionists the most direct answer is **language**. Language allows for culture to be communicated and transmitted [and often changed as well]. Language makes self-talk, the internal conversation, possible.

Language is the bedrock upon which culture exists but interestingly if there is any case to be made for instincts in humans it is with language acquisition. Language will come to us easily and automatically since as humans we have evolved a hard-wired capacity to acquire language. That is, we have a pre-programmed genetically acquired species-wide disposition [instinct if you will] to acquire it and if you take normal infants and put them in a normal developmental situation they will acquire a spoken language—and will acquire it merely by hanging around and being exposed to older people. We know this since humans can't *not* acquire a spoken language given minimal exposure at the correct age.

There are several instances of children who have been raised in social isolation and the negative effects of such isolation include stunted cognitive, social, and moral development. All three of the "classic" cases involved girls. The most recent and most infamous of these cases is that of Genie who as an infant [from about 1.5 years] until after the onset of puberty when she was discovered by the outside world] was confined to a back bedroom of her parents' house. The obvious dysfunctionality of her family life, though perversely fascinating, is beside our point. Even though after her liberation she was given intensive and extensive intervention in attempt to "catch her up" she had passed the critical period [pre-pubertal] of acquiring a first language without ever actually acquiring fluency in one. Consequently, her social, emotional, and of course, mental development was severely stunted. This case should sensitize us to not only the very early window of opportunity for the acquiring of a language but also why in the absence of language acquisition so much else crucial to development is compromised.

One very important implication of this line of reasoning is that language is indispensable to acquiring and fully participating in a culture but because humans are so dependent upon this marvelous instrument it makes all other instincts dispensable. Seen another way language is the means that makes us human but it is our experiences within culture that supply the content of our lives. In turn, language forms, shapes, and otherwise gives meaning to our experiences. The language you speak, in a very real sense, helps shape the reality you live in and thus the experiences you have. This is not to argue that all human behavior and experience are reducible to a spoken language since the fine arts, music, dance, and mathematics [to name some important examples] are not necessarily expressible through words. However, that language is still essential can be seen when we evaluate those who do creative work in those non-linguistic area. The phrases: "he is a terrific sculptor;" "she is a great dancer;" "he is a fine pianist;" and "she is a gifted mathematician" all demonstrate how we may use every day language to communicate about behavior and experience that is not essentially linguistic.

So, to summarize up to this point we can state unequivocally that language is the most fundamental human tool allowing for interaction between humans and interaction within a person and it is this interaction *within* each of us that is the fundamental "stuff" of self. Ok, so what is this fundamental stuff that takes place within us? It is self-consciousness and self-consciousness is literally that: self-awareness—consciousness of one's own sense of being alive. The self is NOT a thing but it is an object to which we can relate. Put another way, there is no self that shows up in an MRI. It is an *awareness* of action, thought, feeling in which the locus of and importance is oneself. One way of seeing this is that *the idea of the self is a person being consciously aware of him/herself.*

Pursuing this a bit brings us to the idea of the **Looking-Glass** nature of self which states that our self-concept is in no small part determined by how we think others view us. A generalization can be stated here: *the more important ideas we have about ourselves will roughly coincide with how we think people who are important to us view* *us.* We view ourselves in a mirror—a mirror of our **significant others**—those who are important to us. However, the mirror itself is distorted by past judgments, evaluations, and the like. To symbolic interactionists there is no self-concept without the "mirror of significant others" but there is no mirror of significant others that is totally accurate in any true sense of the word accurate. Thus, we are, in no small part, the accumulation of the self-distortions.

To be aware of anything assumes a subject as well as an object. In the vocabulary of symbolic interactionism the principle of knowing is termed the "**I**" while the element of yourself about which you are thinking is the "**me**." To put it in terms of grammar the I is the subject and the me is the object of your thinking. The I is "knower" while the me is what is "known" about yourself. Note the reciprocal [and dialectical] nature of this arrangement: the I must have something to be aware of [the me] while the me must have some capacity to be understood [the I]. They are both co-emergent and co-existing: they cannot exist without each other and you can't have one without the other.

That which is truly unique to everyone is the I but the me can refer to what you share with others. As such, the me is social and that is contrasted with the I's uniqueness. Think of it this way: you have no choice but to be both unique as well as social. No one sees the world [literally] as you do but in order for you to have any place in the world; any ability to deal with the world you must be able to communicate and interact with other humans. The me refers to your social dimension—your connectedness with others. In fact, we can risk a generalization: *not only are we all simultaneously unique and social we also can neither be totally unique nor totally social.* While it is true that no matter how socialized we are there will always be a spark of anarchism in each of us it is equally true that no matter how unique we long to see ourselves there will always be a goodly amount of overlap with others. Our selves are thoroughly social. While it is impossible for it to be otherwise being thoroughly social does not mean we are cookie-cutter identical to everyone else. Again, there is a dialectic and reciprocal at work here. We are simultaneously social *and* unique; not social or unique.

In the classic account of childhood socialization by George Herbert Mead there are two stages through which all humans progress in becoming fully functioning adult humans: the play stage and the game stage. With the acquisition of the rudiments of language the **play stage** is engaged. In this stage the child takes the role of specific others—those who are immediate and important to him/her. What is important to note is that the child takes the role [and perspective] of one of these significant others at a time. When engaged in amusement at the play stage the child will typically go back and forth between roles [for example mimicking the parents discussing something or arguing.] It is in this stage that a true self-awareness emerges and the notion of the looking-glass self becomes relevant and so it is in this stage that one's self as an object to oneself emerges. [It is also interesting to note that the fantasy lives of adults are in an important sense a regression back to the play stage wherein one's imaginations can be indulged by alternating roles. However, as adults an entire situation may be fantasized and that is possible because of the game stage.] With the **game stage** participation in social situations becomes more sophisticated; so much so that the child no longer plays at roles but increasingly is able to grasp entire situations—a holistic approach to social life if you will. Here role-taking becomes so much more evolved that single significant others are replaced by a generalized other—which encompasses the entirely of a given situation including understanding all of the roles, rules, and expectations. It's the difference between a five year old relegated to right field standing with an oversized mitt and an outsized cap watching a butterfly and occasionally throwing a ball back to [somewhere] in the infield and an eleven year old noting immediately to pick up the ball and throw to the teammate at second to prevent a single from becoming a double. At the game stage, the game of baseball is grasped as a complex whole of meanings and actions representing a **generalized other** whereas at the play stage the child plays at baseball whose rules and regulations remain pretty much a mystery.

Now possessing a competency in cognition does not guarantee being a moral person. One can have mastered the game stage and be perfectly capable of taking the role of all of the others in a situation and still be bereft of a functioning conscience. Many amoral people are brilliant, shrewd, and highly manipulative of the needs, desires, and weaknesses of others—i.e. they can be excellent practical role-takers—all the better for the predator to seek out and exploit their prey. Alternatively, a great many folk are direct, engaging, and devoid of pretense and quite adept at following Jesus' admonitions from his Sermon on the Mount. So it is obviously not cognitive sophistication alone that allows for morality. Put another way, some rudimentary level of cognitive competence is necessary but not sufficient for morality. What is crucial is the successful internalization and enactment of the rules of generalized others.

Reference group stage. Mead was not completely clear on the subject of the generalized other and so the idea of **reference other** was added. This points to the fact that we do not live in a simple society with a single generalized other but given the successful completion of the game stage we understand that we inhabit a world with many demanding and often conflicting situations each with their own generalized other. So, engaging in different situations means that you will have differing reference groups to take into consideration. For example, the situation of the classroom has fellow students and the professor as the salient reference group[s] while the situation of the wedding will have the bride and groom and relatives and friends as the salient reference group. Hopefully, you will grasp the distinctive generalized other of each situation and not act as a student at a wedding and alternatively you will not act as a boisterous reveler in the classroom. Interestingly, this notion of belonging to multiple groups does not mean that we suffer from multiple personality disorders but most definitely we are challenged by the task of organizing all of the multiple social selves we find ourselves being during the course of a busy day. How do we keep it all straight? Well, we do have a sense of continuity over time and over many social distances and spaces. This continuity underlying all of our diverse experiences gives us a sense that we are truly the same person and that brings us back to a basic point: *self is a person consciously aware of him/herself.* It is this self-awareness over time and space that provides a principle of continuity to our changing and shifting self-concepts.

Of course, there are times of such sudden and significant shifts in perspective that we feel that we are not the same old person we've been up to that point. However, your internal dialogue between the I and me is an indicator that once again you think that it is YOU who has drastically changed; that it is YOU who is no longer the same person. In other words, the idea of you as a person who has undergone a significant change is fundamentally a shift in self-conception. This, in turn, brings us back once again to the concept that the *self is not a noun but a verb: a person being* **consciously aware** *of him/herself as an object of both continuity as well as change.*

SELF KNOWLEDGE

We have already mentioned that what we commonly think of as the "self" is really a collection of beliefs that, over time, we come to hold about ourselves. Self is really something that is called forth in different social settings as part of the social process. For example, the ways that you think about your self when you are in the classroom interacting with a professor and other students is likely very different from the ways that you think about yourself when you are interacting with your peers away from school. For each social setting you occupy a different status. For each status, you have different ways to think about yourself, at least to some degree. Some of us change only very little from situation to situation while others of us can change dramatically as situations vary. Where do these conceptions about the self come from?

Socialization

Socialization refers to the lifelong process of learning your culture. Socialization never ceases because we never cease making transitions in life. Each new stage of life requires us to learn new things, and sometimes to re-learn old things. If you have been married for a long time, and then get divorced, sooner or later you will have to think about dating again, for instance. Socialization is a major source of self concepts.

We will interact with a variety of significant others during our lives that treat us in different ways. These significant others include parents, teachers, friends, and peers. Our experiences with these people can greatly shape our self concept. Parents, for example, are not all the same and we can expect this to be a major source of difference in individuals. Some parents are liberal while others are conservative. Some parents are extremely religious but others are not very religious or maybe even atheists. Some parents are from the upper class and will rely upon Nannies to raise their children. Other parents are from the lower class and will rely upon relatives, perhaps a grandmother, to help raise their children. Parental styles range from extremely permissive to extremely authoritarian. Parenting styles can even change within the same family. My father, for instance, was very authoritarian when I was a child but for my youngest brother, he was permissive because he was a lot older. The point is that our experiences with primary socialization are very influential in shaping our self concepts.

Peer groups are probably the second most important influence in the socialization process related to self concept. Children want to be accepted by their peers. In order to gain acceptance, frequently, children will often adopt the values, attitudes, and behaviors of their peers. Obviously, this will influence self conception. If you want people to know, for instance, that you belong to a certain peer group, you will dress like your peers, talk like your peers, hang out with them, and in general conform to group norms to feel like you belong. Some peer groups are extremely "popular" and some peer groups are labeled as "losers." Which group you identity with can greatly affect your self concept. Even as adults the peer groups we belong to become part of our identity.

Teachers have entirely different influences over us, both positive and negative. Teachers, in many respects, are charged with the task of **cultural assimilation**. The United States is a nation of immigrants. Not every person is of Anglo Saxon ancestry. However, English is the dominant language. English common law is the source of our legal system. Our mores, norms, and folkways and a great many of our values and beliefs are of Anglo Saxon origins. To a large extent, the manifest function of schooling is to ensure that each generation of students is assimilated into our culture. Every child is exposed to the hidden curriculum, which includes standing in line, raising your hand if you want to speak, asking for permission to leave the classroom if you must, being punctual, and turning in work on time, following orders, and so on. These experiences are translated into self conceptions.

In school, some of us are honors students while others of us are vocational students. Whether we are placed in the high, middle, or low ability groups determines how much education we actually receive. High ability students are labeled as "gifted," and get lots of positive feedback in the form of praise for intellectual ability. Low ability students are labeled as "challenged" and research indicates that their self-esteem often suffers as a result of such tracking. Children in the low ability groups are not expected to achieve much intellectually, and thus they get the fewest resources. The labeling that goes on in our educational system is rampant and linked closely to self conceptions.

Socialization is the process through which we become members of a culture. It is the process in which we learn values, norms, beliefs, and ideologies. Our society is highly stratified, in terms of social class, gender, and race and ethnicity. Thus, for each of us, whether we are male or female, upper or lower class, black, white, or brown, makes a difference in the types of social experiences we have. These socialization experiences are highly connected to the self concepts we eventually adopt.

The Looking Glass Self

Self concept comes not only from the thoughts we have about ourselves and our behaviors but also from our impressions of how others view us. On one hand, often we do think directly about our personal qualities, values, beliefs, and behaviors. On the other hand, we also rely upon what we *think* others think of us. Sometimes we are pretty sure about how others view us. Once a student challenged the grade he received in this course. When I did not change his grade he told me "you suck!" Other times we are not so sure, so we are forced to look for clues about their attitude toward us. The point to be clear on is that more often than not we do not have an accurate perception of what others truly think of us. Consequently, our self concepts may be based on incorrect perceptions.

The **looking-glass self** has three phases. In the first phase, we present ourselves to others. **Self presentation** involves our dress, mannerisms, symbols, language, behavior, body language and so on, that we rely upon during interactions with each other. During this phase we are trying to manage the impressions others form of us. In the second phase we imagine how others are evaluating us. Are we seen as intelligent, or attractive, or personable, or are we seen in more negative terms? In the third phase we form an impression about ourselves, based on how we imagine others perceive us. Clearly, self concept can be greatly influenced by our perceptions about how others evaluate us. When we look in the mirror we do not simply see our physical reflection – we also see a person who has certain qualities.

Reflected Appraisals

The looking-glass self refers to our perceptions about how others evaluate. The actual feedback others give is known as **reflected appraisal**. If a man asks a woman to "make out" with him under the bleachers in the gym, and she says that "there's too much light under there – I could *see* you," we understand that she is rejecting him, sarcastically (no one ever really said that to me!). Her sarcastic remark, meant to rebuff him, is a reflected appraisal. His interpretation of her remark refers to the looking-glass self. Thus, reflected appraisals and the looking-glass work hand-in-hand.

For the sake of argument, let us say that you think you are an attractive individual. If one person, perhaps your mother, says that you are good looking, you may or may not believe it. Your mother could be biased, after all. If another person, who is one of your peers, says that you are attractive, you might be more inclined to believe it. If people stare at you and give you the "once over" everywhere you go you will probably begin to believe that you are pretty good looking. On the other hand, if people are rejecting toward you and call you names, or are constantly excluding you and giving you the cold shoulder, you may reach the opposite conclusion, that you are not very good looking. It is also possible that you are good looking but believe you are not because you only look for and pay attention to those who reject you!

We are constantly receiving feedback from others. Parents are often giving us feedback. Sometimes our parents tell us how good we are; other times they tell us how bad we are. Parents give us feedback about our talents, personality, and character. Parental reflected appraisals are important to us in our childhood years and are associated with what type of bond we form with caregivers. Peers are important to us in late childhood and early adolescence. Teachers give us explicit feedback in the form of grades. Often teachers give other forms of feedback, such as comments on our essays, mentoring, letters of reference, and other forms of encouragement. These types of reflected appraisals help us infer our own personal attributes.

Self-Perception

Another way in which we develop an identity and self is through direct reflection about our values, attitudes, and behavior. This is known as **taking the *self* as other**. This is different from **taking the *role* of the other**. Taking the role of the other refers to examining yourself from the point of view of others. When you take your self as other, you are evaluating yourself by comparing yourself to the **ideal self**. The ideal self is your personal idea of the perfect person. Of course, much of what we may think of as the perfect self comes from our cultural definitions of such a person. Nevertheless, the ideal self is not identical for every person and it is possible to compare our actual behavior to our internal standards of behavior.

Taking the self as other is a way in which we infer our personal characteristics from observing and evaluating our own behavior. There are many dimensions along which to think about your self that do not come into our mind very often. In other words, for many values, positions, and attitudes, we do not have a clear picture of where we stand. For example, maybe you are young, not married, and not committed to a relationship. A close friend of yours has become pregnant, is not married and under no circumstances wants to marry the father of the child. She has asked for you advice about an abortion. In the process of thinking about how to respond to this request you will have to clarify your own values. You may not have thought too much about your beliefs, attitudes, and preferences for a great many social issues but you may be able to infer what they are simply from observing the regularities in your own behavior.

The **possible self** is an important type of self perception. Most students sooner or later have to deal with the possible self in connection with choosing a college major. The possible self is based on self conceptions about oneself in the future. When we think about our life goals and career goals we invoke the possible self. For example, when I first started teaching fifteen years ago, I aspired to one day be the chair of a sociology department. I imagined myself in a future role and what it would be like. More importantly, I imagined what I would have to be like in order to achieve that particular goal. Imagining ourselves in the future has implications for self concept in the present. The possible self allows us to deal with our fears about the future, to rehearse future roles, and to pursue our goals and dreams. Possible self allows us to develop a plan to achieve our goals. Possible self also allows us to abandon unrealistic goals.

Social Identity

Social identity refers to the identity that is derived from membership in a group. There are many groups in society to belong to, such as the family, religious groups, ethnic groups, racial groups, and sexual groups. Indeed, there are groups associated with social class, politics, education, leisure, and even age (I recently became old enough to be a member of the American Association of Retired People!). We have discussed previously how childhood socialization is greatly dependent upon membership in groups based on family, social class, and religion. The point here is that self concept and social identity are mutually reinforcing.

Let us use the social identity of gender as the example. Society emphasizes different qualities, behaviors, aptitudes, and even dress for men and women. In terms of human qualities, women are expected to be caring, sensitive, and emotionally responsive. Men are expected to be goal oriented, stoic, and achievement oriented. Women should be concerned with their looks, and making themselves attractive for their man. Men are supposed to be concerned with earning a living and maintaining order and discipline in the household. Women are thought to have an aptitude for communication and cooperation. Men are thought to have an aptitude for math and science. Of course these are just stereotypes but when we think about our qualities as men or women often we compare ourselves to these very stereotypes and try to conform to them. Some actors are more conforming than others. Since we grow up surrounded by these stereotypes it would be difficult not to judge ourselves in relationship to them.

Ethnicity is a major type of social identity. In our culture we are taught from the time we are children on that race and ethnicity matter. Interestingly, research shows that young children do not interact with each other on the basis of race or ethnicity. If you put a bunch of 1 to 2 year olds of different ethnic and racial background together in a room, they will not *see* race or ethnicity. Responding to someone's race or ethnicity is something that must be learned.

For all the language to the contrary, since we do still respond to each other on the basis of race and ethnicity we must be learning it from somewhere. I think the likely culprits are the family, media, and religion. For example, the Mormon Church teaches that Native Americans and other people of color had darker skin as a result of being cursed by God. I have been to Baptist church services in which church members actually put on skits as part of the church service derogating people of color, the poor, and the homeless. The media is full of racist and sexist stereotypes. The main culprit, however, has to be the family. Being raised by racists has to have an effect on a person's self concept.

Living in a culture that encourages people to *see* race, religion, sex, and ethnicity as personal qualities has to have an effect on the self conceptions of people who occupy those categories. Research has identified four types of ethic social identity.

1. **Integrated Ethnic Identity**: This is a bicultural type of ethnic identity. The actor identifies with both the dominant culture and with their particular ethnic group.

2. **Separated Ethnic Identity**: This actor has a strong sense of their ethnic identity accompanied by strong social ties to their ethnic group. However, they have weak ties to the dominant culture. Members of the dominant culture are often threatened by this type of ethnic identity.

3. **Assimilated Ethnic Identity**: In this case the actor has relinquished their ethnic identity and has adopted the identity of the dominant group. This is what members of the dominant group are most likely to desire and the intended function of public education.

4. **Marginal Ethnic Identity**: In this situation, the actor has only weak ties to both their ethnic group and to the dominant culture.

We see that for ethnic identity self concept is reinforced in four different ways. In a racist culture, a strong ethnic identity may lead to self concept problems. Since the desire of the dominant group will run toward assimilation, any individual who actively tries to maintain their ethnic identity will draw attention to themselves. An individual will likely have a strong ethnic identity if their parents have emphasized it in the home and through participation in ethnic organizations. We should point out that too that simply not being white is often enough to be singled out for differential treatment, as the chapter on racial stereotypes will review. It would be difficult *not* to think of yourself in ethnic or racial terms if people are continually interacting with you in a way that makes you conscious of your race or ethnicity. The same could be said about gender. One way for ethnic actors to preserve high self-esteem is to define that way that others treat them as racist, sexist, or otherwise prejudiced.

Self Schemas

Another aspect of self-knowledge is the structured cognitions we all have about ourselves – or **self schemas**. A self schema is a highly organized set of beliefs about oneself. A self schema refers to the usual ways in which we think about ourselves. What are the dimensions along which we can think about ourselves? Here are some examples:

- Morality
- Ethics
- Values
- Beliefs
- Talents, abilities, skills
- Likes and dislikes
- Personality
- Statuses and Roles
- Gender
- Sexuality
- Race or Ethnicity
- Dispositions and temperament

I suspect that each of the students reading this book has highly structured and organized conceptions of themselves for each of the dimensions listed above.

Many situations are schema-relevant, and therefore, often call forth certain behaviors. Teaching is schema-relevant. Being a teacher forces me to consider my ethics, values, and beliefs, in the normal course of preparing lectures, lecturing, writing tests, and assigning grades. As a sociologist, I belong to several professional organizations and I try to follow the American Sociological Association's code of ethics. Often, I find myself thinking about ethical matters in the course of the day. Not surprisingly, since I make ethical decisions on a daily basis, I consider myself to be a highly ethical person.

Other situations call forth other schema-relevant behaviors. Interacting with someone of the opposite sex, for instance, often stimulates self schemas. If a man flirts with a woman he knows is married, she can decide to either encourage him or discourage him. Whether she will or will not encourage him depends on her definition of how important her marriage vows are. We know that sometimes people decide to pursue extramarital affairs, thus there must be some variability in how binding some people define their marriage vows. If you find you are the only man in an all-female group, or only woman, in an all-male group, your gender will be salient to you.

SELF-REGULATION

Let me define self-regulation by using an example. I have a self-concept associated with being a college professor. The dimensions of this self-concept include ethics, values, beliefs, and behaviors. Let us just look at one item in my self-concept: assessing students overall knowledge of the subject matter. I believe that when it comes to assigning a grade, my behavior should be ethical and the assigned grade should be a reflection of the student's *actual* knowledge.

Recently, my self-concept in this regard has been challenged. When class size is limited to fewer than 20 students, I can use a variety of assessment measures, which might include essays, quizzes, research papers, or even student presentations. Under those conditions I am relatively confident about assigning a grade. But what happens to my certainty about any particular student's knowledge when the class size increases from 20 to 30, or to 50, or in some cases more than 100 students? Under these conditions I have to rely on multiple-choice tests. How do I maintain my self-conception as an ethical grader under these conditions? This question implies that, once actors have a relatively stable self concept, they seek to regulate and maintain it.

Here is an example of an extreme form of self-regulation. I was once visited by a student who came to me for advice. He said he was an evangelical with a major problem – the more he tried to be respectful toward women, the more he had thoughts of a sexual nature. It was so bad, he reported, that whenever he talked to a woman he basically saw a "floating head." This was definitely not normal.

I probed and discovered that his beliefs about sexuality and appropriate behavior were highly informed by his church and minister. His minister taught that it was a sin to even have *thoughts* of a sexual nature about anyone you were not married to. He had spoken to his minister about his problem and was advised to study the Bible harder and pray more. Apparently, this was not helping. He also reported that he was a virgin and had never even seen a naked woman. The source of all his guilt seemed to be that he could not help trying to steal a glance at the "secret parts of a woman," such as a woman's breasts if she leaned over. Given the social environment at college, I could understand how he was having difficulty regulating his self-concept as a Christian.

This reminded me of some of the research on drugs (sex can be as addicting as any drug). Wherever marijuana is legal people use it less than if it is criminalized. If it is legal the appeal seems to be diminished. I thought the same might be true in this situation. I gave him some different advice, which I am sure his minister would find appalling – I told him to take a look at some pictures of naked women, readily available on the internet or local newsstand, to see what the entire hubbub was about.

Normal sexuality includes an interest in the opposite sex. After all, how could the human race perpetuate itself through reproduction if we were uninterested in each other sexually? By closing himself off from any form of sexual excitement or gratification, in the name of self-regulation, he had turned himself into what he most feared, someone disrespectful toward women, lurking around trying to glimpse something. Sometimes if the release of tension is not achieved, you are left with increasing levels of tension until you explode! We all know what these explosions look like: abuse, rape, and violence. (Be careful not to read into this example something I did not say. I am not advocating the widespread dissemination of pornography. In this case, the individual's sexual development had been interrupted by religious ideas to the extent that normal development had not occurred. My suggestion was that he stop abusing *actual* women and educate himself about what a woman's body looks like in a way that would accomplish that and provide a release from the sexual tension he suffered from.)

Working Self-Concept

Working self-concept is the part of the self that is relevant to the particular situation you are involved in. Since we each occupy and variety of statuses in society, as we move from status to status throughout the day, our sense of self changes. These changes can be very slight or very dramatic, depending on the situations we find ourselves in. Working self-concept is informed by our overall self-concept, but it is that part of the self that guides our social behavior in specific interactions and situations.

Sometimes the working self-concept conflicts with the **stable self-concept**. I have been following several court cases related to religious values and contraception. Several states are proposing legislation that would allow individual pharmacists to decline to fill prescriptions for contraceptives on religious grounds. The Catholic Church, one among many, for example, rejects the use of contraceptives because the church leadership believes that the role of women is to have children. Contraceptives, from their point of view, diminish the roles of women in families. They may have a point. Imagine how difficult it would be for women to pursue an education or career without contraceptives. The only choice for women who want a career would then be abstinence, which is, of course, the goal of such legislation.

In this situation the conflict for the pharmacists would be between professional ethics and religious values. For a pharmacist, working self-concept would be that part of their self associated with their occupation and the ethics involved in being a pharmacist. Religious values would be part of their overall self-concept. They seem to be asking state legislators to relieve them of the burden of this conflict by making it legal for them to limit opportunities for women.

Here is another example. I teach social workers on a regular basis. Society and the Individual is a class they are required to complete as part of their professional training. Many social work students come from the evangelical religious background. Unfortunately for these students, the social work professional has a code of ethics that requires practitioners of the discipline to set their religious values aside for professional values and ethics, while on the job. This would bring stable self-concept (religious values) and working self-concept (social work values) in to conflict with each other on a regular basis. Many social workers I have worked with have told me that, over time, their stable self-concept comes into line with their working self-concept because it is too difficult to suffer from the cognitive dissonance if their stable self-concept does not change.

Self Complexity

Some people have a **restricted self-concept** – they only think about themselves in one or two ways. Others think of themselves along a variety of dimensions. Those with a simple self-concept are particularly vulnerable to failure in their predominant self-concept. If you have only one or two major dimensions to your self-concept, a failure in one of those areas could cause you a great deal of psychic suffering and discomfort. For example, if you primarily think of yourself in the parental role and your partner divorces you, without other roles in life you will be unable to deflect negative feelings associated with failure.

People who have a variety of dimension along which to think about themselves are better able to deflect a failure associated with one of them. If the person ends up divorced, they can emphasize other areas of their life in which they are successful. This will allow them to continue to keep a positive definition of themselves active in their minds. Perhaps you say to yourself, "yes, I failed at a personal relationship, but I am still really good at being a college professor." **Self-complexity** is a buffer against stressful events in life.

Actors with high levels of self-complexity, think about themselves from a variety of standpoints. The world is not black and white to them. They are generally more creative than people with less self-complexity. If you pay attention, you can spot them. They are constantly cogitating. They find it difficult to turn off the thinking process. Even if they are standing in line at the grocery store, they are reading or thinking about something. They occupy themselves.

People with less self-complexity are less interested in the problems of the world and tend to think about themselves in one or two simple ways. I once knew a woman that, invariably, could only talk about her children, no matter the social circumstances that brought us together. Whatever the occasion no matter the setting – she was bound and determined to talk about her children. Before I became educated I just disliked her because she seemed so self-centered. Now I realize that she just did not have any other dimensions of self to talk about. The point about self-complexity is that if you have a lot of roles in life you can compensate for a failure in one role by turning to the others.

Self-Efficacy

Another form of self-regulation is self-efficacy, which refers to highly specific beliefs we hold about our ability to perform a particular task. Actors with high levels of self-efficacy believe they can accomplish their goals or whatever tasks they have set for themselves. Self-efficacy is related to successes and failures early in life. If you have experienced some successes in the past, likely you will feel more comfortable taking on a goal or task that will entail some risks if you fail. On the other hand, if you have experienced some failures early in life, you may feel that you have little control over achieving your goals or that your fate is in the hands of others. People with high self-efficacy believe that they control their own fate.

Public/Private Self-Consciousness

The last dimension of self-regulation I will discuss is related to public and private self-consciousness. **Public self-consciousness** is the concern we often have with what others think of us. This concern is sometimes unavoidable. In our professional careers we often desire to be promoted and there may even be a process involved in which we have to market ourselves. In these situations you will have to be concerned about how you dress, your manners, your tone of voice and so on. I recall the first time I went to a promotion interview. I felt I should wear a suit so that my appearance would conform to professional standards. I also paid careful attention to how I spoke, to give the impression that I was an intellectual. When we become self-aware, we may try to adjust our behavior to conform to external standards, values, or attitudes.

Private self-consciousness refers to our actual goals and beliefs. Actors with high levels of private self-consciousness are more concerned with their internal goals and try harder to achieve personal standards. I have long since, for example, given up on wearing suits to lecture in. I do not follow many of the norms of "looking" like a college professor. Occasionally, the situation does call for me to be aware of certain standards, such as graduation or other ceremonies. For the most part, actors who are interested in their own standards are less likely to change their demeanor, dress, tone of voice, and so on as the situations change – they are more likely to try to "be themselves," rather than what others want them to be.

CONSISTENT SELF-CONCEPT

We are motivated to maintain a consistent sense of self. This means that we are constantly trying seeking **self-verification**. We seek out self-confirming interactions and situations. If you think of yourself as an intellectual, for example, you might try to maintain that self-concept by playing chess, reading books, or obtaining a college degree. On the other hand, we avoid situations which are at odds with our self-concept. We employ a variety of strategies to maintain and confirm our self-image. We seek out and interact with others who see us as we see ourselves. If you think you are intellectual you will like to hang out with people who also think you are. We choose clothing and other symbols on the basis on the presentation of self we are trying to make. In other words, we try to actively manipulate other's impressions of us.

Self-Presentation

Self-presentation refers to our efforts to control the impression we make on others. We often want people to view us in the way we desire, which is usually positively. We want to be seen as friendly, interesting, attractive, intelligent, and so on. There is plenty of room for variation. Some professors I know want students to *like* them. Other professors want students to *fear* them. Some professors want to be *respected*. I fall into this category. I am aware of one professor who wants to be known as the *"hardest"* professor ever encountered by a student, and this person works really hard to make that impression. Depending upon how we desire to be seen by others, we manipulate our self-presentation.

The way we present ourselves helps us clarify who we are to ourselves. It was not until I had actually stopped wearing a suit to class that I discovered that I really did not care whether the students cared about it or not. That told me something about myself. In many respects self-presentation is an act. It is a performance. Consider what goes into a performance: body language, language, dress, props, and tone of voice, eye contact, and overall demeanor. Think about the college professors you like and those you dislike. I am going to guess that those professors who you like the most give more effective presentations of themselves than those you dislike. In many respects, those who are successful in life understand that the world is a stage and those who can act better go further than those who act poorly.

CULTURE AND SELF

Our sense of self is developed in a social setting. We should not be surprised to discover that self-concept has cultural variations. In some cultures, the emphasis is on the individual and individual achievement. In other cultures, the emphasis is more collective and community oriented, and group success is more valued than individual success. Thus, self-concept will vary depending upon what is stressed by the particular culture you are socialized in. For example, some cultures stress equal opportunity for women and men. In other cultures, the role of women in society is restricted to the home.

Independent Self

In cultures that have a great emphasis on individuality and individual achievement an independent self-concept emerges. Actors socialized in these cultures see themselves as somewhat unique. They pay attention to what makes them different from everyone else, in terms of talents, abilities, or skills. They see themselves as a bounded person, separate from everyone else, as a distinctive whole in their own right. Societies that produce an independent self-concept tend to be described by ideologies related to competition, meritocracy, and individualism.

Interdependent Self

In cultures that emphasize the success of the collective or community, an **interdependent self-concept** emerges. Actors with an interdependent self-concept see themselves as part of an encompassing social relationship. Rather than see themselves as independent from the group, they realize that behavior is greatly determined by the group. The self is only meaningful and complete within the context of the larger social group.

ဆ ၛ ဆ ၛ

REFERENCES

Alicke, M.D., & Largo, E. (1995). The role of the self in the false consensus effect. *Journal of Experimental Social Psychology, 31*, 28-47.

Anderson, S. M., & Chen, S. (2002). The relational self: An interpersonal social-cognitive theory. *Psychological Review, 109*, 619-645.

Armor, D. A., & Taylor, S. E. (1998). Situated optimism: Specific outcome expectancies and self-regulation. In M. P. Zanna (Ed.), *Advances in experimental social psychology*. (Vol. 30, pp. 309-379). New York: Academic press.

Bandura, A. (1986). *Social foundations of thought and action: A social-cognitive theory*. Englewood Cliffs, NJ: Prentice-Hall.

Baumeister, R. F. (1982). A self-presentational view of social phenomena. Psychological Bulletin, 91, 3-26.

Baumeister, R. F. (1993). Understanding the inner nature of low self-esteem: Uncertain, fragile, protective, and conflicted. In R. F. Baumeister (Ed.), *Self-Esteem: The puzzle of low self-regard*. (pp. 201-218). New York: Plenum.

Baumeister, R. F. (1998). The self. In D. T. Gilbert, S. T. Fiske, & G. Lindzey (Eds.), *Handbook of social psychology* (4th ed.) (Vol. 1, pp. 680-740). New York: McGraw-Hill.

Baumeister, R. F., Campbell, J. D., Kreuger, J. I., & Vohs, K. D. (2003). Does high self-esteem cause better performance, interpersonal success, happiness, or healthier lifestyles? *Psychological Science in the Public Interest, 4*, 1-44.

Bohra, K. A., & Pandey, J. (1984). Ingratiation toward strangers, friends, and bosses. *Journal of Social Psychology, 122*, 217-222.

Carver, C. S., Sutton, S. K., and Scheier, M. F. (2000). Action, emotion, and personality: Emerging conceptual integration. *Personality and Social Psychology Bulletin, 26*, 741-751.

Collins, R. L. (1996). For better or worse: The impact of upward social comparison of self-evaluations. *Psychological Bulletin, 119*, 51-69.

Colvin, C. R., & Block, J., & Funder, D. C. (1995). Overly positive self-evaluations and personality: Negative implications for mental health. *Journal of Personality and Social Psychology, 68*, 1152-1162.

Cooley, C. H. (1902). *Human nature and social order*. New York: Scribner's.

Fazio, R. H. (1987). Self-perception theory: A current perspective. In M. P. Zanna, J. M. Olson, & C. P. Herman (Eds.), *Ontario symposium on personality and social psychology* (pp. 129-150). Hillsdale, NJ: Erlbaum.

Fein, S., & Spencer, S. J. (1997). Prejudice as self-image maintenance: Affirming the self through derogating others. *Journal of Personality and Social Psychology, 73*, 31-44.

Fenigstein, A. (1979). Self-consciousness, self-attention, and social interaction. *Journal of Personality and Social Psychology, 31*, 75-86.

Fenigstein, A., & Abrams, D. (1993). Self-attention and the egocentric assumption of shared perspectives. *Journal of Experimental Social Psychology, 29*, 287-303.

Ferrari, J. R. (1991). A second look at behavioral self-handicapping among women. *Journal of Social Behavior and Personality, 6*, 195-206.

Festinger, L. (1954). A theory of social comparison processes. *Human Relations, 7*, 117-140.

Forsyth, D. R., Schlenker, B. R., Leary, M. R., & McCown, N. E. (1985). Self-presentational determinants of sex differences in leadership behavior. *Small Group Behavior, 16*, 197-210.

Frable, D. E. S., Blackstone, T., & Scherbaum, C. (1990). Marginal and mindful: Deviants in social interaction. *Journal of Personality and Social Psychology, 59*, 140-149.

Gangestad, W., & Snyder, M. (2000). Self-monitoring: Appraisal and reappraisal. *Psychological Bulletin, 126*, 530-555.

Geizer, R. S., Rarick, D. L., & Soldow, G. F. (1977). Deception and judgment accuracy: A study in person perception. *Personality and Social psychology Bulletin, 3*, 446-449.

Gilovich, T., Medvec, V. H., & Savitsky, K. (2000). The spotlight effect in social judgment: An egocentric bias in estimates of the salience of one's own actions and appearance. *Journal of Personality and Social Psychology, 78*, 211-222.

Goffman, E. (1959). *The presentation of self in everyday life*. New York: Anchor Books.

Gollwitzer, P. M. (1986). Striving for specific identities: The social reality of self-symbolizing. In R. F. Baumeister (Ed.), *Public self and private self* (pp. 143-160). New York: Springer-Verlag.

Gollwitzer, P. M., Heckhausen, H., & Steller, B. (1990). Deliberative versus implemental mindsets. *Journal of Personality and Social Psychology, 59*, 1119-1127.

Hendricks, M., & Brickman, P. (1974). Effects of status and knowledgeability of audience on self-presentation. *Sociometry, 37*, 440-449.

Hogan, R. (1993). A socioanalytic theory of personality. In M. Page (Ed.), *Nebraska symposium on motivation: Personality – current theory and research* (pp. 58-59). Lincoln: University of Nebraska Press.

Holtgraves, T., & Srull, T. K. (1989). The effects of positive self-descriptions on impressions: General principles and individual differences. *Personality and Social Psychological Bulletin, 15*, 452-462.

Jones, E. E. (1990) *Interpersonal perceptions*. New York: Freeman.

Jones, E. E., & Baumeister, R. F. (1976). The self-monitor looks at the ingratiatory. *Journal of Personality, 44*, 654-674.

Jones, E. E., & Pittman, T. S. (1982). Toward a general theory of strategic self-presentation. In J. Suls (Ed.), *Psychological perspectives on the self* (vol. 1, pp. 231-262). Hillsdale, NJ: Erlbaum.

Leary, M. R. (1986). The impact of interactional impediments on social anxiety and self-presentation. *Journal of Experimental Social Psychology, 22*, 122-135.

Leary, M. R. (1995). *Self-presentation: Impression management and interpersonal behavior*. Madison, WI: Brown & Benchmark.

Leary, M. R., & Kowalski, R. M. (1990). Impression management: A literature review and two-component model. *Psychological Bulletin, 107*, 34-47.

Leary, M. R., & Tangney, P. P. (2003) The self as an organizing construct in the behavior and social sciences. In M. R. Leary, & J. P. Tangney (Eds.), *Handbook of self and identity* (pp. 3-14.). New York: Guilford Press.

Leary, M. R., Tambor, E. S., Terdal, E. S., & Downs, D. L. (1995). Self-esteem as an interpersonal monitor: The sociometer hypothesis. *Journal of Personality and Social Psychology, 68*, 518-530.

Leary, M. R., Tchividjian, L. R., & Kraxberger, B. E. (1994). Self-presentation can be hazardous to your health: Impression management and health risk. *Health Psychology, 13*, 461-470.

Mead, G. H. (1934). *Mind, self, and society.* Chicago: University of Chicago Press.

Mikulincer, M., & Florian, V. (2002). The effects of mortality salience on self-serving attributions – Evidence for the function of self-esteem as a terror management mechanism. *Basic and Applied Social Psychology, 24*, 261-271.

Miller, D. T. (1999). The norms of self-interest. *American Psychologist, 54*, 1053-1060.

Miller, R. S. (1995) On the nature of embarrassability: Shyness, social evaluation, and social sills. *Journal of Personality, 63*, 315-339.

Moskowitz, G. B. (1993). Individual differences in social categorization: The influence of personal need for structure on spontaneous trait inferences. *Journal of Personality and Social Psychology, 65*, 132-142.

Moskowitz, G. B., & Roman, R. J. (1992). Spontaneous trait inferences as self-generated primes: Implications for conscious social judgment. *Journal of Personality and Social Psychology, 62*, 728-738.

Muraven, M., & Baumeister, R. F. (2000). Self-regulation and depletion of limited resources: Does self-control resemble a muscle? *Psychological Bulletin, 126*, 247-259.

Murray, S. L., Rose, P., Bellavia, G. M., Holmes, J. G., & Kusche, A. G. (2002). When rejection stings: How self-esteem constrains relationship-enhancement processes. *Journal of Personality& Social Psychology, 83*, 557-573.

Nadler, A., & Fisher, J. D. (1986) The role of threat to self-esteem and perceived control in recipient reaction to help: Theory development and empirical validation. In L. Berkowitz (Ed.), *Advances in experimental social psychology* (Vol. 19, pp. 81-122). San Diego, CA: Academic Press.

Nezlek, J. B., & Leary, M. R. (2002). Individual differences in self-presentational motives in daily social interaction. *Personality and Social Psychology Bulletin, 28*, 211-223.

Pinker, S. (2000). *The language instinct: How the mind creates language.* New York: Harper Perennial.

Rhodewalt, F., & Augustsdottir, S. (1986). Effects of self-presentation on the phenomenal self. *Journal of Personality and Social Psychology, 50*, 47-55.

Rymer, R. (1994) *Genie: A scientific tragedy.* New York: Harper Perennial.

Schlenker, B. R. (1980). *Impression management: The self-concept, social identity, and interpersonal relationships.* Monterey, CA: Brookes/Cole.

Schlenker, B. R. (2003). Self-presentation. In M. R. Leary, & J. P. Tangney (Eds.), *Handbook of self and identity* (pp. 492-518). New York: Guilford Press.

Schlenker, B. R., & Pontari, B. A. (2002) The strategic control of information: Impression management and self-presentation in daily life. In A. Teser, R. B. Felson, & J. M. Suls (Eds.), *Psychological perspectives on self and identity* (pp. 199-232). Washington, DC: American Psychological Association.

Schlenker, B. R., Dlugolecki, D. W., & Doherty, K. (1994). The impact of self-presentations on self-appraisals and behavior: The power of public commitment. *Personality and Social Psychology Bulletin, 20*, 20-33.

3 | IDENTITY THEORY
by Frank O. Taylor, Ph.D.

STRYKER'S IDENTITY THEORY

Introduction

The key conceptual variable in symbolic interaction is that known as the self (Stryker and Serpe, 1983). The self is a product of society, according to Mead (1934), and Stryker relates the production of the self to the structured relations and social roles among individuals out of which social structure is comprised. The transsituational nature of social activity is the source of significant variability in the self. Mead's thesis states that the self is formed from social relations between people in a complex society; the self, then, must have a structure that reflects the organizational and hierarchical nature of society. However, Mead only conceptualizes the structure of self vaguely and generally. Stryker uses role theory to connect people to social structure and more precisely formulates what the structure of self may be composed of. Stryker employs the concepts of **identity salience** and commitment to develop his Identity Theory.

According to Stryker (1994), Identity Theory is concerned with the explanation of why people make one choice rather than another in situations where choice is possible. Not a complete account of choice, Identity Theory examines "a small set of variables that represent part of the heritage of Mead" (Stryker, 1994:15). Stryker begins with Mead's assertion that society and self are **dialectically** intertwined. The self is shaped by society and, thus, the self influences social behavior. In addition to Mead's basic premise, Stryker incorporates William James' conceptualization of self as a "multiple personality" with as many component selves as there are categories and others to interact with. It is Mead's notion of the self as a social structure, which is a reflection of the individual's particular location within certain groups that is important in Stryker's concept of self. In other words, the self is a reflection of both society generally and an individual's given position specifically.

Identity Theory views the self as "internalized cognitions of positions held in distinctive organized sets of social relations and the behavior expectations associated with those positions" (Stryker, 1993:16). Identities, therefore, are the internalized representations of social positions. Additionally, Stryker presents a modern version of social structure, rather than Mead's somewhat generic and basic ideas in that area. An emphasis on social structure recognizes the complexity and high degree of organization and interrelations among the various components of society. If each position in this complex totality has an associated identity, some being more defined than others, then it is possible that identities can be arranged in a hierarchy of salience. Salience is the tendency of the individual to enact certain identities rather than others over a broad range of social situations. The more salient an identity is for the actor, the likely the actor will engage in behaviors that reflect that identity.

Role Theory

Social role theory will be useful for the discussion of the relationship between the self and social structure; therefore, it will be reviewed here, before discussing Identity Theory in greater detail. The very notion of normative social roles implies statuses within some structured social hierarchy. While role enactment occurs at the individual level, much of that behavior is "expected" or normative behavior. The foundation of social role theory is the idea that an actor's social identity is largely a function of the validated social positions that they occupy (Sarbin and Scheibe, 1983). Sarbin and Scheibe postulate that social survival depends upon the ability of individuals to "locate" themselves in relation to others. Self-location in the role system is an inferential process in which actors ask themselves "who they are" in different situations. Sarbin and Scheibe stress that there is no answer to the question "who am I" without the reciprocal question "who are you" being answered. Thus social structure is implied in every interaction.

Matsueda (1992) further explains this notion of a reciprocal relationship between self and social structure. Symbolic interaction is predicated upon the thesis that social order is produced through the process of social interaction and communication. Shared meanings, behavioral expectations, and reflected appraisals defined by interaction are of central importance. According to Matsueda:

> These shared meanings attach to positions in society and thus link individual conduct to the organization of groups and to social structure. Social structure - the patterned regularities in society - is an ongoing process, built up by social interactions; moreover, social structure in turn constrains the form and direction of these interactions by structuring communication patterns, interests, and opportunities. The specific mechanism linking interaction and social structure is role-taking (Matsueda 1992:1580).

Role taking consists of imagining oneself in the role of the other and appraising, from the standpoint of that role, or social position, "the situation, oneself in the situation and possible lines of action" (Matsueda, 1992). Consensus over goals in differential situations and the normative means of fulfilling those goals is constructed, individual lines of action are coordinated, and concerted action towards achieving the goal takes place due to reciprocal role-taking (Blumer, 1969). What is important from a structural standpoint is that social structure is embedded in role expectations and enactments. Actors in similar positions in the social structure should behave in a similar fashion through the mechanism of "projecting" themselves into the role of others.

Mead (1934) outlined how this process occurs. In the play stage actors serially take the role of "significant others" who are available for interaction. As socialization proceeds, individuals learn to place themselves in the role of "generalized others" (the sum of all possible social roles), which is comprised of norms, rules and the expectations related to the various positions in the social hierarchy (Mead, 1934:152-164). Thus, individuals learn to place themselves systematically in relation to other people; they know, generally, what is expected of them in their roles, and what to expect of others in their roles. This amounts to a "social structure of identity," if identity attaches to the roles individuals engage in throughout their lifetime.

Most importantly, reciprocal role taking leads to cognitive development (Shibutani, 1961). When problems occur, in which some line of action an actor is pursuing is blocked, the cognitive process is called forth. This blockage transforms the self into object, or the "me" (Mead, 1934). In this mode the individual examines the various lines of action available, the possible reactions of others, and the anticipated reflected appraisals of others, or "looking-glass self" (Cooley, 1992). At this point, the actor switches into the "I" mode (Mead, 1934) and decides to either go ahead with a line of action or resist the impulse to act and continues to examine other self-images. In other words, an internal conversation takes place between the self and other self-images. Therefore, Mead (1934) views the act of "thinking" as similar in form and content to role-taking except that it occurs within the actor's mind between the "I" and the "me" (Matsueda, 1992).

Once again, what is important from a structural standpoint is that in similar situations, the "me's" - that part of the self formed when actors take the self as an object – are similar. Ideologically speaking, a common interpellation in late capitalistic societies is that of working class laborer (Althusser, 1971). Althusser indicates that individuals who are interpellated into different categories of subjectivity must be indoctrinated with the appropriate skills and knowledge so that the existing set of social relations may be reproduced. Thus, if the complexity of social structure is to be reproduced through social processes, such as education, and if the self is a reflection of a person's specific interactions in validated groups, some part of the self must therefore be class-based.

It is well documented that when teachers and administrators consider how to best teach their students, they often rely upon a technique known as tracking: separating their students into ability groups (Oakes, 1985). It is not surprising that minorities are over represented in vocational and low ability tracks considering that this is most often the education teachers and administrators feel is "realistically" appropriate. The assumption that most teachers apparently make is that working or lower class children will, at best, be working class in their adult lives and white children from affluent background will be college bound (Oakes, 1985; Bowles and Gintis, 1976).

Teachers and administrators are faced with a systematic problem: how to educate each child and ensure that they receive the knowledge and skill appropriate for their roles later in life. This implies that a system of stratification exists and not all children will have the same outcomes. Therefore, at the outset, it appears that school systems are as much involved in reproducing the social classes as they are in educating students.

The point here is that the vast majority of teachers, when faced with the problem of how to educate a group of children, resort at least informally, if not formally, to separating children in to groups of similar ability. Oakes (1985) indicates that the justifications for this practice are usually altruistic: it is a way to bring the slower children up to at least the level of ability of the average students. However, the outcome is generally the opposite. Children in the slower tracks are exposed to less material and the teachers have lower expectations of them, therefore, they never really catch up. Nevertheless, since most teachers do employ tracking it may be that because they are similar actors in similar roles, they feel that this is a natural solution to the problem and that they acted rationally and realistically.

In addition, the self emerges, as a stable entity because the "I" and "me" employed in one particular situation will resemble the "I" and "me" of similar past situations (Mead, 1934:142). Stryker (1980) uses the term "role-identities" to emphasize the connections to the many roles actors play. Therefore, many role identities are similar, regardless of the individual actors involved. Here again, social structure is explicit.

Social structure impinges upon stable definitions of the self and social identity even more directly when considering that individuals spend a great deal of time in unreflective institutionalized and routinized role enactments (Matsueda, 1992). Problematic situations repeatedly encountered become less problematic over time. The reason for similar "I" and "me" cognitive processes is that actors share a relatively stable and similar "generalized other." Each local world is comprised of social structures which are encountered daily. Work, for example, may be highly routinized for many people. And even for those whose work is not highly routine an objective set of bureaucratic rules usually exists. This is not meant to imply that a new and unique approach to a problem cannot be used by an actor: only that people may be inclined to use schemas known to work and with which they are familiar.

Matsueda (1992) points out that symbolic interaction views the individual as "constrained" by social structures, rather than determined by them. When lines of action are not clearly defined actors are constrained by related norms, values, and beliefs. People can and do violate social norms on a daily basis and experience various sanctions, both positive and negative. However, when problems are encountered, actors must rely upon the generalized other (social structure) in order to imagine alternative lines of action and evaluate the responses of others, thus, even cognitive processes are constrained by social organization. According to Blumer (1969), social structure affects the self by structuring communication and providing reference groups, which makes the act of taking the self as object meaningful in the first place. This process must be at work even for a deviant reference group.

Social Identity

Stryker (1987) has proposed a "structural" version of symbolic interaction theory (Stryker, 1980; Stryker and Serpe, 1982), using **role theory** to connect actors to the larger social structures of society. However, Stryker maintains the symbolic interactionist focus on the self as guiding and organizing behavior and as formed through social interaction. Stryker's argument is that social structures, roles, and statuses embedded in the social structure shape the interactions between individual selves (Stryker, 1987; Stryker and Serpe, 1982; Stryker, 1980). According to Stryker:

> With respect to the former [interactions], it [social identity theory] argues that self-definitions or meanings as well as definitions of others are importantly built around positional and role designations; with respect to the latter [social structure], it argues that these constrain the possibilities for role-making, for the construction rather than the "mere" enactment of behavior, and that they do so by constraining who comes together in what settings to interact for what purposes with what interactional resources (Stryker, 1987:91).

Therefore, according to Stryker, the construction of new roles or lines of action is constrained by the limits of the social structure and the roles and statuses available to actors.

Stryker's (1982; 1987; 1994) conceptualization of the self is one in which the self is a structure composed of differentiated discrete identities. These identities are the characterizations and role-enactments associated with social positions internalized by individuals and validated during social interactions. Drawing upon Mead, Stryker (1982:163) asserts that:

1. Persons seek to create and to maintain stable, coherent identities;

2. Identities motivate behaviors enacting or symbolizing those identities;

3. Identities emerge from social interaction;

4. Concrete behavior develops from a role-making process involving claims of identities and their verification or denial; and

5. Identities are fixed or stabilized through commitments.

Identities, then, are answers to the question "Whom am I?" that individuals reflect upon (Stryker and Serpe, 1982). People answer such questions by naming their positions in the social structure of interpersonal relationships in which they are engaged and the social roles which they enact. These social positions or statuses become the discrete "parts of the self - internalized positional designations that represent the person's participation in structured role relationships" (Stryker and Serpe, 1983:206). These **"role-identities"** are related to the differentiated sets of social positions within the social structure: such as father, mother, employee, homeowner, and so on.

Identity Salience

Stryker (1987) maintains that society produces the self and organizes the behavior of actors by placing them in networks of interaction which are highly differentiated and which produce highly differentiated actors. According to Stryker, "identity theory defines self as a structure of identities reflecting roles played in different networks of interaction, and postulates that the multiple identities involved will be organized in a hierarchy of salience" (1987:91).

This entire commitment to identity salience-role behavior process is understood to be conditioned by the larger social structure affecting objective possibilities for entering or remaining in particular kinds of networks of social relationships. In this way, the larger social structure, including systems of power, social class, sex, age, life course, etc., becomes an integral part of symbolic interactionist-based theorizing (Stryker, 1987:91).

Stryker and Serpe (1994) accept James's (1890) version of multiple selves, rather than a unitary self. This has the effect of organizing the self into a cognitive structure, which is composed of all the possible roles that an actor may enact. Thus, each actor has as many selves as there are other individuals and groups to come into contact with (James, 1890).

This is a theory of self in which the self is organized around multiple identities that are arranged in order of their salience to each particular actor. In other words, selves are hierarchically organized role-identities, some of which, or even one identity, a master status, are more important to the actor than others. Therefore, identity is organized as a "cognitive structure or schema" (Stryker and Serpe, 1994). Identity schemas help us make sense out of a complex world because they help us identify identity relevant information to respond to (Markus and Zajonc, 1985). Moreover, it depends upon which identities an actor is committed to when deciding which identity is selected in situations in which more than one identity option may be appropriate, thus, identity is a "trans-situational personality" variable (Stryker and Serpe, 1994). However, it is clear that many roles force identity-relevant behaviors upon actors.

Commitment

Stryker (1987) defines commitment as the degree to which any particular identity is necessary for the maintenance and definition of the individual as a certain "kind" of person. Thus, a person may be committed to occupying a certain position and playing certain highly defined roles (Stryker and Serpe, 1982). The focus is on the role identities to which people are highly committed and which are related to other important roles the person plays, such that the importance of those other persons requires one to be in certain positions playing certain roles. In others words, the degree to which any particular social role is related to other important social roles in the individual's social networks, that role requires more commitment. In Identity Theory, society impacts the self by placing individuals in reciprocal role relationships, and society impacts behavior through the processes of identity salience and commitment within each individual self.

Stryker and Serpe (1983) postulate that the more committed an individual is to any given identity the more salient that identity will be in the individual's identity salience hierarchy. The individual will, thus, have very positive evaluations of that identity and may base their self-esteem upon it. Additionally, the more central the identity is to valued social networks and relationships, the more salient the identity will be and the more highly committed the individual will be to that identity. If individuals are extremely committed to certain identities their role performances will be close to the expectations associated with that role. Thus, people will take advantage of opportunities to enact salient roles and even seek out such opportunities. Importantly, the more committed an individual is to a salient role the greater their self-esteem will be impacted by role performance, thus, the more likely their performance will reflect normative role expectations. It is this commitment to normative role enactments that reproduces social structure.

According to Thoits (1983), the process of enacting role-identities has two important implications. First, the individual has developed an awareness of the generalized other and of the social positions that they occupy in the social structure, second, "the developed self must be a complex, semi permanent, organized structure" (1983:175). Therefore, when an individual takes the role of the "generalized other," social positions and categories are recognized as well as the "social relations" that appertain to those categories. Each of these positions has a requisite set of role expectations and reciprocal role relationships (Thoits, 1983; Merton, 1957). Thus, Thoits, like Stryker and other structural symbolic interactionists, views the self as a set of differential identities of self-definitions congruent with positions occupied in the social structure.

Identity Accumulation Hypothesis

Social identities are created when people interact with each other on the basis of the statuses in society they occupy (Thoits 1983). These social identities, such as employer, employee, teacher, student, and so on, are governed by rights, duties, and obligations. Thus, social identities are based upon role identities that are relatively permanent and stable, yielding, in turn, a social identity which resembles an organized structure (Stryker and Serpe, 1982, 1983, 1994). The degree of commitment or "network embeddedness," and available time and energy, determines or constrains the hierarchical organization of the social identity (Thoits, 1983). Even more importantly, social positions themselves are ranked culturally and subculturally. Therefore, commitment to an identity should reflect its cultural or subcultural value or worth (Thoits, 1993; Goode, 1960).

Individuals may be more committed to a highly valued position and derive psychological benefits from its enactment or suffer psychological distress from its loss (Thoits, 1983). Thoits hypothesizes that as individuals collect more identities, commitment to any single identity decreases, whereas, if individuals lose identities, commitment to the remaining identities increases. Therefore, even a devalued or "spoiled" identity (Goffman, 1963) is necessary for "existential security" and commitment to it should be high (Thoits, 1983).

Actors with many social roles are well integrated and have many social identities (Thoits, 1983; 1991). On the other hand, actors who are socially isolated and less socially integrated have more to gain from identity accumulation and more to lose from identity loss. According to Thoits:

> The fewer identities claimed and valuated in interaction, the more
> existentially insecure the individual, and the more psychological distress
> he/she will exhibit. Varying degrees of isolation should produce similarly
> varying amounts of disturbance. Losses of positional relationships are the

primary isolating experiences in this formulation. The more important the position, the more committed the individual should be to it, and therefore, the greater should be the psychological impact of its loss...Thus, isolation (a lack of involvement in role relationships) is an essential condition for the subsequent development of psychological distress (Thoits, 1983:178-179).

Thoits explains that, in order for existential reality to exist, individuals must be embedded within networks of reciprocal role-identities. Individuals who are more involved in social networks are more socially integrated and have less psychological distress than less well integrated individuals. Moreover, she stresses that identity-relevant experiences or stressors are more useful predictors of psychological distress than identity-irrelevant experiences.

Macrosocial Influences on the Formation of Social Identities

Gurin, Hurtado and Peng (1994) provide a general framework that highlights the macrosocial conditions that lead to particular microsocial group contacts, which in turn, influence the construction of social identity. Gurin *et al* maintain that elements of the large macrosocial environment produce microsocial conditions that lead to the development of certain psychological processes involved in the formation of social identities. The macrosocial effects on identity formation include ethnicity, language, segregated neighborhoods, and opportunities to interact with others in the same social category or other social categories.

Social categorization and comparison is heightened or lessened by the frequency of intergroup and intragroup contacts (Tajfel, 1981; Turner and Oakes, 1989). Actors may identify with the groups into which they are categorized. Moreover, anything that tends to make social categorization more salient may also increase the salience of the cognitive and motivational processes involved in the creation of a social identity (Gurnin *et al*, 1994). Therefore, inter-group contact should increase the likelihood of the development of some type of social identity because it should increase the salience of social categorization. Frequent intra-group contact might lead to different types of social identities that are based on shared experiences. Minority group contact might encourage the construction of a social identity through the recognition of members of stigmatized groups of the commonality of their treatment (Gurin et al, 1994).

Lau (1989) offers three hypotheses concerning the contextual influence on group identification: 1) the similarity hypothesis, how readily a person is identified as an objective member of a group, 2) the salience hypothesis, the general salience of the group in society as a whole, and 3) the social density hypothesis, the proportion of fellow group members in the local environment. Lau suggests that people will identify with groups based on easily identifiable characteristics. Lau predicts that the probability of group identification is greater at low-density levels because if too many group members are present the salience of group membership is lowered. Lastly, Lau predicts that factors, which increase the salience of group membership, such as gender, race or ethnicity, should increase the probability of identifying with the group. If a person is treated as a member of a group, on the basis of salient characteristics, it is likely that group will become salient to the individual's identity.

Stryker on Social Structure

Stryker accepts the modern sociological definition of social structure as a "complex mosaic of parts, some interrelated and some not" (1994:17). Mead's generic version of social structure, according to Stryker (1982:175), does not recognize the social "strata, institutions, communities, formal organizations, interpersonal networks, and so on down to paired relationships...essential to the task of accounting for social life." Similar to Stryker, my reading of Mead does not agree with certain symbolic interactionists and social psychologists that reject the idea of social structure for a radical constructionism or interpretivism. From a structural standpoint, Stryker's theory is very appealing, due to its balance between Mead's insights about the importance of people's definitions, interpretations and meanings and a modern version of social structure. It is important to realize, as Stryker points out, that people live in local worlds, composed of relatively stable and enduring interactions taking place in small nodes of social relationships.

Identity theory maintains that social structure is complex, differentiated, and related to the key concepts of symbolic interaction: meaning, self, and social interaction (Stryker, 1982).

> I visualize social structure as affecting the probability of particular persons coming together in particular situations at particular times with particular interactional resources, including particular identities and systems of meanings. Accepting the interactionist dictum that self emerges from interaction, identity theory introduces social structure as a constraint on interaction (Stryker, 1982:175).

In addition to this general social structural constraint, Identity Theory stresses the importance of the interpersonal network - the immediate social structural setting in which selves are created and maintained composed of a particular set of individuals coming together under a particular set of circumstances (Stryker, 1982). Nevertheless, social structures are not "fixed" and are, after all, only what individuals happen to be doing in terms of roles. Thus, Stryker introduces the concept of "commitment" to retain the dynamics of the situation. Commitment is presented in terms of the individual's "involvement with or disengagement from particular others" (Stryker, 1982:176). The degree to which any individual is committed to an identity influences identity salience and, thus, one's role choices (Stryker, 1994).

Identity Theory uses the concept of social structure in two ways (Stryker, 1994). First, the theory recognizes that social structures, including age, gender, social class, etc. establish social boundaries. This makes it likely that people with similar material and symbolic resources that are constrained by similar social boundaries will establish networks for given purposes (Stryker, 1994). Social structure influences the formation, duration, and extinction of such social networks. A second manner in which social structure is important in Identity Theory is through the importance placed on the structural links between individuals involved in social networks, some networks being discrete and others overlapping. Social structure, thus, impacts in important ways identities related to positions within it and thereby role choices.

According to Stryker (1980), individuals are "constrained" by the interactional context of the social processes in which they find themselves. An individual's self-conceptualization is constrained by the existing "definitions of the situation, and the behavioral opportunities and repertoires that bound and guide the interaction that takes place" (1980:52). Before a definition of the situation can be constructed by any individual the necessary symbolic resources must be provided by social structure, such as reciprocal role networks, social organization, etc. Therefore, because individuals are born into an on-going social structure considering the impact of society upon the formation of the self is appropriate and any theory of the self must be able to move between the two levels of analysis (Stryker, 1980).

Stryker (1980) outlines a general framework that I will briefly review below.

1. Role enactments require a named and classified social world that gives meaning to behavior and social encounters.

2. The positions in the social structure are designated symbolically and have normative role expectations associated with them.

3. People recognize each other's status positions in prompting behavior expectations.

4. Individuals occupying particular status positions name themselves and in the process internalize behavioral expectations as part of their self.

5. During interaction people define the situation by naming it, themselves and other actors, and thus, know how to behave.

6. Although the interaction is constrained by prior definitions new possibilities may emerge, thus, behavior may be role-making rather than simple role-taking.

7. Some social situations allow for greater role-making than others.

8. When role-making does occur changes in definition, classifications and interaction possibilities may lead to changes in the larger social system.

To summarize, Stryker (1980) views interactions as constrained by the social setting rather than completely determined by it. In situations in which the social setting is relatively closed role enactments are more likely to be played. Conversely, in situations where the social setting is more open, considerable latitude in role enactments may occur, such that actors are more likely to role-make than role-play. Since no social system is completely closed, role making might lead to changes in the social structure.

Language and Symbols

A great deal of human behavior is unproblematic and habitual. According to Stryker (1980), this is due to the individual's earlier behavioral patterns that have, over time, proven successful. In many cases definitions of the situation are readily available. However, when behavior does become problematic individuals "symbolically represent the situation" to themselves and attempt to reach some definition of the situation (1980:53). Individuals rely upon symbols and language in order to develop a definition of the situation and for it to have meaning to them (Stryker, 1980). The use of symbols allows actors to focus upon and recognize the salient factors during an interaction, and thus organize their behavior accordingly. According to Stryker culture may be thought of "as a specification of what is important for interaction by being relevant to goal-oriented activity, a specification representing the cumulative experience of a social unit" (1980:55).

Culture provides linguistic and symbolic systems that signify various natural, biological, and social realities and organize meaningful human action (Stryker, 1989). These significations are usually abstracted from human behavior and are categorical. According to Stryker humans rely upon symbols: "the physical, biological, and social environment in which they live is a symbolic environment" (1980:56). Symbols prompt and organize behavior and are often representative of ready-made definitions.

Nonetheless, there are frequently periods when existing symbolic representations no longer hold, such as during a period of social crisis or change (Stryker, 1980). If social change is rapid and extensive enough the new situation may not be comparable to existing or prior definitions. New definitions must be articulated. These new definitions will be tested against the new social realities and during interactions may be reformulated. Indeed, all definitions, old or new, are tested and reformulated during interactions.

An example of a reformulation of the definition of the situation might be that encountered by newlyweds who, being egalitarian, agree to each contribute 50% to household chores. However, the arrival of the first child introduces a micro-contradiction, as childcare usually falls to the wife. When this micro-definition of egalitarian marriage is put to the test against the new reality, the definition is reformulated. From an Althusserian standpoint, the ideologies of capitalism, patriarchy, and egalitarianism have condensed into a contradiction. Since husbands are usually the highest paid earner in the family it seems logical for the couple to agree upon a more traditional childcare arrangement. From Stryker's standpoint, the old definitions held by the couple must undergo a reformulation.

Therefore, during interactions, whether they are interpersonal or macro discourses, definitions are challenged or validated and may even compete with other definitions (Stryker, 1980). Competing definitions may be modified further by definitions that emerge during the interaction. According to Stryker, "it is not unreasonable to conceptualize such interaction as involving a battle...over whose and which definitions are to prevail as the basis for future interaction" (1980:57).

Role

In order to define a situation individuals name themselves and others (Stryker, 1980). A social "position" (status) refers to categories of actors widely recognized as such. Thus, individuals are able to symbolically place themselves in relationship to other actors, understand what behavior is expected of them, and predict the behavior of others. Positional labels prompt certain behavioral expectations associated with various positions called "roles" (Stryker, 1980).

According to Stryker (1980), some role expectations are rigidly defined and require specific enactments. Other role expectations are merely outlines within which there is wide latitude for actors to experiment and improvise. Role expectations may pertain only to a limited number of interactions or to all of an actor's interactions. Additionally, role expectations "may attach to positions informally organized social structure or relate to informal social relationship" (Stryker, 1980:58). In many instances, due to the complexity of the social structure, actors are faced with conflicting and contradictory role expectations. Often that situation allows actors to improvise solutions.

Self

Stryker (1980) makes an interesting point concerning the self when behavior is purely reflexive and unproblematic: in these situations there may be no self. Self-reflective activity, taking oneself as an object, requires that actors view themselves objectively, from the point of view of others (reflected-appraisals). Therefore, self-reflection has implications for behavior. To have a self, then, requires that actors define themselves in relation to others based on "socially recognized categories and corresponding roles" (Stryker, 1980:59). In the complex social structure there are many positions, some more defined than others, and their attendant role requirements, some of which require precise enactments and others that only loosely defined. Therefore, any individual has many selves, corresponding to the positions they occupy in the social structure (Stryker, 1980).

Identity

As part of the self, identity is positional internalization that organizes behavior based on structured role relationships. According to Stryker, an actor has an identity when they "appropriate and announce" an identity and are placed as a social object by others in the same terms (1980:60). The actual number of identities an actor may have is limited only by the number of structured role relationship they participate in.

Theoretically, the self can be conceptualized as constructed of discrete identities arranged in a hierarchy of salience (Stryker, 1980). According to Stryker:

> It is likely that an identity's location in a salience hierarchy will lower or raise its "call up" threshold in interaction with other defining characteristics of situations. To the degree that a situation is structurally isolated - has no implications for other interactive situations - it is less likely that more than one identity will be invoked. But to the degree that there is structural overlap among situations - i.e., when analytically distinct sets of social relationships do impact with one another - different identities are likely to be concurrently called up. If different identities are called up, they may or may not carry conflicting or contradictory expectations. If they do their relative location in the identity salience hierarchy becomes a potentially important predictor of subsequent behavior (Stryker, 1980:61).

Role-Taking and Socialization

Role expectations are important to the "structure of the self" (Stryker, 1980:62). Interactions are defined through the process of placing oneself in relationship to others based on positional designations, and other physical and behavioral clues. During socialization actors learn what identities are possible within the culture, subcultural variations, statuses and their attendant roles, the degree to which creativity and innovation can be used in the definition of any given role, and counter positions which are not occupiable (Stryker, 1980).

Role-taking is the process of imagining oneself in the place of another by using symbols (Stryker, 1980). In this manner individuals are able to anticipate the responses and behaviors of others with whom they are interacting. Individuals rely upon symbols, past experiences, and particular or comparable others in order to develop a particular definition of others attitudes, responses, and future responses. During the interaction process old definitions are tested, non-valid definitions are reformulated or discarded.

Although shared experiences and symbols are not universal, and may in some cases be contested, they are part of collective reality and, to a large degree, they are the basis of social life (Stryker, 1980). Actors are repeatedly "cast" into roles by others who provide cues meant to elicit role-enactments.

To the degree that the person comes to incorporate societal definitions of appropriate role behavior into self and to internalize their accompanying expectations, the person is effectively controlled. There are at least two mechanisms implicated in this process. First, persons will generally seek confirmation or validation of their identities - by behaving in ways that elicit validating responses from others. Thus, having an identity that is premised on societal definitions will tend to produce behavior that conforms to those definitions. Second, self-esteem becomes tied to behaving in accord with a salient identity (Stryker, 1980:64).

The processes by which actors learn to conform are not different from those by which they learn to be deviant (Stryker, 1980). In a highly complex and differentiated society, in which there are a host of subcultural local worlds with different norms and values, the process of socialization can also produce non-conformity.

Social Structure

Human interaction is characterized by patterned regularities (Stryker, 1980). Most interactions between individuals occur within their local world with relatively stable groups of people. These interaction networks, including families, co-workers, and neighbors, tie individuals together through regular and predictable interactions. There is a pattern to every interaction we engage in. These pattered interactions can be thought of as social structures. Thus, local worlds are connected to collective reality by the more abstract components of social structure, such as "class structure, power structure, age structure, ethnic structure, and so on" (Stryker, 1980:66).

Therefore, according to the above discussion, one of the consequences of a differentiated and complex social structure is that individuals are not randomly thrown together in interactions (Stryker, 1980). The opportunities for interaction and association are not randomly distributed and most interactions take place within an actor's typical situations and settings. Hence, the social structure provides the opportunities and conditions of interaction. However, this is not a static relationship. If social actors change the patterns of interaction then social structures also change.

I am reminded of the experiences of several friends of mine who were able to beat their addictions to alcohol only by completely restructuring their local worlds to the extent that they no longer maintained contact with friends who used alcohol or frequented drinking establishments. They were able to reinforce their alcohol-free lives by establishing new social networks with non-drinkers. It is important to note that these people were able to *use* social structure to their advantage and actively restructure their role relationships at the local level simply by seeking out new friends and social settings. Nevertheless, they had to have the desire to quite drinking in the first place. Since their social environments included interactions with many individuals who used alcohol it is hard to see how the impulse to quite drinking could have arisen from a social network that validated using alcohol. The desire to beat an addiction implies a self that is active.

I maintain that in order for an individual to have a self there must be a generalized other that is apprehended as a social structure of positions and corresponding role requirements. Individuals develop existential security by becoming embedded in reciprocal interaction networks. Moreover, these interaction networks must be relatively stable and non-problematic. Since interaction networks are not randomly distributed and are influenced by variables such as social class, race or ethnicity, gender and community, the existential security of any individual is dependent upon the location of the local world within the existing social structure. Therefore, the objective social structure provides opportunities for and limits upon the interaction networks that make up an individual's local world.

Additionally, individuals experience reality in their local worlds, through daily, repetitive and stable interaction networks. Thus, particular local worlds are likely to become the basis of individuals' "reference reality": the collection of social experiences and interaction networks an individual refers to when making judgments about the nature and order of reality. Since reference reality is dependent upon interaction networks in local worlds, which are themselves structurally differentiated, upon this structural variable alone I predict that it is possible for multiple "reference realities" to exist. Moreover, "reference reality" becomes the basis of interpreting "collective reality." Thus, collective reality, the real foundation of local worlds and interaction networks, are so far removed from immediate and daily interaction networks that it becomes an abstract and symbolic representation.

This is what Althusser means when he maintains that individuals "imagine" their relationship to their real conditions of existence. Individuals imagine collective reality by referring to their interaction networks within their local worlds. In considering the importance of the family in the socialization process of children, Stryker and Serpe (1983) note that the behaviorist, Freudian and functionalist theories of socialization grant omnipotent status to the role of parents. In the structural-functionalism of Parsons (1951; and Parsons and Bales, 1960), social structure is granted the preeminent position and the family simply reflects the functional requirements of the social system. In any case, the above theories of socialization fail to note the limits of the family and parents in the socialization process (Stryker and Serpe, 1983). On the other hand, and equally misguided according to Stryker and Serpe, is the tendency of symbolic interactionists following Blumer to view social life as emergent, constructed and unfolding without any reference to social structure. Socialization does not occur in a vacuum and families are part of the social structure. Moreover, there are certain structured patterns involving socialization. Stryker insists that the emergent and constructed qualities of social life deserve to be recognized but the "socially structured constraints on what can emerge and on what is constructed" not only obviously exist but also deserve to be recognized by symbolic interactionist (Stryker and Serpe, 1983:51).

As is apparent by now, Stryker follows Mead's assertion that the self and society are dialectically related, each determines the other. The interactionist contention that the person and society are mutually determinative leads directly, then, to an image of the person as a structure of positions and roles. Internalized, that structure is the self. The relation of the self and society, however, is not static; thus, the issue now becomes how a dynamic relationship between individual and society is to be dealt with conceptually, theoretically, and analytically (Stryker and Serpe, 1983:51).

If society is composed of a complexity of highly differentiated and interrelated groups then that level of complexity must be reflected in the self. This is implied by Mead but not very well developed. Stryker and Serpe (1983) address the question of the dynamic relationship between self and society by viewing self as a cause of social behavior rather than simply a consequence of it. This is suggested by the symbolic interactionist premise that reciprocal role relations exist "among three conceptual entities: interaction, society, and self" (Stryker and Serpe, 1983:52). Reciprocities are not instantaneous, uniform in direction, intensity or in any sense equal. From this perspective, the self is necessary for the explanation of behavior. In other words, behavior in the social setting requires not just social stimuli but also a self. Again, Stryker incorporates identity salience and commitment to valued identities to give the self-dynamic qualities.

Social networks are the media that link discrete actors to the larger social structure. According to Stryker and Serpe:

> Networks are located in some institutional context: families in the kinship institutions of society, work networks in the economic institutions, and so on. Institutions, as well as the multiple broad social strata - class, status, power, and age - both provide content to network relationships and constrain the kinds of persons who enter, the kinds of social meanings from which interaction proceeds, and the interactional resources available to network members. These networks may be highly specialized or heavily overlapping in personnel and other features...(1983:53).

Local worlds, thus, are comprised of the networks of interaction located with the institutions and social structures of society. Any particular family, for example lives in a certain neighborhood. Neighborhoods are zoned for certain types of dwellings, apartments or single family. Of course, social class is indirectly related to the ownership of a home because zoning laws specify what homes may cost, out of what materials they shall be built, what types of roofs they may have, etc. Since income is related to occupation and social class it is likely that others in the neighborhood have similar incomes and social class positions.

It is not enough to suggest that any individual's local world exists within the institutional context without recognizing that even deeper structures exist. For example one may have an interactional network at one's work place and, thus, be institutionally involved in the economy. However, the economy rests upon other factors as well, such as Capitalism and the Protestant work ethic. Therefore, individuals not only have interactions in their networks but those interactions have ideological components. Ideology is practice, i.e. behavior. If the self is a cause of behavior ideology becomes a tool. Selves use ideology as much as they are influenced by ideology. More, ideologies related to highly valued identities to which individuals are highly committed are more likely to be useful than ideologies associated with identities to which individuals are not committed.

This analogy can be carried out for all social institutions. Children attend specific schools; those schools are part of the social institution of education. There are ideologies associated with education such as meritocracy, competition, individualism, etc. One may work at a specific job at a factory or office, within in the blue-collar, white collar or pink-collar occupations; these jobs exist within the social institution of the economy. Certain ideologies are related to the economy. One may attend a specific church; that church is part of the social institution of religion. Ideologies associated with religion may include traditional patriarchal gender roles, heterosexuality, etc. Thus, the ideologies associated with the various institutions within which local worlds are situated become part of the "generalized other."

Social Change

An important aspect of role enactment which role theory often neglects is that, frequently, social roles are ambiguous (Stryker and Serpe, 1983). Additionally, it is not always clear which role is appropriate for the situation, making role enactment somewhat difficult. Roles and statuses are, after all, only concepts. In reality, concepts have a way of loosing their boundaries, of dissolving into chains of relatedness and in-order-to relationships. The upshot of this is that role enactments are quite often very problematic. Stryker (1994) points out the degree of randomness and chance in human social interaction.

While it is true that behavior is constrained by social organization the very complexity of society leads to a certain degree of ambiguity. People don't always behave according to role expectations. Additionally, a person may be so highly committed to an identity that they allow it to determine their behavior in situations where it may not be appropriate, such as invoking the fatherhood role at work. Thus, it is important to apply Mead's concept of "mind" to situations in which role performance is so ambiguous as to really be role-making. This implies an active self. Mind emerges in response to problematic situations; the "I" is called forth by such situations and under these circumstances role performance is really role-making.

Mead insists that, although such self-reactions may be infinitely small, role-making changes social structure. This emphasis on role-making preserves the emergent qualities of the self and social interaction. I suggest that since ideologies are really behaviors and that there are a multitude of ideologies associated with the institutions within which individuals act in their local worlds there is bound to be certain contradictions among them. Ideological contradictions, thus, also call out the "I" because of their problematic nature. Indeed, under such circumstances new reactions to social stimuli may emerge.

CONCLUSION

Summary Statements

1. The transsituational nature of society is the source of significant variability in the self.

2. The self must have a structure that reflects the organizational and hierarchical nature of society.

3. The structure of the self reflects the structure of society generally, and, more specifically, the groups in which the individuals carry on interactions.

4. A person's social identity is related to validated social positions that they occupy.

5. Individuals locate themselves inferentially in the social hierarchy by asking themselves "who" they are in different situations.

6. There is a reciprocal relationship between self and social structure: social structure is composed of patterns of regularity that emerge from social interaction; in turn, social interaction is constrained by these patterns.

7. Agency is facilitated by social structure, coordinated and concerted action by groups of individuals, and reciprocal role-taking.

8. Reciprocal role-taking leads to cognitive development as individuals "take the role of the other" in problematic situations.

9. The self emerges as a stable identity in as much as the "I" and "me" processes employed in one situation resemble those of past situations.

10. "I" and "me" processes *between* individuals are similar to the extent that individuals share a relatively stable "generalized other."

11. Social structures, roles, and statuses shape the interaction between individuals by constraining whom it is possible to interact with and under what conditions.

12. Macrosocial influences on identity formation include ethnicity, language, segregated neighborhoods, and opportunities to interact with others from different social categories.

13. Social structure is complex, including social strata, institutions, such as marriage and family, education, etc., communities and neighborhoods, interpersonal networks, such as those at work or school, and more abstract structures such as age, gender, and ethnicity.

14. Social structure constrains the probability of people interacting in particular settings, creating social boundaries.

15. In situations where the social setting is less constrained individuals may engage in considerable role-making; in situations where the social setting is more constraining, individuals are more likely to give appropriate role-performances, especially if the situation is associated with a valued identity.

16. The self is a structure composed of differentiated and discrete identities internalized by individuals through validated role-enactments and social interactions.

17. The self is a structure of identities associated with an individual's specific networks of interaction; there are as many identities as networks one is involved in; identities are organized in a hierarchy of salience.

18. The salience of any identity in an individual's identity salience hierarchy is conditioned by the larger social structure that constrains the opportunities for interaction in particular kinds of networks.

19. The more committed an individual is to any given identity the more salient that identity will be, especially if the identity is central to valued social networks.

20. As individuals collect more identities commitment to any single identity may decrease, while on the other hand, as individuals' loose identities, commitment to remaining identities may increase.

21. In order for individuals to be "existentially secure" they must be involved in networks of reciprocal role identities.

22. In order for a situation to be defined individuals name themselves and others by referring to their respective social statuses and role expectations.

23. To have a self requires that individuals encounter problematic situations in which self-reflective activity is called forth, which implicates social structure in as much as individuals take themselves as an other based on their social networks.

24. Individuals seek validation of their identities by giving appropriate role-performances.

25. Human interaction is characterized by patterned regularities occurring in reciprocal role networks in local worlds.

26. Local worlds are located within institutional settings that connect them to the collective reality.

ℰ ℭ ℰ ℭ

REFERENCES

Althusser, L., & Balibar, E. (1970). *Reading capital*. London: New Left.
Althusser, L. (1969). *For Marx*. London: New Left.
Althusser, L. (1971). *Lenin and philosophy*. New York: Monthly Review Press.
Berger, P. L., & Luckmann, T. (1967). *The social construction of reality: A treatise in the sociology of knowledge*. New York: Anchor Books, Doubleday & Co.
Berger, P. L. (1963). *Invitation to sociology: A humanistic perspective*. Garden City, NY: Doubleday.
Blumer, H. (1969). *Symbolic interactionism: Perspective and method*. Englewood Cliffs, NJ: Prentice-Hall.
Bowles, S., & Gintis, H. (1976*). Schooling in capitalist America*. New York: Basic Books.

Burke, P. J. (1991). Identity processes and social stress. *American Sociological Review, 56,* 863-849.

Callero, P. (1994). From role-playing to role-using: Understand role as resource. *Social Psychological Quarterly, 3,* 228-243.

Carlton, E. (1984). Ideologies as belief systems. *International Journal of Sociology and Social Policy, 4(2),* 17-29.

Charon, J. M. (1989). *Symbolic interactionism: An introduction, an interpretation, an integration.* (3rd ed.), Englewood Cliffs, NJ: Prentice Hall.

Cohen, J. L. (1985). Strategy or identity: New theoretical paradigms and contemporary social movements. *Social Research, 52,* 663-716.

Cookson, P. W., & Persell, C. H. (1985). *Preparing for power: America's elite boarding schools.* New York: Basic Books.

Cooley, C. H. (1922). *Human nature and the social order,* (Rev. ed). New York: Scribners.

Goffman, E. (1963). *Stigma: Notes on the management of a spoiled identity.* Englewood Cliffs, NJ: Prentice-Hall.

Goldstein, J., & Rayner, J. (1994). The politics of identity in late modern society. *Theory and Society, 23*(3), 367-384.

Goode, W. J. (1960). A theory of role strain. *American Sociological Review 25,* 483-496.

Gurin, P., Hruado, A., & Peng, T. (1994). Group contacts and ethnicity in the social identities of Mexicanos and Chicanos. *Personality and Social Psychology Bulletin, 20,* 521-532.

James, W. (1890). *Principles of psychology.* New York: Holt.

Josephs, R. A., Markus, H., & Tafarodi, R.W. (1992). Gender differences in the source of self-esteem. *Journal of Personality and Social Psychology, 63,* 391-402.

Lau, R. R. (1989). Individual and contextual influences on group interaction. *Social Psychological Quarterly, 52,* 220-231.

Markus, H. R., & Zajonc, R. B. (1985). The cognitive perspective in social psychology. In *The Handbook of Social Psychology* (Vol. 1, pp. 137-230) Gardner Lindsey and Elliot Aronson (Eds.), New York: Random House.

Markus, H. R., & Kitayama, S. (1994). A collective fear of the collective: Implications for selves and theories of selves. *Personality and Social Psychology Bulletin, 20,* 568-579.

Matsueda, R. L. (1992). Reflected appraisals, parental, labeling, and delinquency: Specifying a symbolic interactionist theory. *American Journal of Sociology, 97,* 1577-1611.

McCarthy, E. D. (1994). The uncertain future of ideology: Rereading Marx. *Sociological Quarterly, 35(3),* 415-429.

Mead, G. H. (1932). *The philosophy of the present.* Chicago: University of Chicago Press.

Mead, G. H. (1934). *Mind self and society.* Chicago: University of Chicago Press.

Melucci, A. (1988). Getting involved: Identity and mobilization in social movements. *International Social Movement Research, 1,* 329-348.

Merton, R. K. (1957). *Social theory and social structure.* New York: Free Press.

Oakes, J. (1985). *Keeping track: How schools structure inequality.* New Haven, CT: Yale University Press.

Sarbin, T. R., & Scheibe, K. E. (1983). A model of social identity. In Sarbin, T. R., & Scheibe, K. E. (Eds), *Studies in social identity.* New York: Praeger.

Shibutani, T. (1961). *Society and personality.* Englewood Cliffs, NJ: Prentice Hall

Somers, M. R. (1994). The narrative constitution of identity: A relational and network approach. *Theory and Society, 23*(5), 605-649.

Stryker, S. (1988). Substance and style: An appraisal of the sociological legacy of Herbert Blumer. *Symbolic Interaction, 11*(1), 33-42.

Stryker, S., & Craft, E. A. (1982). Deviance, selves and others revisited. *Youth and Society, 14*(2),159-183.

Stryker, S., & Serpe, R. T. (1994). Identity salience and psychological centrality: Equivalent, overlapping, or complementary concepts? *Social Psychology Quarterly, 57*, 16-35.

Stryker, S., & Serpe, R. (1983). Toward a theory of family influence in the socialization of children. *Research in Sociology of Education and Socialization, 4*, 47-71.

Stryker, S. (1972). Symbolic interaction theory: A review and some suggestions for comparative family research. *Journal of Comparative Family Studies, 3*(1), 17-32.

Stryker, S. (1977). Developments in "Two social psychologies": Toward and appreciation of mutual relevance. *Sociometry, 40*(2), June, 145-160.

Stryker, S. (1978). Status inconsistency and role conflict. *Annual Review of Sociology, 4*, 57-90.

Stryker, S. (1980). *Symbolic interactionism: A social structural version.* Menlo Park, CA: Benjamin/Cummings.

Stryker, S. (1982). A review symposium: Symbolic interactionism: A social structural version. *Symbolic Interaction, 5*(1), 139-165.

Stryker, S. (1987). The vitalization of symbolic interactionism. *Social Psychology Quarterly, 50*(1), 83-94.

Stryker, S. (1989). The two psychologies: Additional thoughts. *Social Forces*; *68*(1), 45-54.

Stryker, S. (1994). Identity theory: Its development, research base, and prospects. *Studies in Symbolic Interaction, 16*, 9-20.

Tajfel, H. (1981). *Human groups and social categories: Studies in social psychology.* London: Cambridge University Press.

Tajfel, H. (1981). *Human groups and social categories: Studies in social psychology.* Cambridge: Cambridge University Press.

Thoits, P. (1983). Multiple identities and psychological well-being: A reformulation and test of the social isolation hypothesis. *American Sociological Review, 48*, 174-187.

Thoits, P. A. (1991). On merging identity theory and stress research. *Social Psychology Quarterly, 54*,101-112.

Thoits, P. A. (1993). Multiple identities and psychological well-being: A reformulation and test of the social isolation hypothesis. *American Sociological Review, 48*, 174-187.

Thoits, P. (1991). On merging identity theory and stress research. *Social Psychology Quarterly, 57*, 101-112.

Turner, J. C., & Oakes, P. J. (1989). Self-categorization theory and social influence. In P. B. Paulus (Ed.), *The Psychology of group influence* (2nd ed. pp. 322-75). Hillsdale, NJ: Lawrence Erlbaum.

Turner, J. C., & Oakes, P. J. (1989). Self-categorization theory and social influence. In P. B. Paulus (Ed.), *The Psychology of Group Influence* (2nd ed., pp. 233-257) Hillsdale, NJ: Lawrence Erlbaum.

Turner, R. H. (1969). The theme of contemporary social movements. *British Journal of Sociology, 20*, 390-405.

Turner, R. H., & Killian, L. M. (1987). Toward a theory of social movements. In *Collective Behavior*, (3rd ed, pp. 241-261). Englewood Cliffs, NJ: Prentice-Hall.

PART TWO: SOCIETY AND THE INDIVIDUAL

4 | THE INDIVIDUAL, GROUPS, AND SOCIAL INFLUENCE
by Frank O. Taylor, Ph.D. with Alexander F. Rice

THE IMPORTANCE OF GROUPS

What is a social group? Let us start by defining what a group is not. A group is different from an aggregate. If you go to the mall you will see hundreds of people gathered there to window shop and cruise the stores but beyond the need to shop for something there is no underlying purpose that makes them special in any way. An aggregate is simply a bunch of people who happen to be in one place at the same time.

A **group** is at least two people who interact with each other based on shared norms, values, and beliefs. People in groups have a sense of belonging or a shared identity based on the expectation of interacting together. Common groups include the family, peer groups, sororities and fraternities, professional associations, clubs, and so on. Groups are characterized by norms of behavior. Larger groups usually have formal rules of behavior written down somewhere. Groups are also characterized by positions within the group, known as **statuses**. Mother, father, brother, and sister, are statuses within the family. Each status in the group has an associated range of behaviors that define it. These are known as **roles**. Sociologists are interested in groups because a great deal of socialization takes place in groups. Groups play an important role in the transmission of culture across generations.

TYPES OF GROUPS

Primary and Secondary Groups

A small group characterized by face-to-face interaction is known as a **primary group**. Primary groups are of long duration. For example, you will be a member of your family for your entire life. In general, we are loyal to our primary groups because they tend to define "who" we are. Primary groups fulfill many emotional needs, such as a sense of belonging, a sense of togetherness, and a sense of personal worth. These are *expressive goals*. Along with the family, the peer group is a common primary group. We usually have a very strong identification with our peers and derive a good deal of our identity from interaction with peers. Behavior in primary groups is governed by traditions. Each family or each peer group creates their own traditions but they are often a reflection of the norms of society.

A group that is large and impersonal with a formal organization is a **secondary group**. You will be a member of a good many secondary groups during your lifetime. When you are in the classroom at college you are a member of a secondary group. We come together at college, not for expressive or emotional reasons, but for *instrumental goals* – to achieve formal education. In very large secondary groups we may not even have the opportunity to meet everyone involved, let alone get to know them as people. They are anonymous to us and our relationship to them is mostly formal. Secondary groups often define "what we do."

In-Groups and Out-Groups

In-groups and out-groups establish social boundaries. They also engender a lot of social conflict between groups. A group, which we hold in high esteem, is considered an in-group. An **in-group** may be a group you desire to become of member of or a group you already belong to. A consequence of in-group membership is that out-groups are implied. In groups foster feelings of superiority over out-groups.

An **out-group** is a devalued group. Out-groups often are opposed to your in-group. For example, if you are a Republican, the Democrats and Greens are probably out-groups for you. Frequently out-groups have a **spoiled identity**. Spoiled identity refers to groups of people often ridiculed by society or held up as examples of bad behavior. Common out-groups with spoiled identities include welfare mothers, prisoners, the homeless, and often the mentally handicapped.

In 1999 in Littleton Colorado, two members of an out-group called the Trenchcoat Mafia, who resented the teasing and taunting they were subjected to by the Jocks, attacked and killed students and teachers. This incident left 15 dead. Often adolescents feel rejected by classmates and overwhelmed by academic responsibilities. When they are pumped up by media images of violence and messages about revenge and retribution, derogated actors may lash out against perceived in-groups. Although society cannot forgive this behavior, in order to prevent future episodes of violence we should strive to understand in-group/out-group dynamics.

Reference Groups

Group membership affects nearly every aspect of our lives. It is related to patterns of speech, dress, interaction, leisure, and so on. A reference group is a group individuals use as a standard of evaluating themselves. As a college professor, for example, I often consider how I am doing in my professional career. In this respect, my reference group is comprised of the other sociologists I went to graduate school with, the professors who taught me, the members of my department, and in a broader sense, sociologists in general. I use these people as a bell-weather for gauging how successful I am. Of course, I have other reference groups as well, some related to leisure pursuits and some related to family life.

Reference groups, such as an adolescent peer group, have great ability to influence behavior. If you want to join a reference group you will have to conform to their standards of conduct, values, and beliefs. If you want to join a peer group of "gamers," for example, other people who like to play video games, you will have to play the same video games they do, dress like they do, and have similar attitudes and values, and so on. Across the normal life cycle, you can expect to belong to a variety of reference groups. When you are 45, for example, it is unlikely that you will still measure yourself against a reference group you used in adolescence.

Interaction and Group Size

The simplest of all social groups, and the most unstable, is the dyad. A **dyad** is a two-member group. A common dyad is the wife/husband dyad. The level of intimacy that can be achieved in a dyad cannot be replicated in any other type of group. Dyads also have a lot of freedom to construct their role relationships however those involved wish. If the couple desires egalitarian roles they may establish them. Conversely, if the couple wants to base their roles on traditional arrangements they may do so. Dyads have a great deal of flexibility in this regard.

Role expectations refer to those roles society generally expects people to perform. For example, in my role as a professor, students have fairly concrete expectations of the behaviors I should engage in. These include lecturing, writing tests, grading, reading in preparation of lecturing, and so on. They expect every professor to perform these roles. But role expectation and role performance are two different concepts. **Role performance** refers to flair, style, or personality. Not every college professor lectures in exactly the same way – each has a style somewhat their own. In dyads such as marriage, society will have role expectations. However, especially in dyads, the actors involved will have great flexibility to create unique performances. Performances involve symbols, dress, tone-of-voice, gestures, props, and language.

The problem for dyads is that they are unstable. If one person leaves the group the group is finished. On the other hand, even the addition of one extra person changes the group dynamics completely. A **triad**, or group of three people, is much more complex than a dyad because the opportunity for other roles is increased. In a triad the new person may become a mediator, who resolves conflicts between the other two members. Or they may play a divisive role, by trying to win one or the other members to their point of view in a dispute. Lastly, the third member may play a unifying role.

If the new member of the group is a baby, role-performances in the group become much less flexible. Our society is structured around certain patriarchal assumptions. Work arrangements are based on the assumption of a male breadwinner and female caregiver. Once children arrive couples will be forced to adopt role strategies that are more in line with cultural expectations.

Even small groups have informal patterns of interaction and communication. As group size gets larger, those most active at communication will have to work harder. A person who dominates in a group of 3 or 4 will be even more dominating in a larger group. For example, in a small group it is hard to ignore the wishes of the members. But in a group of 15 or more, some members can be ignored and some viewpoints disregarded.

Coalitions develop in larger groups. A coalition is an alliance forged to meet a common goal. Coalitions can be based on broad or narrow goals and can take on a variety of different objectives. In the movie *The Great Outdoors*, two families who are related vacation together in a cabin in the woods. Throughout the movie the two fathers, Roman and Chet, vie with each other over what activities they will be involved in. Chet wants to rent a pontoon boat, so the entire family can motor leisurely around the lake while barbequing. Roman, on the other hand, wants a jet-boat so they can enjoy water skiing. Roman manages to get Chet's children to vote for the ski boat, effectively forming a coalition within the family for a very short-lived goal. Other coalitions come together for long-term goals. For example, community-based organizations often band together to achieve improvements in their neighborhoods. Often these coalitions last for months, years, or even decades.

Bureaucracy

A bureaucracy is a special type of group, a formal organization designed to achieve maximum efficiency. Bureaucracies are structured in such a way as to make the management of large-scale operations easier. They have rules, regulations, hierarchies or rank, and are meant to make management as efficient as possible. Bureaucracies are characterized by five principles:

1. Division of Labor: A division of labor refers to the extreme level of specialization that characterizes modern bureaucracies. People work at specific tasks and the overall product is dependent upon hundreds of people doing this specialized work.

2. <u>Impersonality</u>: Imagine the typical office scene, where hundreds of employees sit in tiny cubicles, and people perform their duties without the need of forming friendships or knowing each other personally.

3. <u>Technical Qualifications</u>: Obtaining work in one of the major corporations usually depends upon having the correct training – represented by a college degree or other vocational certificate. Job performance and evaluations are supposed to be based on technical ability. Getting promoted often means having to possess the correct certificate.

4. <u>Hierarchy of Authority</u>: A hierarchy of authority refers to a chain-of-command. At this college, for example, the President is ultimately in charge. Underneath the president are the vice presidents, one of whom is the Provost. The academic deans answer to the Provost. Directly under the Dean of Liberal Arts come the department chairs. Bureaucratic hierarchies are like a power pyramid – as you move toward the top, more and more power is concentrated in fewer and fewer hands.

5. <u>Written Rules and Regulations</u>: Bureaucracies are governed by a formal set of rules. These rules define each employee's duties and obligations, and even occasionally their rights. These are rule of conduct. In most universities there are very strict rules that govern promotion and tenure. Students in most universities are governed by a code of ethics usually specified in a student handbook.

While the overall tenor of formal organizations is one of impersonality many people have friends within the workplace, helping to make the experience of work inside a bureaucracy less alienating.

CONFORMITY TO GROUPS

Just how much influence do groups have over us? **Conformity** refers to the tendency to change our behavior to be consistent with the group. Within group settings, we often comply with what we are asked to do even if we do not necessarily agree with the request. Some people have the **legitimate authority** to ask for our compliance or to grant that authority to their agents. These people generally include the representatives of the government, such as the police, firefighters, and so on, doctors, and many others. The business of legislators, for example, is to write laws, most of which limit or constrain our behavior in some manner.

Milgram Study

In a previous chapter we reviewed several experiments designed to test the extent to which people succumb to group pressure. I will briefly review one of those experiments here, the Milgram experiment. Milgram was testing whether or not he could get ordinary people to inflict harm on others if told to do so by someone in legitimate authority, in this case a doctor. Research subjects were told that they were going to administer an electric shock to someone performing a task in another room, as a form of reinforcement. The subjects could not see the other person but could hear them over a loudspeaker in the laboratory. Milgram was able to get many of the subjects to administer what they thought were lethal doses of electric shocks. In actuality no one was in fact electrocuted and the experiment was only a simulation, nevertheless, the subjects did think that they were electrocuting people and many suffered psychological distress later. Our point here is that many people do submit to legitimate authority or group pressure. This is a common finding in many experiments.

Why People Conform

The Desire to Be Right

The behavior of others often influences our own behavior. For one thing, they may possess information that we do not. In unfamiliar situations, we often look to others for clues about what to expect or how to behave. The more ambiguous the situations the more likely people are to conform. The more we trust the group, as is often the case with peer groups, the more likely we are to go along with the group. Anything that increases the level of trust in the group also increases conformity. In many situations we do not feel particularly confident in our abilities. In that case, we are more likely to conform. Thus, people are likely to conform to group norms and behaviors because they desire to make the right choice or decision.

The Desire to Be Liked

Another major influence over our behavior is the desire to be liked. We like to have the approval of our friends and other people and we avoid disapproval and those who disapprove of us. The desire to be liked by a certain group may lead us to alter our behavior in order to conform to group standards. Often we fake interest in things peers and friends are interested in because we want them to like us. Ultimately, if you hang around with a peer group long enough you may actually change your views and behaviors.

When People Conform

There are several factors that influence when people will decide to conform to the group:

1. Group Size: Conformity generally increases as the size of the group increases, especially if there is a unanimous majority.

2. Group Unanimity: A unanimous majority places great pressure on individuals to conform. In this situation, if one person disagrees they are likely to stand out. Some people do not like to stand out and thus will decide to conform even if they think the group is wrong.

3. Commitment to the Group: In general, people who are more committed to the group are more likely to conform to group norms.

4. Desire for Individuation: Sometimes, people desire to stand out and in that case they are less likely to conform to group standards and norms. Such individuals tend to be more critical, less socially compliant, and less polite.

Social Power and Conformity

Often, we decide to conform because there are rewards involved if we do so. There are six bases of social power:

1. Reward Power: We often decide to conform because some type of reward is involved if we do. Rewards can be almost anything, from a pat on the back, to verbal praise, or a promotion at work. Sometimes, we just find hanging out with certain people to be rewarding because of the positive **reflected appraisals** we get.

2. Coercion: Other times we decide we have little choice but to conform because punishments are involved. Much like reward power, coercion can be almost anything, from a cold shoulder, rejection, or ejection from the group, to other sanctions such as fines and imprisonment.

3. Expertise: Occasionally we conform to group norms and expectations because the people in the group have the knowledge we either need or rely on. This often describes the student/teacher relationship. Students conform to classroom

norms for a variety of reasons, including coercion and reward power, but also because they desire to gain the knowledge they need to obtain a degree in their major.

4. <u>Information</u>: Some social situations are ambiguous – it is not clear what is going on. In that case, we often follow the lead of the group because we rely on them to interpret what is happening. When I was in the Navy, for example, we once encountered a major storm that generated 50 foot high waves. I was not sure whether or not we were actually in danger. By observing what the old-hands were doing, I concluded that we were not.

5. <u>Referent Power</u>: Many times in life you will need someone's help in terms of a job reference, news about potential job openings, or help meeting someone you are interested in and the like. Thus, we sometimes conform when the group has this ability.

6. <u>Legitimate Power</u>: As mentioned above, some people have the power to ask us to conform to their wishes because they have the legitimate authority to do so.

BASIC FEATURES OF GROUPS

Group Structure

All groups have **statuses** and **roles**. A status is a position within the group, such as wife or husband, if we think of a marriage. Each status has a variety of roles to play. For instance, wives usually are responsible for major caregiving roles and homemaking, although they may also work in the paid labor force. Husbands generally are responsible for breadwinning and helping out around the house. Husbands may have some chores to do, such as mowing the lawn and taking out the trash. Wives are generally expected to be the **relationship-monitors** in the family – they are aware of the emotional state of family members and the health of the relationships. Fathers are generally expected to be in charge of making major decisions and discipline. Of course, each family creates its own patterns and norms.

Every group has a **status set**, which describes all of the statuses within the group. In general, there are more and less powerful members and leaders and followers. There may be a single leader and a great many followers. The point is that each status within the group will have a set of roles that make it different from the other statuses. The sociology club, for example, is a type of group. Within the club there are ordinary members, who by and large are sociology majors, and officers. As in most groups of this type, there is a President, a Vice-President, Secretary, and Treasurer. That makes five separate statuses. Although most of the time everyone is doing similar things, officers have differential and greater responsibilities.

For a good many groups, such as formal clubs and organizations and marriages, among a wide variety of other groups, social norms highly influence group norms. **Social norms** are shared rules and expectations about how members of certain groups, such as families, should behave. Although families can and do create their group norms and no family is exactly the same in this regard, society does have certain expectations about family norms. The most basic norm is probably the wife/caregiver and husband/breadwinner social norm. But it does not end there. **Social roles** are clusters of norms that apply to anyone in a particular position in a group, such as the family. Thus, not only are wives expected to be the caregivers, the exact behaviors associated with caregiving are highly prescribed by society. The same is true for breadwinning.

In every university around the nation, we expect to find several different divisions, such as Liberal Arts, Natural Science, Humanities, and so on. Within each of these areas we also expect to find a variety of majors. In Liberal Arts you would expect to find Anthropology, Geography, or Sociology. In the Natural Sciences you would hope to find Biology or Physics. In the Humanities you would find Philosophy and History. In each of these majors you would find a group of professors and a department chair. We would expect then, due to social norms and social roles, to find a great deal of similarity in the behaviors of those who occupy the positions of Dean, department chair, and professors, who are ranked from instructor to full-professor. On the other hand, due to role performance, there would also be room for different teaching styles and personality.

Group Cohesiveness

Some groups are more enduring than others. Membership in your family generally lasts for your lifetime whereas membership in peer groups changes over your lifetime. You may have a variety of jobs over your lifetime, which is entirely normal. However, unless you marry outside of your religious group, you will probably remain in whatever religious denomination you were raised in.

There are many positive factors for membership in a highly cohesive group. Sometimes adult peer groups are of very long duration. For example, college professors often have a "peer group" within their department. Here we find a group of professors who have professional relationships but also friendships with each other. In other words, they do things together. If the group is cohesive interaction among members will be harmonious and effective. Additionally, members of cohesive groups help each other achieve instrumental goals. For college professors, these goals may be related to tenure, promotion, research, election to office of a professional organization, or publications. The more cohesive the group the more positive the outcomes are for members.

Of course, there are negative factors associated with a highly cohesive group as well. Members of cohesive groups are more likely to succumb to group pressure. This is because cohesive groups often have a group-identity. It is hard to go against that. The costs of leaving the group will be high emotionally. There may be other costs involved as well. If you leave a group that is the source of rewards and reference power your career may suffer.

BEHAVIOR IN THE PRESENCE OF OTHERS

Social Facilitation and Social Inhibition

Sometimes we perform better when others are present. A few years ago the students in this course worked on a group experiment. They decided to form a "cheer-squad" for the women's basketball team. Wherever the team played this group of students would follow and cheer them on. They worked with the cheer leaders on special cheers and generally tried to create as much enthusiasm as possible. The team began to win more games, on average, than they had in previous years. As part of the experiment, the "cheer-squad," for one game, stayed home. The students in the course then interviewed the women on the basketball team about the effect of the absence of the "cheer squad." Not surprisingly, their absence had a negative effect, according to the basketball players not only on the morale of the team, but also on their performance (the cheer squad picked a game that had no effect on the team's conference standing, as an ethical concern). The next game, the cheer squad was back and followed the women's basketball team to the end of the semester. That year, the basketball team won the championship. When performance is improved by the presence of others it is referred to as **social facilitation**.

On other occasions, the presence of others hinders performance. Have you ever had to make a speech? The first time you are asked to do so, perhaps for a class, most people report absolute fright. I've seen students so freaked out by having to stand in front of the class and give a presentation that they can barely speak! It depends upon the complexity of the task. On a simple task or for tasks at which the actor is already an expert the presence of others facilitates performance, as we saw with the basketball players. But on more complex tasks, or tasks for which the actor is not an expert, the presence of others hinders the actor's performance. I remember being in algebra class in high school and being asked to go to the board to solve an equation. As was true for many of the other students in the class, I often had difficulty when others were watching.

When performance is hindered by the presence of others it is referred to as **social inhibition**.

Evaluation Apprehension

Sooner or later most students will graduate from college and seek employment in an area related to their major, hopefully. When you go on your job interview, you are likely to be concerned about making a good impression. Normally, when people get ready for a job interview, they concern themselves with their manners, their dress, body language, and tone of voice in order to make a good impression. In other words, **evaluation apprehension** refers to the apprehension you may feel when you know you are going to be evaluated. For simple tasks, awareness of being evaluated often leads to greater effort. But for more complex tasks, the pressure of evaluation may harm performance.

Distraction-Conflict

At the basketball games mentioned earlier, the cheer-squad would shout, scream, and stamp their feet whenever a woman from the opposing team got a free throw. They tried to distract the player so she would miss. I thought this rather unethical behavior until I realized that opposing fans were doing the same thing to our players. The point is that the presence of others can often be distracting. Here again, on easy tasks, the presence of others can lead to more concentration and a better performance. The players, on both our team and the opponents, rarely missed. This is likely because throwing a basketball is not all that difficult and they were experts anyway. On harder tasks this type of distraction may hinder performance. If the task at hand is very demanding and difficult, paying attention to the audience will be a hindrance.

Social Loafing

I find that a good many students absolutely hate working in groups, especially if there is a grade involved. On the other hand, some students, especially if there is a grade involved, relish the prospect of working in a group, because they do not intend to work. They are **social loafers**. When students work in groups they feel that it is hard to evaluate the contribution of any single person, and some are thus inclined to work less. Students feel anonymous in groups. If you feel no one will notice, you may be inclined to work less hard. Social loafing is known to increase with the size of the group. If there are only three students working on a project with a clear division of labor regarding who is to do what, it is harder to loaf. If there are seven or eight students, or even more, and confusion related to the division of labor, some students will work less hard than others. People tend to loaf more around strangers than with their friends.

Friends can sanction you for social loafing if your loafing harms their grade. All male groups tend to loaf more than all female groups. Social loafing occurs in all groups.

Social Compensation

As you might suspect, some people are more concerned about *their* grade, on group projects, than *your* grade. Some people work harder in a group to compensate for perceived social loafing. Two conditions are usually operating when this happens. First, the actor must believe that everyone else in the group is performing poorly. And second, the actor must feel that the quality of the product is important, which it will be if the project is for a grade or related to employment. Under these conditions, some actors decide to try and compensate for the lack of effort of others. This is particularly true for students with low interpersonal trust. They expect others to loaf no matter what and try to work harder. In some cases, social compensators try to prevent you from making a contribution because they do not trust you. When people care about the group's performance and perceive that their co-workers are social loafers, they often try to compensate.

Social Impact Theory

Social Impact Theory studies how strong an influence, positive or negative, the presence of others has on our performance. According to this theory, three factors are particularly important in determining the influence others have on us. The first factor is related to the number of observers. The impact of the audience increases as the number of people gets larger and larger. Secondly, the strength of the social forces involved can influence our performance. In many cases, we are being evaluated by important or powerful people in social settings governed by rules and norms. For example, your employer could be the person evaluating you for a job promotion. The immediacy of the audience is the third factor. The further away the audience is, the less impact they have on our performance. Many college professors teach courses over the Internet, in which case, their students are nowhere near them geographically and they may not even communicate in the same day. In large classes on campus the students and professor are together in the classroom. Imagine having to make a presentation to the other students in a large class who are in the same room with you as opposed to making the same presentation via the Internet to fellow students who are completely remote to you and you get the idea.

Deindividuation

Sometimes the presence of others causes deindividuation. **Deindividuation** refers to the temporary loss of your individual identity and social self. Deindividuation can be caused by **social contagion**. A good example of losing personal identity in a group is often seen in rioting behavior. During riots, a breakdown of norms and social conventions occurs. Because riots generally involve very large groups, the individual not only begins to feel anonymous, but begins to feel less personally responsible for what is going on around them. In this situation, personal identity can be replaced by the goals and actions of the crowd. This seems to have been the case during the social unrest in Los Angeles following the acquittal of the police officers on trial for beating a Black motorist senseless.

In such crowds, where others are rioting, breaking into stores, looting, setting fire to cars, and so on, the actor may be less aware of their personal values and ethics. Additionally, during a riot, the actor is less concerned about the consequences of their actions, as they seem anonymous. This, in turn, leads to a diminished sense of self-awareness. In a mob people seem to blend together. This reduced sense of self-awareness and sense of anonymity can induce deindividuation.

GROUP PERFORMANCE

Up to now, we have been examining the performance of individuals in groups. We now examine the performance of groups themselves. There are four types of group activities related to group performance. The first type is the **complex task**. In this type of group, there is a division of labor such that each group member is given a critical task to complete and an equal, or nearly so, amount of work. In order for the group to be successful, each member must complete the tasks assigned to them. Under the complex task process, each member of the team is generally assigned his or her task by a supervisor. This makes social loafing less of an issue although it may still occur.

A second type of group activity is known as the **additive task**. In this type group process, the supervisor or professor just assigns the task to the entire group and group activity is the sum of effort from each member. To be successful, group members must coordinate their own efforts effectively. College students are often challenged by this particular strategy. Frequently, when they are unable to coordinate their efforts they fail. Here again some individuals will be social loafers. If one member of the group is a social loafer, group success will be at risk of failure. In this case, a social compensator often steps in, completes the work of the loafer, and the group is still successful.

In the complex task and the additive task, if social loafing occurs it can be compensated for by other members. No so for the **conjunctive task**. In this type of group process each member has individual expertise. The other members of the group do not possess the knowledge, talent, or abilities you do. Likewise, you do not possess the appropriate knowledge, training, or ability necessary to complete tasks assigned to the other group members. In order for the group to be successful, all members of the group must succeed. In this group process, group productivity is only as good as the least competent member. The development of the atomic bomb during World War II is a good example of this type of group process. In order for the United States to be able to develop this weapon, for good or ill, a multitude of separate groups and individuals, working on vastly different tasks and in different locations, all had to be successful.

The last type of group activity we will examine is the **disjunctive task**. In this group process, only one person needs to be successful in order for the entire group to succeed. Here success depends on the skills of the most competent member of the group. I remember playing football in Middle School. Our team had a player who was unusually large for his age. Essentially, all that had to be done was to hand off the football to this guy. He was so much larger than the rest of the players on both teams it was not even necessary to block or execute complex plays. Once he had the ball he literally ran through the opposing team because they were too small, comparatively, to stop him. Of course, as time went by the other players did eventually begin to catch up to him in size but right up until we were seniors in high school he could run-over just about anyone!

GROUP DECISION MAKING

Decision Rules

Groups often have to decide what course of action to take – they have to make decisions. **Decision rules** are rules that groups use in arriving at a decision. There are three types of decision rules. The first type is known as the **Unanimity Rule**. Basically, no course of action can be decided upon and no decision made unless all the members of the group agree unanimously. The unanimity rule works best in smaller groups, obviously. A very large group, where there are a variety of opinions and options about decisions, would have a difficult time reaching unanimity. Additionally, if the group has a dissenting minority, their views become more important and compromise is more likely to be reached. Of course, sometimes compromises are hard to reach and this type of decision making can fail.

A second type of decision rule is the **Majority-Wins Rule**. In many groups the decision is related to a familiar topic and there are few alternatives, or the alternatives provide no obviously correct solution. If a simple majority (51%) of members vote for a particular course of action, the discussion about what to do is over. Obviously, this may cause resentment if there is a dissenting minority because their input may not be necessary for the group to reach a decision.

The third type of decision rule is the **Truth-Wins Rule**. In this situation, there is likely an obvious or correct proposal which makes more sense than other proposals that are flawed. The Truth-Wins rule is likely to be agreed upon for extremely important decisions where the costs of making a mistake would be very negative. For example, I was reading in the local newspaper recently that the City Council was reviewing a proposal that had been made about moving to a single interview for children who were the victims of rape, incest, or violent crime, as a matter of public policy. This is because multiple interviews with a variety of professionals had been discovered to be psychologically traumatizing for children. In order to avoid damaging the child, in that situation, social workers proposed streamlining the process. This is an example of the Truth-Wins Rule because the decision was based upon what was known to be the best outcome for children.

Group Polarization

Sometimes groups become polarized. This means that more extreme decisions are taken as a result of group discussion than individuals would undertake by themselves. In the not-too-distant past, the United States and The Soviet Union nearly started a nuclear war over the presence of Soviet missiles, with nuclear capabilities, deployed in Cuban missile silos. During the discussion about what to do in response to the threat, President Kennedy's advisors almost succumbed to the **Risky Shift**. The risky shift occurs when groups make decisions collectively which the individuals involved would consider too risky. In this case, they were about to launch a preemptive nuclear strike against Cuba and the Soviet Union. The President's Cabinet was only *just* talked out of this action by a persistent minority. And luckily so, since documents released decades later by the Soviet's reveal the presence of Soviet nuclear submarines off our coast, with orders to launch their nuclear missiles if the U.S. attacked.

Why do groups drift to the "risky" decision when individuals do not? For one thing, in a group discussion there are usually a large number of arguments made initially. Eventually, people have to decide and commit to their position. They then talk others into their position until only two positions remain: the majority position and the minority position. At this point, those in the minority are often viewed as the "opposition," rather than members of the same group who just disagree. Additionally, people often do not want to be seen as "going against the group." In this case, they are likely to agree with a risky decision in a group context when they would not make the same decision on an individual basis. Lastly, for decisions such as these, there is often an "us against them" mentality that takes over. It is easy to imagine, during the Cuban missile crisis, the President's advisors wanting to "strike first," before the Soviets did – it is "us against them." Such thinking also has the function of solidifying group identity.

COMPETITION OR COOPERATION IN GROUP INTERACTION

What determines whether individuals in a group will compete with each other or cooperate? Researchers have concocted a variety of experiments to test this and have discovered that frequently, those involved would be better served by cooperation rather than competition. It turns out that middle-class, white, college students are most likely to compete, even when cooperation would be more rewarding.

This has to do with the perceived reward structure. If the rewards are structured in such as to make one person's loss another's gain, people will compete. For example, let us say that, regardless of overall grades or performance, those with the 10 highest point averages in this course receive an A, and those with the 10 lowest point averages receive an F, even if no student has lower than 75%, which is normally at least a C. This is known as **competitive interdependence**. In other words, it takes all of us to make this course in sociology be an educational experience but the outcomes for individuals are independent of each other.

The opposite of competitive interdependence is **cooperative interdependence**. In this situation, the outcomes of group members are all linked to each other. In order for a single individual to succeed, everyone in the group must succeed. For example, let us say that I have at least one group project required and if one person in the group fails, everyone in the group fails. In this case, students must cooperate to succeed and they generally do.

There are other factors associated with cooperation and competition too. One factor is individual differences in competitiveness. Not everyone is highly competitive. Those who are not are more likely to cooperate. Additionally, when communication patterns in the group are highly functional competition is reduced and more cooperation takes place. The **norm of reciprocity** also helps reduce competition. According to the norm of reciprocity, if someone helps you on a project, the ethical thing to do is to return the favor and help them, which has the function of reducing competition.

Cultural Values help determine levels of competition and cooperation. There are at least three value orientations. **Cooperators** have internalized a value system in which maximization of group rewards is the most desirable. **Competitors** have a value system that stresses individual gains relative to the group. Competitors try to maximize their rewards at the expense of the group. **Individualists** are simply concerned with their own gains period, and are not concerned about the group.

THE GROUP AND SOCIAL DILEMMAS

A **social dilemma** is a situation where an outcome desirable for you is undesirable for the group. These situations arise occasionally. For example, belonging to a union often places union members in the situation where going on strike, while it may preserve pay and benefits in the long run, equals the loss of pay and benefits in the short run. This may be particularly true for newer members who may not have built up a savings account that would buffer the loss of income while on a job action or strike.

A **Free Rider** is someone who enjoys group membership but either did not make the initial sacrifices the other members of the group did or is unwilling to do so if called upon. I often ask students the following questions and always receive affirmative responses: "do you believe that women who perform the same work men should earn the same income as a man;" "do you believe that women should be able to vote;" "do you believe that women should be safe from unwanted sexual harassment at work;" "do you believe that women can think for themselves without a man telling them what to do?" These, of course, were the achievements of the women's movement. Liberal feminists struggled for decades to win these and other liberties. Yet, when I ask how many feminists there are in the class, many women, who only moments before were enthusiastically endorsing the goals and achievements of the women's movement, are no longer willing to raise their hands and be recognized. If they are unwilling to be recognized as feminists, but like the liberties and freedoms the feminists won for all women, as a group, they are free riders.

ഏ ഓ ഏ ഓ

REFERENCES

Aldag, R. J., & Fuller, S. R. (1993). Beyond Fiasco: A reappraisal of the group-think phenomenon and a new model of group decision processes. *Psychological Bulletin, 113,* 533-552.

Alvero, E. M., & Crano, W. D. (1997). Indirect minority influence: Evidence for leniency in source evaluation and counterargumentation. *Journal of Personality and Social Psychology, 72,* 949-964.

Asch, S. E. (1955). Opinions and social pressures. *Scientific American, 193,* 31-35.

Baron, R. S. (1986). Distraction-conflict theory: Progress and problems. In L. Berkowitz (Ed.), *Advances in experimental social psychology* (pp. 1-40). Orlando, FL: Academic Press.

Baron, R. S., & Roper, G. (1976). Reaffirmation of social comparison views of choice shifts: Averaging and extremity effects in an autokinetic situation. *Journal of Personality and Social Psychology, 33,* 521-530.

Barry B., & Stewart, G. L. (1997). Composition, process, and performance in self-managed groups: The role of personality. *Journal of Applied Psychology, 82,* 62-78.

Bartol, K. M., & Martin, D. C. (1986). Women and men in task groups. In R. D. Ashmore, & F. K. Del Boca (Eds.), *The social psychology of female-male relations: A critical analysis of central concepts* (pp.

259-310). New York: Academic Press.

Baumeister, R. F., & Leary, M. R. (1995). The need to belong: Desire for interpersonal attachments as a fundamental human motivation. *Psychological Bulletin, 117*, 497-529.

Blasovich, J., Ginsberg, G. P., & Howe, R. C. (1975). Blackjack and the risky shift, II: Monetary stakes. *Journal of Experimental Social Psychology, 11*, 224-232.

Bond, C. F., & Titus, L. J. (1983). Social Facilitation: A meta-analysis of studies using Asch's line judgment task. *Psychological Bulletin, 94*, 265-292.

Brauer, M., Judd, C. M., & Jacquelin, V. (2001). The communication of social stereotypes: The effects of group discussion and information distribution on stereotypic appraisals. *Journal of Personality and Social Psychology, 81*, 463-475.

Brickner, M. A., Harkins, S. G., & Ostrom, T. M. (1986). Effects of personal involvement: Thought provoking implications for social loafing. *Journal of Personality and Social Psychology, 51,* 763-770.

Brownstein, A. L. (2003). Biased predecision processing. *Psychological Bulletin, 129*, 545-568.

Caporeal, L. R., & Baron, R. M. (1997). Groups as the mind's natural environment. In J. A. Simpson, & D. T. Kenrick (Eds.), *Evolutionary social psychology* (pp. 317-344). Hillsdale, NJ: Erlbaum.

Clark, R. D., III (1990). Minority influence: The role of argument refutation of the majority position and social support for the minority position. *European Journal of Social Psychology, 20*, 489-497.

Cohen, S. G., & Bailey, D. E. (1997). What makes teams work: Group effectiveness research from the shop floor to the executive suite. *Journal of Management, 23*, 239-290.

Coon, C. S. (1946). The universality of natural groupings in human societies. *Journal of Educational Sociology, 20*, 163-168.

Cottrell, N. B. (1968). Performance in the presence of others: Mere presence, audience, and affiliation effects. In E. C. Simmel, R. A. Hoppe, & G. A. Milton (Eds.), *Social facilitation and imitative behavior* (pp. 91-110). Boston: Allyn & Bacon.

Cottrell, N. B., Wack, D. L., Sekerak, G. J., & Rittle, R. H. (1968). Social facilitation of dominant responses by the presence of an audience and the presence of others. *Journal of Personality and Social Psychology, 9*, 245-250.

Davis, J. H. (1969). Group performance. New York: Addison-Wesley.

Davis, J. H. (1973). Group decision and social interaction: A theory of social decision schemes. *Psychological Review, 80,* 97-125.

DeDreu, C. K. W, & West, M. A. (2001). Minority dissent and team innovation: The importance of participation in decision making. *Journal of Applied Psychology, 86*, 1191-1201.

Diener, E., Fraser, S. C., Beaman, A. L., & Kelem, R. T. (1976). Effects of deindividuation variables on stealing among Halloween trick-or-treaters. *Journal of Personality and Social Psychology, 33*, 178-183.

Driskell, J. E., Hogan, R., & Salas, E. (1987). Personality and group performance. In C. Hendrick (Ed.), Group processes and intergroup relations (pp. 91-112). Newbury Park, CA: Sage.

Eagly, A. H. (1983). Gender and social influence: A social psychological analysis. *American Psychologist, 38*, 971-983.

Eagly, A. H., & Karau, S. J. (1991). Gender and the emergence of leaders: A meta-analysis. *Journal of Personality and Social Psychology, 60*, 685-710.

Eagly, A. H., & Karau, S. J. (2002). Role congruity theory of prejudice toward female leaders. *Psychological Review, 109*, 573-598.

Eagly, A. H., Karau, S. J., & Makhijani, M. G. (1995). Gender and effectiveness of leaders: A meta-analysis. *Psychological Bulletin, 117*, 125-145.

Earley, P. C. (1989). Social loafing and collectivism: A comparison of the United States and the People's Republic of China. *Administrative Science Quarterly, 34*, 565-581.

Eby, L. T., & Dobbins, G. H. (1997). Collectivistic orientation in teams: An individual and group-level analysis. *Journal of Organizational Behavior, 18*, 275-295.

Festinger, L., Pepitone, A., & Newcomb, T. (1952). Some consequences of deindividuation in a group. *Journal of Abnormal and Social Psychology, 47* (#2 Supp.), 382-389.

Festinger, L., Schachter, S., & Back, K. (1950). *Social pressures in informal groups.* Stanford, CA: Stanford University Press.

Forsyth, D. R. (1990). *Group dynamics* (2nd ed.). Pacific Grove, CA: Brooks/Cole.

Gabrenya, W. K., Jr., Wang, Y. E., & Latané, B. (1985). Social loafing on an optimizing task: Cross-cultural differences among Chinese and Americans. *Journal of Cross-Cultural Psychology, 16,* 223-242.

Goethals, G. R., & Zanna, M. P. (1979). The role of social comparison in choice shifts. *Journal of Personality and Social Psychology, 37,* 1469-1476.

Gordijn, E., De Vries, N. K., & DeDreu, C. K. W. (2002). Minority influence on focal and related attitudes: Change in size, attributions, and information processing. *Personality and Social Psychology Bulletin, 28,* 659-670.

Guerin, B. (1993). *Social facilitation.* Paris: Cambridge University Press.

Gully, S. M., Devine, D. J., & Whitney, D. J. (1995). A meta-analysis of cohesion and performance: Effects of level analysis and task interdependence. *Small Group Research, 26,* 497-520.

Harkins, S. G., & Jackson, J. M. (1985). The role of evaluation in eliminating social loafing. *Personality and Social Psychology Bulletin, 11,* 457-465.

Herek, G. M., Janis, I. L., & Huth, P. (1987). Decision making during international crises: Is quality of process related to outcome? *Journal of Conflict Resolution, 31,* 203-226.

Hertel, G., Kerr, N. L., & Messe, L.A. (2000). Motivation gains in performance groups: Paradigmatic and theoretical developments on the Kohler effect. *Journal of Personality and Social Psychology, 79,* 580-601.

Ingham, A. G., Levinger, G., Graves, J., & Peckham, V. (1974). The Ringelmann effect: Studies of group size and group performance. *Journal of Personality and Social Psychology, 10,* 371-384.

Isenberg, D. J. (1986). Group polarization: A critical review and meta-analysis. *Journal of Personality and Social Psychology, 50,* 1141-1151.

Janis, I. L. (1972). *Victims of groupthink.* Boston: Houghton Mifflin.

Janis, I. L. (1983). *Groupthink: Psychological studies of policy decisions and fiascoes* (2nd ed.). Boston: Houghton Mifflin.

Karau, S. J., & Williams, K. D. (1993). Social loafing: A meta-analytic review and theoretical integration. *Journal of Personality and Social Psychology, 65,* 681-706.

Karau, S. J., & Williams, K. D. (2001). Understanding individual mutation in groups: The collective effort model. In M. E. Turner (Ed.), *Groups at work: Theory and research* (pp. 113-141). Mahwah, NJ: Erlbaum.

Konrad, A. M., Ritchie, J. E. Jr., Lieb, P., & Corrigall, E. (2000). Sex differences and similarities in job attribute preferences: A meta-analysis. *Psychological Bulletin, 126,* 593-641.

Lamm, H., & Myers, D. G. (1978). Group-induced polarization of attitudes and behavior. In. L. Berkowitz (Ed.), *Advances in Experimental Social Psychology* (Vol. 11, pp. 145-195). Orlando, FL: Academic Press.

Latané, B., Liu, J. H., Nowak, A., Bonevento, M., & Zheng, L. (1995). Distance matters: Physical space and social impact. *Personality and Social Psychology Bulletin, 21,* 795-805.

Levine, J. M., & Moreland, R. L. (1998). Small groups. In D. T. Gilbert, S. T. Fiske, & G. Lindzey (Eds.), *The handbook of social psychology* (4th ed.) (Vol. 2, pp. 415-469). Boston: McGraw-Hill.

Lewin, K., Lippitt, R., & White, R. K. (1939). Patterns of aggressive behavior in experimentally created "social climates." *Journal of Social Psychology, 10,* 271-279.

Liang, D. W., Moreland, R., & Argote, L. (1995). Group versus individual training and group performance: The mediating role of transactive memory. *Personality and Social Psychology Bulletin, 21,* 384-393.

Likel, B., Hamilton, D. L., & Sherman, S. J. (2001). Elements of a lay theory of groups: Types of groups, relationship styles, and the perception of group entitavity. *Personality and Social Psychology Review, 5*, 129-140.

Maass, A., & Clark, R. D. (1984). Hidden impact of minorities: Fifteen years of minority influence. *Psychological Bulletin, 95*, 428-450.

Maass, A., & Clark, R. D., III, & Haberkorn G. (1982). The effects of differential ascribed category membership and norms on minority influence. *European Journal of Social Psychology, 12*, 89-104.

Mackie, D. M., & Goethals, G. R. (1987). Individual and group goals. In C. Hendrick (Ed.), *Group processes* (pp. 144-166). Newbury Park, CA: Sage.

Mann, L. (1980). Cross-cultural studies of small groups. In H. Triandis, & R. Brislin (Eds.) *Handbook of cross-cultural psychology: Social psychology* (Vol. 5, pp. 155-209). Boston: Allyn & Bacon.

Martin, R., Gardikiotis, A., & Hewstone, M. (2002). Levels of consensus and majority and minority influence. *European Journal of Social Psychology, 32*, 645-665.

Maznevski, M. L. (1994). Understanding our differences: Performance in decision-making groups with diverse members. *Human Relations, 47*, 531-552.

McCauley, C. (1989). The nature of social influence in groupthink: Compliance and internalization. *Journal of Personality and Social Psychology, 57*, 250-260.

McGrath, J. E. (1984). *Groups: Interaction and performance*. Englewood Cliffs, NJ: Prentice Hall.

McLeod, P. L., & Lobel, S. A. (1992, August). *The effects of ethnic diversity on idea generation in small groups*. Presented at the 52nd annual meeting of the Academy of Management, Las Vegas, Nevada.

Meister, A. (1979). Personal and social factors of social participation. *Journal of Voluntary Action Research, 8*, 6-11.

Moreland, R. L. (1987). The formation of small groups. In C. Hendrick (Ed.), *Group processes* (pp. 80-110). Newbury Park, CA: Sage.

Morrison, J. D. (1993). *Group composition and creative performance*. Unpublished doctoral dissertation, University of Tulsa, Tulsa, OK.

Moscovici, S., & Zavalloni, M. (1969). The group as a polarizer of attitudes. *Journal of Personality and Social Psychology, 12*, 125-135.

Mugny, G. (1982). The power of minorities. New York: Academic Press.

Mugny, G. (1983). Operationalizing the effect of the group on the individual: A self-attention perspective. *Journal of Experimental Social Psychology, 19*, 295-322.

Mullen, B., Anthony, T., Salas, E., & Driskell, J. E. (1994). Group cohesiveness and quality of decision making: An integration of tests of the groupthink hypothesis. *Small Group Research, 25*, 189-204.

Mullen, B., & Copper, C. (1994). The relation between group cohesiveness and performance: An integration. *Psychological Bulletin, 115*, 210-227.

Postmes, T., Spears, R., & Cilhangir, S. (2001). Quality of decision making and group norms. *Journal of Personality and Social Psychology, 80*, 918-930.

Prentice-Dunn, S., & Rogers, R. W. (1980). Effects of deindividuating situational cues and aggressive models on subjective deindividauting and aggression. *Journal of Personality and Social Psychology, 39*, 104-113.

Prentice-Dunn, S., & Rogers, R. W. (1982). Effects of public and private self-awareness on deindivuation and aggression. *Journal of Personality and Social Psychology, 43*, 503-513.

Sargis, E. G., & Larson, J. R., Jr. (2002). Informational centrality and member participation during group decision making. *Group Processes and Intergroup Relations, 5*, 333-347.

Schmitt, B. H., Gilovich, T., Goore, N., & Joseph, L. (1986). Mere presence and social facilitation: One more time. *Journal of Experimental Social Psychology, 22*, 242-248.

Schulz-Hardt, S., Jochims, M., & Frey, D. (2002). Productive conflict in group decision making: Genuine and contrived dissent as strategies to counteract biased information seeking. *Organizational Behavior and Human Decision Processes, 88*, 563-586.

Shafer, M., & Crichlow, S. (1996). Antecedents of groupthink: A quantitative study. *Journal of Conflict Resolution, 40,* 415-435.

Sheppard, J. A., & Taylor, K. M. (1999) Social loafing and expectancy-value theory. *Personality and Social Psychology Bulletin, 25,* 1147-1158.

Smith, B. N., Kerr, N. A., Markus, M. J., & Stasson, M. F. (2001). Individual differences in social loafing: Need for cognition as a motivator in collective performance. *Group Dynamics, 5,* 150-158.

Steiner, I. D. (1972). *Group process and productivity.* New York: Academic Press.

Stoner, J. A. F. (1961). *A comparison of individual and group decisions involving risk.* Unpublished master's thesis, Massachusetts Institute of Technology.

Szymanski, K., & Harkins, S. G. (1987). Social loafing and self-evaluation with social standard. *Journal of Personality and Social Psychology, 53,* 891-897.

Tindale, R. S., & Davis, J. H. (1983). Group decision making and jury verdicts. In H. H. Blumberg, A. P. Hare, V. Kent, & M. F. Davies (Eds.), *Small groups and social interaction* (Vol. 2, pp. 9-38). Chichester, UK: Wiley.

Triandis, H. C. (1995). *Individualism and collectivism.* Boulder, CO: Westview Press.

Wallach, M. A., Kogan, N., & Bem, D. J. (1962). Group influence on individual risk taking. *Journal of Abnormal and Social Psychology, 65,* 75-86.

Watson, W., Michaelsen, L. K., & Sharp, W. (1991). Member competence, group interaction, and group decision making: A longitudinal study. *Journal of Applied Psychology, 76,* 803-809.

Wegner, D. M. (1987). Transactive memory: A contemporary analysis of the group mind. In B. Mullen and G. R. Goethals (Eds.) *Theories of group behavior* (pp. 185-208). New York: Springer-Verlag.

Whyte, G. (1989). Groupthink reconsidered. *Academy of Management Review, 14,* 40-56.

Williams, K. D., Harkins, S., & Latané, B. (1981). Identifiability as a deterrent to social loafing: Two cheering experiments. *Journal of Personality and Social Psychology, 40,* 303-311.

Wood, W., Lundgren, S., Ouellette, J. A., Busceme, S., & Blackstone, T. (1994). Processes of minority influence: Influence effectiveness and source perceptions. *Psychological Bulletin, 115,* 323-345.

Zaccaro, S. J. (1984). Social loafing: The role of task attractiveness. *Personality and Social Psychology Bulletin, 10,* 99-106.

Zaccaro, S. J., & Lowe, C. A. (1988). Cohesiveness and performance on an additive task: Evidence for multidimensionality. *Journal of Social Psychology, 128,* 547-558.

Zajonc, R. B. (1965). Social facilitation. *Science, 149,* 269-274.

Zander, A. (1985). *The purposes of groups and organizations.* San Francisco: Jossey-Bass.

5 | *THE INDIVIDUAL AND PERSONAL RELATIONSHIPS*
by Frank O. Taylor, Ph.D.

PERSONAL RELATIONSHIPS

There is a cultural imperative for human beings. What this means is that we rely on culture for our survival. Human children are completely helpless when they are born. Children cry when they are hungry or uncomfortable, but crying, a biological response, does not automatically provide food and comfort. Parents must learn how to care for their children. There is no nurturing instinct because there are no culturally universal caregiving practices. Cultures differ widely on what is considered appropriate in the way of caregiving.

The Benefits of Social Relationships

It is clear that humans rely upon social relationships for survival. As we grow and mature, our social needs become more complex. In childhood we become attached to the people who take care of us and interact with us frequently. Eventually, we come to define these tender interactions, which include hugging, kissing, caring, and touching, as love. **Attachment** serves two social functions. First, attachment reassures children when they are afraid. Second, children look to the adults they are attached to for guidance and help in interpreting the situation. We are not born with any instincts to guide us or ensure our survival. Thus, as humans, we depend upon personal relationships.

Social integration is another benefit of social relationships. This refers to having a place in society. Largely, **social integration** is part of the process of socialization, through which we eventually acquire a self, identity, personality, and occupation. Society must replace members. Moreover, a society as complex as ours, with literally thousands of occupations in the division of labor, if it is to continue to exist, must raise and train generation after generation, or replacement members. Social integration also refers to gender, sexuality, and social class. Social integration refers to membership in a community. The first community we experience is our family. As we mature we experience integration into friendships and other personal relationships.

Human beings are emotional creatures. Social relationships help us achieve a sense of worth and self esteem. Being a member of a family, having friends, loving and being loved, are important aspects of reality for us. Personal relationships help us create meaning in our lives and give us a sense of security and belonging.

Fundamentally, humans cannot survive without social support. Social support refers to the interpersonal exchanges we engage in to assist each other. These interpersonal relationships establish the patterns of interaction that give rise to religion, the family, the economy, and other social institutions. **Instrumental social support** is related to providing goods and services for each other. **Informational social support** is related to guidance, advice, and mentoring. **Emotional social support** is the basis of self-esteem.

FRIENDSHIPS AND PERSONAL RELATIONSHIPS

As humans we are motivated by a strong desire for affection from others. Friendships are fundamental to human interaction. Sometimes we feel compelled to talk to complete strangers, perhaps just to pass the time while we wait in the line at the supermarket. Most of us have a number of acquaintances. Often we really do not know these people very well but we are comfortable enough around them to discuss matters related to health, family, career, politics, and even the weather. Mostly though, we desire close relationships with friends, family, and lovers. This drive was identified by William James as the **affiliation motive**.

Friendship

Friends are people who have affection for each other. Researchers have discovered that people define friendship in a variety of ways but there is wide agreement about what friendship is. For example, most people agree that friends help each other out in times of need. Also, we tend to feel that our friends understand us and we try to understand our friends in return. Trust is big element in most friendships. We trust our friends to act in our best interests and not to betray us. We often confide in our friends and allow them to confide in us. Friends are accepting of our values and beliefs and respectful of our feelings. Friends like to hang out and enjoy each other's company. Friends often have similar interests. Of course, not every friendship has all of these qualities but most friendships have some of them.

The Personal Characteristics of Liking

Who do we like? Are there some characteristics associated with friendship, liking, and love? For one thing, we tend to like people who have higher levels of personal warmth. We like people who are friendly and have a positive outlook on life. Warm people care about us. They ask us for advice, question us about our opinion, and, in general, they are people we like to be around. Cold people are rejecting, pessimistic, and negative.

We also like people who are competent. Competent people can be very helpful indeed. When you struggled with your algebra homework, did you turn to a friend who was mathematically challenged? Of course not! Competent people have good social skills. They are easy to converse with and seem to know a little about almost everything. Competent people are intelligent and self-assured. Of course, people are competent in different respects and our level of feeling comfortable around them depends upon our relationship to them.

Physical attractiveness is a personal characteristic. People who are physically attractive benefit from the **halo effect**. We often think that a person who has one positive attribute, such as good looks, has other positive attributes. Just as often, we are mistaken. However, we tend to like to be around people who are good looking. Physically attractive people are generally evaluated more positively in a variety of situations.

Physical attractiveness seems to be an important aspect of dating, particularly for males. Even gay men prefer more attractive partners. However, physical attractiveness seems to be less important after the initial interaction habituates. The importance of attractiveness tends to decline over time. This suggests that those who are less attractive physically can improve their potential as friends or mates by simply managing to hang around long enough for their other characteristics to be noticed.

Similarity often is the basis of friendship, and later intimate relationships and marriage. This is known as the **Matching Principle**. It is no surprise to find that we tend to prefer people who have similar attitudes, likes and dislikes, and similar experiences. **Definition of the situation** is a concept sociologists use to explain how human activity takes place. Before we act, we must define what is happening. People who have similar levels of education and who come from similar neighborhoods and social class backgrounds share the same definitions, making it easier for interaction to take place. People who are similar find it easy to get along. However, when people from different backgrounds do interact, religious and ethnic differences are often transcended.

Proximity

The more important factor associated with making friends and finding mates is proximity. This is the **Propinquity Principle**. It is very difficult to meet, date, or marry someone from another state or faraway community, unless potential partners are brought together for some purpose, such as education. Proximity is very likely based on similarity, such as income, occupation, or social class. Additionally, proximity increases familiarity. Thus, people who are near to us are available for interaction, are usually similar to us, and become more familiar to us.

Theories of Affiliation

Humans are social creatures. We spend our lives in the company of other people. Being around others can help us deal with anxiety and fear. Children often seek the comfort of a parent, for example, when they become afraid. There are two theories about why we seek out friendships. The **reinforcement-affect model** stresses that the major goal in affiliation is the desire to feel good. Consequently, we tend to like people we associate with warm feelings or positive rewards and tend to dislike people we associate with negative feelings. Thus, we like to affiliate with people who have attitudes and values similar to our own and who agree with us on a variety of issues.

A second explanation of affiliation is offered by **social exchange theory**. This theory suggests that affiliation and friendship are motivated by the desire to maximize rewards and minimize costs. From this perspective, people are rational beings who calculate the costs and benefits of affiliation, much like a financial transaction.

CLOSE RELATIONSHIPS

Equity and Fair Exchanges

Exchange theory shows that the benefits of affiliation can be related to understanding, shared activities, communication, affection, companionship, and even sex. Obviously, there are other possible benefits, such as the provision of actual economic rewards such as money. Sometimes relationships can provide instrumental rewards, favors, promotions, or letters of reference. Rewards can be tangible or symbolic. Additionally, the value of a reward often lies in who gives it. We tend to crave rewards from people we like or love.

Relationships also involve certain costs. The **norm of reciprocity** suggests that in order to receive rewards we must be prepared to give them in return. Relationship costs can involve things such as stress, worry, and anxiety. Additionally, relationships involve some loss of freedom. We may become dependent upon a partner or a partner may become dependent upon us. Men tend to worry more about monetary costs and investments of time. Women, on the other hand, tend to worry more about becoming dependent upon someone who may turn out to be unreliable. Women also worry that they will give up too much of their identity.

Social exchange theory suggests that we evaluate our personal relationships by keeping track of the rewards and costs. If the costs outweigh the rewards, we may consider ending the relationships. Much like a financial investor, we consider whether or not the relationship is profitable. There are a variety of ways in which we might perform a cost/benefit analysis. Often, we compare our relationship to other relationships, such as those of our parents or friends. Alternatively, we may analyze the quality of the relationship, comparing it to our schema of an ideal relationship. Lastly, we might consider the alternatives available in terms of relationships with other people.

The **equity rule** is frequently applied by partners to see if the relationship is fair. No personal relationship is entirely equitable; some inequality is bound to exist. In every relationship needs are relative. Thus, partners may consider what is fair, more than outright equality. If one partner works full time, for example, and the other does not, the non-working partner may feel that it is acceptable to do a larger share of the household labor. If one or both partners begin to perceive that needs are not being met and inequity become intolerable, conflict may develop.

Partners may become distressed when the relationship is not fair. The partner receiving disproportionate rewards may experience guilt while the partner getting fewer rewards may become angry. When we perceive that we are putting more into a relationship than we are getting out of it we generally feel less satisfied. Relationship satisfaction is greatest when partners feel the distribution of rewards and outcomes are fair. The perception of fairness can often be restored either by changing behaviors or by changing our perception of fairness.

Correspondent Outcomes and Roles

If partners share the same interests, maintaining a close, personal relationship can be easier than if partners have little in common. When both partners are receiving similar rewards from the relationship, they have **correspondent outcomes**. However, non-correspondent outcomes implies that the partners have different values and interests and had a difficult time finding activities that both like and find rewarding. Non-correspondent outcomes often lead to conflicts. These types of conflict can be dealt with if the partners find less preferred alternatives acceptable to each.

Partners who have achieved **role congruency** generally report the most equity in their relationships. Role congruency is related to agreement about the statuses and roles in the relationship. For example, a man and a woman who both have traditional attitudes toward gender roles are likely to agree about who does what in the relationship. They will have similar attitudes about discipline, the household division of labor, leisure activities, decision-making, and other duties and responsibilities. On the other hand, a woman with liberal attitudes and a man with traditional attitudes may experience a great deal of conflict over the roles in the relationship. In this case, one or both may perceive inequity in the relationship because their role attitudes are incongruent.

Self-Disclosure and Intimacy

The capacity for symbolic communication is the foundation of being human. Human beings converse with each other. Sharing through conversation is a large part of relationships. **Self disclosure** refers to conversations with significant others in which we share intimate details about our hopes and dreams, fears, personal experiences, attitudes, and expectations. Descriptive self disclosure occurs when we describe our self to another. In this case, you are describing yourself to another in terms of your likes, dislikes, attitudes, beliefs, hobbies, and the like. Evaluative self disclosure involves sharing our assessments or evaluations about people or situations.

Self disclosure serves a variety of functions. It allows us to express our feelings and innermost thoughts. Self disclosure also allows us to gain clarity over our thoughts on certain situations by talking through them. This often happens when we try to figure out what our position is on an issue we have not given much thought. Often self disclosure allows us to validate our position on an issue when our significant other agrees with us. Perhaps the most important aspect of self disclosure is that it allows intimacy between partners to grow. As we become more and more attached to another, we are more likely to increase the level of self disclosure.

As the relationship becomes more intimate, the partners begin to reveal more to each other. They begin to share intimate details. This is known as **social penetration**, trying to get to know our partner's inner self. The depth of the disclosure may increase, and personal information about our inner most thoughts and emotions are shared. Similarly, the breadth of disclosure increases as a wider range of topics is discussed. There is a close relationship between intimacy and self disclosure in relationships. In our culture, generally, a higher level of self disclosure is widely considered to be the foundation of a good relationship.

Self disclosure is not without risks. The person we would like to know better may be indifferent to our attempts to become intimate. When we share personal details we give up some control and the information could be used to hurt us. Of course, sometimes personal information we have shared with someone is used against us and we are betrayed by the person we trusted. The greatest risk is rejection. We may reveal an attitude or belief that the person we are attracted to finds unacceptable. In the process of developing a relationship, we use self disclosure to help us decide whether to continue increasing the level of intimacy or not.

Gender and Self Disclosure

A popular myth about gender is that men are from Mars and women are from Venus. Stereotypes about men and women suggest that men are emotionally repressed while women, on the other hand, like to talk and gossip. There is little support for such stereotypes. However, researchers have discovered that women do reveal slightly more than men. In male-female disclosures, women tend to reveal their emotions and weaknesses. Men, on the other hand, tend to hide their weaknesses and reveal their strengths and aggressive tendencies. Overall, men tend to disclose less than women. Both men and women tend to disclose more to romantic partners than to anyone else.

Power and Relationships

Social norms, or rules of behavior, generally allow men to have more power than women. This social system is known as **patriarchy**. Traditional gender roles and laws protecting men's power in families are a reflection of patriarchy. Until very recently, for example, there were no laws in the United States making spousal rape illegal. Historically, women were expected to defer to their husbands within their households. The Women's Movement ushered in many advances for women both in the household and in civil society, however, complete equality with men was never achieved and conservative forces continue to try and rollback the gains of the movement. The struggle over abortion rights is a prime example. Even today, in spite of the advances gained by women, as a group, women earn less then men and are more likely to be order-takers than order-givers in the workplace.

Patriarchy ensures that men have more relative resources than women. Those with more resources have more power, not only in their personal relationships, but in society. Resources can be almost anything, including status, money, occupation, and even physical appearance. Less attractive men, for example, are often able to use money to offset what they lack in physical appearance. This is less likely to be the case for unattractive women. Additionally, even attractive women are less appealing to men as they age, whereas the reverse is true for men. Today, the majority of married women work but usually do not earn as much as their husband's, which means, even though their income may be important for the family's financial well-being, their ability to survive outside the marriage is more restricted than their husbands'.

In most relationships, the partner less interested in continuing the relationship generally has greater power. This is known as the **principle of least interest**. The partner that is more dependent upon the other is usually the one more interested in continuing in the relationship. What would make you the less interested partner? You may feel that you are very attractive. Perhaps, you know other people who are interested in you. You may be the main breadwinner in the relationship. In terms of the equity rule, you may be the partner receiving most of the rewards and positive outcomes. There are many ways in which power operates in relationships.

Relationship Conflict

Conflict is a natural part of all relationships. Partners should understand that conflict can be managed and there are some positive functions of conflict. For one thing, conflict provides opportunities for clarifying disagreements. **False consciousness** is a sociological concept usually associated with misunderstanding your social class position in society. However, false consciousness can also operate in relationships. You may be unaware that you are, in fact, the dependent partner or the partner receiving fewer rewards and positive outcomes. Conflict often clarifies one's position in the relationship and can lead to changed expectations. In other words, conflict can move the relationship in a more equitable direction. Of course, conflict can get out of control but partners should strive to exercise positive conflict management. If one partner is unwilling to deal with conflict relationship exit may be the only option.

There are three general categories of conflict in relationships: specific behaviors, norms and roles, and personal dispositions. Often conflict is associated with specific behaviors. One partner may find certain things the other partner does extremely annoying and hard to deal with. For example, if one partner is expected to be in charge of the budget and paying the bills, continually forgetting to make one monthly payment or another may lead to conflict. This may be resolved by changes in responsibilities. However, if the person paying the monthly expenses perceives that responsibility as a positive outcome in the relationship, simply changing responsibilities may not solve the problem. Another approach is to change the behavior itself. This implies, of course, that the person is willing to change.

Another area in which conflict emerges is associated with norms and roles in the relationship. As mentioned previously, role-congruency leans against this type of conflict. When the rights, duties, and obligations of each partner are worked out role-congruency is high and conflict is minimized. However, this is usually a process. Over time, partners can work this out. Sometimes, people just refuse to change. A traditional man may simply view it as his prerogative not to participate in roles associated with child rearing, such as changing diapers or feeding the children. This may cause conflict.

A third area in which conflict often emerges involves the personal dispositions and personalities of the partners. People with a conflict-habituated personality, for example, thrive on conflict and may seek to introduce stress into their relationships deliberately. Some may have personality quirks that, over time, become difficult to adapt to. For example, some people are grouchy. Other people are aggressive or intimidating. Some people are too avoiding of conflict and disagreement, so much so that difficulties are never resolved. Some people bottle-up their emotions. Some people want to disclose too much information. Over time, most partners manage to work out conflict related to personal dispositions.

Worthy of mention is that change is inevitable. The situation often changes, forcing partners to reexamine roles already worked out. For example, partners who have an equitable division of household labor will be challenged when children arrive and they discover our social organization is predicated on the assumption that women will stay home and care for children. Another common situation is change at work. Job loss, promotions, moving a household and uprooting the family due to geographical relocations associated with work, downsizings, or periods of unemployment, are fairly common occurrences in relationships. During these episodes, specific behaviors, norms and roles, and personal dispositions can all be affected and relationship conflict may increase.

Healthy Communication Rules

Effective communication is the key to successfully managing relationship conflict. There are seven rules for healthy communication:

1. When your partner asks you to do something, say exactly what you can or want to do – not what you cannot or do not want to do.

2. When your partner does a chore, show appreciation – do not nitpick.

3. Always greet each other with a warm hello and leave with a warm goodbye.

4. Do not psychoanalyze everything – you'll be a know-it-all no one likes!

5. Always speak for yourself.

6. When you have an opinion be direct, do not beat around the bush.

7. If you do not have something nice to say shut up – you will just make everything worse.

Relationship Satisfaction and Commitment

Relationship satisfaction refers to the overall quality of the relationship. Partners tend to have greater satisfaction if the relationship is equitable. People who are happy in their personal relationship avoid trading insults. For these partners, if one person is upset and makes a negative comment the other person does not take offense and may infer that their partner is just having a bad day. Generally, satisfied partners attribute grouchiness and negative comments to external pressures, rather than internal personality characteristics. Happy partners give each other the benefit of the doubt. Dissatisfied partners tend to attribute negative comments to their partner's personality, rather than to external pressures, and respond in kind. Arguments often start with trading insults.

Couple's, who stick it out, through the good times and the bad, have high levels of commitment. There are two ways to think about commitment. One is **constraint commitment**. In this type of commitment, the partners lack other choices. This type of commitment is really based on external forces, such as lack of time, energy, emotion, or money. The partners are stuck with each other and make the best of it. The other type of commitment is **personal dedication**. This couple has a "we" identity. Their personal sense of self includes the other person. They prefer not to do something if the other cannot for some reason. The identity of both involves the identity of the other.

There are healthy and unhealthy responses to relationship dissatisfaction. **Voice** refers to raising an issue for discussion. When a problem is voiced, committed partners try to rescue the relationship by talking about the problem. **Neglect** is destructive. Less committed partners often passively let the relationship deteriorate, ignoring, or refusing to discuss the issue. **Loyalty** is constructive. Committed partners wait for the situation to improve and attempt to maintain the relationship through effective communication. **Exit** refers to the ultimate destruction of the relationship with the partners ending it.

Relationship Exit: Breaking Up Is Hard To Do

People who are rejected by a lover go through three stages of detachment, if they are still in love with the person who rejects them:

1. **Protest:** crying, complaining, making further demands, requests for an explanation, acting unreasonably, and in general refusing to accept the rejection – occasionally some rejected lovers go berserk.

2. **Despair:** feelings of sadness, depression, loss of self-esteem, and passivity.

3. **Detachment:** spurned lovers often derogate those who reject them. In this sense, the rejected lover changes their perception of their former partner, defining the person in negative terms, and eventually detaches emotionally.

LOVE AND ROMANCE

How do you know if you are in love? You may be in love if you can interpret your partner's body language. If you are interested in another's opinions, feelings, emotional state, and well being, you may be in love. If you are willing to make financial and emotional sacrifices for someone, you may be in love. If you can tolerate someone's personality quirks, you may be in love. If the level of self disclosure in the relationship is high, you may be in love. Love generally implies a distinctive cluster of thoughts you have regarding another person that you do not have for other people.

Progress toward Marriage

There is a sequence of events generally associated, at least in heterosexual relationships, with progress toward marriage. Generally, partners start out by spending time together. Dating activities include going out to eat or to the movies, and other activities that allow the partners to be together. Usually, partners begin to hold hands while dating and engage in mild forms of "petting," such as kissing. Referring to each other as "boyfriend" or "girlfriend" indicates that the relationship is exclusive and that the partners agree not to date other people.

As the relationship becomes more serious the partners may begin to discuss what their "future" together will be like. This is an important part of the progress toward a committed relationship and allows the partners to discuss their expectations and roles. Many people who rush into marriage later discover, to their regret, that their partner has different, and unacceptable, ideas about what their roles should be. Eventually, the couple becomes "engaged," at which point plans for marriage are generally made and discussed. Often couples who reach this stage take a vacation together or cohabitate.

Defining Love

Not everyone means the same thing when they say "I love you." Researchers have identified six different definitions of love.

1. Romantic Love: This type of love is often described as an all-consuming emotional experience. When the lover is absence, a nearly physical experience of loss or separation is felt.

2. Possessive Love: An obsessive type of love that is also emotionally intense and often accompanied by jealousy on the part of the possessive lover. The possessive lover fears rejection and is controlling.

3. Best Friends Love: This type of love is based on companionship and a high level of trust and comfort with each other. A best friend's lover is thoughtful, caring, and warm.

4. Pragmatic Love: This type of love is based mostly on compatibility. The partners are suitable for each other based on expectations, interests, and similarity.

5. Altruistic Love: A type of love that is unconditional and based on duty and obligation. It is often the basis of parental love for a child. The altruistic lover is caring, forgiving, and willing to place the happiness of the loved one first.

6. Game-Playing Love: This type of love is often preferred by those who see life as a game to be won. Relationships based on game-playing love often do not last long.

We can contrast two major types of love, passionate love and companionate love. **Passionate love** is highly emotional. In this type of love the focus is on the "chemistry" the couple experiences. Passion refers to the desire the individuals feel for each other. Here, there is a preoccupation with the other and an interest in pursuing sexual desires. As you may guess, passionate love frequently burns out quickly.

Companionate love, on the other hand, is a more practical type of love. Couples who experience companionate love emphasize trust, caring, and friendship. Their lives are deeply intertwined and their activities are highly coordinated. As time goes by, these couples discover each other's strengths and weakness and learn to live with each other's flaws. Companionate love is the basis of long-term relationships.

Triangle Theory of Love

Robert Sternberg has proposed a theory of love that views love as a mixture of the various types of love discussed above, rather than simply one or the other. In other words, in Sternberg's view, it is possible to experience his three main ingredients of love, intimacy, passion, and commitment, all at once and different levels of each.

Passion, according to Sternberg, is the emotional state characterized by arousal, sexual desire, and excitement. **Intimacy** refers to the close feelings people develop for each other. Intimate couples know each other very well and care deeply about each other's welfare. **Commitment** refers to the conscious decision to stay together through thick-and-thin. Sternberg believes that every relationship has different levels of all three ingredients.

Defining love as a mixture of passion, intimacy, and commitment allows Sternberg to identify other types of love. **Compassionate love**, for example, has high levels of intimacy and commitment, but very little passion. **Romantic love** has high levels of intimacy and passion but very little commitment. **Empty love**, is mostly commitment but little passion or intimacy. **Infatuation** is mostly passion but little intimacy and commitment. **Consummate love** has nearly equal parts of intimacy, passion, and commitment. In our society, consummate love is often seen as the ideal type for which all couples should strive.

Jealousy

Jealousy is a reaction to a perceived threat to the relationship. The quality of the relationship could be threatened or the threat could be to the continuation of the relationship. Insecure people tend to be more susceptible to feelings of jealousy and a perceived threat to the relationship could be a blow to their self-esteem. The person more dependent upon the relationship, and who has fewer alternatives, is more likely to feel threatened when one partner develops other relationships.

Adult Romantic Attachments

Have you noticed that, when trying to develop relationships with others, some people are easy to get to know while other people are uncomfortable with your interest or try to avoid you entirely? Attachment theory studies two dimensions of attachment, anxiety and avoidance. Anxiety refers to attitudes you may have about yourself while avoidance refers to attitudes you may have about others.

Looking at attachment in this manner allows us to identify four types of attachment. **Secure attachment** refers to adults who are low on both anxiety and avoidance. These adults are more open and easy to get along with. They are not particularly worried about being abandoned by their partner, think positively about their partners, and describe their relationships as happy. They have high levels of trust and share feelings and ideas. Adults characterized by secure attachments tend to have happy, satisfying, and intimate relationships.

The second type is **attachment anxious/ambivalent** attachment (more recently referred to as preoccupied attachment). In this category of attachment people desire closer relationships but have high levels of anxiety about themselves. Anxious people are preoccupied with their faults and shortcomings and fear that those they are close to will discover their negative traits. Consequently, they try too hard to be sensitive and supportive, to the extent that they can be seen as controlling. In other words, anxious/ambivalent types are more likely to be supportive out of concerns about their own shortcomings rather than genuine concern for others.

The third type of attachment is called **dismissing avoidant attachment**. People characterized by this type of attachment can seem aloof and distant. They are slow to disclose personal feelings and ideas because they are distrustful of others. They have love anxiety but high avoidance. In other words, they have positive attitudes about their attributes but see others, including their partners, as unreliable and uncaring. In their personal relationships they are distant, less committed, and less able to enjoy the relationship. Compared to secure or anxious/ambivalent types, they provide less care and support in their marriages and relationships.

Given the fact that attachment is fundamental to humanness, avoidant individuals are hard to fathom. It is possible that early in life these individuals had a rejecting or distant parent, possibly a mother. Or, perhaps, they experienced an early failure of a relationship or romantic rejection. In any case, they desire relationships but fear getting to close to anyone. In that sense, they desire companionship but not too much intimacy.

The last type of attachment is called **fearful avoidant attachment**. Individuals in this category score high on both anxiety and avoidance. These people not only have negative attitudes about themselves they view others as untrustworthy and uncaring. These individuals worry that they are unlovable and try to keep others at a distance.

Romance and Biology

Is there a romantic love gene? Some socio- and evolutionary biologists think so. They have proposed that love is genetic or at least an artifact of evolution. They argue that a romantic love gene would ensure that humans fall in love, have sex, and thus, perpetuate the species. For example, these theorists argue that we fall in love with our children because they have disproportionately large eyes, which makes them "cute."

Additionally, these evolutionary assumptions tend to be based on the idea that the nuclear family is natural. The problem is that the nuclear family is not a cultural universal, which you would expect to find if love and family type were evolutionary or genetic. The nuclear family is sociologically, historically, and culturally specific. If you are involved in a non-nuclear family type, such as single parent family or extended family, do you not love the people you live with?

There are a variety of questions raised by the hypothesis that love may be genetic. First, what about homosexual relationships? Are we ready to believe that gay men and women are not in love or that they cannot experience love? What about the types of love that are not romantic, such as pragmatic or altruistic love? If love romantic love was genetic how could the other forms of love exist? How can the genetic hypothesis explain why partners in "love" beat the crap out of each other, let alone child abuse or elder abuse? How can a love gene explain "who" we fall in love with?

I propose that love is not genetic or evolutionary at all - it is the product of human interaction. Love arises out of the symbolic capacities of human beings. Love is defined and negotiated. Love means different things to different people. Certainly, without sexual activity and emotional attachment human beings could not exist. Thus, humans invented culture to solve these problems.

80 CB 80 CB

REFERENCES

Abend, T. A., & Williamson, G. M. (2002). Feeling attractive in the wake of breast cancer: Optimism matters, and so do interpersonal relationships. *Personality & Social Psychology Bulletin, 28*, 427-436.

Allen, K. M., Blascovich, J., Tomaka, J., & Kelsey, R. M. (1991). Presence of human friends and pet dogs as moderators of autonomic responses to stress in women. *Journal of Personality and Social Psychology, 61*, 582-589.

Allen, R. W., Madison, D. L., Porter, L. W., Renwick, P. A., & Mayes, B. T. (1979). Organizational politics: Tactics and characteristics of its actors. *California Management Review, 22*, 77-83.

Allport, G. W., & Postman, L. (1947). *The psychology of rumor.* New York: Henry Holt.

Andersson, J., & Roennberg, J. (1997). Cued memory collaboration: Effects of friendship and type of retrieval cue. *European Journal of Cognitive Psychology, 9*, 273-287.

Aron, A., Melinat, E., Aron, E. N., Vallone, R. D., & Bator, R. J. (1997). The experimental generation of interpersonal closeness: A procedure and some preliminary findings. *Personality and Social Psychology Bulletin, 23*, 363-377.

Aseltine, R. H., Jr., Gore, S., & Colten, M. E. (1994). Depression and the social developmental context of adolescence. *Journal of Personality and Social Psychology, 67*, 252-263.

Bank, B. J., & Hansford, S. L. (2000). Gender and friendship: Why are men's best same-sex friendships less intimate and supportive? *Personal Relationship, 7*, 63-78.

Baumeister, R. F., & Leary, M. R. (1995). The need to belong: Desire for interpersonal attachments as a fundamental human motivation. *Psychological Bulletin, 117*, 497-529.

Baumeister, R. F., Twenge, J. M., & Nuss, C. K. (2002). Effects of social exclusion on cognitive processes: Anticipated aloneness reduces intelligent thought. *Journal of Personality & Social*

Psychology, 83, 817-827.

Beach, S. R. H., Tesser, A., Fincham, F. D., Jones, D. J., Johnson, D., & Whitaker, D. J. (1998). Pleasure and pain in doing well, together: An investigation of performance-related affect in close relationships. *Journal of Personality and Social Psychology, 74*, 923-938.

Berscheid, E., & Reis, H. T. (1998). Attraction and close relationships. In D. T. Gilbert, S. T. Fiske, & G. Lindzey (Eds.), *Handbook of Social Psychology* (4th ed.) (Vol. 2, pp. 193-281). New York: McGraw-Hill.

Blascovich, J., Mendes, W. B., Hunter, S. B., & Salomon, K. (1999). Social "facilitation" as challenge and threat. *Journal of Personality & Social Psychology, 77*, 68-77.

Bogart, L. M., & Helgeson, V. S. (2000). Social comparisons among women with breast cancer: A longitudinal investigation. *Journal of Applied Social Psychology, 30*, 547-575.

Bolger, N., & Eckenrode, J. (1991). Social relationships, personality, and anxiety during a major stressful event. *Journal of Personality and Social Psychology, 61*, 440-449.

Bornstein, R. F. (1989). Exposure and affect: Overview and meta-analysis of research, 1968-1987. *Psychological Bulletin, 106*, 265-289.

Bowlby, J. (1969). *Attachment and loss. Vol. 1 Attachment.* New York: Basic Books.

Brisette, I. S., Scheier, M. S., & Carver, C. S. (2002). The role of optimism in social network development, coping and psychological adjustment during a life transition. *Journal of Personality & Social Psychology, 82*, 102-111.

Buckingham, J. T., & Alicke, M. D. (2002). The influence of individual versus aggregate social comparison and the presence of others on self-evaluations. *Journal of Personality & Social Psychology, 83*, 1117-1130.

Bugental, D. B. (2000). Acquisition of the algorithms of social life: A domain-based approach. *Psychological Bulletin, 126*, 187-219.

Bukowski, W. M., Hoza, B., & Boivin, M. (1994). Measuring friendship quality during pre- and early adolescence: The development and psychometric properties of friendship qualities scale. *Journal of Personal and Personal Relationships, 11*, 471-484.

Buunk, B. P., & Verhoeven, K. (1991). Companionship and support in organizations: A microanalysis of the stress-reducing features of social interaction. *Basic and Applied Social Psychology, 12*, 242-258.

Buunk, B. P., Doosje, B. J., Jans, L. G. J. M., & Hopstaken, L. E. M. (1993). Perceived reciprocity, social support, and stress at work: The role of exchange and communal orientation. *Journal of Personality and Social Psychology, 65*, 801-811.

Buunk, B. P., Gibbons, F. X. & Visser, A. (2002). The relevance of social comparison processes for prevention and health care. *Patient Education and Counseling, 47*, 1-3.

Byrne, D. (1971). The Attraction Paradigm. New York: Academic Press.

Campbell, J. D., & Tesser, A. (1985). Self-evaluation maintenance processes in relationships. In S. Duck, & D. Perlman (Eds.), *Understanding personal relationships: An interdisciplinary approach* (pp. 107-135). Beverly Hills, CA: Sage.

Campbell, L., Simpson, J. A., Kashy, D. A., & Rholes, W. S. (2001). Attachment orientations, dependence, and behavior in a stressful situation: An application of the actor-partner interdependence model. *Journal of Social and Personal Relationships, 8*, 821-843.

Cannon, W. B. (1932). *The wisdom of the body.* New York: Norton.

Cantril, H. (1940). *The invasion from mars.* Princeton, NJ: Princeton University Press.

Caporeal, L. R. (1997). The evolution of truly social cognition: The core configurations model. *Personality and Social Psychology Review, 1*, 276-298.

Carli, L. L. (1989). Gender differences in interaction style and influence. *Journal of Personality and Social Psychology, 56*, 565-576.

Case, R. B., Moss, A. J., & Case, N. (1992). Living alone after myocardial infarction: Impact on prognosis. *Journal of the American Medical Association, 267*, 575-85.

Chartrand, T. L., & Bargh, J. A. (1999). The chameleon effect: The perception-behavior link and social interaction. *Journal of Personality and Social Psychology, 76*, 893-910.

Chen, F., & Kenrick, D. T. (2002). Repulsion or attraction: Group membership and assumed attitude similarity. *Journal of Personality & Social Psychology, 83*, 111-125.

Chen, S., Lee-Chai, A. Y., & Bargh, J. A. (2001). Relationship orientation as a moderator of the effects of social power. *Journal of Personality & Social Psychology, 80*, 173-187.

Christensen, P. N., & Kashy, D. A. (1998). Perceptions of and by lonely people in initial social interaction. *Personality and Social Psychology Bulletin, 24*, 322-329.

Cialdini, R. B., Borden, R., Thorne, A., Walker, M., Freeman, S., & Sloane, L. T. (1976). Basking in reflected glory: Three (football) field studies. *Journal of Personality and Social Psychology, 34*, 366-375.

Clark, M. S., & Chrisman, K. (1994). Resource allocation in intimate relationships. In A. H. Weber, & J. H. Harvey (Eds.), *Perspectives on close relationships* (pp. 176-192). Boston: Allyn & Bacon.

Clark, M. S., & Jordan, S. D. (2002). Adherence to communal norms: What it means, when it occurs, and some thoughts on how it develops. In B. Laursen, & W. G. Graziano (Eds.), *Social sxchange in development. dew directions for child and adolescent development* (pp. 3-25). San Francisco: Jossey-Bass/Pfeiffer.

Clark, M. S., Mills, J. R., & Corcoran, D. M. (1989). Keeping track of needs and inputs of friends and strangers. *Personality and Social Psychology Bulletin, 15*, 533-542.

Clark, M. S., Ouellette, R., Powell, M. C., & Milberg, S. (1987). Recipient's mood, relationship type, and helping. *Journal of Personality and Social Psychology, 53*, 94-103.

Clore, G. L., & Byrne, D. (1974). A reinforcement-affect model of attraction. In T. L. Huston (Ed.), *Foundations of interpersonal attraction* (pp. 143-170). New York: Academic Press.

Collins, N. L., & Miller, L. C. (1994). Self-disclosure and liking: A meta-analytic review. *Psychological Bulletin, 116*, 457-475.

Colvin, C. R., Vogt, D., & Ickes, W. (1997). Why do friends understand each other better than strangers do? In W. J. Ickes (Ed.), *Empathic acccuracy* (pp. 169-193). New York: Guilford.

Condon, J. W., & Crano, W. D. (1988). Inferred evaluation and the relation between attitude similarity and interpersonal attraction. *Journal of Personality and Social Psychology, 54*, 789-797.

Cutrona, C. E. (1982). Transition to college: Loneliness and the process of social adjustment. In L. A. Peplau, & D. Perlman (Eds.), *Loneliness: A sourcebook of current theory, research, and therapy.* New York: Wiley-Interscience.

Cutrona, C. E., Cole, V., Colangelo, N., Assouline, S. G., & Russell, D. W. (1994). Perceived parental social support and academic achievement: An attachment theory perspective. *Journal of Personality and Social Psychology, 66*, 369-378.

Czikszentmihalyi, M., Larson, R., & Prescott, S. (1977). The ecology of adolescent activity and experience. *Journal of Youth and Adolescence, 6*, 281-294.

Daly, M., Salmon, C., & Wilson, M. (1997). Kinship: The conceptual hole in psychological studies of social cognition and close relationships. In J. A. Simpson, & D. T. Kenrick (Eds.), *Evolutionary social psychology* (pp. 265-296). Mahwah, NJ: Erlbaum.

Davis, K. E., & Todd, M. J. (1985). Assessing friendship: Prototypes, paradigm cases, and relationship description. In S. Duck, & D. Perlman (Eds.), *Understanding personal relationships: An interdisciplinary approach* (pp. 17-38). Beverly Hills, CA: Sage.

de Waal, F. B. M. (1989). *Chimpanzee politics: Power and sex among apes.* Baltimore: Johns Hopkins University Press.

DePaulo, B. M., & Kashy, D. A. (1998). Everyday lies in close relationships. *Journal of Personality and Social Psychology, 74*, 63-79.

DePaulo, B. M., Kashy, D. A., Kirkendol, S. E., Wyer, M. M., & Epstein, J. A. (1996). Lying in everyday life. *Journal of Personality and Social Psychology, 70*, 979-995.

Derlega, V. J., Metts, S., Petronio, S., & Margulis, S. J. (1993). *Self-disclosure.* Newbury Park, CA: Sage.

Diener, E. (2000). Subjective Well-Being: The science of happiness and a proposal for a national index. *American Psychologist, 55*, 34-43.

Dindia, K., & Allen, M. (1992). Sex differences in self-disclosure: A meta-analysis. *Psychological Bulletin, 112*, 106-124.

Ensari, N., & Miller, N. (2002). The outgroup must not be so bad after all: The effects of disclosure, typicality, and salience on intergroup bias. *Journal of Personality & Social Psychology, 83*, 313-329.

Festinger, L., Schachter, S., & Back, K. (1950). *Social pressures in informal groups.* Stanford, CA: Stanford University Press.

Fiske, A. P. (1992). The four elementary forms of sociality: Framework for a unified theory of social relations. *Psychological Review, 99*, 689-723.

Foa, E. B., & Foa, U. G. (1980). *Resource theory: Interpersonal behavior as exchange.* In K. J. Gergen, M. S. Greenber, & R. H. Willis (Eds.), *Social exchange: Advances in theory and research* (pp. 77-94). New York: Plenum.

Forgas, J. P. (1995). The affect-infusion model (AIM). *Psychological Bulletin, 117*, 39-66.

Forgas, J. P., Levinger, G., & Moylan, S. (1994). Feeling good and feeling close: mood effects on the perception of intimate relationships. *Personal Relationships, 2*, 165-184.

Friedmann, E., Katcher, A. H., Lynch, J. J., & Thomas, S. A. (1980). Animal companions and one-year survival of patients after discharge from a coronary care unit. *Public Health Reports, 95*, 307-12.

Gable, S. L., & Reis, H. T. (1999). Now and then, them and us, this and that: Studying relationships across time, partner, context, and person. *Personal Relationships, 6*, 415-432.

Gardner, W. L., Gabriel, S., & Hochschild, L. (2002). When you and I are "We," you are not threatening: The role of self-expansion in social comparison. *Journal of Personality & Social Psychology, 82*, 239-251.

Gardner, W. L., Pickett, C. L., & Brewer, M. B. (2000). Social exclusion and selective memory: How the need to belong influences memory for social events. *Personality and Social Psychology Bulletin, 26*, 486-496.

Geary, D. C., & Flinn, M. V. (2002). Sex differences in behavioral and hormonal response to social threat: Commentary on Taylor et al. (2000). *Psychological Review, 109*, 745-750.

Gerard, H. B., & Rabbie, J. M. (1961). Fear and social comparison. *Journal of Abnormal and Social Psychology, 62*, 586-592.

Gottlieb, B. H. (1994). Social support. In A. L. Webber, & J. H. Harvey (Eds.), *Perspectives on close relationships* (pp. 307-324). Boston: Allyn & Bacon.

Greenberg, J., & Baron, R. A. (1993). *Behavior in organizations* (4th ed.). Boston: Allyn & Bacon.

Greenberg, M. S., & Westcott, D. R. (1983). Indebtedness as a mediator of reactions to aid. In J. D. Fisher, A. Nadler, & B. M. DePaulo (Eds.), *New directions in helping behavior* (Vol. 1, pp. 113-141). San Diego: Academic Press.

Gump, B. B., & Kulik, J. A. (1997). Stress, affiliation, and emotional contagion. *Journal of Personality and Social Psychology, 72*, 305-319.

Hall, J. A., & Halberstadt, A. G. (1986). Smiling and gazing. In J. S. Hyde & M. C. Linn (Eds.), *The psychology of gender: Advances through meta-analysis* (pp. 136-158). Baltimore: Johns-Hopkins University Press.

Harlow, R. E., & Cantor, N. (1994). Social pursuit of academics: Side effects and spillover of strategic reassurance seeking. *Journal of Personality and Social Psychology, 66*, 386-397.

Harmon-Jones, E., & Allen, J. J. B. (2001). The role of affect in the mere exposure effect: Evidence from psychophysiological and individual differences approaches. *Personality & Social Psychology Bulletin, 27*, 889-898.

Harvey, J. H., & Omarzu, J. (1997). Minding the close relationship. *Personality and Social Psychology Review, 1*, 224-240.

Haslam, N. (1997). Four grammars for primate social relations. In J. A. Simpson, & D. T. Kenrick (Eds.),

Evolutionary social psychology (pp. 297-316). Mahwah, NJ: Erlbaum.

Hatfield, E., Greenberger, E., Traupmann, J., & Lambert, P. (1982). Equity and sexual satisfaction in recently married couples. *Journal of Sex Research, 18*, 18-32.

Hatfield, E., Traupmann, J., Sprecher, S., Utne, M., & Hay, J. (1985). Equity and intimate relationships: Recent research. In W. Ickes (Ed.), *Compatible and incompatible relationships* (pp. 1-27). New York: Springer-Verlag.

Helgeson, V. S., Shaver, P., & Dyer, M. (1987). Prototypes of intimacy and distance in same-sex and opposite-sex relationships. *Journal of Social and Personal Relationships, 4*, 195-234.

Hill, K., & Hurtado, A. M. (1993). Hunter-gatherers in the new world. In P. Sherman, & J. Alcock (Eds.), *Exploring animal behavior* (pp. 154-160). Sunderland, MA: Sinauer.

Hofstede, G. (1980). *Culture's consequences: International differences in work-related values.* Beverly Hills, CA: Sage.

Hsu, F. L. K. (1983). *Rugged individualism reconsidered.* Knoxville: University of Tennessee Press.

James, W. (1890). *Principles of psychology.* New York: Henry Holt.

Joiner, T. E., Alfano, M. S., & Metalsky, G. I. (1992). When depression breeds contempt: Reassurance seeking, self-esteem, and rejection of depressed college students by their roommates. *Journal of Abnormal Psychology, 101*, 165-173.

Joiner, T. E., Jr. (1994). Contagious depression: Existence, specificity to depressed symptoms, and the role of reassurance seeking. *Journal of Personality and Social Psychology, 67*, 287-296.

Jones, W. H., & Carver, M. D. (1991). Adjustment and coping implications of loneliness. In C. R. Snyder, & D. R. Forsyth (Eds.), Handbook of Social Clinical Psychology (pp. 395-410). New York: Pergamon.

Jones, W. H., Cavert, C. W., Snider, R. L., & Bruce, T. (1985). Relational stress: An analysis of situations and events associated with loneliness. In S. Duck, & D. Perlman (Eds.), *Understanding personal relationships: An interdisciplinary approach* (pp. 221-242). Beverly Hills, CA: Sage.

Jones, W. H., Freemon, J. E., & Goswick, R. A. (1981). The persistence of loneliness: Self and other determinants. *Journal of Personality, 49*, 27-48.

Jones, W. H., Hobbs, S. A., & Hockenbury, D. (1982). Loneliness and social skill deficits. *Journal of Personality and Social Psychology, 42*, 682-689.

Jones, W. H., Sansone, C., & Helm, B. (1983). Loneliness and interpersonal judgments. *Personality and Social Psychology Bulletin, 9*, 437-441.

Kafetsios, K., & Nezlek, J. B. (2002). Attachment styles in everyday social interaction. *European Journal of Social Psychology, 32*, 719-735.

Kameda, T., Takezawa, M, Tindale, R. S., & Smith, C. M. (2002). Social sharing and risk reduction: Exploring a computational algorithm for the psychology of windfall gains. *Evolution and Human Behavior, 23*, 11-33.

Kameda, T., Takezawa, M., & Hastie, R. (2003). The logic of social sharing: An evolutionary game analysis of adaptive norm development. *Personality and Social Psychology Review, 7*, 2-19.

Kanter, R. M. (1977). *Men and women of the corporation.* New York: Basic Books.

Kashy, D. A., & DePaulo, B. M. (1996). Who lies? *Journal of Personality and Social Psychology, 70*, 1037-1051.

Kelly, A. M., Klusas, J. A., von Weiss, R. T., & Kenny, C. (2001). What is it about revealing secrets that is beneficial? *Personality and Social Psychology Bulletin, 27*, 651-665.

Kenny, D. A., & DePaulo, B. M. (1993). Do people know how others view them? An empirical and theoretical account. *Psychological Bulletin, 114*, 145-161.

Kenrick, D. T., & Johnson, G. A. (1979). Interpersonal attraction in aversive environments: A problem for the classical conditioning paradigm? *Journal of Personality and Social Psychology, 37*, 572-579.

Kenrick, D. T., Li, N. P., & Butner, J. (2003b). Dynamical evolutionary psychology: Individual decision-rules and emergent social norms. *Psychological Review, 110*, 3-28.

Kenrick, D. T., Montello, D. R., Gutierres, S. E., & Trost, M. R. (1993). Effects of physical attractiveness on affect and perceptual judgment: When social comparison overrides social reinforcement. *Personality and Social Psychology Bulletin, 19*, 195-99.

Kiecolt-Glaser, J., Garner, W., Spreicher, C., Penn, G., Holliday, J., & Glaser, R. (1985). Psychosocial modifiers of immuno-competence in medical students. *Psychosomatic Medicine, 46*, 7-14.

Kirkcaldy, B. D., Shephard, R. J., & Siefen, R. G. (2002). The relationship between physical activity and self-image and problem behavior among adolescents. *Social Psychiatry and Psychiatric Epidemiology, 37*, 544-550.

Kirkpatrick, L. A., & Shaver, P. (1988). Fear and affiliation reconsidered from a stress and coping perspective: The importance of cognitive clarity and fear reduction. *Journal of Social and Clinical Psychology, 7*, 214-233.

Klein, K., & Hodges, S. D. (2001). Gender differences, motivation and emphatic accuracy: When it pays to understand. *Personality & Social Psychology Bulletin, 27*, 720-730.

Kors, D. J., Linden, W., & Gerin, W. (1997). Evaluation interferes with social support: Effects of cardiovascular stress reactivity in women. *Journal of Social and Clinical Psychology, 16*, 1-23.

Kraut, R., & Kiesler, S. (2003). The social impact of internet use. *Psychological Science Agenda, 16*, 8-10.

Kraut, R., Patterson, M., Lundmark, V., Kiesler, S., Mukhopadhyay, T., & Scherlis, W. (1998). Internet paradox: A social technology that reduces social involvement and psychological well-being? *American Psychologist, 53*, 1017-1031.

Kulik, J. A., & Mahler, H. I. M. (1990). Stress and affiliation research: On taking the laboratory to health field settings. *Annals of Behavioral Medicine, 12*, 106-111.

Kulik, J. A., & Mahler, H. I. M. (2000). Social comparison, affiliation, and emotional contagion under threat. In J. Suls, & L. Wheeler (Eds.), *Handbook of social comparison: Theory and research* (pp. 295-320). New York: Kluwer Academic Publishers.

Kulik, J. A., Mahler, H. I. M., & Earnest, A. (19940. Social comparison and affiliation under threat: Going beyond the affiliate-choice paradigm. *Journal of Personality and Social Psychology, 66*, 301-309.

LaFrance, M., Hecht, M. A., & Paluck, E. L. (2003). The contingent smile: A meta-analysis of sex differences in smiling. *Psychological Bulletin, 129*, 305-334.

Lepore, S. J., Ragan, J. D., & Jones, S. (2000). Talking facilitates cognitive-emotional processes of adaptation to an acute stressor. *Journal of Personality & Social Psychology, 78*, 499-508.

Liden, R. C., & Mitchell, T. R. (1988). Ingratiatory behaviors in organizational settings. *Academy of Management Review, 12*, 572-587.

Lino, M. (2000). *Expenditures on children by families, 1999 Annual Report*. U.S. Department of Agriculture (Miscellaneous Publication #1528-1999). Washington, DC: USDA.

Lott, A. J., & Lott, B. E. (1974). The Role of reward in the formation of positive interpersonal attitudes. In T. L. Huston (Ed.), *Foundations of interpersonal attraction* (pp. 171-192). New York: Academic Press.

Lyubomirsky, S., & Ross, L. (1998). Hedonic consequences of social comparison: A contrast of happy and unhappy people. *Journal of Personality and Social Psychology, 73*, 1141-1157.

Magdol, L. (2002). Is moving gendered? The effects of residential mobility on the psychological well-being of men and women. *Sex Roles, 47*, 553-560.

Magdol, L., & Bessell, D. R. (2003). Social capital, social currency, and portable assets: The impact of residential mobility on exchanges of social support. *Personal Relationships, 10*, 1149-1169.

Maines, D. R., & Hardesty, M. J. (1987). Temporality and gender: Young adults' career and family plans. *Social Forces, 66*, 102-120.

Marsh, K. L., & Webb, W. M. (1996). Mood uncertainty and social comparison: Implications for mood management. *Journal of Social Behavior and Personality, 11*, 1-26.

Martin, R. (1997). "Girls don't talk about garages!" Perceptions of conversations in same- and cross-sex friendships. *Personal Relationships, 4*, 115-130.

Marx, E. M., Williams, J. M G., & Claridge, G. C. (1992). Depression and social problem solving. *Journal of Abnormal Psychology, 101,* 78-86.

McGowan, S. (2002). Mental representations in stressful situations: The calming and distressing effects of significant others. *Journal of Experimental Social Psychology, 38,* 152-161.

McKenna, K. Y. A., Green, A. S., & Gleason, M. E. J. (2002). Relationship formation on the internet: What's the big attraction? *Journal of Social Issues, 58,* 9-31.

McWilliams, S., & Howard, J. A. (1993). Solidarity and hierarchy in cross-sex friendships. *Journal of Social Issues, 49,* 191-202.

Mesquita, B. (2001). Emotions in collectivist and individualist contexts. *Journal of Personality and Social Psychology, 80,* 68-74.

Moghaddam, F. M., Taylor, D. M., & Wright, S. C. (1993). Social psychology in cross-cultural perspective. New York: W. H. Freeman.

Myers, D. G. (2000). The funds, friends, and faith of happy people. *American Psychologist, 55,* 56-67.

Nakao, K. (1987). Analyzing sociometric preferences: An example of Japanese and U.S. business groups. *Journal of Social Behavior and Personality, 2,* 523-534.

Neuberg, S. L, Smith, D. M., Hoffman, J. C., & Russell, F. J. (1994). When we observe stigmatized and "normal" individuals interacting: Stigma by association. *Personality and Social Psychology Bulletin, 20,* 196-209.

Nezlek, J. B. (1993). The stability of social interaction. *Journal of Personality and Social Psychology, 65,* 930-941.

Nezlek, J. B., & Derks, P. (2001). Use of humor as a coping mechanism, psychological adjustment, and social interaction. *Humor: International Journal of Humor Research, 14,* 395-413.

Nezlek, J. B., Richardson, D. S., Green, L. R., & Schatten-Jones, E. C. (2002). Psychological well-being and day-to-day social interaction among older adults. *Personal Relationships, 9,* 57-71.

Orive, R. (1988). Social projection and social comparison of opinions. *Journal of Personality and Social Psychology, 54,* 953-964.

Oswald, D. L., & Clark, E. M. (2003). Best friends forever? High school friendships and the transition to college. *Personal Relationships, 10,* 187-205.

Owens, L., Shute, R., & Slee, P. (2000). "Guess what I just heard!": Indirect aggression among teenage girls in Australia. *Aggressive Behavior, 26,* 67-83.

Paloutzian, R. F., & Ellison, C. W. (1982). Loneliness, spiritual well-being and the quality of life. In L. A. Peplau, & D. Perlman (Eds.), *Loneliness: A sourcebook of current theory, research, and therapy* (pp. 224-237). New York: Wiley.

Parkinson, B., Briner, R. B., Reynolds, S., & Totterdell, P. (1995). Time frames for mood: Relations between momentary and generalized ratings of affect. *Personality and Social Psychology Bulletin, 21,* 331-339.

Pataki, S. P., Shapiro, C., & Clark, M. S. (1994). Children's acquisition of appropriate norms of friendships and acquaintances. *Journal of Personal and Personal Relationships, 11,* 427-442.

Pellham, B. W., Mirenberg, M. C., & Jones, J. T. (2002). Why Susie sells seashells by the seashore: Implicit egotism and major life decisions. *Journal of Personality and Social Psychology, 82,* 469-487.

Pennebaker, J. W., Barger, S. D., & Tiebout, J. (1989). Disclosure of traumas and health among Holocaust survivors. *Psychosomatic Medicine, 51,* 577-589.

Pennebaker, J. W., Hughes, C. F., & O'Heeron, R. C. (1987). The psychophysiology of confession: Linking inhibitory and psychosomatic processes. *Journal of Personality and Social Psychology, 52,* 781-793.

Penninx, B. W. J. H., Rejeski, W. J., Pandya, J., Miller, M. E., DiBari, M, Appelegate, W. B., & Pahor, M. (2002). Exercise and depressive symptoms: A comparison of aerobic and resistance exercise effects on emotional and physical function in older persons with high and low depressive syptomatology. *Journals of Gerontology B: Psychological Sciences and Social Sciences, 57B,* 124-132.

Peplau, L. A., Russell, D., & Heim, M. (1979). The experience of loneliness. In I. H. Frieze, D. Bar-Tal, & J. S. Carroll (Eds.), *New approaches to social problems: Applications of attribution theory*. San Francisco: Jossey-Bass.

Petronio, S. (2002). *Boundaries of privacy: Dialectics of disclosure*. Albany: State University of New York Press.

Pietromonaco, P., & Feldman-Barrett, L. (1997). Working models of attachment and daily social interactions. *Journal of Personality and Social Psychology, 73*, 1409-1423.

Pittman, T. S. (1998). Motivation. In D. T. Gilbert, S. T. Fiske, & G. Lindzey (Eds.) *Handbook of social psychology* (4th ed.) (Vol. 1, pp. 549-590). New York: McGraw-Hill/Oxford University Press.

Putnam, R. D. (2000). *Bowling alone: The collapse and revival of the American community*. New York: Simon & Schuster.

Rawlins, W. K. (1992). *Friendship matters: Communication, dialectics, and the life course*. New York: Aldine DeGruyter.

Reis, C. D., & Singer, B. (2000). Interpersonal flourishing: A positive health agenda for the New Millennium. *Personality & Social Psychology Review, 4*, 30-44.

Reis, H. T., & Gable, S. L. (2000). Event-sampling and other methods for studying everyday experience. In H. T. Reis, T. Harry, & C. M. Judd (Eds.), *Handbook of research methods in social and personality psychology* (pp. 190-222). New York: Cambridge University Press.

Reis, H. T., & Wheeler, L. (1991). Studying social interaction with the Rochester Interaction Record. *Advances in Experimental Social Psychology, 24*, 269-318.

Reis, H. T., Collins, W. A., & Berscheid, E. (2000). The relationship context of human behavior and development. *Psychological Bulletin, 126*, 844-872.

Reis, H. T., Senchak, M., & Solomon, B. (1985). Sex differences in the intimacy of social interaction: Further examination of potential explanations. *Journal of Personality and Social Psychology, 48*, 1204-1217.

Reis, H. T., Sheldon, K. M., Gable, S. L., Roscoe, J., & Ryan, R. M. (2000). Daily well-being: The role of autonomy, competence, and relatedness. *Personality & Social Psychology Bulletin, 26*, 419-435.

Roney, C. J. R., & Sorrentino, R. M. (1995). Uncertainty orientation, the self, and others: Individual differences in values and social comparison. *Canadian Journal of Behavioural Science, 27*, 157-170.

Rosen, S, & Tesser, A. (1970). On the reluctance to communicate undesirable information: The MUM Effect. *Sociometry, 33*, 253-262.

Rosenbaum, M. E. (1986). The repulsion hypothesis: On the nondevelopment of relationships. *Journal of Personality and Social Psychology, 61*, 1156-66.

Russell, D., Peplau, L. A., & Cutrona, C. E. (1980). The revised UCLA Loneliness Scale: Concurrent and discriminant validity evidence. *Journal of Personality and Social Psychology, 39*, 472-480.

Salmon, P. (2001). Effects of physical exercise on anxiety, depression, and sensitivity to stress: A unifying theory. *Clinical Psychology Review, 21*, 33-61.

Salovey, P., Rothman, A. J., & Rodin, J. (1998). Health behavior. In D. T. Gilbert, S. T. Fiske, & G. Lindzey (Eds.), *Handbook of social psychology* (4th ed.) (Vol. 2, pp. 633-683). New York: McGraw-Hill.

Sarason, B. R., Sarason, I. G., & Gurung, R. A. R. (1997). Close personal relationships and health outcomes: A key to the role of social support. In S. Duck (Ed.), *Handbook of personal relationships* (2nd ed.) (pp. 547-573). New York: Wiley.

Sarnoff, I., & Zimbardo, P. (1961). Anxiety, fear, and social affiliation. *Journal of Abnormal and Social Psychology, 62*, 356-363.

Schimel, J., Pyszczynski, T., Greenberg, J., O'Mahen, H., & Arndt, J. (2000). Running from the shadow: Psychological distancing from others to deny characteristics people fear in themselves. *Journal of Personality and Social Psychology, 78*, 446-462.

Schwarz, N. (1990a). Assessing frequency reports of mundane behaviors: Contributions of cognitive psychology to questionnaire construction. In C. Hendrick, & M. S. Clark (Eds.), *Research methods in personality and social psychology* (pp. 98-119). Newbury Park, CA: Sage.

Schwarz, N., & Clore, G. L. (1983). Mood, misattribution, and judgments of well-being: Informative and directive functions of affective states. *Journal of Personality and Social Psychology, 34*, 513-523.

Sedikides, C., & Skowronski, J. J. (1997). The symbolic self in evolutionary context. *Personality and Social Psychology Review, 1*, 80-102.

Sedikides, C., & Skowronski, J. J. (2000). On the evolutionary functions of the symbolic self: The emergence of self-evaluation motives. In A. Tesser, R. B. Felson, & J. Suls (Eds.). *Psychological perspectives on self and identity*. Washington, DC: American Psychological Association.

Segal, M. W. (1974). Alphabet and attraction: An unobtrusive measure of the effect of propinquity in field setting. *Journal of Personality and Social Psychology, 30*, 654-657.

Shaffer, J. W., Graves-Pirrko, L., Swank, R., & Pearson, T. A. (1987). Clustering of personality traits in youth and the subsequent development of cancer among physicians. *Journal of Behavioral Medicine, 10*, 441-447.

Shulman, S., Elicker, J., & Sroufe, L. A., (1994). Stages of friendship growth in preadolescence as related to attachment history. *Journal of Personal and Personal Relationships, 11*, 341-361.

Shulman, S., Laursen, B., Kalman, Z., & Karpovsky, S. (1997). Adolescent intimacy revisited. *Journal of Youth and Adolescence, 26*, 597-617.

Siegel, J. M. (1990). Stressful life events and use of physician services among the elderly. *Journal of Personality and Social Psychology, 58*, 1081-1086.

Snyder, C. R., Lassegard, M., & Ford, C. E. (1986). Distancing after group success and failure: Basking in reflected glory and cutting off reflected failure. *Journal of Personality and Social Psychology, 51*, 382-388.

Solano, C., Batten, P. G., & Parish, E. A. (1982). Loneliness and patterns of self-disclosure. *Journal of Personality and Social Psychology, 33*, 435-441.

Stone, A. A., Broderick, J. E., Porter, L. S., & Kaell, A. T. (1997). The experience of rheumatoid arthritis pain and fatigue: Examining momentary reports and correlates over one week. *Arthritis Care and Research, 10*, 185-193.

Strack, S., & Coyne, J. C. (1983). Social confirmation of dysphoria: Shared and private reactions to depression. *Journal of Personality and Social Psychology, 44*, 798-806.

Suls, J., Lemos, K., & Stewart, H. L. (2002). Self-Esteem, construal, and comparisons with the self, friends, and peers. *Journal of Personality & Social Psychology, 82*, 252-261.

Swann, W. B., Jr., Wenzlaff, R. M., Krull, D. S., & Pelham, B. W. (1992) Allure of negative feedback: Self-verification strivings among depressed persons. *Journal of Abnormal Psychology, 101*, 293-306.

Tamres, L. K., Janicki, K., & Helgeson, V. S. (2002). Sex differences in coping behavior: A meta-analytic review and an examination of relative coping. *Personality and Social Psychology Bulletin, 6*, 2-30.

Tan, D. T. Y., & Singh, R. (1995). Attitudes and attraction: A developmental study of the similarity-attraction and dissimilarity-repulsion hypotheses. *Personality and Social Psychology Bulletin, 21*, 975-986.

Taylor, S. E. (2002). *Health psychology*. (5th ed.). New York: McGraw-Hill.

Taylor, S. E., Klein, L. C., Lewis, B. P., Gruenwald, T. L., Gurung, R. A. R., & Updegraff, J. A. (2000b). Biobehavioral responses to stress in females: Tend-and-befriend, not fight-or-flight. *Psychological Review, 107*, 411-4293.

Thibaut, J., & Kelley, H. H. (1959). *The social psychology of groups*. New York: Wiley.

Thompson, L., & Fine, G. A. (1999). Socially shared cognition, affect, and behavior: A review and integration. *Personality and Social Psychology Review, 3*, 278-302.

Tietjan, A. M. (1994). Children's social networks and social supports in cultural context. In W. J. Lonner, & R. Malpass (Eds.), *Psychology and culture* (pp. 101-106). Boston: Allyn & Bacon.

Townsend, M. A., McCracken, H. E., & Wilton, K. M. (1988). Popularity and intimacy as determinants of psychological well-being in adolescent friendships. *Journal of Early Adolescence, 8*, 421-436.

Triandis, H. C. (1994). *Culture and social behavior.* New York: McGraw-Hill.

Twenge, J. M., Catanese, K. R., & Baumeister, R. F. (2002). Social exclusion causes self-defeating behavior. *Journal of Personality and Social Psychology, 83,* 606-615.

Veitch, R., & Griffitt, W. (1976). Good news, bad news: Affective and interpersonal effects. *Journal of Applied Social Psychology, 6,* 69-75.

Wegner, D. M. (1987). Transactive memory: A contemporary analysis of the group mind. In B. Mullen, & G. R. Goethals (Eds.), *Theories of group behavior* (pp. 185-208). New York: Springer-Verlag.

Wheeler, L., Reis, H., & Nezlek, J. (1983). Loneliness, social interaction, and sex roles. *Journal of Personality and Social Psychology, 45,* 943-953.

Williams, K. D., & Sommer, K. L. (1997). Social ostracism by coworkers: Does rejection lead to loafing or compensation? *Personality and Social Psychology Bulletin, 23,* 693-706.

Wisman, A., & Koole, S. L. (2003). Hiding in the crowd: Can mortality salience promote affiliation with others who oppose one's world views? *Journal of Personality and Social Psychology, 84,* 511-526.

Zajac, R. J., & Hartup, W. W. (1997). Friends as coworkers: Research review and classroom implications. *Elementary School Journal, 98,* 3-13.

Zjonc, R. B. (1968). Attitudinal effects of mere exposure. *Journal of Personality and Social Psychology Monographs, 9* (2, part 2), 1-27.

6 | *THE INDIVIDUAL AND THE OTHER SIDE OF LOVE*
by Frank O. Taylor, Ph.D.

VIOLENCE AND ABUSE IN INTIMATE RELATIONSHIPS

There is a prevalent myth that the family is a sanctuary from the trials and tribulations of the outside world. This myth may lead to the distorted belief that very little violence occurs in the family. When I think about this myth I am reminded of several television shows from my youth, such as *Leave it to Beaver* or *Father Knows Best*, in which the family was portrayed as a warm and loving refuge. The typical scenario was that of the hard-working breadwinner, always the father, coming home from a hard day at work to the warmth of the family home, where he was met at the door by his wife, who did whatever was necessary to look after his emotional and physical needs. Invariably, in each episode the father would solve some family problem involving his wife or children.

Unfortunately, violence in the family is not rare. Nor is it rare on the television today. Violence in the family may be more common than any other type of crime in the United States. Consider the following:

- Every 12 to 15 seconds an act of family violence occurs.

- Two thirds of all marriages will experience at least one incidence in which violence occurs.

- Martial violence is given as the reason for divorce in over 20% of *middle class* marriages.

- Millions of children are punched, kicked, beaten, and sometimes even attacked with a gun or knife by their parents annually.

- On average, in the United States, four (4) children die each day as a result of injuries sustained from violence and abuse.

The picture that emerges from the research about the family does not bear out the myth that the home is a refuge and place of safety. In fact, it is within marriage and family that women and children are most likely to experience violence, including rape and murder. In this chapter we will consider several types family violence, including wife rape, battering, child abuse, incestuous assault, child neglect, and elder abuse.

DOMESTIC VIOLENCE

Wife Rape

Wife rape is reported to be more common than stranger rape, date rape, or acquaintance rape. Many women fear being raped by a stranger while about 12% of married women report that their husbands have raped them. That adds up to more than 43 million women in the United States. This figure places wife rape in the running for the most common type of violence faced by women, as a group. More women have been victimized by their husbands than by any other type of perpetrator! The more intimate the relationship the greater the likelihood a rape will take place. Thus, women should least fear stranger rape, because they are more likely to be raped by an acquaintance and most likely to be raped by a husband.

In one study of Boston-area women, conducted by Finkelhor and Yllo, 10% of the women interviewed reported that they and been raped at least once by a husband or ex-husband. Additionally, 10% reported that they had been raped by a date. Only 3% of the women interviewed reported being the victim of stranger rape. This clearly bears out the fact that sexual assaults by intimates, especially husbands, are far more common than sexual assaults by strangers. In this study, sexual assault was not simply an isolated incident but rather characteristic of the marriage. Half of the women who reported being raped by their husbands indicated that they had been raped more than twenty times. Other researcher's find that over 70% of the victims of wife rape have been raped more than once, confirming the findings of Finkelhor and Yllo. About one-in-seven women who experience rape are raped by ex-husbands.

There seems to be a close correlation between wife rape and wife beating. Interpersonal violence occurs in about 50% of all intimate relationships. Not surprisingly, therefore, violence often accompanies wife rape. Research suggests that about 36% of women experience a beating in conjunction with the rape. Many women report that they were beaten as often as they were raped. The assaults reported are often extremely brutal. One woman reported that her husband jumped her in the dark and raped her in the anus. Another woman reported that she was gang-raped by her husband and his friends. One husband kidnapped his child in order to force his estranged wife to have sex with him.

Sexual assault often occurs without the use of violence or physical force. Women are much more likely to be economically dependent upon their husbands, for example. In this situation, husbands often have more forms of power at their disposal than their wives. Additionally, social norms dictate that wives should defer to their husbands. Thus, sexual intercourse between a husband and wife can be coercive. Husbands many threaten to withhold money in order to obtain sexual gratification. If a husband

113

asks for sex before granting some favor asked of him by his wife, coercion may be involved. This situation may arise in which a woman feels that she needs her husband's permission before doing something, making a purchase, entertaining friends, or going on a trip, for instance. In these circumstances, a husband may threaten to withhold money, favors, or permission in order to obtain sex. Such demands as these are not indicative of a healthy marital relationship.

Wife Beating

In any given year, 1.8 million wives are beaten by their husbands. Between 25-33% of heterosexual couples experience wife battery. The amount of wife battering is probably higher than this figure indicates due to **the norm of social desirability**. This norm pressures people to try to *appear* to be as close to the ideal norm as possible, for any given situation. Thus, when researchers show up at the door, during interviews people often give inaccurate answers to questions about abuse because they want to avoid the stigma of being a victim. Of course, some women may not report the abuse out of fear of further beatings if their husbands find out. Moreover, sadly, the woman often discovers that authorities, who are often male, are not much inclined to help her. In any case, it is estimated that only one in ten battered women actually reports the abuse to the police.

Many women are beaten repeatedly over a period of years. Beatings frequently escalate over time from simple slapping and shoving to serious forms of abuse. Women are often stabbed, burned, frequently with cigarettes, or shot. Severe internal injuries often occur as a result of serious beatings. Teeth are fractured and bones broken. Often, the woman is beaten during a pregnancy, with a miscarriage as the result.

Heterosexual wife battery happens in every social class. However, it is not equally distributed across society. Some women are more at risk than others. For example, married women are more likely to be beaten than unmarried women. Younger women, particularly between the ages of 18-34, are more likely to be beaten than women of any other age group. Women in the lower class are more likely to be beaten than women from the upper classes. Passive and non-assertive women are more likely to experience battery than more assertive and aggressive women.

What explains these patterns? **Social norms**, related to both gender and the family certainly contribute. Gender norms and scripts encourage women to be more passive than men and to be order-takers in the workplace and home. In general, girls experience more parental monitoring, in terms of their activities and behaviors, than boys do. Girls are encouraged to believe that their main role in life is to be wives and mothers. These norms grant men a lot of power over their wives. Family norms also encourage men to see themselves as the order-givers, breadwinners, and disciplinarians. Men often see it as their *responsibility* to control their wives and children. Additionally, many religious norms stress that women are to defer to their husbands. In other words, women are encouraged by social norms to submit to their fathers and husbands, especially in a **patriarchal society**.

Men who batter share some characteristics. For one thing, low-income men are more likely to assault their wives than men in higher income groups. Unemployed men are more likely than either employed or part-time employed men to abuse their wives. Battering men are more likely to be violent and aggressive to begin with. We see two patterns here. First, if the major social role for men, regarding the family, is breadwinning, men who are failing at that role may become frustrated and lash out at the women closest to them, particularly if the family is under economic strain or the woman complains. Second, hyper-masculine men may view controlling their wives as a demonstration of their manliness.

Husband Beating

Not all violence in the home is directed toward wives. Children and elderly parents also experience violence, as do some husbands. A second prevalent myth associated with the family is that men are equally likely to be the victims of domestic violence. Husbands do suffer from abuse at the hands of the wives but we must qualify this by realizing that 85% of the victims of domestic violence are women and women are much more likely to actually suffer physical harm than are men. Nevertheless, a minority of victims of domestic violence are husbands.

When a woman commits murder, for example, it usually occurs in her home and the victim is usually her husband or significant other. In fact, it is not uncommon for the murdered husband to actually have initiated the violence that ultimately culminated in his death. This seems to indicate that many forms of violence, such as throwing something at a husband or hitting a husband with an object, and other forms of violence, such as slapping, kicking, or biting, may actually be self-defense on the woman's part. Thus, while it is possible that a small number of men are in fact the victims of abuse, very few police reports in domestic violence cases cite the woman as the initiator of the violence.

Homosexual Partner Battering

Domestic violence is not limited to heterosexual relationships – homosexual relationships also experience violence and abuse. About 20% of men in the gay community are battered each year. Battering in lesbian relationships is equal to and perhaps higher than in heterosexual relationships. About 33% of lesbian relationships experience significant levels of violence annually. Victims of homosexual domestic violence may stay in abusive relationships for reasons similar to those of heterosexual women.

Male Rape

A third prevalent myth associated with violence in relationships is that men cannot be raped. This is nonsense. Male-on-male rape in prisons is a widespread problem. However, male rape is not limited to the prison environment. Men who are raped face the same issues as women who are raped, including feelings of guilt and shame. In fact, when it comes to men who are raped, cultural norms and myths surrounding the issue may prevent victims from receiving the emotional and psychological support they may be in dire need of. All victims of this crime, female and male, need to have support mechanisms in place to help deal with the trauma. A rape crises center in Memphis, Tennessee, for example, over a two-year period of time noted that 6% of their clients were men! Rape, whether it involves men or women, is a crime of violence. Most researchers agree that issues of power and control underlie both female and male rape, not sexual desire.

Effects of Domestic Violence

Beating people up has little to do with sexual desire and more to do with attempts to dominate and control one's partner. Battery is associated with the attempts to control one's behavior, speech, decisions, the clothes one wears, one's group of friends, and even decisions and thoughts! Battered and sexually abused women should be thought of as *survivors*. As a society, we do not expect people who have survived war, natural disaster, the ravages of diseases, or other forms of calamity to be without emotional, physical, and psychological scars. Nor do we blame them for their problems. We should treat people who have lived with abuse as survivors because they are survivors.

Physical and Emotional Scars

There are many negative effects associated with physical and sexual abuse. Physical effects are probably the most visible and include problems such as broken bones, blackened eyes, and even more serious problems such as scars and permanent disfigurement and, in its extreme form, death.

The psychological and emotional scars may be less visible but are no less damaging. Many women who survive abusive relationships suffer from low self-esteem, self-hate, depression, to the point of suicide, and emotional dependence upon others. Also, many of these women have a very low sense of self-worth, many to the point where they feel as if they somehow deserved the abuse they suffered. Some women blamed themselves and tried to change themselves. Women who survive abuse often feel helpless and suffer from low self-efficacy. They also struggle with hopelessness, alienation, and apathy.

Psychological and Emotional Strategies

Most psychological and emotional strategies employed by women to deal with physical and sexual abuse are based on attempts to avoid future attacks, or to redefine the abuse as not serious enough to end the relationship. Sometimes women are able to use sex to distract their partner from aggression. Others try to figure out what, exactly, triggers the violence, and to avoid any behaviors associated with the violence. Often, however, the abuse is unpredictable and can be triggered by almost anything. More extreme forms of coping involve dreams or fantasies about ending the relationship or even killing their mate. Some women simply repress or block out their experiences and refuse to deal with them, a strategy that often fails in the long run.

Self-Destructive Behaviors

For many women, self-destructive behaviors, almost always harmful and ineffective, are how they cope with physical and sexual violence. Women engage in a variety of self-destructive behaviors, including attempted suicide, cutting, over-eating, and drug abuse.

Suicide

Battering and suicide are highly correlated. Battered women account for about 42% of all attempted suicides. Hospitals report that about 25% of female suicides attempts are the result of physical abuse. Of those women, 80% had previously attempted suicide and had at least one injury associated with abuse prior to their first attempt. It is estimated that one-half of African American women who attempt suicide are victims of abuse.

Drug and Alcohol Addiction

Drug and alcohol dependency is another problem faced by women trying to cope with physical and emotional abuse. As you may suspect, this solution is hardly effective and may even contribute to the abuse. Researchers have tried to determine, for abused women, which problem came first, alcohol and drug addiction, or abuse. It appears that, for three-fourths of abused women, abuse precedes alcoholism. A similar picture emerges for other drugs. Here researchers find that abused women are nine times more likely to become addicted to drugs *after* the abuse occurs, whereas prior to the onset of abuse there are no significant differences in drug abuse between abused women and other women. This tends to indicate that for the majority of women drugs and alcohol are used as escape mechanisms and as a way of dealing, ineffective as it is, with abusive mates.

Fighting Back

As mentioned above, some women fight back in self-defense. Most fighting back involves less serious behaviors, such as hitting or shoving. However, occasionally more serious violence emerges, such as biting, hitting with an object, shoving him down stairs, cutting him with a knife, or shooting him. Some women eventually kill their abuser. When this happens the result is almost always incarceration by the criminal justice system, although a handful of women have been exonerated on the grounds of self-defense. Generally there is ample evidence that the woman has suffered years of serious abuse. In any case, killing is an exceptional situation. In general when woman resort to violence, it is much less serious and less likely to result in harm then when the perpetrator is male.

Fighting back does not necessarily entail resorting to violence. Many women, in spite of limited resources and great personal danger find a way to leave the abuser. Many women are able to use education, assistance programs, women's shelters, and family and friends to leave the abusive relationship.

WHY MANY WOMEN DO NOT LEAVE

Given the destructive emotional, psychological, and physical harm staying in an abusive relationship can incur, many people wonder why women, and some men, do not leave abusive partners. One impediment to leaving is economic dependency. Many women are economically dependent upon a husband. If the woman has remained at home, and out of the labor market, she may have very few skills that would help her find employment. It is very difficult to leave an abusive situation without the necessary economic resources to set up a new household somewhere else. Even women who have work experience and an education will find it economically challenging if they have children, for a number of reasons. The more children she has the more she will require financially to leave. Also, women with children often find that the time they have to spend in childrearing duties interrupts their career, resulting in fewer promotions and often less pay. Thus, even if a woman wants to leave an abusive relationship, she will usually face a variety of economic problems.

Fear is another factor that influences the decision to leave an abusive relationship. The woman may simply be too afraid to leave. Women, who have been raped or beaten in the past, obviously have something to fear. Specifically, they may be afraid that their husbands will find them and injure them more severely. She may also be afraid for the safety of her children. Some husbands are not above specifically threatening to harm their children in order to achieve control over their wives. Additionally, there is the fear of the unknown. Moving out requires solving a lot of problems regarding where to live, what to take with you, where to work, whether or not you can live on what you earn, who to turn to for help, and so on. These questions, by themselves, can be overwhelming for someone not experiencing abuse. Adding abuse inserts a huge complication into the survival equation.

Unfortunately, **learned helplessness** is another reason why women remain in abusive situations. During socialization, girls learn that women are expected to defer to their husbands, if not obey them. Many women feel that they belong in the home, whether or not their partner is abusive. Also, some women experience guilt and shame to the degree that they feel they deserve no better. Some women even blame themselves for the abuse. In any case, when women are raised to think that their fathers and husbands have the right to control their lives, we should not be surprised to find women enduring abusive relationships.

Lastly, we cannot forget that love is often a factor in why some women choose not to leave an abusive spouse or significant other. As remarkable as it may seem, abused women often report that they do not like the abuse but they love the person they are with. Often, they can point out other positive characteristics. Some women report that love for their children and the desire not to uproot their children's lives takes precedence over getting out of an abusive relationship.

CHILDREN AND ABUSE

Child Abuse

It is estimated that 24 out of 1000 children are physically abused annually. Some of this abuse is extreme. Annually 110 children per 1000 are beaten with some type of object. Child abuse was not always "defined" as a social problem. For example, in the not too distant past many parents, if not most, believed in the axiom that stated "spare the rod – spoil the child." This belief literally means that if a child was not beaten with a stick for behavioral infractions the child would be somehow "spoiled." Of course, today we define beating people with sticks as a form of assault. An infant should certainly never be spanked with anything, let alone a stick! Child abuse began to come to the attention of general society in the 1960s when pediatric radiologists began to observe broken bones and other abnormalities in children as a result of X-ray technology.

Child abuse comes in three forms, physical abuse, psychological abuse, and emotional abuse. Recently, for example, I read about two cases of child abuse that occurred in my community. In one case a mother had used a belt to beat her infant child whenever it cried, resulting in the child's death. In another case, a woman withheld food from her infant. Her child eventually died of starvation. Elsewhere in this text we have reviewed the necessity for children to form secure attachments emotionally to their caregivers. Thus, for the children in these two examples, the abuse involved all three types. Beating a child and starving a child are forms of physical abuse. Refusing to nurture a child, or comfort a child, however, are forms of emotional abuse. When children cry they are trying to convey information, such as being afraid, or soiled, or hungry. Ignoring the infant interrupts the bonding process, which causes psychological harm. It is important to remember that not all forms of abuse are physical.

As with wife abuse and rape, most physical and sexual abuse of children occurs within the family. However, the media have perpetuated the myth that most abuse of children, especially sexual abuse, occurs outside the family. Almost nightly, we are exposed to media coverage of child molesters lurking around elementary school waiting to prey upon unsuspecting children. There have been many television specials featuring a variety of tricks used by pedophiles to lure children into their vehicles, for example. A current version of this type of programming is seen in the programs that focus on Internet chat rooms. In these television specials adults, posing as children, try to lure child molesters, or potential molesters, to a child's home, where the "molester" is confronted by the news personality. In spite of the message of this programming, children are most likely to be victimized by people with whom they live.

Child Neglect

Child neglect is defined as injury or impairment resulting from a parent or guardian's inattention to a child's basic needs for health, nutrition, shelter, education, supervision, affection, or protection. Child neglect, thus, is a broader type of offense than child abuse. Whereas child abuse, such as beating a child with a belt, results in obvious injury, the results of child neglect can be harder to see. If a child is skinny is it the result of the child's metabolism or neglect? If a child is left at home for hours everyday because the parent is a work, is that neglect? The issue of what constitutes child neglect can be difficult to determine and is best left to experts.

Child neglect is much more prevalent than child abuse, though with consequences that can be just as serious. Here are some examples. If a child has dental problems, such as an abscessed tooth, which leads to an infection, it is child neglect if the parent has dental insurance but, for whatever reason, fails to obtain appropriate medical attention for the child. If a child is undernourished because a parent refuses to buy food for the household, in spite of having ample income to do so, it is child neglect. Whenever a child's general welfare is ignored, in spite of the fact that it is within the parent or guardian's ability to do so, neglect may be a factor.

Child neglect comes in many forms:

- Refusal or delays in providing physical or mental health care.
- Refusal to supervise the child.
- Refusal to accept custody of the child.
- Abandonment or desertion of the child.
- Failure to provide a stable home environment.
- Neglect of personal hygiene.
- Failure to remove hazards in the home.
- Inadequate sanitation.
- Failure to provide nutrition.
- Educational neglect.

You may ask, for example, how lack of a stable home environment could be a form of child neglect. For one thing, when a child is sexually abused, usually by the father, it would be child neglect if the mother was aware of the abuse but did nothing to stop it. Many children are poisoned every year because parents do not think to move poisonous materials out of the reach of children. Child neglect associated with personal hygiene can run from failure to change a child's soiled diapers to not treating head lice. Thus, there are a variety of ways in which a child's welfare can be ignored.

Large numbers of children experience some or all of the forms of neglect mentioned here. Approximately 39 out of 1000 children annually suffer from some form of child neglect. Girls are more likely than boys to suffer from abuse – whereas, boys are more likely than girls to suffer from neglect. For both boys and girls the risk of abuse or neglect increases as they get older.

Who is more likely to abuse or neglect children, mothers or fathers? It appears that abuse and neglect is about evenly distributed between women and men. However, about half of the neglect and abuse is committed by the parent who is generally least responsible for children.

Sexual Abuse

Incestuous assault can hardly be called a rare occurrence in the American family. It is estimated that as many as one- third of all women have had a sexual encounter, of some sort, with an adult male while they were children. Researchers estimate that as much as 12% of women have had a sexual experience with a male relative, usually a father or stepfather. It is not uncommon for researchers to find that about 16% of women have experienced at least one instance of incest before the age of 18. Perpetrators are overwhelmingly male, usually the father.

Most victims of incest, about 70%, are daughters under the age of 18. The majority of victims are either the oldest child or the only daughter. Incestuous assault generally begins between the ages of 6 and 9 for girls, and earlier for boys. Girls tend to be victimized longer than boys. The sexual assaults are repeated and tend to last three years or longer. If the victim has not yet reached puberty, sexual contact is generally limited to fondling and masturbation. If the victim is past puberty, sexual intercourse is more likely to occur.

Father-daughter incestuous assault is the most common form of incest. This type of incest is most likely to occur in families with traditional male-dominant and authoritarian attitudes. Traditional/authoritarian men expect sexual, housekeeping, and childrearing services from their wives. When the wife is unwilling or unable, for some reason, such as mental or physical disability, to provide those services, traditional/authoritarian men are more likely than other men to turn to their daughters for those services. Responsibility usually falls to the oldest daughter, who is used for housekeeping services and sexual relations.

The Experience of Incestuous Assault

The victim experiences incestuous assault as coercive. In other words, children, even infants, are *forced* to have sex and will not completely understand what is happening. Eventually, however, as children get older they begin to understand that something "different" is happening. At this point, they may experience guilt and self-blame. Victims of incest experience fear, anxiety, depression, anger, and difficulties in school. Often, the victims of incest run away from home in an attempt to end the abuse. Victims report that they remain frightened for years afterward, and many have difficulty achieving normal sexual development and healthy sexual relations later in life.

Researchers have discovered a link between prostitution and incestuous assault. Many prostitutes report that their first sexual experience was an incestuous assault, by a male in their family, in the family home. A common experience among prostitutes is the use of a bribe from a father or stepfather in return for sex. These bribes may include clothes, toys, permission to do something, such as obtaining a driver's license, a car, and even affection. From bribes such as these, prostitutes learned early in life that sex can be traded for favors. The result of this deviant form of socialization is that some women learn that they can trade their bodies for commodities.

Father-daughter incest seems to cause the most damage. When the oldest daughter is the victim, she often experiences shame, guilt, and social isolation. Often, the father tries to keep his daughter in line by making feel as if she is "holding the family together," by keeping the secret. Daughters find it difficult to avoid this type of incest when the father is their sole provider. Additionally, fathers are more likely to force vaginal intercourse on their daughters than are other incest perpetrators. Fathers abuse their daughters more frequently than other incest perpetrators or relatives and are more likely to use physical force to obtain sex.

SEXUAL INFIDELITY IN MARRIAGE

Infidelity

Infidelity is defined as sexual contact outside of the marital relationship. Infidelity is known by many titles, such as extramarital sex, adultery, cheating, or having an affair or fling. Nationally representative surveys tend to find that 3-4% of married people have had a sexual partner besides their spouse in any given year. If we look across the life of a marriage, these figures increase to 14-15% of married individuals. Husbands tend to have higher rates of infidelity than wives. About 23% of husbands, as opposed to 12% of wives, report having a sexual partner other than their spouse. Since the 1980s, levels of extramarital affairs have tended to remain stable, with about 5% of husbands, and 2.5% of wives engaging in sexual activity outside the marriage.

Correlates of Extramarital Affairs

What predicts who will engage in extramarital behaviors? Age is one factor. It is more common for younger adults, who have been married for shorter periods of time, to report engaging in extramarital affairs than older adults. This is probably because, after having multiple sex partners, monogamy may be hard to adjust to in the short run. Not surprisingly, infidelity is higher among men than women. So gender plays a role. Race also plays a role, with infidelity being more common among Blacks than other racial groups. Infidelity is also more common in the lower class, among those who attend church less frequently, and among those who have been separated or divorced previously.

Attitudes about Extramarital Affairs

Most Americans are disapproving of extramarital affairs. In 1977, 76% of Americans said they believed adultery was morally wrong. There appears to have been a slight loosening of attitudes about extramarital affairs since the 1970s, however. By the 1990s researchers estimate that 25% of husbands and 15% of wives had engaged in the activity. Still, currently, about 95% of Americans view having sex with a prostitute as a form of adultery. Some people view even having a sexually explicit conversation with someone other than the spouse as adultery. About 45% of Americans view holding hands and flirting as adulterous behavior. Thus, in spite more liberal attitudes towards sexual mores, in general, extramarital affairs are still frowned upon.

Predicting Extramarital Affairs

What predicts who is most likely to engage in extramarital affairs? Two factors seem to be important, sex-drive and marital happiness. Individuals with a strong urge to have sex are more likely than individuals with a weaker sex-drive to seek out sex outside of marriage. This may be especially true if the sex within marriage is unsatisfactory or one partner has become bored with their sexual relationship. Also, individuals who are not happy in their marriage or present relationship are more likely than those who are happy to look outside of the relationship for happiness.

Short and Long Term Extramarital Involvements

Extramarital affairs can range from one-night stands, to full-fledged affairs that last for weeks, months, and even years. As you may suspect, there are differences between men and women in the type and duration of extramarital involvements preferred. Interestingly, some extramarital involvements do not involve sex.

Short-Term Extramarital Involvements

Short-term extramarital affairs often begin at office parties, out of town meetings, or when bumping into an old flame. Men are frequently looking for sex without the strings of "love" attached. Often men enjoy the feeling of conquest and sexual excitement associated with one-night-stands. Women, on the other hand, often engage in extramarital behavior because they are angry with their husbands or seeking revenge for his infidelity. For women, even short-term extramarital involvements often involve love.

Long-Term Extramarital Involvements

People get involved in long-term extramarital affairs, obviously, for entirely different reasons than short-term affairs. Some of the reasons for this behavior, discussed here, while sociologically relevant, may make people uncomfortable. For instance, there may be some positive functions of long-term extramarital affairs from the sociological standpoint.

Marriage Maintenance

I admit that it is strange to claim that some forms of extramarital affairs are positive. Nevertheless, one motive for having a long-term extramarital affair is to provide something that the marriage itself is lacking. As people get older they often change, for example, especially if they obtain an education. Thus, an extramarital affair may actually help sustain the marriage if companionship, sex, interests, and other activities are lacking in the marriage. For example, it is not uncommon for one spouse in the marriage to get a college education while the other does not. The educated partner may feel he/she has to look outside the marriage for intellectual stimulation. Perhaps one partner has become physically disabled and unable to sexually satisfy their spouse.

Intimacy Reduction

Intimacy reduction is another function of extramarital affairs with some positive function, if it helps maintain the marriage. Some people feel emotionally stifled by a spouse that is extremely dependent and needy. Perhaps a spouse is not giving their partner enough "personal space," to enjoy leisure time activities or friendships. Some spouses are so dependent they cannot make decisions for themselves and in extreme cases, cannot even talk on the telephone or even drive a car. In this situation, the non-dependent spouse can begin to feel "boxed in" – that they constantly have to be there to take care of someone who cannot take care of themselves. Seeking affairs outside the marriage can be a way of enjoying sex without too much intimacy.

Reactive

Sometimes people begin to feel unattractive, or less attractive. Typically, this occurs in middle-age, when our youthful looks and vitality begin to flag. Some people are better at dealing with the effects of aging than others. Attractive individuals, faced with getting old, may begin to question their sexuality. In this case, engaging in extramarital affairs is a way to gain reassurance about youthfulness and sexual vitality.

Hedonistic

The hedonistic affair is least justifiable as a form of marriage maintenance. Hedonistic people are often perfectly happy and sexually fulfilled in their marriages. To the hedonist affairs are playful acts. They do not mean to hurt anyone, necessarily. Hedonists like the adventure, excitement, and allure of extramarital affairs. They are essentially self-centered people who care a lot about their own sexual fantasies and fulfillment. They often feel that as long as the sex is consensual no one is harmed.

Affairs without Sex

Sometimes affairs are emotional and do not involve sex. The partners involved in the affair drain off emotional energy that would otherwise be invested in their spouses. Some people have more emotional energy, in other words, than their spouses can deal with and they look outside the marriage to vent it. Thus, partners involved in this type of affair have sex with their spouses but somehow are unfulfilled in other important aspects of human relationships. These other areas may include communication, sharing of interests and hobbies, intellectual pursuits, companionship, or whatever is missing in the marriage. Over the long run, these relationships often do evolve into extramarital sex, but frequently they do not.

Consequences of Extramarital Sex

Some marriages might be held together by an affair. Generally, however, this measure is only a short-term solution to serious marital problems. Once the affair is revealed the result is almost always a major crisis. Revelations of infidelity often end in divorce. Even if the marriage does not end in divorce, the offended spouse is likely to lose trust in the offender, even if they eventually forgive them. Revelations of cheating often lead to further reductions in the level of intimacy between the spouses. For example, if he admits that he had an affair, she may insist that he move out of the bedroom. Affairs, obviously, introduce conflict into the marriage. If both partners desire to mend the relationship and carry on, any reaction that lowers relationship intimacy would not be productive.

The offended spouse will most certainly suffer emotional heartbreak and psychological pain. Frequently, the offended spouse will feel inadequate. If their spouse went outside of the marriage, they may feel that it is because they lack something. They may worry that they are unattractive or uninteresting. The offended spouse may become anxious or depressed. They may also experience anger and lash out against the offender.

Personal Factors Associated with Infidelity and Divorce

Now let us consider who is more likely to engage in extramarital affairs. There are a variety of reasons why a married individual might engage in this behavior.

Communication Problems

If a couple has faulty or poor communication skills, issues go unresolved over time. This may lead to the feeling, on the part of one or both spouses, that the other spouse "does not know or understand them."

Spousal Infidelity

When one spouse cheats on the other, the offended spouse will feel that "he/she has broken my heart or trust." When infidelity occurs, husbands are more upset that she had sex, whereas, wives are more upset that he is emotionally attached to someone else.

Conflict

When the level of conflict in the marriage is high, one or both spouses may feel that "we never get along." Marital conflict can occur over chores, discipline of children, controlling behaviors, or finances, among other issues, and lead to an affair outside the marriage to escape the constant bickering.

Emotional Abuse

If the marriage is marred by emotional abuse it may lead to thoughts that "he/she does not treat me well." Husbands tend to view a wife's moodiness, criticism, and negativity as emotionally abusive. Husbands also, in general, tend to respond poorly to not talking and easily hurt feelings. Wives tend to resent moodiness, not talking, not being home enough, and irritating habits. While some of these issues may not rise to the level of actual emotional abuse, if one or both spouses define their experience as emotional abuse, they my get "turned-off" of the marriage and look for an affair or divorce.

Falling Out of Love

Sometimes people change. You may start out your marriage with similar values and beliefs but over time, diverge from each other. This is particularly true under certain circumstances, such as getting an education or experiencing a religious conversion. Over the life course, people who once enjoyed each other may come to dislike each other. They may no longer enjoy being with each other or doing the same kinds of things together. Sometimes partners grow apart. Sometimes we do not like how our partner has changed. When couples no longer have much in common, the marital relationship is weakened. This is frequently the case for women who seek a college education but are married to a traditional/conservative man who has only a high school degree.

Unsatisfactory Sex

When people begin to feel like "the thrill is gone" in the bedroom, especially if they have a strong sex-drive, they may seek out an extramarital affair. Boredom with sex is the number one reason why people enter into extramarital affairs.

Physical Abuse

The ultimate form of disrespect is physical abuse. Other forms of abuse are also disrespectful. When one partner abuses the other, the offended partner may begin to wonder what the benefit of remaining married is. If they define the situation as no longer beneficial, they may seek an extramarital affair or divorce.

Boredom

When one or both spouses feels that their "life is the same old same old," they may seek an extramarital affair for the sake of excitement. Often, marriages get boring. There are no more romantic dinners, trips, dates, vacations, and so on. Life becomes dull, routine, and repetitive. When partners fail to find pleasurable experiences in the marriage they may look outside the marriage.

Falling In Love with Someone Else

Sometimes we meet people we are attracted to. If they take an interest in us we may begin to ask ourselves some questions, such as "is this the person I should have married?" Obviously, falling in love with someone may lead to an affair with that person, and eventually to a divorce from the person to whom you are married.

ဢ ඥ ဢ ඥ

REFERENCES

Abbot, J., Johnson, R., Koziol-McLain, J., & Lowenstein, S. (1995). Domestic violence against women: Incidence and prevalence in an emergency department population. *The Journal of the American Medical Association, 273*, 1763-68.

ACADV. (2006). *Barriers to leaving.* Retrieved on July 14, 2006 from http://www.acadv.org/barriers.html

Ambert, A. (2001). Families in the new Millennium. Boston: Allyn & Bacon.

American Humane Fact Sheets. (2004). *America's children: How are they doing? Child fact sheets.* Retrieved on July 19, 2006 from http://www.americanhumane.org/site/PageServe.

American Psychological Association. (2001). *Understanding childhood sexual abuse: Education, prevention, and recovery.* Office of Public Communications, Washington DC. PsycNET. Retrieved on January 19, 2002 from http://www.apa.org/releases/sexabuse/homepage.html.

Amnesty International. (2004, March 5). *Making violence against women count: Facts and figures.* Media Briefing. Retrieved on July 7, 2006 from http://web.amnesty.org/library/index/ENGACT770362004.

Andersen, M. (1988). *Thinking about women: Sociological Perspectives on sex and gender* (7th ed.). Boston: Allyn & Bacon.

AsherMeadow, (2001). The many faces of MSP. *MSP Magazine.* Retrieved on January 24, 2002 from http://www.ashermeadow.com/amm/notes2.htm.

Athealth. (2006). Domestic violence fact sheet. Retrieved on July 13, 2006 from http://www.athealth.com/consumer/disorders/domviolfacts.html.

Atwater, L. (1982). *The extramarital connection: Sex, intimacy, identity.* New York: Irvington.

Avon Foundation. (2006). *Speak out against domestic violence.* Retrieved on July 26, 2006 from http://www.avoncompany.com/women/speakout/informational_materials/pa.

Bannister, S. A. (1991). The criminalization of women fighting back against male abuse: Imprisoned battered women as political prisoners. *Humanity and Society, 15*(4), 400-416.

Barnett, O. W., Miller-Perrin, C. L., & Perrin, R. D. (1997). *Family violence across the lifespan.* Thousand Oaks, CA: Sage.

Barr, M. (2005). *Shaken baby syndrome is real and based on medical evidence.* National Center on Shaken Baby Syndrome. Retrieved on July 19, 2006 from www.dontshake.com.

Benokraitis, N. V., & Feagin, J. R. (1986). *Modern Sexism.* Englewood Cliffs, NJ: Prentice Hall.

Brown, G., & Andersen, B. (1991). Psychiatric morbidity in adult inpatient with childhood histories of sexual and physical abuse. *American Journal of Psychiatry, 148*, 55-61.

Bureau of Justice Statistics Crime Data Brief. (2003).

Challam County Courts. (2006). Domestic violence. Retrieved on July 12, 2006 from http://www.clallam.net/courts/html/court_domesticviolence.htm.

Chandy, J., Blum, R., & Resnick, M. (1996). History of sexual abuse and parental alcohol misuse: Risk, outcomes, and protective factors in adolescents. *Child and Adolescent Social Work Journal, 13*, 411-434.

Chang, J., Saltzman, C., & Herndon, J. (2005). Homicide: A leading cause of injury deaths among pregnant and postpartum women in the United States, 1991-1999. *American Journal of Public Health, 95*(3), 471-477.

Childhelp. (2005). National child abuse statistics. Retrieved on July 15, 2006 from http://www.childhelpusa.org/resources/learning_center/statistics.

Children's Defense Fund. (2001b). Moments in America for children. Retrieved on January 5, 2002 from http://www.childrensdefensefund.org/factsfiguresmoments.htm.

Clark County Prosecuting Attorney. (1999). *Myths and facts about domestic violence.* Retrieved on June 1, 1999 from http://www.clarkprose...html/domviol/myths.htm.

Clothesline Project, The. (1995, August 26). *Bearing witness to violence against women.* Retrieved on June 4, 1999 from http://home.cybergrrl.com/dv/orgs/ep.html.

Coalition to End Family Violence. (2006). *Myths and reality.* Retrieved on July 11, 2006 from http://www.thecoalition.org/education/myths.html.

Coval, S. (2003). The heart never forgets. *American Demographics, 25,* 16.

Daly, M. (1978). Gyn/Ecology: *The metaethics of radical feminism.* Boston: Beacon Press.

DeMillo, A. (2001, August 25). Home violence study reveals police findings. *Washington Post,* p. B01.

DHHS. (2000). *Domestic violence.* U. S. Department of Health and Human Services, Administration for Children and Families. Retrieved on January 8, 2002 from http://www.acf.dhhs.gov/programs/opa/facts/domsvio.htm.

DHHS. (2005). *Child Maltreatment 2003.* U. S. Department of Health and Human Services, Administration for Children, Youth and Families. Washington, DC: U.S. Government Printing Office, Online Summary. Retrieved on July 11, 2006 from http://www.acf.hhs.gov/programs/cb/publications/

Doyle, J. A., & Paludi, M. A. (1995). *Sex and gender: The human experience.* Dubuque, IA: William C. Brown.

Doyle, J., & Paludi, M. (1997). *Sex and gender: The human experience.* (4th ed.). Blacklick, OH: McGraw-Hill.

Dutton, D. G. (1988). *The domestic assault of women.* Boston: Allyn & Bacon.

Edelhart, C. (1996, June 1). Male rape survivors also deal with myths. *Chicago Tribune* p.4.

Fahim, K., Farmer, A., & Moyniham, C. (2006, June 29). Mother is charged in killing 3-year-old Brooklyn girl. *New York Times,* p. B4.

Family Violence Prevention Fund. (1999). *General statistics.* Retrieved on June 2, 1999 from http://www.fvpf.org/the_facts/stats.html.

Family Violence Prevention Fund. (2006a). *The facts on domestic violence.* Retrieved on June 30, 2006 from http://www.endabuse.org/resources/facts/.

Family Violence Prevention Fund. (2006b). *Celebrity watch: Hall of shame.* Retrieved on July 11, 2006 from http://www.endabuse.org/celebritywatch/index.php?Fame=N.

Fayette County Government. (2004). *Domestic violence.* Retrieved on June 30, 2006 from http://www.admin.co.fayette.ga.us/courts/solicitor/domestic_violence.htm.

FBI Uniform Crime Report. (1999). Retrieved on September 20, 2001 from http://www.fbi.gov/ucr/99hate.htm.

Feldman, M. (2001). *Parenthood betrayed: The dilemma of Munchausen Syndrome by Proxy.* Retrieved on January 24, 2002 from http://www.shpm.com/articles/parenting/hsmun.html.

Finkelhor, D., & Yllo, K. (1995). Types of marital rape. In Patricia Searls and Ronald Berger (Eds.), *Rape and society: Readings on the problem of sexual assault* (pp. 152-159). Boulder, CO: Westview Press.

Frazer, J. (1995). *Community justice course.* Retrieved on December 12, 1995 from http://www.tafe.lib.rmit.edu.au/judy/overview.html.

Fulcher, J. (2002, Summer). Domestic violence and the rights of women in Japan and the United States. *Human Rights Magazine, 29,* 3. Section of Individual Rights and Responsibilities, American Bar Association, Washington, DC. Retrieved on July 11, 2006 from http://www.abanet.org/irr/hr/summer02/fulcher.html.

Gaudin, J., Polansky, N., Kilpatrick, A., & Shilton, P. (1996). Family functioning in neglectful families. *Child Abuse and Neglect, 20*(3), 63-77.

Gelles, R. J. (1995). *Contemporary families: A sociological view.* Thousand Oaks, CA: Sage.

Gelles, R. J. (1995). *Maternal employment and violence toward children.* In R.J. (Ed.), Family Violence (pp. 108-125). Newbury Park, CA: Sage.

Gelles, R. J. (1997). *Intimate violence in families* (3rd ed). Thousand Oaks, CA: Sage

Gelles, R. J. (1997). *Intimate violence in families* (3rd ed.). Thousand Oaks, CA: Sage.

Gelles, R. J., & Hargreaves, E. F. (1987). Maternal employment and violence toward children. In R. J. Gelles (Ed.), *Family Violence* (pp. 108-125). Newbury Park, CA: Sage.

Gelles, R. J., & Straus, M. (1987). Is violence toward children increasing? A comparison of 1975 and 1985 national survey rates. *Journal of Interpersonal Violence, 2*, 212-222.

Gelles, R. J., & Straus, M. (1987). Is violence toward children increasing? A comparison of 1975 and 1985 National survey rates. *Journal of Interpersonal Violence, 2*, 212-222.

Gelles, R. J., & Straus, M. (1988). *Intimate violence: The definitive study of cases and consequences of abuse in the American family.* New York: Simon & Schuster.

Ghista, G. (2005). Marital rape. *World Prout Assembly.* Retrieved on July 17, 2006 from http://www.world-proutassembly.org/archives/2005/05/marital_rape.html.

Gillespie, M. (2001). Americans consider infidelity wrong, but acknowledge its prevalence in society. *The Gallup Organization.* Retrieved November 4, 2001. http://www.gallup.com/poll/releases/pr010709b.asp.

Griffin, S. (1979). Rape: The power of consciousness. San Francisco: Harper & Row.

Haddocks, R. (1995). Live-in relationships more prone to violence. *Standard Times 3,* [online].

Iazetto, D. (1989). *When the body is not an easy place to be.* Ph. D diss., Union Institute, Cincinatti, OH.

Jenny, C., Hymel, K., Ritzen, A., Reinert, S., & Hay, T. (1999). Analysis of missed cases of abusive head traumas. *Journal of the American Medical Association, 281*(2), 621-626.

Johnson, A. G. (1980). On the prevalence of rape in the United States. *Signs, 6,* 136-146.

Kaminer, W. (2001, November 25). Virtual Rape. *The New York Times Magazine,* 70-73.

Karp, S., Silber, D., Holmstrom, R., & Stock, L. (1995). Personality of rape survivors as a group and by relation of survivor to perpetrator. *Journal of Clinical Psychology, 51,* 587-592.

Kempe, C. H., Silverman, F. N., Steele, B., Droegemueller, W., & Silver H. K. (1962). The battered child syndrome. *Journal of the American Medical Association, 181,* 17-24.

Lasch, C. (1977). *Haven in a heartless world: The family besieged.* New York: Basic Books.

Levinson, D. (1981). Physical punishment of children and wife beating in cross-cultural perspective. *Child Abuse and Neglect, 5*(4), 193-196.

Levy, B., (Ed.). (1991). *Dating violence: Young women in danger.* Seattle, WA: Seal Press.

Maginnis, R. L. (1995). Marriage protects women from violence. *Insight.* Washington, DC: Family Research Council, 1-3.

McCloskey, L., Figueredo, A., & Koss, M. (1995). The effects of systemic family violence on children's mental health. *Child Development, 66,* 1239-1261.

McNeal, C., & Amato, P. (1998). Parents' marital violence: Long-term consequences for children. *Journal of Family Issues, 19,* 123-140.

Mendel, M. (1995). *The male survivor: The impact of sexual abuse.* Thousand Oaks, CA: Sage.

Mignon, S., Larson, C., & Holmes, W. (2002). *Family abuse: Consequences, theories, and responses.* Boston: Allyn & Bacon.

National CASA Association. (2000). *Statistics on child abuse and neglect, foster care, adoption, and the CASA Association.* Retrieved on January 26, 2002 from http://www.casa.net.org/library/abuse/abuse-stats98.htm.

North Carolina Coalition against Domestic Violence. (2002). *A fact sheet on sexual assault.* Retrieved on January 8, 2002 from http://www.ncadv.org/handouts/sexual_assault.htm.

Pagelow, M. D. (1988). Marital Rape. In V. B. Van Hasselt, R. L. Morrison, A. S. Bellack, and M. Hersen (Eds.), *Handbook of Family Violence* (pp. 207-232). New York: Plenum.

Pan-American Health Organization. (2006). *Domestic violence during pregnancy.* Retrieved on July 13, 2006 from http://www.paho.org/English/AD/GE/VAWPregnancy.pdf.

Parnell, T., & Day., D. (Eds.). (1998). *Munchausen by Proxy Syndrome.* Thousand Oaks, CA: Sage.

Pizzey, E. (1974). *Scream quietly or the neighbors will hear.* Harmondsworth, England: Penguin.

Pleck, E. (1989). Criminal approaches to family violence. In L. Ohlin and M. Tonry (Eds.), *Family Violence* (pp.19-58). Chicago: University of Chicago Press.

RAINN. (2006). *Statistics.* Retrieved on July 15, 2006 from http://www.rainn.org.

Schoen, C., Davis, K., Collins, K., Greenberg, L., DesRoches, C., & Abrams, M. (1997). *The Commonwealth Fund Survey of the health of adolescent girls.* Retrieved on January 19, 2002 from http://www.cmwf.org/programs/women/adolehl.asp.

Schoen, C., Davis, K., DesRoches, C., & Shekhdar, A. (1997). *The heatlh of adolescent boys: Commonwealth Fund Survey findings.* Retrieved on January 19, 2002 from http://www.cmwf.org/programs/women/boysv27.asp.

Scott, B., & Schwartz, M. A. (2006). *Sociology: Making sense of the social world.* Boston: Pearson/Allyn Bacon.

Scott, J. (1994). Social and cultural issues related to violence. *Vital Signs, 10*(2), 8.

Sims, S. (1989, June 11). Violent. *Chicago Tribune,* sec. 6,1,6.

Soroka, M. P. & Bryjak, G. J. (1995). *Social problems: A world at risk.* Boston: Allyn & Bacon.

St. George, D. (2004, December 19). Pregnant women murdered at an alarming rate. *The Washington Post.*

Stark, E. & Flitcraft, A. (1988). Violence among intimates: An epidemiological review. In V. B. Van Hasselt, R. L. Morrison, A. S. Bellack, and M. Hersen (Eds.), *Handbook of Family Violence* (pp. 293-318). New York: Plenum.

Stayton, W. R. (1984). Lifestyle spectrum 1984. *Sex Information and Educational Council of the U.S. Reports (SIECUS), 12*(3), 1-4.

Steinmetz, S. (1977). The battered husband syndrome. *Victimology: An International Journal, 2*(3/4), 499-509.

Straus, M. & Donnelly, D. (2001). *Beating the devil out of them: Corporal punishment in American families and its effects on children.* New Brunswick, NJ: Transaction.

Suhr, J. (2006, June 26). Illinois doctor who killed sons, self accused wife of cheating. WBBM News Radio 780 Chicago. *Associated Press News.*

Tower, C. (2004). *Understanding child abuse and neglect* (6th ed.). Boston: Allyn & Bacon.

Trauma Intervention Program. (2006). *Facts about domestic violence.* Retrieved on July 13, 2006 from http://www.tipnational.org/node/262.

U. S. Department of Health and Human Services, National Center on Child Abuse and Neglect. (2006). *Third National Incidence Study of Child Abuse and Neglect: Final Report* (NIS-3). Washington, DC: U.S. Government Printing Office.

U. S. Department of Health and Human Services, National Center on Child Abuse and Neglect. (2001a). *Child maltreatment 1999: Reports from the states to the national child abuse and neglect data system.* Washington, DC: U.S. Government Printing Office.

U. S. Department of Health and Human Services, National Center on Child Abuse and Neglect. (2004). Child maltreatment 2004. *Administration for Children and Families.* Retrieved on July 19, 2006 from http://www.acf.hhs.gov/programs/cb/pubs/cm04/chapterone.htm

U. S. Department of Health and Human Services, National Center on Child Abuse and Neglect. (2000b). Sexual assault of young children as reported to law enforcement: Victim, Incident, and offender characteristics. *Bureau of Justice Statistics.* Retrieved on January 7, 2002 from http://www.ojp.usdoj.gov/bjs/abstract/saycrle.htm.

U. S. Department of Health and Human Services, National Center on Child Abuse and Neglect. (2001b). Criminal victimization 2000: Changes 1999-2000 with trends 1993-2000. *Bureau of Justice Statistics.* Retrieved on January 18, 2002 from http://www.ojp.usdoj.gov/bjs/cvict_v.html.

U. S. Department of Health and Human Services, National Center on Child Abuse and Neglect. (2000b). Criminal victimization in the United States. *Office of Justice Programs, Bureau of Justice Statistics.* Retrieved on July 15, 2002 from http://www.ojp.usdoj.gov/bjs/cvict.htm.

U. S. Department of Health and Human Services, National Center on Child Abuse and Neglect. (2000b). Criminal victimization: Summary findings. *Office of Justice Programs, Bureau of Justice Statistics.* Retrieved on July 8, 2006 from http://www.ojp.usdoj.gov/bjs/pubalp2.htm.

U.S. Department of Veteran Affairs. (2006). *Child sexual abuse.* Retrieved on July 19, 2006 from http://www.ncptsd.va.gov/facts/specific/fs_child_sexual_abuse.html.

Violence kills more U.S. kids. (1997, February 7). *San Francisco Chronicle,* A1.

Walker, L. (1978). Treatment alternatives for battered women. In J. R. Chapman and M. Gates (Eds.), *The victimization of women* (pp. 143-174). Beverly Hills, CA: Sage.

Walker, L. (1984). *The battered woman syndrome.* New York: Springer.

Wallace, H. (2004). *Family violence: Legal, medical, and social perspectives* (4th ed.). Boston: Allyn Bacon.

Weise, D., & Daro, D. (1995). *Current trends in child abuse reporting and fatalities: The results of the 1994 Annual Fifty States Survey.* Chicago: National Committee to Prevent Child Abuse.

Weitzman, S. (2001). *"Not people like us": Hidden abuse in upscale marriages.* New York: Basic Books.

Wellesley Centers for Women. (1998). *The wife rape information page.* Retrieved on July 17, 2006 from http://www.wellesley.edu/wcw/projects/mrape.html.

Wilsnak, S., Vogeltanz, N., Klassen, A., & Harris, T. (1997). Childhood sexual abuse and women's substance abuse: National survey findings. *Journal of Studies on Alcohol, 58,* 264-272.

Yllo, K. (1999). Wife rape: A social problem for the 21st century. *Violence Against Women, 5,* 9.

7 | THE INDIVIDUAL AND PEER GROUPS
by Frank O. Taylor, Ph.D.

Peer groups are a reflection of other types of groups in society. In theory, a **peer group** is a collection of individuals who are each other's equals. But in reality, just like in any social group, group dynamics are always in play. Within the peer group some individuals will occupy leadership roles while other individuals will be followers. Some individuals will be decision-makers and wield more power whereas others will be order-takers and have comparatively little power.

In the classroom there are generally two or three statuses: professor, graduate assistant, and students. **Statuses** are names of positions in the social hierarchy that people occupy. Professors are interchangeable. However their roles are very similar. Professors may change but there is a structure to what they do: lecturing, testing, writing tests, and grading tests and research papers. **Roles** refer to the behaviors that are associated with statuses. Peer groups have statuses. There will be leaders and decision-makers, but there will be arbitrators and mediators as well. The larger the peer groups the wider the range of possible roles within the peer group.

Peer groups are formed on the basis of several factors, such as age. For one thing, very young children are dependent upon their parents to arrange play dates. As children get a little older they can play with other children in the neighborhood. Once children are old enough to go to school the possibilities for new friends and involvement in new peer groups greatly increases. Gender is another important dimension of peer groups. Younger children tend to prefer same sex peer groups. Additionally, social norms about the type of play and social activities appropriate for girls and boys will influence their activities. Female peer groups will be encouraged to engage in expressive activities while male peer groups will be encouraged to pursue activity oriented activities. As children get older another factor that influences peer groups are hobbies and interests. Peer groups based on interest in sports, academics, hobbies, music, and gaming are fairly common. Lastly, parental influences are important in peer group formation. Parents may encourage or discourage their children from playing with neighborhood children. Parents often want their children to be interested in intramural sports, like soccer, or activities related to church or school. Peer groups do a lot of things that require parental involvement, such as letting friends visit after school, on weekends, spending the night, and parties.

Sociologists are interested in peer groups because of the functions they perform for society. Are certain aspects of peer groups useful for society? What are the positive benefits of peer groups? At the end of the chapter we will consider some of the negative effects of peer groups. Here, we will focus on the positive. Interaction in peer groups helps children develop a wide range of social skills. These skills include cooperation, learning to get along, reciprocity, empathy, decision-making, and communicative skills. Additionally, participation in peer groups meets many emotional needs, such as a sense of worth, belonging, and social identity. **Reflected appraisals** from peer's help children discover "who" they are. If your peers praise your guitar-playing talent, for example, you may come to think you are talented musically. Peer groups help children acquire self-knowledge about their personal qualities and characteristics. Lastly, as we will discover, peer groups help children achieve social, cognitive, and psychological development.

Today, due to the women's increased participation in the paid labor force, children are increasingly likely to find themselves in group settings, such as day care. This means that modern children will begin interacting with peers earlier in life than children of even a generation ago. Additionally, today's children will interact with peers over a longer period of their lives. Peer groups, therefore, are an important and integral part of the socialization of children.

SOCIALIZATION AND THE PEER GROUP

Peer Groups and Normative Development

Belonging to groups helps meet basic human needs. Family, friends, and peers are essential to self-development. In earlier chapters we reviewed the stages of self development, including the preparatory stage, the play stage, the game stage, and the references stages of development. In general, as children move through these stages of development, they develop mind and self by interacting with others. First, they imitate other roles models. As they get a little older they begin playing simple games, which is a form of role-playing. They play house, or dress up, or other games where they imitate adults. As they get even older, they learn to play games that involve several players, formal rules, and to be successful you must predict how others are going to behave.

During all of these stages of self-development, children are receiving reflected appraisals from significant others. Children develop a **Looking-Glass self** from these interactions. In other words, they begin to have conceptions about their qualities and abilities as they get feedback from others. Peer groups are fundamental to this process. In their peer groups, children experiment with role performances, role expectations, norms, innovations, and the like. They begin to get a sense of the **generalized other**, or the status structure of society.

Infancy and Toddler Years (Birth to Age 2)

Self-development occurs first within the family as children interact with parents, siblings, and other kinfolk. Since children are completely dependent upon adults for their care, the nature of the parent-child bond is very important for later emotional, psychological, and social development. Thus, it is important whether or not the child is securely bonded to the caregiver. Let us consider two types of childhood attachment: **secure attachment** and **insecure attachment**.

Securely Attached

Certain parenting styles are associated with raising children who are securely bonded to the caregiver. Securely attached children have caregivers who provide consistent, quality, parenting. These parents are usually authoritative in their parenting style (discussed more fully below). They are neither too lenient nor to controlling and allow their children some role in setting rules. There are open lines of communication between the parent and the child. The main thing is that they are consistent. They are also sensitive to the child's needs.

Children who are securely bonded to their caregivers come to feel that they can count on the parent to help them if they get in trouble or to comfort them if they get hurt. When the child falls down and cries, for example, the sensitive parent does not ignore the child or lecture the child about "taking it like a man," if the child is male, or "crying like a sissy," if the child is female. The sensitive parent expresses concern and comforts the child. Children can then develop a sense of security – that they are safe. Securely bonded children can use these experiences later in their own lives as a model for intimate relationships. Securely attached children like to explore their environment because, as long as the caregiver is nearby, they feel safe to do so. They make friends easier because they are less fearful. They have positive expectations about meeting new people. In their peer groups, securely attached children are often the leaders and others like to be friends with them because they are friendly children.

Insecurely Attached

As you may guess, children whose parent's use inconsistent and insensitive parenting styles are likely to be insecurely attached to the caregivers. Here again, the problem is consistency – sometimes the parent is available, sometimes the parent is not. Oftentimes such parents have other problems that interfere with their ability to be consistent or sensitive, such as struggling with the emotional stress of divorce, or other problems, including physical or mental disability, or drug and alcohol problems. If the parents are poor there may be a lot of financial stress involved, which can be very debilitating. In any case, the child comes to feel that the parent or caregiver is unreliable.

Insecurely attached children have many difficulties in their normative development. They often have negative expectations towards friends and peers, for example. Experiences of disappointment and neglect at home leads to the further expectation of disappointment and neglect. These children often withdraw from interactions in order to avoid more disappointment. Sometimes they become aggressive toward other children. Not having developed a sense of security, they are much less likely to explore their surroundings, have negative expectations of others, and lack a positive relationship with caregivers to bases adult intimate relationships on.

Early Childhood (Ages 2 to 6)

For preschool children, opportunities for interaction with other children are limited. The research seems to indicate that children who have early interactions with other children have higher levels of social competence. Parents have to be willing to provide such opportunities for their children. Other children in the neighborhood are usually the child's playmates. Preschool children need to be supervised, so parents will have to be willing to arrange play-dates or otherwise supervise the interactions. However, if the neighborhood is full of retirees, preschool children may be scarce. Parents in this situation may have to look to neighborhood organizations or church for opportunities for their child to interact with other children. Thus, some parents will take the child to the park, church, to the homes of other children, or other places were children are, such as day care.

Parenting Styles are associated with children's competence with peers. There are a variety of parenting styles which we will now review.

Authoritative

Authoritative parenting is a democratic style of interaction. Parents discuss rules and behavior with their children. These parents get informed and educate themselves concerning childhood development. They have a sense of what is and is not appropriate for the child's level of cognitive ability. They often discuss issues and behaviors with their children. Children are somewhat involved in the decision-making process. Authoritative parents are highly involved. These parents often let their children pick their own friends and peers but are involved in the decisions. If the child makes a poor decision the parent is likely to become more involved. Children raised in the authoritative style of parenting often have high levels of social competence. These parents let their children make mistakes but try to help them learn a lesson through discussion and role-modeling.

Authoritarian

My son had a friend whose step-father was very strict. He laid down the law with no explanation or discussion. Whatever he said was the rule – no exceptions. He was also a harsh disciplinarian. Infractions of his rules involved loss of privileges, grounding, and spankings, when the child was younger. Because the punishments were harsh and often applied for trivial infractions this child was often insecure and uncertain. His parents chose his friends for him. This is the **authoritarian style of parenting**. Unsurprisingly, children with authoritarian parents have few opportunities to develop social competence. They are not allowed to learn from mistakes, they are punished for them. Thus, they tend to stop trying to learn how to use their own judgment and instead consider first how their parents will react. Often, these children rebel against their parents when they reach their teenage years. These children often behave like they are out on parole in social settings. They become loud, aggressive, and rambunctious whenever they are out from under their parent's control. The school yard bully often has an authoritarian father.

Indifferent

Some parents are completely indifferent to their children. They leave their children to their own devices. They do not monitor their child's peers and friends. Not surprisingly, their children often get into trouble with the authorities. Children of indifferent parents often look for missing emotional bonds by joining deviant peer groups, such as gangs. Children raised by indifferent parents are often shy, withdrawn, and socially awkward. They often suffer from low self-esteem and are easy to recruit into gangs or even cults. My son had another good friend who was raised by indifferent parents. In his teenaged years he was beginning to get into legal trouble and was eventually taken away from his parents and became a ward of the state.

Permissive

The authoritative and authoritarian styles of parenting are parent driven. The **permissive style of parenting** is child driven. The child is more in control than the parents. These parents are very indulgent. Children raised by permissive parents are also less socially competent compared to children raised by authoritative parents. These children are often pushy, bossy, arrogant, and conceited. In this situation, it is not that the parents do not care, as in indifferent parenting; they indulge the child to the extent that learning life lessons is difficult. The parent's can always be counted on to bail the child out of a difficult situation.

We should bear in mind that there is a cycle to life. Our parents have lives to live too and periodically life events intrude into their parenting styles. While some parents can be placed in one style or another for most of their life as a parent, some parents fluctuate between styles. For example, I was raised by an authoritative mother and an authoritarian father. As my parents had more and more children, they both became permissive parents. After all, raising five children can wear anyone out. Authoritative mothers may become indifferent under the stress of divorce for a short period of time, typically a year or two. If this happens while the child is between the ages of 2 to 6, some negative socialization effects may occur. Authoritarian and permissive parents are more involved than indifferent parents. Many children in the upper class are raised by **proxy parents**, such as nannies, and their biological parents are indifferent to them.

Middle Childhood (Ages 6 to 13)

At this age children start school. Once children start school parents become less important in their children's lives. School provides a variety of opportunities for children to interact with each other. Children increasingly want to spend time with their friends and parents will have to try to accommodate these types of interactions, such as letting children come over to play after school, shuttling children to school activities, such as chorus, plays, and sporting events, or weekend sleepovers.

The opportunities for interaction among peers, once children start school, increase. Children will need their parents less and less as they begin to take over the organization of their own activities. Of course, effective parenting does not include handing over parental responsibilities entirely to children; they will still have to be monitored. However, children will begin to look more to their peers for approval rather than their parents and this is entirely normal. Children will adjust better if their parents remain involved. This means helping children make friends by encouraging them to get involved in sports, school activities, and other social activities.

Adolescence (Age 13 to 18 or 19)

Adolescents tend to belong to several peer groups ranging from most to least intimate. The **"best friends" peer group** has the highest levels of intimacy. This peer group is comprised of the one or two people they are closest to. Adolescents are also often in a **"clique."** Here we find six or seven friends, sometimes more, they organize activities with. This peer group also has relatively high levels of intimacy. The **"crowd"** is a larger group of people the adolescent identifies with. Adolescents tend to like to "hang out" with the crowd, which is essentially their in-group, a group of people who have similar attitudes and interests, and may even dress alike.

PEER GROUPS AND PSYCHOLOGICAL DEVELOPMENT

Interaction in peer groups helps children develop normative social skills. There are many social skills involved when children interact with each other in peer groups. Interaction involves communication. Also, children have to learn that in order to get along with others they have to cooperate. As children get older, they discover that if they are unwilling to play by the rules they may be excluded. Another social norm involved in peer groups is the **norm of reciprocity**, which means that if a friend does you a favor they have a right to expect you to return it. Peer interactions, especially in the play stage of self development, involve lots of role-playing, pretending, and creativity. In peer group interactions children use their imaginations. Also, children begin to learn about the dynamics of power while interacting with their peers. Peer groups often have a pecking order with some peers being more powerful than others. Children who experience poor peer group relationships often have poor psychological adjustment in later life.

DEVELOPING SOCIAL COMPETENCE

Social competence refers to the ability to recognize one's different roles in different situations - to interact successfully in a variety of situations. Some behaviors are appropriate in certain social settings but not in others. Competitive behaviors, for example, may be appropriate for team sports but not in most intimate interactions.

Group life is highly structured. Children have to learn to take turns, to share, to comfort each other, to be respectful to those in authority, such as parents and teachers, and what the roles of a good friend are. It is in the play stage of self-development, when children are in their first peer groups, where children first begin to take the role of the other. To imagine the other's point of view and take account of it. Interactions in peer groups help the child develop a sense of the generalized other. The socially competent child has at least a general sense of how to behave in a variety of settings, such as church, school, the family, or the peer group. This is the **generalized other** – a general set of internalized rules of behavior.

Sometimes children should conform to peer pressure. It is appropriate not to cheat when playing Monopoly and we expect children to conform to some basic expectations during their interactions. On the other hand, sometimes children should not conform to peer pressure, especially when peers are encouraging deviant behavior, such as drinking alcohol or smoking tobacco. The degree to which children conform to the peer group depends on three factors, cognitive ability, the social setting, and psychological factors.

Cognitive Ability and Age

Very young children, of course, have limited cognitive ability and are not likely to experience too much peer pressure. Peers have the most influence over children in middle childhood, when they are just beginning to develop critical thinking skills. Peer influence begins to decline in adolescence because by age 13 – 15 children are beginning to understand the consequences of their behavior and develop attitudes and values. Too, they have very likely sorted themselves into peer groups on the basis of their values by then. Thus, deviants tend to hang out with other deviants and children not inclined to go shoplifting are hanging out with other children of similar values.

Children aged 7 to 13 are most likely to experience **peer pressure**. Children in this age group often go along with the group even when they know the group is wrong. Researchers have discovered that children of this age will often change their answers in testing experiments to go along with the group even when they know their answers are incorrect. However, after age 13 the effect of peer pressure begins to decline as children begin to have a more concrete sense of their identity, values, and attitudes. Conformity to anti-social behavior tends to peak in the ninth grade. Conformity to pro-social behavior tends to peak in the sixth grade.

Social Setting

The second factor influencing peer pressure is the social setting. Children often find themselves in situations where appropriate behavior is uncertain or ambiguous. In this situation, children tend to conform to the behavior of others in their peer group. In other words, if the child is unsure as to appropriate behavior, they are more likely to follow the lead of their peers.

Psychological Factors

Whether or not people conform to group expectations depends in large part on their particular values. If the child feels the behavior is wrong they are less likely to engage in it. Of course, values tend to become clearer with age, so there is some overlap between the three factors. Children raised by authoritative parents are often more certain about their values than children raised by the other types of parents because they have been encouraged to think about their values.

SOCIAL COGNITION AND SUSCEPTIBILITY TO PEER PRESSURE

As children get older and have more social experience their ability to deal with complex issues increases. Under the age of 7, children do not possess the cognitive skills to take the role of the other. They have only a rudimentary ability to understand the other's point of view or how their behavior affects others. Also, they do not have the ability to imagine how others perceive them, as in the **Looking Glass Self**.

Cognition refers to critical thinking skills and children have to have hundreds of thousands of interactions with parents and peers in order to develop them. **Social cognition**, thus, refers to thoughts about social reality. Social cognition refers to the link between social development and critical thinking skills. Social interaction helps children develop the skills necessary for reflection about self, and self in a variety of interactions and social settings..

Let us consider three different groups to which most 7 year old children belong: family, peer group, and classmates. Interaction in each of these social settings helps the child learn about the structure of social reality. For each group there are some statuses – names of positions within the group. Statuses in the family include parent and child; in the peer group they include at least two equals; in the classroom they include teacher and student. The child has to learn the roles associated with not only their position in each setting but the position of everyone else. There is a structure to their relationships in different social settings. To achieve social cognition is to understand what those relationships are. Teachers expect children to behave in ways that are different from peers or parents.

Age is related to social cognition. Younger children are experimenting with their social identity. Children have to learn how to be masculine or feminine, for example. Peer groups provide cues about how to dress. Boys wear pants and girls wear skirts. Girls play certain games, such as skip-rope, Barbie, and dress-up and boys play other games, such as ball games and sports-oriented out-of-doors games. Peer groups are great at reinforcing gender stereotypes. Peer groups also help define attitudes and definitions of right and wrong.

Younger children tend to be more conforming than older children. Children aged 7 to 11 are just beginning to understand the structure of social reality. They have the capacity to understand the patterns of social reality and the statuses associated with the groups they belong to. However, they lack the cognitive skills to differentiate between actual reality and their assumptions of reality. Once, while watching the Winter Olympics with me, my youngest son, who was about eight years old, was surprised to see a woman competing in the downhill skiing event. He insisted that "girls could not ski" even though he was watching it happen.

Young children make assumptions about reality without considering all the available facts. At this age, they are know-it-alls who tend to be overconfident in how smart and clever they are. They resist parental efforts to correct them. They are beginning to think logically but have not developed the capacity to make inferences.

From around age 11 and older, children have the beginnings of abstract thought. They begin to understand concepts, such as love, responsibility, and friendship. At this point children can begin to evaluate the strength of an argument or point of view and the associated facts. While a 7 year old cannot understand the implications of an assumption, a 15 year old can.

As children get older they begin to have access to symbolic and conceptual realities. Things are no longer black and white. This causes adolescents to become less sure of their positions and more sensitive to the need to test their assumptions against the generalized other. For example, my eight year old son just ignored the evidence of his eyes and continued to believe that there were things girls could not do just because they were girls. By age 15, of course, he was able to test that assumption against any number of examples of female athletes at school. Thus, he learned that "in general" there are lots of women who are good at sports. As children become more knowledgeable about the generalized other, they become more cognizant of possible conflicts between peer pressure and the norms of the broader society – and therefore less likely to succumb to peer pressure.

PRINCIPLES OF PEER GROUP SOCIALIZATION

There are a variety of social processes at work in peer groups that encourage conformity. According to Social Learning Theory, reinforcement, modeling, fear of rejection, and social learning are the mechanisms through which learning takes place.

Reinforcement

Reinforcement basically means to look for a certain behavior and try to encourage it (or discourage it). Peers influence each other's behavior through reinforcement. Positive reinforcement refers to a pat on the back, a smile, praise, a laugh, or other response that engenders feelings of inclusion and acceptance. Thus, if the child is seeking acceptance and a certain behavior, such as a joke, is rewarded with laughter, and the laughter makes the child feel accepted and invokes a sense of belongingness, they are apt to repeat the behavior and tell more jokes. Conversely, negative reinforcement, such as disapproval, threats of rejection or expulsion, and even aggression can be used to obtain peer group conformity.

Modeling

Role models engage in certain behaviors – they model behavior for observers. Children often imitate a role model. Modeling has several social functions. First, children can learn to do something new by watching others do it. Secondly, if the modeled behavior is positively reinforced children are more likely to try to imitate it. If the behavior has negative consequences, children are less likely to imitate it. Thus, children can learn the consequences of certain behaviors by watching others model it. Thirdly, children can learn how to behave in new or uncertain social situations by taking their cues from others.

Three important factors influence whether or not children will imitate a model. The situation in which the modeling takes place is important. Passive behavior is less likely to be imitated than active behavior. Characteristics of the model are also important. If the model is similar to the observer and has desirable traits, children are more likely to imitate the behavior. Characteristics of the observer play a role as well. The observer must be physically and cognitively capable of imitating the modeled behavior. Preschool children do a lot of verbal and physical imitating that is both positive and negative. Imitating role models tends to decline after age 10.

Fear of Rejection

The fear of being excluded, rejected, or teased is another way peers exert pressure over group members. Indeed, fear of rejection may be the basic element of conformity to peer pressure. In most peer groups there is a pecking order – some members have higher status than others and one individual may be the leader. Bullies tend to be aggressive, dominant, angry, and impulsive and have low tolerance for frustration. Children lower down in the pecking order tend to be shy, passive, withdrawn, and insecure and often have difficulty asserting themselves in groups.

Social Learning

Children learn from each other and this is another way peer groups influence our behavior. I have been a musician all of my adult life. When I think back on the matter I realize that most of what I know about music I learned from other musicians in my peer group. I remember that I struggled with a particular Led Zeppelin Song but a friend of mine showed me how to play it on guitar. He also taught me several ZZ Top guitar licks and some standard blues turnarounds. It was not long before I was playing in a band because one friend of mine took the time to pass on a little knowledge.

If you think about it you will be able to identify all kinds of things, some useful and some not so useful, you learned from your peers – knowledge about sexuality, making out, how to dance, how to ask someone out, how to break up with a boyfriend or girlfriend, and any number of social skills you now take for granted. Novice peer group members learn from their more skilled peers. In the peer group, old hands teach newcomers all kinds of deviant behavior. I learned a lot from my peers: tips on how to cheat on examinations, how to file down a penny so vending machines would count it as a dime, how to hold my breath when "toking" on a "j," really cool moves to get to "third base" with your date, and some street-fighting techniques, like the "sucker punch," how to "trick" my "wheels" so it would go faster, and where to buy a Penthouse, among lots of other things, all of which seemed important at the time!

SOCIAL SKILLS AND PEER GROUPS

To be successful in life requires certain social skills. You will need to be able to communicate effectively. Sometimes cooperation is better than competition. People do not like a sore loser. It takes some work to learn that you cannot always get your way. Interaction in peer groups helps children develop these important social skills. Children cared for in day care are generally more socially competent than children cared for at home. This is because they have experience interacting with other children. They have already had to learn some hard lessons about getting along, cooperation, and sharing. Children with early experiences in group settings are slightly more aggressive because they have learned to stand up for themselves.

Morals and Values and Peer Groups

Children need to develop morals and values. **Morals** are conceptions of right and wrong. Values are standards that society holds up as desirable. Not stealing is moral imperative because we teach children that stealing is wrong. Obtaining a college degree is a value position because society holds up education as desirable. Children need to interact with others in order to develop morals and values – there is an indirect connection: group life is governed by norms and rules - morals and values both establish rules of conduct.

Between ages 3 -7 when children play together the rules are ambiguous – each child may have different views about how a game is played. Between ages 7 -8 children learn that everyone needs to play by the same rules but their understanding of the rules may be vague. By age 12 children understand the rules and apply them to everyone – if you want to play the game or be in the group you must follow the established rules. So we see in game-playing the social function of acquiring morals. Children move from the position that certain behaviors violate the rules of a particular game, to the position that certain behaviors violate the rules of most games, to the position that certain behaviors, like cheating, are wrong in general, which is a moral position. Thus, through interaction in the game-stage children learn that "rules" are constraints upon behavior just like morals.

Two Types of Morality

Morality of Constraint

Morality of Constraint places restraints on behavior that arise from respect for authority figures. Children learn that certain people have the right to be respected and minded. These people include parents, teachers, and religious leaders, if the family is church-going. This type of morality is fostered in adult-dominated social settings.

Morality of Cooperation

Morality of Cooperation places restraints on behavior that arise from the mutual desire between individuals to continue their group. In a dyad, for example, where there are only two people, if one person leaves the group the relationship is over. Thus, in order to preserve these types of "best friends" peer groups there must be respect between peers. Of course, the morality of cooperation may apply to groups larger than a dyad. This type of morality is fostered in peer dominated social settings. To be successful socially children need to develop both types of morality.

There is a relationship between parenting style, peer group experiences, and how much influence peers have over children. Authoritative parenting, combined with extensive and positive peer group experiences, tends to produce children with high levels of social competence and autonomy. Autonomous individuals think for themselves and are less likely to succumb to pressure from their peers. Authoritarian or Permissive parenting, combined with extensive peer group experiences, tends to produce children who are peer conformists. These children are more likely to succumb to pressure from peers.

PEER GROUPS AND SOCIAL ROLES

Interaction in Group Settings

Adults play many roles in life: employee, parent, sibling, spouse, and best-friend, to name a few that are common. Often adults experience role conflict and role strain. **Role conflict** refers to the stress associated with two statuses that compete with each other – say parent and breadwinner. **Role strain** refers to conflicts that arise from the behaviors associated with one status – such as loving parent and disciplinarian. Children, of course, will have difficulty sorting this out. They have to learn which roles are appropriate in different social settings. When is empathy called for? When should one conform? When should one compete? Does the situation call for passivity or assertiveness? Children learn how to deal with these issues and how to resolve conflicts from their experiences in peer groups. One of the main functions of peer groups is to prepare children for role-enactments later in life.

Gender Roles

Gender roles are a major part of everyday life. Sex refers to the biological differences between women and men. Gender, on the other hand refers to the social definitions of masculinity and femininity, which children learn through the process of socialization. Society places great emphasis on gender. Did you ever wonder why parents dress their children in different colors? Pink is for little girls and blue is for little boys? An infant has no idea of what color they are dressed in. The purpose is a social exercise. The color of the child's apparel signals to everyone who interacts with the child what sex it is. Once you know whether the child is male or female, the gender scripts associated with masculine and feminine are called forth and you begin to interact with the child according to those scripts. In other words, we treat little boys differently from little girls and this treatment begins while children are infants.

Parents are highly involved in the process of creating "gendered" children. First, they decide on the child's name. Names, for the most part, imply gender. Even when the name is gender neutral most times by looking at how the name is spelled you can decide whether the child is female or male. Parents decide what clothes will be bought for their children and what color the clothes will be. Of course, it is somewhat hard to avoid these stereotypes. Increasingly, the only places to shop are large retail chains that only have sex-stereotyped clothes to choose from. The toys boys and girls are encouraged to play with are clearly gendered. Toys for boys include trucks, balls, cars, and pretend weapons, unless you happen to be opposed to your child playing with plastic guns and knives. Toys for girls, on the other hand, include Barbie dolls, dress up clothes, pretend makeup, and lots of imitation household items, such as ovens, irons, and ironing boards. When parents decide on names, clothes, and toys they are actively creating 'gendered' children.

There is a lot of sex-segregation in peer groups. In other words, girls tend to play with girls, whereas boys tend to play with other boys. Girl peer groups have different social experiences than boy peer groups. I suggest that these differential experiences in childhood are correlated with different expectations and outcomes as adults. By the time children are 3 they have fairly concrete ideas about gender. They get their gender definitions from a variety of sources, such as the media, the family, and observation of others. Unfortunately, much of this information is not only stereotypical but flawed. Sex-segregation in peer groups, where children interact with each other on the basis of social gender scripts, is one of the main ways in which children internalize gender stereotypes, which they apply to themselves and others.

Girl peers are encouraged to role play caregiving and homemaking activities. Girls play house, dress up, dolls, cooperative games, and otherwise have peer group interactions that emphasize rules associated with caregiving. Playing dress up with Barbie and Ken dolls engenders a whole different range of behaviors than playing war with G.I. Joe dolls. For example, Barbie and Ken dolls facilitate communicative skills. Superhero dolls encourage aggressive behavior. Expressive toys encourage the development of expressive skills. Of course, girls do a lot of other things in their peer groups and even roughhouse with boys. However, a lot of what girls do in their peer groups is anticipatory socialization for homemaking and caregiving.

Boy peers are encouraged to get outside and play at wide-ranging competitive activities. You do not often see girls involved in the basketball and football games boys are encouraged to play. These games have explicit rules and the goal is to "win." Playing competitive games encourages boys to learn a different set of skills than girls who play with Barbie dolls. While girls are learning to communicate, boys are learning to compete and developing motor skills and physical strength and coordination. Have you ever watched a boy play with a toy dump truck? They load dirt or sand into the truck and pretend they are actually the driver, who has to move the contents to a different location and dump it. This is an instrumental skill or way of thinking – it is goal oriented: moving dirt, or getting the job done. These are entirely different skill sets. The play girls are engaged in develops **expressive skills** useful for homemaking, whereas the play boys are engaged in develops **instrumental skills** useful for work and breadwinning.

Sexuality

Children learn about sexuality from a variety of sources, including the mass media, role models in their family, like their parents, who usually model heterosexual sexuality, and they get hands-on experience at school and in their peer groups. The media, for example, glamorizes sex. Sex is used to sell products, to keep our attention when programming is on, it is in magazines, books, music, on television and movie screens and so on – the media is saturated with sex. Rarely, however, are the consequences of sexually transmitted diseases or unwanted pregnancy discussed or considered. Additionally, the media tend to perpetuate sexual stereotypes.

Sexuality is also associated with the family. Imagine all the cues about heterosexuality children are able to observe in their parent's behavior. Surely you must have seen your parents kiss or hug. Unless your parents were completely prudish, it is impossible to hide every sexual behavior.

What would a sociologist expect a child to observe regarding sexuality? For one thing, parents have conversations with each other. Research indicates that women speak more often and attempt to maintain the flow of conversation. Men, on the other hand, interrupt more and are more likely to change the subject. Parents interact physically with each other. There is hugging, kissing, pinching, and squeezing going on, in many families. The next time you see a couple pay attention: who has their arm around the other, who is holding whose hand? Of course, in some families, there is much less physical interaction in public.

Much parental behavior, available for children to observe, is gender stereotypical. Mothers, for example, tend to do most of the cooking and cleaning whereas fathers tend to do things like take out the trash and mow the lawn. In fact, in most families there are gendered spheres of influence – the garage is Dad's area and the kitchen is Mom's area. During social gatherings, for example, the men often congregate in the living room near the television, or outside near the barbeque and the women seek each other out in the kitchen. Fathers are generally responsible for earning the income while mothers are generally responsible for contributing to the family income and caring for the home and children. When chores are assigned, girls are generally assigned to the female sphere and boys to the male sphere. In other words, girls wash dishes and help with laundry while boys take out the trash, rake leaves, wash the car, or mow the lawn. Mothers and fathers worry about different things too—Dads may worry about the bills while Moms worry about the children's health.

It is not just the observation of immediate family through which children begin to pick up on sexuality. Children see lots of other people role modeling sexuality. Older siblings are easy to observe. They can see older children in a variety of social settings engaged in sexual relationships, such as holding hands, kissing, or even petting. When your child visits the home of a friend to play it is likely that they will encounter the identical, or nearly identical, heterosexual script. What I mean is that mothers and fathers in other families tend to be engaged in similar behaviors. As mentioned earlier, by age 3 children have observed literally thousands, perhaps hundreds of thousands gendered interactions.

And then there is the peer group. Think back on it – how much did you learn about sexuality from your peers? In actuality, the younger the children involved the less experienced they are and the more incomplete and distorted their ideas about sexuality are. A lot of what I believed as an adolescent was just plain wrong. Nevertheless, peer groups establish norms about initiating sexual activity. Peers discuss love, intercourse, masturbation, petting and every other aspect about sexuality. There is even role-playing related specifically to sexuality. We played Twister with the girls for the excitement derived from close physical proximity! Other games, such as *spin the bottle*, and *truth or dare* are also opportunities for adolescents to experiment with sexuality.

I remember in elementary school, about the fourth grade, some girl chased me down, sat on me, and kissed me! She went on and on about how much she "loved" me. My guy friends all thought I had cooties for sure, although no one knew exactly what cooties were. But whatever they were – they were bad! I remember the girls were always talking about which boy was cute and who they wanted to marry. As for the boys, our attitude was basically to avoid the girls at all costs. Somehow, around adolescence the boys discovered the girls were not so bad after all.

In general, peers greatly influence the onset of sexual behavior. Teens on academic tracks in school, rather than vocational tracks, tend to be less sexually active. Of course, school is one of the main venues for peer group formation. Teens who date earlier, for example, tend to have sex sooner than teens who hold off on dating until later in life. In my day, boys tended to have sex earlier than girls, or at least claimed to. Research indicates that the gap between the onset of sexual activity for boys and girls is closing, as girls are also now having sex earlier. The lower the socioeconomic status of the teens the earlier they tend to engage in sexual activity. It is likely that working class teens do not expect to go to college and therefore see no reason to put off sexual activity for an academic career.

Social Identity

Social identity refers to characteristics such as gender, ethnicity, and race, but also to religious groups and social class, and other personal characteristics that peers associate with particular individuals. For instance, some personal characteristics might include being a good athlete, a good listener, a great friend, a practical joker, introverted or extroverted, and so on. In addition to a variety of characteristics associated with group membership, such as religion, every child has relatively stable personality characteristics. Peer groups help children choose between conflicting images of self. Peer groups allow children to achieve **self-validation**. For instance, if you think you are a good athlete and you get positive feedback from teammates, the coaches, fans, and peers, you probably are. Thus, peer groups are an important aspect of social identity formation. We come to have certain beliefs about our talents, abilities, and attributes, in large part, because we get lots of feedback from peers.

In part, claiming a social identity can be achieved by adopting the behavior, dress, and attitudes of peers. In college, it is relatively easy to tell what types of peer groups people belong to. Women who belong to a sorority, for example, often wear a blouse or sweatpants with the Greek letters splashed all over them. Still others have liberal or progressive leanings, and through their dress and mannerisms you can see that they are members of vegetarian, environmental, or other left-leaning peer groups. There are bikers, musicians, gamers, jocks, and ROTC peer groups. In part, people get involved in peer groups for a sense of empowerment. You can feel like you are in control of what is going on around you if you are affiliated with like-minded people. They dress in similar ways and may even have a certain lingo, code words they use to communicate with each other.

PEER GROUP DYNAMICS AND INTERACTION

Unfortunately, not every child is accepted into the peer groups they may desire to be part of. For instance, it took me a long time to become accepted into the music crowd. I was always commenting that "Those guys can *jam* man!" Not only is there a pecking order within peer groups but between peer groups as well. The *popular crowd* is generally at the top of the pecking order. There are lots of wannabes who would love to join this peer group. But there are lots of other peer groups higher or lower in social status. Of course, not everyone wants to be in the 'popular' group.

When I was in high school there were several peer groups: Jocks, Cheerleaders, Nerds, Heads, Musicians, Hippies, Thespians, Motor Heads, and Curbies, to name a few. The Nerds were those poor people who were interested in academic achievement. We felt sorry for them at the time but I suspect they pity us now!

I moved between several peer groups, including the Musicians, the Motor Heads, and the Curbies. The Musicians all had long hair and played one instrument or another and tried to "look cool." Many of us were actually in bands or played in the school jazz or stage band. Musicians often hung out with Heads. The Motor Heads (sometimes called Jammers) were basically guys who liked cars and spent a lot of time in shop classes "tricking" their cars out. The Curbies were a bunch of people who liked to hang out downtown and got in lots of trouble with the authorities. They seemed to most enjoy sitting on the curb, from where the name is derived, just off school property where they could smoke cigarettes in plain view of the authorities. None of these people were jocks so there was not much anyone could do about it. Curbies hated "*the man.*" If you messed with one Curbie you had a major problem with every Curbie.

As I moved between these peer groups, the activities I engaged in, the attitudes I affected, the clothes I wore, and even the lingo I spoke changed somewhat, sometimes dramatically. For instance:

- "Jammin'," meant to go fast when Motor Heads used the term, but to Musicians it also meant getting together to play our guitars. "Let's jam!" i.e. play lots of fast solos.

- "Riff" referred to a musical passage, such as a lead guitar part. "Smokin' riff!"

- "Gear" is what musicians had, in terms of amplifiers, guitars and so on, but was mostly used to indicate *superior* equipment or equipment that was not too shoddy. "That's gear!" A Gibson guitar or Marshall Amplifier was "gear, man, gear."

- "Bug out" was a term Curbies used to indicate the "man" was coming. "Let's bug."

- "Heavy" was used by nearly everyone to indicate a deep thought or statement. "That was heavy."

- "Bad" meant good. "She's bad!"

- "Profile" To profile meant to be seen "cruzin'," as in seen from the side as you drive by someone on the street. We loved to profile in tee shirts, in my 1957 Ford 2 door, with the sleeves rolled up and elbows out the window. I had "way-cool" "meats" in the back, which referred to the gargantuan size of my rims and tires.

- "Breeze" was another nearly universal term that meant to leave one place for another, as in "let's breeze." Sometimes it was used to refer to breaking up with someone, as in "give her the breeze."

- "Hang" meant to hang out together.

Some of this crazy lingo used by your ancient professor is still relevant today! There was even a geographic aspect to some of these terms. For instance, we understood that "hang 10," was a surfer reference but we never had occasion to use it. When I was in the Navy I learned an interesting term, "FUBAR." You will learn about that at some point in your life. Today, text messaging has led to the evolution of many more catch phrases such as "LOL," which means laugh out loud.

Characteristics of Acceptance

Not surprisingly, there are some characteristics associated with acceptance and rejection by peers. Prosocial characteristics are highly correlated with acceptance by peers. Being helpful, empathetic, and cooperative are highly desired characteristics. After all, peers do things together and to be part of the group you have to cooperate. Social competence and intelligence are also characteristics generally associated with acceptance by peers. People who are socially competent understand how to behave in almost any social setting and make good role models for others in the group. People who are intelligent are good problem-solvers and can often help others in the group with academic or other types of problems. It does not hurt to be physically attractive either. Research indicates that good looking people are evaluated more positively on a wide range of issues.

Characteristics of Rejection

You may guess by now that if prosocial behaviors are associated with acceptance by peers, anti-social characteristics would predict rejection by peers. You would be correct in that assumption. I once played a board game with a boy I knew from my neighborhood. When it became obvious he was going to lose, he brushed all the chess pieces off the board. Not only did I never play another board game with him, I never invited him over again. People hate poor losers. Children who are bossy, disruptive, or aggressive often have a hard time making friends or joining peer groups. Research indicates that those with lower levels of social competence, low intellectual ability, or who are physically unattractive, are more likely to be rejected by peers. The socially incompetent just do not know how to get along in groups. If they are disruptive or too aggressive games that require cooperation are difficult to play. It is just easier not to invite them to play. Of course, when peers do this it tends to reinforce their negative attributes. If you do not have many social skills, being excluded from peer groups is not going to help you develop them.

Recall that parenting styles sometimes swing, depending upon the social situation of the parent, between positive and negative parenting styles. The same is true for peer group's dynamics. Sometimes, depending upon what the child is going through, they are more likely to be rejected. There are a variety of situational problems that can damage children's peer relations. When parents divorce, for example, all kinds of problems can develop for a child. The stress of the situation may change their personality or how they interact with their friends. They may become depressed or withdrawn. They may even have to move away from their peers depending upon custody and living arrangements. Children may be abused. Parents may become addicted to drugs or alcohol. There are many factors in the child's social environment that can impact how successfully they interact in their peer groups.

Development of Friendships

Making Friends in Childhood

As children mature the complexity of their interactions with friends increases. Very young children have not fully developed their cognitive abilities. Thus, research confirms that for 13-24 month old children, a friend is basically whoever is available to play with. Children this age, while not able to understand complex rules of play are nevertheless usually happy to see each other and like to be in each other's presence. Between 24-36 months, children begin to have friends for different purposes and activities, such as emotional support or different activities.

Early Childhood

Momentary playmates best describes the friendships in early childhood. Children under the age of 4 have not mastered taking the role of the other. Thus, they are unable to see themselves from the point of view of other children. Children this age are very egoistic, they can only consider what they want from a friend, not what a friend may want from them. For children this age, a friend is someone they know who lives nearby. These "friends" often have some material possession they like to play with, such as a swing set, dolls, or other interesting toys. In this stage, a friend is whoever is available.

Early to Middle Childhood

One-way assistance best describes the friendships in early to middle childhood. Between the ages of 4 and 9 children begin to be influenced by the opinions of their friends. Still, a friend is someone who complies with their wishes or someone who will share with them, not the other way around. But they are beginning to get the idea that being a friend involves give and take. In this stage, a friend is whoever will share with you.

Middle Childhood

Fair-weather cooperation basically describes friendships in middle childhood. Between 6 and 12 children learn that friendship involves give and take, two-way interactions. In other words, children learn that they must share and cooperate if they want others to share and cooperate. This is a major developmental step. In this stage, however, children are not quite capable of understanding friendship in universal terms – that friendship is a social relationship independent of those involved. It is not too long before children move from sharing with particular friends because they like to play with them, to sharing as something associated with all human relationships. In middle childhood, a friend is someone who shares with you and with whom you share and get along with.

Middle Childhood to Adolescence

Friendships in late childhood to adolescent are intimate, mutually-shared-relationships. By this time children understand the abstract aspects of friendship. Between 9 and 15 children come to view friendship as something that has to be nurtured for its own sake. In this stage, friendships often involve possessiveness and jealousy. For instance, if a "best friend" goes to a party you are not invited to you may experience jealousy or be emotionally upset. Friendships in this stage involve more complex principles of equality and reciprocity.

Adolescence to Adulthood

Friendships in late adolescence to young adulthood are characterized by autonomous/interdependent relationships. Young adults begin to understand that sometimes friends need to have time for themselves away from everyone. In this stage, if you invite a friend to do something with you, and they decline because they need some "alone time," you are not likely to get upset with them. There are gender differences in types of friendships in young adulthood. Boys, and young men, tend to prefer a best friend who is a good companion. In other words, boys are activity-driven – they want to do things together, such as play basketball or other sports-related activities. Girls and young women view a best friend as someone who is true to them and who they can share intimate conversation with.

Bullies and Their Victims

Bullying is a problem in school. Bullying takes many negative forms, including harassment, threats, name-calling, and other negative interactions, including physical beatings. Bullies have some recognizable characteristics. They need to feel powerful and dominate others. Often, bullies are impulsive and have little tolerance for frustration. They can not resist teasing and name-calling. They show little empathy for their victims. It is not unusual for bullies to be physically athletic and aggressive. Schools are beginning to pay more attention to this problem as research is demonstrating a connection between school shootings and bullying.

Victims also have some recognizable characteristics. Usually, victims are physically weaker than bullies. While bullies tend to have relatively high self esteem, victims tend to have relatively low self esteem. They are cautious, passive, and submissive. Typical victims also have difficulty asserting themselves. These children often relate better to adults than to peers.

Deviant Peer Groups

A deviant peer group is one that is engaged in antisocial behavior. These behaviors range from status offenses, such as skipping school, smoking, fighting, and so on, to criminal behavior, such as selling drugs, shoplifting, stealing, and other serious criminal activity. We should realize that there is a vast range between the "wrong crowd," or a "rough crowd," and a gang. Hanging around with the wrong crowd can mean engaging in relatively harmless activities, such as staying out late, occasionally skipping-school, and perhaps some drinking and smoking. While those behaviors can be bad enough, and parents usually discourage their children from making friends among those kids, being in a gang generally involves serious infractions of the law.

Family factors are the single best predictor of gang involvement. Children attracted to gangs are lacking family support and socialization. If a child's emotional, social, and economic needs are not met in the home, he/she may turn to gangs to fulfill them. Additionally, some parental styles are more likely to produce children who favor gangs than others. For instance, highly permissive or highly punitive parenting styles are often associated with gang-membership. Families in which children experience low levels of concern and affection are more likely to produce children susceptible to deviant peer groups. Single-parent and step-parent families are also more likely to see their children involved in gangs. Children who have few positive adult role-models are more likely to be attracted to deviant peer groups and gangs. Thus, gangs can provide things that are often lacking in the home.

Family factors are not independent of other social factors. Families do not exist in a vacuum. Families are influenced by a variety of important social factors. Perhaps the most important social factor that predicts gang involvement is the lack of educational and economic opportunities. When neighborhoods are dilapidated, schools are failing, and economic opportunities are nearly nonexistent, children are much more likely to seek out deviant peer groups. Another important factor is the presence of deviant adult subcultures. Gang leadership is adult. When the neighborhood is full of unemployed adults and adults with gang ties who may also have criminal backgrounds, they end up being role-models for younger children. Additionally, gangs need to recruit and train new members and it is generally the adults who are engaged in this activity. Therefore, social factors are also important in determining which children will find gangs acctractive.

Personality characteristics of individuals are important too when it comes to participation in deviant peer groups and gangs. Gangs tend to be more attractive to antisocial children. Children who are attached to normative social structures, such as family, church, or school, are less likely to be attracted by the gang subculture. Children who are in trouble in school and who are relatively uninvolved in their families, churches, and schools are more likely to become gang members. These children are impulsive, defiant, cannot get along well with others, and generally have lower self esteem than children more attached and involved in normative social structures.

Thus, we see that gang membership is a complex issue. It may be that a child has some of the personality characteristics usually associated with gangs, but lives in a middle class neighborhood and has authoritative parents. Without the negative social and parental factors, such children may never become involved in gangs. A family history of gang membership, lack of positive male role-models, an economically depressed and run-down neighborhood, and antisocial personality characteristics can combine to produce children susceptible to gang recruitment.

Gangs

Gangs are a group of people who form an allegiance for the purpose of deviant behavior. Gangs provide members with a social identity. They have names and are often identified by certain clothes, colors, tattoos, hand signs, and slang language. Gangs can often perform some of the functions of the family. They meet the emotional, and sadly, sometimes the economic needs of their members. Because of this, much like families, gangs can achieve high levels of loyalty and solidarity. There is an "us" against "them" flavor to gang membership. For the gang member, the gang is the "in-group" and the "reference group," and other gangs and society in general is the "out-group." Gangs are appealing because they offer a sense of belongingness, just like a family. Gangs also provide guidance, protection, and even excitement.

Certain personal attributes are associated with gang membership. Race is an important correlate of gang membership. Gangs are usually homogenous in terms of race. There are Hispanic gangs and African American gangs. Of course, gangs have a long history in this nation. There have, in the past, been Jewish, Irish, and Italian gangs. Socioeconomic status is correlated with gang activity. Gang members are generally from poor families in inner cities. Recently, however, gangs have been fanning out across the nation in cities that have not seen the problem before. As mentioned previously, family structure is associated with gang activity. Many gang members come from families where relatives are also in the gang or the family has a history of gang membership. There is also a correlation between lack of adult supervision and gang membership. Other family factors include female-headed families and two-adult families where the child has a negative relationship with a stepfather or mother's boyfriend. Lastly, certain belief systems are correlated with gang activity. People who have developed an injustice frame, the belief that society has screwed them and they are justified in breaking the rules to survive, are more likely to find gangs attractive.

ಶಿ ಄ ಶಿ ಄

REFERENCES

Abramovitch, R., & Grusec, J. E (1978). Peer interaction in a natural setting. *Child Development, 49*, 60-65.

Adams, G. R., & Crane, P. (1980). Assessment of parents' and teachers' expectations of preschool children's social preferences for attractive or unattractive children and adults. *Child development, 51*, 224-231.

Adams, G. R., Gullotta, T. P., & Markstrom-Adams, C. (1994). *Adolescent life experiences* (3rd ed.). Pacific Grove, CA: Brooks/Cole.

Adler, P. A., & Adler, P. (1998) *Peer power: Preadolescent culture and identity.* New Brunswick, NJ: Rutgers University Press.

Ainsworth, M. D. S. (1979). Infant-mother attachment. *American Psychologist, 34*, 932-937.

American academy of Pediatrics. (2002). *Peer Groups and Cliques.* http://www.aap.org/.

Asher, S. R. (1982). Some kids are nobody's best friend. *Today's Education, 71(1)*, 23.

Asher, S. R., & Coie, J. D. (1990). *Peer rejection in childhood.* New York: Cambridge University Press.

Asher, S. R., Gottman, J. M., & Oden, S. L. (1977). Children's friendships in school settings. In E. M. Hetherington, & R. D. Parke (EDS.), *Contemporary readings in child psychology.* New York: McGraw-Hill.

Bagwell, C. L, J, D., Terry, R. A., & Lochman, J. E. (2000). Peer clique participation and social status in preadolescence. *Merrill-Palmer Quarterly, 46(2)*, 280-305.

Baker, A. K., Barthelemy, K. J., & Kurdek, L. A. (1993). The relation between fifth and sixth graders' peer-rated classroom social status and their perceptions of family and neighborhood factors. *Journal of Applied Developmental Psychology, 14*, 547-556.

Bandura, A. (1989). Social cognitive theory. In R. Vasta (Ed.), *Annals of child development: Vol. 6. Six Theories of Child Development: Revised Formulations and Current Issues.* Greenwich, CT: JAI Press.

Baumrind, D. (1973). The development of instrumental competence through socialization. In A. Pick (Ed), *Minnesota symposium on child psychology (Vol. 7).* Minneapolis: University of Minnesota Press.

Berenda, R. (1950). *The influence of the group on the judgment of children.* New York: King's Crown Press.

Berk, L. E., & Winsler, A. (1995). *Scaffolding children's learning: Vygotsky and early childhood education.* Washington, DC: National Association for the Education of Young Children.

Berndt, T. J. (1979). Developmental changes in conformity to peers and parents. *Developmental*

Psychology. 15, 608-616.

Berndt, T. J. (1983). Correlates and causes of sociometric status in childhood: A commentary on six current studies of popular, rejected and neglected children. *Merrill-Palmer Quarterly, 29,* 439-448.

Berndt, T. J., & Ladd, G. W. (1989). *Peer relationships in child development.* New York: Wiley.

Best, R. (1983). *We've all got scars: What boys and girls learn in elementary school.* Bloomington: Indiana University Press.

Bogenschneider, K., Wu, M., Rraffaelli, M., & Tsay, J. C. (1998). Parental influences on adolescent peer orientation and substance use: The interface of parenting practices and values. *Child Development, 69,* 1672-1688.

Brooks-Gunn, J., & Furstenberg, F. F., Jr. (1989). Adolescent sexual behavior. *American Psychologist, 44(2),* 249-257.

Brown, B. B., Clausen, D. R., & Eicher, S. A. (1986). Perceptions of peer pressure, peer conformity dispositions and self-reported behavior among adolescents. *Developmental Psychology, 22,* 521-530.

Burton, C. B. (1985). Children's peer relationships. ERIC *Digest.*

Clarke-Stewart, K. A. (1992.). Consequences of child care for children's development. In A. Booth (Ed), *Childcare in the 1990s; Trends and consequences.* Hillsdale, NJ: Erlbaum.

Cohen, R., Bornstein, R., & Sherman. R. C. (1973). Conformity behavior of children as a function of group make-up and task ambiguity. *Developmental Psychology, 9,* 124-131.

Coie, J. D., & Cillesen. A. (1993). Peer rejection: Origins and effects on children's development. *Current Directions in Psychological Science, 2,* 89-92.

Coie, J. D., & Dodge, K. A. (1998) Aggression and antisocial behavior. In W. Damon (Ed.), *Handbook of child psychology* (5th ed., Vol. 4). New York: Wiley.

Coie, J. D., Dodge, K. A., & Kupersmidt, J. B. (1990). Peer group behavior and social status. In S. R. Asher, & J. D. Coie (Eds.), *Peer rejection in childhood.* New York: Cambridge University Press.

Coleman, J. (1961). *The adolescent society.* New York: Macmillan.

Condroy, J. C., & Simon, M. L. (1974). Characteristics of peer- and adult-oriented children. *Journal of Marriage and the Family, 36,* 543-546.

Cooley, C. (1964). *Human nature and the social order.* New York: Schocken. (Original Work Published 1909).

Devereaux, E. C. (1970). The role of peer group experience in moral development. In J. P. Hill (Ed.), *Minnesota symposia on child psychology* (Vol. 4). Minneapolis: University of Minnesota Press.

Dishion, T. J., McCord, J., & Poulin, F. (1999). When interventions harm: Peer groups and problem behavior. *American Psychologist, 54(8),* 755-764.

Dodge, K. A. (1983). Behavioral antecedents of peer social status. *Child Development, 54,* 1386-1399.

Dodge, K. A. (1986). A social information processing model of social competence in children. In M. Perlmutter (Ed.), *Minnesota symposia on child psychology* (Vol.18). Hillsdale, NJ: Erlbaum.

Eder, D. (1995). *School talk: Gender and adolescent school culture.* New Brunswick, NJ: Rutgers University Press.

Elkind, D. (1981a). Egocentrism in children and adolescents. In D. Elkind (Ed.), *Children and adolescents: Interpretive essays on Jean Piaget* (3rd ed.). New York: Oxford University Press.

Erikson, E. H. (1963). *Childhood and society.* New York: Norton.

Fagot, B. I. (1985). Beyond the reinforcement principle: Another step toward understanding sex-role development. *Developmental Psychology, 21,* 1097-1104.

Farrington, D. P., & Loeber, R. (2000). Epidemiology of juvenile violence. *Juvenile Violence, 9,* 733-748.

Foster-Clark, F. S., & Blyth, D. A. (1991). Peer relations and influences. In R. M. Lerner, A. C. Petersen, & J. Brooks-Gunn (Eds.), *Encyclopedia of adolescence* (Vol. 2). New York: Garland.

Furman, W., & Masters, J. C. (1980). Affective consequences of social reinforcement, Punishment, and Neutral Behavior. *Developmental Psychology, 16,* 100-104.

Goldstein, A. P. (1991). *Delinquent gangs: A psychological perspective.* Champaign, IL: Research Press.

Gottman, J., Gonso, J., & Rasmussen, B. (1975). Social interaction, Social competence, and friendship in children. *Child Development, 46,* 709-718.

Greenfield, P. M., & Suzuki, L. K. (1998). Culture and human development: Implications for parenting, education, pediatrics, and mental health. In W. Damon (Ed.), *Handbook of child psychology* (5th ed., Vol. 4). New York: Wiley.

Grusec, J. E., & Lytton, H. (1988). *Social development: History, theory, and research.* New York: Springer-Verlag.

Harris, J. R. (1998). *The nurture assumption: Why children turn out the way they do.* New York: Free Press.

Hartup, W. W. (1983). Peer relations. In P. H. Mussen (Ed.), *Handbook of child psychology* (4th ed., Vol. 4). New York. Wiley.

Harup, W. W. (1989). Social relationships and their developmental significance. *American Psychologist, 44*(2), 120-126.

Harup, W. W. (1996). The company they keep: Friendships and their developmental significance. *Child Development, 67,* 1-13.

Havighurst, R. (1972). *Human development and education* (3rd ed.). New York: McKay.

Howes, C. (1988). Peer interaction of young children. *Monographs of the Society for Research in Child Development, 43*(1, Serial No. 217).

Howes, C., Matheson, C. C., & Hamilton, C. E. (1994). Maternal, teacher, and child care history correlates of children's relationships with peers. *Child Development, 65,* 264-273.

Hymel, S., Bowker, A., & Woody, E. (1993). Aggressive versus withdrawn unpopular children: Variations in peer and self-perceptions in multiple domains. *Child Development, 64,* 879-896.

Jackson, R. K., & McBride, W. D. (1985). *Understanding street gangs.* Sacramento, CA: Custom.

Jacobson, J. L., & Willie, D. E. (1986). The influence of attachment pattern on developmental changes in peer interaction from the toddler to the preschool period. *Child Development, 57,* 338-347.

Katchadourian, H. (1990). Sexuality. In S. S. Feldman, & G. R. Elliot (Eds.), *At the threshold: The developing adolescent.* Cambridge, MA: Harvard University Press.

Kemple, K. M. (1991). Research in review: Preschool children's peer acceptance and social interaction. *Young Children, 46*(5), 47-54.

Kerns, K. A., Contreras, J. M., & Neal-Barnett, A. M. (2000). *Family and peers: Linking two social worlds.* Westport, CT: Praeger.

Kindermann, T. (1998). Children's development within peer groups: Using composite social maps to identify peer networks and study their influences. In W. M. Bukowski, & A. H. Cillesen (Eds.), *New directions for child development* (No. 80). San Francisco: Jossey-Bass.

Ladd, G. W. (1999). Peer relationships and social competence during early and middle childhood. *Annual Review of Psychology,* 333-344.

Ladd, G. W., & LeSieur, K. D. (1995). Parents and peer relationships. In M. H. Bornstein (Ed.), *Handbook of parenting* (Vol. 4). Mahwah, NJ: Erlbaum.

Ladd, G. W., & Pettit, G. S. (2002). Parenting and the development of children's peer relationships. In M. H. Bornstein (Ed.), *Handbook of parenting* (2nd ed.). Mahwah, NJ: Erlbaum.

Lamb, M. E. (1998). Nonparental child care: Context, quality, correlates, and consequences. In W. Damon (Ed.), *Handbook of child psychology* (5th ed., Vol. 4). New York: Wiley.

Landre, R., Miller, M. & Porter, D. (1997). *Gangs: A handbook for community awareness.* New York: Facts on File.

Langlois, J. H. (1986). From the eye of the beholder to behavioral reality: Development of social behavior and social relations as a function of physical attractiveness. In C. P. Herman, M. P. Zanna, & E. T. Higgins (Eds.), *Physical behavior: The Ontario Symposium* (Vol. 3). Hillsdale, NJ: Erlbaum.

Lever, J. (1976). Sex differences in the games children play. *Social Problems, 23,* 478-487.

Maccoby, E. E. (1990). Gender relationships: A developmental account. *American Psychologist, 45,* 513-520.

Maccoby, E. E. (2002). Perspectives on gender development. *International Journal of Behavioral Development, 24*, 398-406.

Martin, G., & Pear, J. (2003). *Behavior modification: What it is and how to do it* (7th ed.). Upper Saddle River, NJ: Prentice-Hall.

Mead, G. H. (1934). *Mind, self, and society.* Chicago: University of Chicago Press.

Miller, B. C., Christopherson, C. R., & King, P. K. (1993). Sexual behavior in adolescence. In T. P. Gullota, G. R. Adams, & R. Montemayor (Eds.), *Adolescent sexuality.* Newbury Park, CA: Sage.

National Research Council. (1993*). Losing generations: Adolescents in high-risk settings.* Washington, DC: National Academy Press.

Olweus, D. (1993). *Bullying at school: What we know and what we can do.* Cambridge, MA: Blackwell.

Park, K. A., & Waters, E. (1989). Security of attachment and preschool friendships. *Child Development, 60*, 1076-1080.

Parker, J. G., & Asher, S. R. (1987). Peer relations and later adjustment: Are low-accepted children "At risk"? *Psychological Bulletin, 102*, 357-389.

Patterson, G. R., Reid, J. B., & Dishion, T. J. (1992). *Antisocial boys.* Eugene, OR: Castilia.

Piaget, J. (1952). *The origins of intelligence in children* (M. Cook, Trans.). New York: American Library.

Piaget, J. (1965). *The moral judgment of the child* (M. Gabain, Trans.). New York: Free Press.

Pitcher, E. G., & Schultz, L. H. (1983*). Boys and girls at play: The development of sex roles.* New York: Bergin and Garvey.

Ritts, V., Patterson, M. L., & Tubbs, M. E. (1992). Expectations, impressions, and judgments of physically attractive students: A review. *Review of Educational Research, 62*, 413-426.

Rubin, K. H., Bukowski, W., & Parker, J. G. (1998). Peer interactions, relationships, and groups. In W. Damon (Ed.), *Handbook of child psychology* (5th ed., Vol. 3). New York: Wiley.

Ruble, D., & Martin, C. L. (1998). Gender development. In W. Damon (Ed.), *Handbook of child psychology* (5th ed., Vol. 3). New York: Wiley.

Rutter, M. (1971). Parent-child separation: Psychological effects on the children. *Journal of Child Psychology and Psychiatry*, 12, 233-256.

Rutter, M., Giller, H., & Hagell, A. (1998). *Antisocial behavior by young people.* Cambridge, UK: Cambridge University Press.

Sandstrom, M. J., & Coie, J. D. (1999). A developmental perspective on peer rejection: Mechanisms of stability and change. *Child Development, 70*, 955-966.

Schneider, B. H., Atkinson, L., & Tardif, C. (2001). Child-parent attachment and children's peer relations: A Quantitative Review. *Developmental Psychology, 37*, 86-100.

Selman, R. L., & Selman, A. P. (1979). Children's ideas about friendships: A new theory. *Psychology Today, 12*(4), 71-80.

Serbin, L. A., Powlishta, K. K., & Gulko, J. (1993). The development of sex typing in middle childhood. *Monographs of the Society for Research in Child Development, 58*(2), Serial No. 232).

Shantz, C. U. (1983). Social cognition. In P. H. Mussen (Eds.), *Handbook of Child Psychology* (4th ed., Vol. 3). New York: Wiley.

Small, S., & Luster, T. (1994). Adolescent sexual activity: An ecological risk-factor approach. *Journal of Marriage and the Family, 56*, 181-192.

Steinber, L. (1996). *Beyond the classroom: Why school reform has failed and what parents need to do.* New York: Touchstone.

Steinberg, L. (1987). Single parents, step parents, and the susceptibility of adolescents to antisocial peer pressure. *Child Development, 58*, 269-275.

Thompson, W. E., & Dodder, R. A. (1986). Containment theory and juvenile delinquency: A reevaluation through factor analysis. *Adolescence, 21*, 365-376.

Thornburg, H. D. (1981). The amount of sex information learning obtained during early adolescence. *Journal of Early Adolescence, 1*, 171-183.

Thorne, B. (1993). *Gender play: Girls and boys in school.* New Brunswick, NJ: Rutgers University Press.

Troy, M., & Sroufe, L. A. (1987). Victimization among preschoolers: Role of attachment relationship history. *Journal of the American Academy of Child and Adolescent Psychiatry, 26,* 166-172.

U. S. Department of Justice. (2000, August). Youth gangs in school. *Juvenile Justice Bulletin.* Washington, DC: U.S. Government Printing Office.

Wang, A. Y. (1994). Pride and prejudice in high school gang members. *Adolescence, 29,* 279-291.

Wentzel, K. A., & Erdley, C. A. (1993). Strategies for making friends: Relations to social behavior and peer acceptance in early adolescence. *Developmental Psychology, 29,* 819-826.

Wilson, S., & Mishra, R. (1999, April 28). In high school, groups provide identity. *Washington Post,* p. A1.

Youniss, J., & Volpe, J. (1978), A relational analysis of children's friendship. In W. Damon (Ed.), *Social cognition.* San Francisco: Jossey-Bass.

Zarbatany, L., Hartmann, D. P., & Rankin, D. B. (1990). The psychological functions of preadolescent peer activities. *Child Development, 61,* 1067-1080.

8 | THE INDIVIDUAL, VALUES, AND BELIEFS
by Alexander F. Rice

THE INDIVIDUAL AND BELIEFS

A **belief** is a state of mind or conviction in the truth or reality of some phenomenon. When you have great trust and confidence in some thing or someone, you may be said to have belief. Beliefs are related to our assessment as to the truth or falsity of certain matters. One such matter is the existence of God. Ultimately, the existence of God cannot be decided. This is an excellent example of pure belief; which is to say that pure belief is an assertion without empirically verifiable proof. To think that a God does indeed exist in spite of the lack of concrete proof is the essence of belief.

However, it is also true that when enough evidence is marshaled, even though ultimate proof may never be attained, people may begin to believe that something is true. An example of this is global warming. Scientific evidence indicates that the Earth is warming as a result of human behavior but ironclad evidence is still pending. When the signs point in a certain direction, people begin to believe that something is happening.

We believe in a great many things. Early in life, most children believe in the infallibility of parental judgment. Whatever parents say is true, for children, because they do not have the cognitive ability to reject or test the claims their parents make. I, for example, believe in the American Sociological Association's (ASA) code of ethics. There is abundant evidence that acting in an unprofessional or unethical manner causes harm to research subjects. However, there is ultimately no proof that the ASA's code of ethics is any better than the ethics of any other group. Liberals tend to believe that most people, in the core of their self, are fundamentally good. Conservatives, on the other hand, tend to be suspicious of that claim. Some people believe that government can serve society in ways that are ultimately good. Other people see government, at best, as a necessary evil, and at worse, as just plain evil, which will be discussed later in the chapter. There is also no proof that heaven or hell exists but many of us are convinced that every person has one or the other as his or her final destination.

Often various groups get together and decide on a formal belief system. For Christians, this happened in 325 A.D., at the Council of Nicea. The Roman emperor Constantine realized that a strong centralized Catholic Church could serve a political function by uniting all Romans under one belief system, thus strengthening the empire. To this end, he supervised the effort to create, out of all the different varieties of Christianity, a core belief system that would serve both political and religious functions. Certain Gospels

163

were included in the Bible, while others were excluded. Even the historical order of the Gospels was changed to meet Constantine's political objectives. The Church that emerged from the Council of Nicea supported Constantine's goals because it became the "official" Church of Rome and was vested with great powers and wealth. The big losers in this battle of beliefs were the Gnostics, who were far from the Roman power center in Constantinople. Many academics today believe that the Gnostics may have been closer to the actual teachings of original Christians.

The Protestant Ethic

There are three other important "belief systems" that operate in the United States today, including The Protestant Ethic, Individualism, and Meritocracy. In sociology, we refer to a more or less coherent system of beliefs that explains social inequality as an **ideology** and ideologies are very powerful indeed.

The relationship between values and beliefs and human behavior was of major interest to another important figure in sociology, the German sociologist Max Weber. In his book *The Protestant Ethic and the Spirit of Capitalism*, he analyzed the relationship between the values embodied in the Protestant ethic of the early Puritan sects and social and economic institutions that evolved out of those beliefs in the United States and Europe. Weber documented a relationship between economic success and membership in Protestant sects, particularly the Puritan, Mennonite, Baptist, Methodist and Quaker sects. Economic success was an unanticipated consequence of a Protestant lifestyle. Weber pointed out that some of the values and beliefs associated with Protestantism were also associated with success in the economic areas of life.

Early Protestant Reformers, such as Luther and Calvin, stressed that individuals could have a direct personal relationship with God. This was at odds with the bureaucracy of the Catholic Church, in which a hierarchy of clergy acted as intermediaries between the faithful and God. However, if one has a personal relationship with God, it may be hard to know whether or not one is in God's favor. Additionally, the Protestant emphasis on hard work, diligence, saving, and thrift, associated with a lifestyle of asceticism, strict self-denial as a measure of spiritual discipline, happened to also be helpful in achieving economic success. Calvin taught that some individuals were predestined to be saved, while others were predestined to damnation. These three Protestant "ideals" turned out to be quite helpful to capitalism in general. If you are unsure of God's favor, you can look for signs in your everyday life, such as good fortune in matters related to family and business. And since the lifestyle Protestants practiced for spiritual reasons also happened to be correlated with economic success it would not be hard to impute God's favor.

Today, of course, the spiritual side of the Protestant ethic is deemphasized while the exhortation to work-hard, be thrifty, and save money is still around. In other words, the Protestant ethic has been secularized. Weber's point is that the United States was, partly, colonized by a group of Protestants with a certain belief system and lifestyle. These beliefs and the associated lifestyle tended to compliment capitalism. Although the spiritual dimensions of the Protestant ethic have declined in importance, Americans still tend to believe in the basic principles associated with hard work.

There is a peculiar relationship between religious beliefs and values and the inequalities embedded in our system of stratification. Calvin's "Doctrine of the Elect," seems to suggest that no matter what individuals do during their lifetimes, some are destined for hell. In a sense he proposed religious "castes" in which the elect were saved and everyone else damned. Also, in Christian Sunday schools all over the United States, children are taught a variety of lessons about heaven and hell and who goes to each and why. Sinners go to hell; the faithful go to heaven. So, in a sense, some religious beliefs and values tend to support the spirit of inequality.

The inequality of salvation is perhaps the first lesson taught to kids. It is no major leap from the inequality of salvation to social inequality in general. If you teach children that inequality is natural in the religious realm, you should not be surprised to discover they are willing to tolerate inequality in the social realm. Additionally, many people believe what religious leaders teach them, in so far as suffering and misery being associated with damnation. Here again, it is no great leap to also believe that suffering is natural. These religious beliefs are easily translated into the social beliefs that the poor are somehow bad or immoral people, who, if they would only change their ways, could pull themselves out of poverty. The misery and suffering associated with poverty can be seen as not only natural but as the appropriate inducement to change one's behaviors. From the point of view of religious beliefs and values, poverty can be seen as an indication of God's disfavor and the misery that accompanies it as the punishment.

Individualism

Individualism is an ideological doctrine that holds that the rights and interests of the individual are, or ought to be, equal if not greater than those of the group. A society that practices individualism will favor individual effort, motivation, and action over policies that benefit the entire group. For example, returning to the issue of poverty, an individualistic society will view poverty as an individual problem, rather than a social problem, and expect individuals to take care of themselves. The belief in individualism in the United States grew out of the frontier experience, where settlers had to rely upon their own ingenuity and initiative to survive. To a great extent, individualism is widely popular in the United States as is evidenced by the debates surrounding the future of

165

Social Security. Many conservatives believe that people ought to be responsible for their own welfare, especially in retirement.

One important aspect of the ideology of individualism is the belief that each person has a set of uniquely personal talents, skills, characteristics, and abilities. A society organized on the principles of individualism would emphasize the differences between people that make them stand out, rather than the similarities between people. In our culture, children are taught to see certain creative and artistic interests as indicators of talent not widely shared throughout society.

Many people see themselves as rugged individualists who could, if it became necessary, survive on their own. Indeed, the leisure industry depends upon people who believe they personally possess these qualities. The products associated with hunting, fishing, camping, rock-climbing, and exploring we see on the shelves of our favorite department stores cater to people who see themselves as possessing these individualistic qualities. When parents are asked why they are teaching their children how to hunt or can goods they often remark that they want their children to be "self-sufficient," like our ancestors. Of course, one wonders how successful our ancestors would have been without the guns, knives, wheels, and other products that made the conquest of the frontier possible.

Meritocracy

The ideology of meritocracy is based on a system of beliefs that create a system in which the talented are chosen for social promotion and advancement based on their achievements. In a true meritocracy, appointments and promotions would entirely be based on individual competence rather than favoritism, nepotism, or politics. Even a cursory examination of the stratification system in the United States should be enough to dispel any notion that meritocracy actually exists. Nevertheless, we tend to believe that rewards and punishments should be a reflection of the qualities and actions of individuals. Here, of course, there is a close relationship between the Protestant ethic and meritocracy. We tend to view the qualities associated with the Protestant ethic as the very qualities most meritorious.

The ideology of meritocracy is clearly part of the institution of education in the United States, and the system of grading reflects it. As a child, perhaps you questioned why someone you know received a better grade than you did on an assignment. If you asked your teacher why this was so the answer you received was very likely the embodiment of meritocracy. The answer probably went something like this: Mary received an A because she worked harder on her project than you did on yours and the quality of her project was better. In other words, favoritism on the part of the teacher, or failure to fully explain the project to all the students, or unwillingness to help certain students, are never part of the reason one person gets a lower grade than another. Meritocracy translates failure into a personal characteristic.

Of course, it may be true that you did not work as hard as you could have on the assignment. But it may also be true that the failure was on the part of the teacher or the educational system. The ideology of meritocracy tends to mask institutional problems. Additionally, meritocracy is a subtle form of social control. If society has marked certain groups of people for, if not outright failure, then fewer social rewards, it makes for a more peaceful society if those receiving fewer social rewards actually believe they deserve less.

In a society where the ideology of meritocracy holds sway, the explanation for the success of Bill Gates, the computer software entrepreneur, will be based on innovation, drive, hard-work, and creativity, rather than stealing, illegality, and monopolistic manipulation of the market. To a large degree, the social function of private boarding schools and Ivy League college education for the children of the elite is to turn social class advantages into the myth of personal achievement. This is often described as "being born on third base and claiming you've hit a triple." You may feel that the children of the affluent have unfair advantages. But they can respond that they had to go to college and work very hard. In other words, even though the upper classes do have advantages, they try to mask those advantages by appealing to meritocracy.

Inequality and the Intersection of Ideologies

Every system of stratification is legitimized by a corresponding belief system. Otherwise, people would be quick to rebel. Stratification systems tend to be fairly stable because people internalize the ideologies that support them. Once this **internalization** has taken place, people tend to believe that they are deserving of their place in life and the social rewards they are receiving. This internalization is probably less true for those at the very bottom of the stratification system, but it is certainly true for those at the top and everyone else who is relatively well off. Even for those at the bottom of the stratification system, who are actually suffering from the effects of poverty, it would take a good deal of cognitive work to see through the ideologies they have grown up with, and internalized as part of their personalities, as the mechanisms of social control they are. Even if a small number of citizens actually achieved the **class-consciousness** necessary to see ideology for what it is and began to agitate for reforms, so long as the majority of the population still subscribe to the ideologies of social control the protestors can simply be interpreted as trouble makers.

Clearly, one explanation of poverty and inequality is that opportunities are not equally distributed. The children of the upper classes are more likely to be able to take advantage of educational opportunities, for example, than the children of the poor. If people became aware of the structural nature of inequality they might begin to argue for structural solutions, such as widening the opportunities for everyone. However, these structural explanations are hidden by ideological justification for inequality.

From the point of view of the Protestant ethic, people are poor because they cannot put off instant gratification and they do not work hard enough or save for the future. From the point of view of meritocracy, if you help the poor, you are only enabling them to remain lazy. Lazy people are not deserving of our help. From the point of view of individualism, it is natural to expect some people to be wealthier and more successful than others because they are more creative, or have developed more useful skills that make them more worthy of wealth and comfort than others. From the point of view of the three ideologies discussed here, people are poor because they have maladaptive values, they are lazy, and they are ignorant. However, we must ask ourselves if is correct to paint the pre-school aged children of the poor with these labels.

THE INDIVIDUAL AND VALUES

The Key Values

Values are culturally derived judgments of good or bad. The United States is a diverse nation, in terms of religious groups, ethnic groups, social classes, and educational levels. Although many argue that individualism is the most important American value (Bellah et al., 1985), there are many different values woven throughout the American social fabric. It would be incorrect to assume that everyone subscribes to the same values and beliefs. However, sociologists have discovered that some values are widely accepted:

- Equal Opportunity
- Achievement
- Material Comfort
- Hard Work
- Practicality and Efficiency
- Progress
- Science

- Democracy

- Free Enterprise

- Freedom

- Individualism

- Humanitarianism

- Education

- Religious Freedom

- Environmentalism

- Ethnocentrism and American Exceptionalism

- Leisure

In our culture, people value equal opportunity but realize that through achievement and success, everyone will not be equal. Since we also value humanitarianism, there is a general feeling that those who live in poverty, or with disability and illness are deserving of our help. Clearly, part of the American Dream is related to material comfort as can be seen by the emphasis on home-ownership. However, material comfort also means having food, shelter, and adequate health care. We also value progress, activity, work, and practicality. Our daily lives have been greatly enriched by advances in science, especially in the areas of nutrition and medicine. We also believe in attaining a literate society of critical thinkers. We value democracy and the freedoms associated with it. Leisure has also become a very important value in our society.

Recently, we have come to place great emphasis on time away from work to be with family and friends and to engage in the leisure activities that make life rewarding. Take the weekend for example. It has become such an important part of American culture that most people believe that without it we would not be able to survive.

> It's the time we think of as our own. On the weekend we dress differently, we "go away," we build weekend retreats, we sleep in, we go out, we linger over the Sunday paper. We become different people. Yet why, when asked, "What did you do on the weekend?" do we often answer "The usual" (Rybczynski, 1991, p1)?

This is interesting because it shows that the work ethic is so deeply ingrained into our psyche that we turn our leisure time into little organized rituals. This is often visible during the traditional vacation period. It is supposed to be a vacation, a time to relax, but when you look at the behavior of some people; you wonder where the leisure time is. They are so determined to have a good time that they work themselves into a frenzy planning activities. Take my family for example. This author thought that it would be nice to plan a vacation with other members of the family that had since moved away. The vacation spot? Where else? The wonderful world of Disney, of course! We rented a villa for the three families. Little did I know that the other families were bringing extra people with them. Fourteen people sharing one residence, each with their own plans for what we should do. Needless to say, there were no relaxation days. Every day was filled with activities. I could not wait to return to work! I needed the rest!

One other major value requires special attention: **ethnocentrism**. Americans tend to view our solutions to problems as the best, or most reasonable or intelligent, and our particular way of life as superior to that of other cultures. The tendency to value your own group's beliefs and norms over those of others is known as ethnocentrism. In point of fact, our way of life evolved over hundreds of years and includes a history of genocide and slavery. We value men over women, white people over people of color, those of Anglo-Saxon decent over other ethnic groups. How do we know that some groups are more "valued" than others – by comparing lifestyles, such as level of education, income, wealth, and so on, of various groups. When thinking about how to best help the people of other cultures, out of the spirit of humanitarianism, we often feel that they should try to be "more like us."

Cultural relativism suggests that we try to understand other people's culture and history on their own terms. Also, Americans often believe that the activities of the United States elsewhere in the world are always benevolent. Some people even believe that the United States is God's chosen land, and our motives are always above reproach. This is often displayed in our political system, which in turn creates value conflict.

Value Conflict

Because of the diversity of our culture the values of one group are often in conflict with the values of other groups. Value flashpoints occur in relation to governmental issues, social issues, religious issues, and economic issues. Religious values issues currently focus on the role of women in the church, contraception, abortion rights, school prayer, the relationship of the church to the state, and issues associated with evolution. Those with traditional religious values and beliefs believe that the function of sex is reproduction; therefore women should not use contraception. For one thing, contraception might prevent childbearing, which is widely viewed as the traditional role for women. Secondly, contraception allows recreational sex to take place. While not every religious group supports school prayer, some of the more right-leaning denominations do, setting up **value conflicts** among religious groups and between secular groups and some religious groups. Most religious denominations subscribe to the creation story but some religious groups are more ardent than others, and would like to see the teaching of evolutionary science banned completely. Others would like to see creationism introduced into the classroom. Because of the great diversity among religious denominations there is disagreement between religious denominations on all of these issues.

A variety of social issues give rise to value conflicts. The rights of women in society have been greatly debated. Do women have the right to control their bodies? If so, does this extend to abortion rights? Do women have the right to equal pay with men? Do women have a right to labor in a workplace free from sexual harassment? If your answer is yes to most of these questions and you believe that women are the equals of men, you are probably a liberal feminist.

There are other value conflicts. These conflicts center on issues of bilingual education, immigration, affirmative action, civil liberties, the powers of the police, unions, and even globalization. Should gay couples be allowed to adopt? Do gay couples have the right to get married, or should they be restricted to civil unions? What about insurance and health care for gay partners? Should marijuana be legalized for medicinal purposes? Should the death penalty be abolished? As you can see, the list of value conflicts is long indeed. Your particular position on all of these values depends upon whether or not you are more or less liberal, whether or not you are male or female, whether or not you are more or less religious, what your particular religion is, and other important variables. The point is that the conflict over value issues is not likely to abate any time soon. Let us look more closely at some of these political conflicts.

Liberal-Conservative Conflict

Political socialization refers to the influences and experiences that lead people to define their political orientation as liberal or conservative. Young adults do not come into the political arena as blank slates. They are socialized with values and beliefs throughout their lives. So, the process of political socialization combines elements of both early and later influences. Thus, ideologies are formed and one associates themselves with liberal or conservative values and beliefs. Let's now look at the differences between the two camps.

Liberals believe in governmental action to achieve equal opportunity for all, and that it is the duty of the state to alleviate social ills and to protect civil liberties and individual and human rights. They believe the role of the government should be to guarantee that no one is in need. Liberals also believe that people are basically good. Liberal policies generally emphasize the need for the government to solve people's problems. Conversely, conservatives believe in personal responsibility, limited government, free markets, individual liberty, traditional American values, and a strong national defense. They believe the role of government should be to provide people the freedom necessary to pursue their own goals. Conservative policies generally emphasize empowerment of the individual to solve problems. Let us look at some of the flashpoint topics that create the most controversy between the two orientations.

Controversial Topics

Liberals believe in governmental action to achieve equal opportunity and equality for all, and that it is the duty of the state to alleviate social ills and to protect civil liberties and individual and human rights. They believe the role of the government should be to guarantee that no one is in need. Liberals also believe that people are basically good. Liberal policies generally emphasize the need for the government to solve people's problems.

Conservatives believe in personal responsibility, limited government, free markets, individual liberty, traditional American values, and a strong national defense. They believe the role of government should be to provide people the freedom necessary to pursue their own goals. Conservative policies generally emphasize empowerment of the individual to solve problems.

Abortion

Conservatives are more likely than are liberals to believe that human life begins at conception and, assuming that, believe that abortion is the murder of a human being. Nobody has the right to murder a human being. Conservatives also supported legislation to prohibit **partial birth abortions**, called the "Partial Birth Abortion Ban." The bill (HR760) passed both chambers of Congress: 281–142 in the House of Representatives on October 2, 2003, and 64–34 in the Senate on October 21, 2003, and was signed into law by President George W. Bush on November 5, 2003. Most liberals disagree with the conservative view of abortion believing that a fetus is not a human life—at least not in the early stages of embryonic development. The decision to have an abortion is a personal choice of a woman regarding her own body and the government should stay out of it. Women should be guaranteed the right to a safe and legal abortion, including partial birth abortion. In other words, control over her body.

Affirmative Action

Conservatives believe that people should be admitted to schools and hired for jobs based on their ability. They believe it to be unfair to use race as a factor in the selection process. Conservatives caution that reverse discrimination is not a solution for racism. Conversely, liberals believe that due to prevalent racism in the past, minorities were deprived of the same education and employment opportunities as whites and that our society needs to make up for that. They support affirmative action based on the belief that America is still a racist society. Minorities still lag behind whites in all statistical measurements of success. Also, the presence of minorities creates diversity.

Death Penalty

Most conservatives believe in the death penalty. They consider the death penalty a punishment that fits the crime; it is neither "cruel" nor "unusual." They believe that executing a murderer is the appropriate punishment for taking an innocent life, whereas most liberals believe that we should abolish the death penalty. They believe the death penalty is inhumane and is "cruel and unusual" punishment. It does not deter crime; therefore, imprisonment is the appropriate punishment. Every time a person is executed we run the risk of killing an innocent person.

Economy

Conservatives believe that the free market system, competitive capitalism, and private enterprise afford the widest opportunity and the highest standard of living for all. Free markets produce more economic growth, more jobs, and higher standards of living than those systems burdened by excessive government regulation. Liberals favor a market system in which government regulates the economy. They believe we need government to protect us against big businesses. Unlike the private sector, the government is alleged to be motivated by public interest and we need government regulation to level the playing field.

Education

School vouchers are a major concern when it comes to education. Conservatives believe that school vouchers will give all parents the right to choose good schools for their children, not just those who can afford private schools. Parents (who pay the taxes that fund the schools) should decide how and where to educate their child. But liberals are not in agreement. They consider that school vouchers are untested experiments. Liberals believe that we need to focus on more funding for existing public schools and to raise teacher salaries and reduce class size.

173

Environment

Conservatives desire clean water, clean air, and a clean planet, just like everyone else. However, they believe that extreme environmental policies destroy jobs and damage the economy. They allude to the belief that changes in global temperatures are natural over long periods of time. They also contend that so far, science has not shown that humans can affect permanent change to the earth's temperature. Liberals are very vocal about the views of the conservative on this issue. Liberals believe that conservatives don't care about protecting the environment. Liberals are concerned that industrial growth, without environmental protection policies, can damage the environment. Global warming is caused by an increased production of carbon dioxide, and since the U.S. is a major contributor to global warming because it produces 25% of the world's carbon dioxide, we should enact laws to significantly reduce that amount.

Gun Control

Conservatives propose that the Second Amendment gives the individual the right to keep and bear arms. They contend that gun control laws do not thwart criminals and that you have a right to defend yourself against criminals. Their conception is that more guns mean less crime. If one were to actually read and interpret the constitution accurately they would realize that the Second Amendment gives no individual the right to own a gun. It allows the state to keep an armed militia such as the National Guard.

Health Care

Conservatives believe that free healthcare provided by the government (socialized medicine) only means that everyone will get the same poor-quality healthcare. The rich will continue to pay for superior healthcare, while all others will receive poor-quality free healthcare from the government. They believe that health care should remain privatized. Liberals, on the other hand support universal government-supervised health care. Since there are millions of Americans who can't afford health insurance, they are being deprived of a basic right to healthcare. This is a serious matter deserving of a chapter all to itself.

Immigration

This is a very touchy matter at the moment. Conservatives support legal immigration at current numbers, but do not support illegal immigration. They contend that government should enforce immigration laws. Many conservatives oppose President Bush's amnesty plan for illegal immigrants. They believe those who break the law by entering the U.S. illegally should not have the same rights as those who obey the law by entering legally. If there were a decrease in cheap, illegal immigrant labor, employers would have to substitute higher-priced domestic employees, legal immigrants, or perhaps increase mechanization. Liberals support legal immigration and increasing the number of legal immigrants permitted to enter the U.S. each year. They support blanket amnesty for current illegal immigrants and believe that regardless of how they came to the U.S., illegal immigrants deserve U.S. government financial aid for college tuition and visas for spouse and children to come to the U.S. Liberals believe that most illegal immigrants do the jobs that Americans do not want to do

Religion

Conservatives comment that the phrase "separation of church and state" is not in the Constitution. The First Amendment to the Constitution states "Congress shall make no law respecting an establishment of religion, or prohibiting the free exercise thereof..." Therefore this prevents the government from establishing a national church. However, it does not prevent God from being acknowledged in schools and government buildings. Conservatives oppose the removal of symbols of Christian heritage from public and government spaces and contend that government should not interfere with religion and religious freedom. Liberals support the separation of church and state. They believe that religious expression has no place in government and support the removal of all references to God in public and government spaces.

Same-Sex Marriage

As for same sex marriage, conservatives believe that marriage is between one man and one woman, although opinions differ on support for the creation of a constitutional amendment establishing marriage as the union of one man and one woman. Many conservatives believe that requiring citizens to sanction same-sex relationships violates moral and religious beliefs of millions of Christians, Jews, Muslims and others who believe marriage is the union of a man and a woman. Liberals are much more likely to believe that marriage should be legal for gay, lesbian, bisexual and transgender couples to ensure equal rights for all. All individuals, regardless of their sex, have the right to marry. Liberals believe that prohibiting same-sex citizens from marrying denies them of their civil rights. Again, opinions differ on whether this issue is equal to the importance of civil rights for African Americans.

Social Security

Conservatives are very vocal about the nature and future of the Social Security system. They believe the current Social Security system is in serious financial trouble.

Conservatives believe that changes are necessary because the U.S. will be unable to maintain the current system it in the future. They support proposals that allow a portion of Social Security dollars withheld be used in an account chosen by the individual, not the government. Liberals generally oppose change to the current Social Security system. Of course, opinions vary on whether the current system is in financial trouble. Many liberals believe that changing the current system will cause people to lose their Social Security benefits. Liberals also support a cap on Social Security payments to the wealthy.

Taxes

Conservatives support lower taxes and a smaller government. Lower taxes create more incentive for people to work, save, invest, and engage in entrepreneurial endeavors. Most conservatives believe that money is best spent by those who earn it. Liberals have a different view on taxes. Liberals support higher taxes and a larger government. Higher taxes help fund social welfare programs and create jobs for the poor.

War in Iraq

Conservatives pronounce that the attack on Iraq was a preemptive strike to protect the U.S. All intelligence indicated that Saddam Hussein possessed and used weapons of mass destruction (WMDs) in the past and was prepared to use them again. He would not allow United Nations weapons inspectors to confirm his claim that he had destroyed his WMDs, so there was no other option. Conservatives believe that a democracy can succeed in Iraq if the people are given the opportunity to create one, and that all people want to live in freedom. The liberal view is much different. Many liberals believe that this is George Bush's war for oil and that Saddam Hussein was no real threat. We have not found weapons of mass destruction (WMDs), therefore it is believed that Saddam did not have any. Liberals believe that President Bush lied about WMDs and the dangers posed by Saddam, and that we should have given the UN more time. We have alienated the rest of the world by our unilateral action, the "go it alone" attitude. A democracy can't succeed in Iraq if they do not want to live in one.

Welfare

Most conservatives oppose long-term welfare. They believe that we need to provide opportunities to make it possible for poor and low-income workers to become self-reliant and that it is far more compassionate and effective to encourage a person to become self-reliant, rather than keeping them dependent on the government for money. Liberals generally support welfare. They believe that welfare provides (minimally) for the poor—

especially for the poor who cannot work. We have welfare to bring fairness to American economic life. Without welfare, life below the poverty line would be intolerable.

Basically, liberals and conservatives differ on many topics but one must remember that there is a lot of overlap between the two. Those in office are usually members of the affluent classes, so although liberals are more in favor of helping the poor, they are not often willing to give up much if any of their own wealth.

ॐ ॐ ॐ ॐ

REFERENCES

Bachrach, P., & Baratz, M. S. (1962). Two faces of power. *American Political Science Review, 56,* 947-52.

Barlett, D. L., & Steele, J. B. (1994). *America: Who really pays the taxes.* New York: Simon & Schuster.

Barlett, D. L., & Steele, J. B. (1998, November 9). Corporate welfare. *Time,* Vol. 152, No. 19, 36-54.

Barlett, D. L., & Steele, J. B. (2000, May 15). Soaked by Congress. *Time,* pp. 64-75.

Barlett, D. L., & Steele, J. B. (2000, February 7). How the little guy gets crunched. *Time,* pp. 40-43.

Blau, P. M. (1964). *Exchange and power in social life.* New York: John Wiley & Sons.

Beeghley, L. (2000). The Structure of Social Stratification in the United States, 3rd ed. Boston: Allyn and Bacon.

Bellah, R. N., McNeely, M.R., Sullivan, W. M., Swindler, A. & Tipton, S.A. (1985). *Habits of the heart: Individualism and commitment in American life.* Berkeley: University of California Press.

Connolly, W. E. (1969). *The Bias of Pluralism.* New York: Lieber-Atherton.

Cunningham, F. (1975). Pluralism and Class Struggle. *Science and Society, 39,* 385-416.

Dahl, R. A. (1982). *Dilemmas of Pluralist Democracy.* New Haven, CT: Yale University Press.

Dahrendorf, R. (1958). Toward a theory of social conflict. *Journal of Conflict Resolution, 2,* 178-83.

Dahrendorf, R. (1959). *Class and class conflict in industrial society.* Stanford, CA: Stanford University Press.

Emerson, R. M. (1962). Power-dependence relations. *American Sociological Review, 27,* 31-41.

Gans, H. J. (1968). *More equality.* New York: Vintage Books.

Gerth, H. H., & Mills, C. W. (Eds.). (1962). *From Max Weber: Essays in Sociology.* New York: Oxford University Press.

Getter, L. (2004, May 4). Bush, Kerry awash in money. *Los Angeles Times.*

Higley, J., & Moore, G. (1981). Elite integration in the United States and Australia. *American Political Science Review, 75,* 581-97.

Bill H.R. 760 Report No. 108–58 108th Congress. Retrieved June 3, 2007 from http://frwebgate.access.gpo.gov

Huffingtion, A. (2003). *Pigs at the trough: How corporate greed and political corruption are undermining America.* New York: Crown.

Hurst, C. E. (1995). *Social inequality: Forms, causes, and consequences* (2nd ed.).Needham Heights, MA. Allyn & Bacon.

Ivins, M. (2000, May15). Capitalism gets a really bad name. *Progressive Populist,* pp. 22-23.

Jansson, B. S. (1990). *Social welfare policy: From theory to practice.* Belmont CA: Wadsworth.

Judis, J. B. (1990, January 21). Pulling U.S. strings: Japanese money buys influence. *Akron Beacon Journal,* pp. E1, E4.

Keller, S. (1969). Beyond the ruling class – Strategic elites. In C.S. Heller (Ed.), *Structured Social*

Inequality (pp. 520-524). New York: Macmillan.

Lindblom, C. E. (1977). *Politics and Markets.* New York: Basic Books.

Martin, R. (1971). The concept of power: A critical defense. *British Journal ofSociology, 22,* 240-257.

Manley, J. F. (1983). Neo-Pluralism: A class analysis of pluralism I and pluralism II. *American Political Science Review, 77,* 368-383.

McFarland, A. S. (1987). Interest groups and theories of power in America. *British Journal of Political Science, 17,* 129-147.

Mills, C. Wright. (1956). *The power elite.* New York: Oxford University Press.

Mosca, G. (1939). *The ruling class.* New York: McGraw-Hill.

Parenti, M. (1978). *Power and the powerless* (2nd ed.). New York: St. Martin's Press.

Parenti, M. (2002). *Democracy for the few* (7th ed.). New York: Bedford/St. Martian's Press.

Presthus, R. (1962). *The organization society.* New York: Vintage Books.

Phillips, K. (1995, December 22). Today's 'Gingrichomics' echoes GOP eras of old. *Christian Science Monitor.*

Phillips, K. (2002). *Wealth and Democracy: A political history of the American rich.* New York: Broadway Books.

Piven, F. F. (1996). Welfare and the transformation of electoral politics. *Dissent, 43,* 61-67.

Piven F. F, & Cloward, R. A. (1971). *Regulating the poor.* New York: RandomHouse.

Rybczynski, W. (1991). *Waiting for the weekend.* New York: Viking.

178

9 | *THE INDIVIDUAL AND RELIGION*
by Frank O. Taylor, Ph.D. and Lawrence J. Mencotti, Ph.D.

Our major concern in this chapter is to turn the sociological perspective on the institution of religion. Which is to say sociologists approach the phenomenon of religion in a way very different from theologians, clergy, or the laity. That is, sociologists do not address the truth or validity of religious practices or practitioners. Rather, and please heed this warning, sociologists analyze religions, religious belief, religious ritual, and religious behavior as fundamentally no different than that of any other social institutions. Where true believers see their religion, religiosity, and religious life in terms of the sacred sociologists consider religions to be, at bottom, human creations. Thus rather than supernatural awe sociologists' approach religion as a fascinating but ultimately naturally occurring phenomenon.

Undoubtedly the sociological analysis of religion is distasteful to some readers and perhaps to others downright sacrilegious. So be it, since sociology as a discipline is certainly not to everyone's taste. So with those caveats in place let us proceed.

A SOCIOLOGIST'S VIEW OF RELIGION

Sociologists are less interested in the origins of religion and are more interested in religion as a social and group phenomenon. Sociologists believe that religious beliefs, faith, and religious behaviors derive their meaning, and become meaningful, from group interaction. In other words, individuals who are tightly bound to religious groups and interact with members of the group frequently, are more likely to claim higher levels of religiosity than individuals who are not members of religious groups and organizations. Thus, sociologists are interested in the group dynamics, process, and interactions that take place in religious groups as people "become" religious.

One day I was out in the neighborhood in which I live taking a walk. I happened to pass a Catholic priest who was changing the catch-phrase posting on the marquee, a tactic used to get passersby to think about some religious message. This particular saying went like this: "First God; then love." I stopped and pointed out to the priest that I thought he had it wrong. He asked me what I thought the sign should say. My suggestion was: "First Mom; then love; then God." I think this surprised him somewhat as he was probably expecting me to say something stupid. He thought about it for a moment and said it was interesting but missed his point, which he explained was that unless you had a personal relationship with God and Jesus you could not really know what love was. Just to be argumentative, because I enjoy it, I pointed out that lots of children probably experience the love of their mother, and love their mothers, as well as other close relatives, long before he or she posses the ability for abstract thought, which would be a requirement to believe in God. At this point the priest began to frown a little, sensing I had a valid point. I pointed out, further, that until one mastered language and understood symbols, both of which require interaction with significant others, such as mothers and later teachers, one could hardly have any kind of relationship with God, at least not one you could personally be aware of. My point is that without socialization, mind and self would not develop. Without mind, one would lack the imagination to perceive an abstract concept like "god." Therefore, no mother no God. The priest chuckled and remarked that the point was taken. He then proceeded to put the sign up just as he had intended.

The French sociologist Emile Durkheim, one of the founders of sociology, argued that the pattern for religion is society itself. This is immediately evident. We live in a patriarchal society in which men have great power. God is widely perceived to be male. We believe in discipline before forgiveness. Catholics teach that people who are essentially saved, but have committed a variety of lesser sins, must go to purgatory before they can be admitted to heaven, where they will experience punishment. We have a system of unequal rewards resulting in a system of stratification. You know – an upper class and a lower class. In heaven, we are often taught, there are many rooms, some closer to God, and some further away. Your mind, housed both in your brain and between you and the people you interact with, is the location of many wonderful thoughts. Your feet, as you get older, ache, and sometimes even stink. Your head is up; your feet are down. Heaven is often thought of as being above us while hell is below us.

Durkheim's point is that the real object of worship in any religion is actually society itself. Even the idea of a soul is a symbolic representation of the **a priori** nature of society – it exists prior to us, and it continues to exist after we are dead. Many of you were named after members of your family who have died. This is how, in part, the departed live on long after they are dead. Religion, in this respect, is something that society invents to legitimate its values and norms. It is interesting to note the religious similarities among many ancient cultures. The myth concerning a god-man who is born of humble origins, of a mortal man and virgin mother, who offers his followers a path to salvation, is persecuted, executed, and finally resurrected, was part of ancient pagan religious beliefs in Egypt, Greece, and Persia. In Egypt the god-man was Osiris. In Persia he was known as Mithras. In Greece he was known as Dionysius. In the ancient world, death and resurrection were common religious themes, which suggest a concern with the ultimate survival of humanity.

Durkheim suggested that religion serves many beneficial social functions. First, every member of society must pass through a cycle of life or phases. Society must prepare individuals for their future roles. Largely, that is why you are reading this book. Rituals impose self-discipline, which is necessary for social life. Second, society can only continue to exist if people are bonded to it and respect it. Thus, ceremonial rituals help individuals achieve a sense of belonging and connection to society and the past. Third, religious ceremonies and rituals help make people aware of their shared heritage. Fourth, when faced with disaster or calamity, such as was experienced after the terrorist attacks on 9/11 or in the wake of Hurricane Katrina, religion helps people reestablish a sense of order and well being.

Guy Swanson builds on Durkheim's theory. Swanson defines spirits as organized clusters of statuses and roles. Each spirit stands for a set of patterns already present in society. God largely reflects the social script for most fathers. Fathers are expected to provide for their family's welfare, including housing, food, clothing, security and so on. The Virgin Mary largely reflects the social script for mothers. Mothers are charged with love, devotion, and nurturing. Swanson points out that reincarnation is more likely to develop in communities characterized by intimate long-lasting and interdependent social relations. In these types of societies, the intimate social relationships survive the members who were involved at any given time – the memory of the departed tends to linger on.

Rational choice theory in sociology suggests that people try to maximize social rewards in any economy they happen to find themselves in through rational choices. In other words, people try to figure out what the rules are and maximize their returns within whatever framework they interact, economic, social, or religious. People try to achieve a range of goals from those available to them and understand the costs needed to get there. Over time, people develop schemas associated with past successes and failures to which they refer when making decisions. Religion is just another aspect of life that requires reasoned decision making.

BECOMING RELIGIOUS

People are not born with religious instincts. People become religious through a process of socialization and learning. Human infants may be predisposed toward interaction with other humans, known as **sociation**. But the nature of that interaction will be socially conditioned by whatever group the individual happens to be born into. The infant learns religious beliefs much like anything else, such as language or gender scripts. A child born to a family with no religious affiliations can be expected to receive very little in the way of informal or formal religious socialization. On the other hand, a child born to a Catholic family, for example, that has intense interactions with the church can be expected to experience greater levels of both informal and formal socialization.

On the informal side, families with religious involvements and beliefs often pray together, attend church together, and perhaps attend other social functions at church. Formal religious socialization is often in the hands of Sunday school teachers and priests or ministers. Quite often, religious bodies hold seminars for their teachers and publish lessons and books in which church doctrine is elaborated. Sermons, for example, are often used to elaborate and teach, as well as reinforce what church members can reasonably be expected to already know. The point is that becoming religious is fundamentally a group process through which new members are inducted and existing members are maintained.

Sociologists refer to the range of behaviors associated with religion and the intensity of religious beliefs as **religiosity**, which refers to the issue of how religious people are. Obviously, one can be more religious or less religious. People with high levels of religiosity can be expected to exhibit more religious behaviors, such as attending church services and other social events, are more likely to be involved in ritual observances, such as participating in the Sacrament, are more likely to contribute financially to their church, and overall, participate more actively in congregational life. Someone who attends church less frequently, who does not contribute financially, and almost never participates in their church's religious rituals, except for maybe Easter and Christmas, can be said to have lower levels of religiosity.

We must be careful when trying to measure religiosity, sociologically speaking. Some individuals may attend church very little but have extremely deep and intense beliefs; others may attend church frequently but have superficial beliefs. There are two popular methods for measuring religiosity among sociologists: comparison between groups and within groups, and the individual approach. Some sociologists who take the group affiliation approach try to predict and observe differences in people's behavior and attitudes based on their religious affiliations. Many sociologists have studied the differences between major religious families, such as Protestant, Catholic, or Jewish on attitudes toward homosexuality, the right to die, and prayer in public schools. Other sociologists have used religious affiliation to examine differences in attitudes and behaviors between groups within the same religious family on important dimensions or religiosity. For example, Catholics and Protestants are from the same religious family, both are Christian. Additionally, Protestant denominations range from extremely conservative to extremely liberal and have differing positions on important doctrinal issues, such as the divinity of Jesus, the virgin birth, and the miracles described in the bible.

Some sociologists take the individual approach, which is more narrowly defined as the degree and type of commitment to religious values and norms. This approach recognizes the diversity among members of the same group relative to commitment and intensity of belief. These sociologists are interested in several measures of individual participation, such as the frequency of church attendance, attendance at other activities, such as prayer groups and dinners, and how often such individuals take communion. The general feeling is that if the person is more involved in these activities than not, they can be said to have higher levels of religiosity. There are other measures of individual participation, such as frequency of prayer, and even self-identification on religiosity surveys on a question or range of questions concerning the intensity of beliefs. These surveys typically ask the respondent to evaluate how important religion is to them personally. Clearly, religiosity is not one-dimensional. People are religious in different ways. One person may rank high on one or more measures of religiosity but low on others.

Looking at individual measures of religiosity, Joseph Fichter identified four ways in which a person could be Catholic. He labeled those highly involved in parish life as **Nuclear Catholics**. Those who generally observe the rituals, such as not eating meat on Fridays and Lent, and attend mass most of the time, he labeled as **Model Catholics**. Some Catholics almost never attend church beyond weddings, funerals, and occasionally at Christmas. They are **Marginal Catholics**. **Dormant Catholics** are not members of any particular church but were baptized and confirmed as Catholics and will probably want to be married by a Catholic priest and have the priest administer their last rites.

Glock and Stark were interested in how people experience religion and how the same individual can be more religious on one measure than on another. They identified five dimensions of religiosity. The experiential dimension refers to the degree to which the individual is emotionally attached to the supernatural. The ritualistic dimension refers to the rate of participation in religious activities. Glock and Stark divided the ritualistic dimension into two other categories: ritual, which refers to formal religious activities, and devotion, praying and studying sacred books and religious writings.

I have mentioned that children internalize religion in much the same manner as they learn language, sex roles, and other important roles associated with self and identity. What we are interested in here can be called growing up religious. Involvement in any agent of socialization, such as the family, the school, and the mass media is linked to the development of one's personality and self-concept. It is no different for religion. Children learn how others expect them to behave and begin to see themselves from various perspectives and various roles as they are exposed to the agents of socialization. Thus, when children are formally and informally socialized in religious settings they begin to internalize a religious attitude and the values associated with their particular congregation. This is a fairly complex process. In the beginning children are only capable of mimicking and emulating their parents. Nevertheless, they begin to learn a great deal about their religions. They start with simple group identification and from there, through socialization, they learn more about their particular group and differences from other religious groups. As the person matures they learn more about other groups and can begin to identify the other religious groups and some of their beliefs. Eventually, as a young adult they begin to understand the abstract values and beliefs of their religious group. Thus, children attain a religious orientation long before they confront such issues in the form of religious doctrines and ideas. For example, children learn the differential behaviors and duties associated with women and men in their church long before they understand that these behaviors are associated with inequality in the broader culture.

Initially, then, religious socialization takes place almost exclusively in the home and is informal in nature. Later, as the child matures, informal socialization is replaced by formal learning in-group settings. The family is an important location of religious socialization for most children. If the family has some religious affiliation, even if only weakly, a significant portion of religious socialization may take place. Some religious groups have programs specifically aimed at helping families with the religious socialization of their children, although some studies indicate that they may not be very effective. Families can include religious practices in their everyday interactions – such as praying at the dinner table and saying prayers in the evenings. Additionally, families can filter out religious influences for other groups. For instance, many religious groups have missionaries who go door-to-door and try to gain converts. However, if there is a gate-keeper in the household, their message cannot make it beyond the front door. Some families send their children to religious or other parochial schools, which try to reinforce formal religious doctrine.

However, many families tend to fall far short of the expectations of the various religious groups they are involved with when it comes to the reinforcement of formal religious socialization. It turns out that some factors are more important than specialized parochial schools. Most important for young people is the presence of peers they like to interact with. If the child has peers involved in religious activities they are more likely to join in. Also, children whose parents attend church regularly are much more likely to have higher levels of religiosity then children whose parents do not attend church regularly.

Not everyone grows up experiencing religious socialization as a matter of fulfilling parental wishes. Some people convert to one religion or another. Conversion often occurs during adolescence and may be related to sexual guilt and anxiety that may accompany the development of sexual identity (sexual desires and propensities, although entirely normal, come in for special attention by most religious groups). Age, thus, is a major factor in conversion but not the only one. People most likely to convert share some important characteristics. For most of them, religious influences existed prior to their conversion. Family members may already be part of the religious group they are interested in and, in fact, the individual may already be involved in the lifestyle of the group. Many people eventually convert to religions they are essentially "trying out." Groups are interested in gaining more members so it is not surprising that they attempt to control the conditions potential members encounter and manipulate the interactions.

There are generally three important factors involved in religious conversion. First are predisposing conditions. The convert may be experiencing emotional tension and stress. This stress may be related to job loss, illness, educational failure, relationship problems, and the like. However, traditional solutions to stress are closed off. The person is not able to seek counseling and they do not have other statuses to which they can shift their focus. People with a variety of interesting statuses can often deal with stress by de-emphasizing the stress related status and emphasizing other statuses. Thus, the person has few avenues available to relieve the stress. Situational factors are also important. Commonly, the tipping point in some crisis has been reached. They are looking for help. If affective relationships outside the group are weak and the person has been intensively involved with the group and has formed close bonds with people in the group, under these conditions they are extremely likely to convert.

There are a variety of ways and conditions in which people decide to convert to religious groups. People may start by intellectually investigating the group. Here they read what they can find about the group and become familiar with the group's values and beliefs. Some people report having a mystical conversion, in which they experienced a high level of emotional arousal. Other people convert based on experimentation with a number of groups or one group over a period of time. Some people form affectional bonds with members of a particular group. Some people attend church revivals and convert to a religious group in a public and dramatic fashion. Lastly, some people are simply the victims of brainwashing or programming. Researchers agree about two things. First, people who have prior affective bonds to one or more group members, a family member for instance, is a member of the group, are more likely to convert. Second, conversion is frequently a result of intensive interaction with the group.

Very frequently, people decide to withdraw from religious life and activities. In other words, they deconvert. Deconversion is likely when individuals disengage from the social activities of the group or disassociate from those within the group they were bonded to. Like any other group, religious groups have to "deliver the goods," so to speak. They have to provide members with a meaningful framework, solutions to problems, security, and other similar goals. When groups can no longer provide those goods membership may decline.

RELIGION POLITICS AND VOTING BEHAVIOR

At first glance, you may wonder how religion could possibly impact voting behaviors. However, just look at the long list of issues that have religious overtones: abortion rights, school prayer, God in the Pledge of Allegiance, and American intervention around the world, often based on the belief that God is at work in the destiny of the United States and that we have a duty to bring about God's work for humankind. The theology and doctrine of any particular religious group will dictate its stand on any of these issues. Some religious groups support political activism and defend it as a legitimate area in which believers can be active. When these issues become part of the political process or legislation is proposed related to these religious flashpoints, religion can and does affect people's voting behavior.

Religion not only affects peoples voting rate, it affects who people vote for and how they vote in regard to proposed legislation. One's beliefs about God, morality, ethics, and other religious values, influence the political choices one makes. Oftentimes, candidates try to get the vote of specific groups of religious people, such as the "Evangelical vote," or the "Catholic vote." Also, voting patterns can be affected by social class. If the denomination is predominately working class, members of the congregation are more likely to vote for Democrats. Conversely, denominations that are more upper class are more likely to vote for Republicans. In general, Protestants are more likely to vote Republican whereas Catholics are more likely to vote Democrat. However, it is important to note that in recent years, there has been some waning of support for the Democrats among Catholics due to theological issues--especially abortion. The Democratic Party is much more likely to support abortion rights, for example. In spite of the conservative political positions of the Catholic Church, however, more Catholics than Protestants subscribe to liberal social and political viewpoints. Jews are even more likely than Catholics to vote for Democrats. It is important to remember that many variables affect how we vote and at no time has voting been strictly religious.

RELIGION AND CONFLICT

A functional analysis of religion will point out all ways in which religion is functional and beneficial for society. Religion helps people deal with the unknown and unknowable. It provides a framework for living. Religion also gives meaning to life. Frequently, social cohesion is enhanced by religion. But there is a flip-side to this coin as well. An analysis of religion based on the ideas of conflict theory will point out the negative aspects of religion for individuals and society. It does not take much effort to realize that religion has been at the heart of a great deal of conflict and war, for example. The list of religious conflicts is long indeed, and includes wars between the Israelites, who believed they were God's chosen people, and the others who they tired to deprive of their land, the holy wars or crusades between Christians and Muslims, the Catholic church's use of the Inquisition to subdue dissent, the Protestant-Catholic guerrilla war in Northern Ireland, and the current Israeli-Palestinian conflict, just to name a few.

On an individual level, religion often creates unique forms of stress, worry, and anxiety. Feelings of guilt, or having sinned, often accompany high levels of religiosity. And as mentioned above, religion is often related to sexual hang-ups. Most religions, and certainly the Christian denominations, see sex primarily as a means for reproduction of the species, not as an avenue for pleasure. In modern Western society, sexual mores have undergone a long process of liberalization. In the new sexual script it is perceived as acceptable to have sex for sex's sake, so long as precautions are, hopefully, taken and the activity is consensual. Additionally, religious doctrine is often at the heart of other conflicts between individuals and groups, on a whole range of issues, such as abortion rights, homosexuality, the death penalty, and euthanasia, separation of church and state, and prayer in school.

Telling people that their natural state is one of sin, and that only the activities of ordained specialists can cleanse them of their sins, certainly guarantees the status and position of the ordained. In this sense, religion can be used to exploit others. This is the point of view of Karl Marx, who viewed religion as the opium of the people. His argument was that religion can be used to deflect the legitimate dissatisfaction of those who are sick, poor, hungry, overworked, or mistreated by those in power, for their own personal gain, to some future reward received in heaven. Marx's point was that the "will of God" is not the cause of human suffering and misery, economic policies and the activities of the affluent are. Marx was not saying that the bible says the poor are to blame for their problems. Marx was pointing out that religion can be used to tell people to accept their fate and place in life as the will of God. This becomes easier to accomplish if people believe that their suffering on Earth will be rewarded in heaven and that those who exploited them on Earth will be punished. The message that people should work hard and perform their job to the best of their ability and look for a reward in heaven is used by the elite class to keep the poor in their place and to prevent the possibility of social mobilization of the poor. In short, religion can be used as a tool to keep poor people from recognizing their common misery and taking action, namely revolt.

Modern individuals, who are virtually surrounded by scientific advancements and the technology born of that science, must, if they are even slightly religious, deal with internal conflicts that surround religious teaching. These conflicts are an example of **cognitive dissonance**. It is nearly impossible to dispute the advances of modern science. How difficult then, is it to believe in some of the teachings in the bible that are part and parcel of the doctrine of major Christian denominations. For example, how was it possible for Moses to part the red sea, or to call forth any of the plagues he supposedly did to punish the Egyptian pharaoh, particularly in light of modern scientific explanations of such events? To take another example was blood responsible for the Nile River turning red or was it an algae bloom? Likewise, is it really possible for a person to live in the belly of whale, as we are told Jonah did? Is it possible for a virgin to conceive? Can wine and bread really, actually, be the body and blood of Christ? And those are just some of the lower level issues. Some issues seem to be even more abstract, such as the issue of the proper mode of baptism or whether or not children should be baptized. Once one begins to question the lower level issues it is but a short leap to the higher level questions. Did Jesus really live? If he did, was he married and did he have children? Was he resurrected and will he return again? These questions lead directly to the big one, is there a God?

It should be pointed out that many people do not necessarily believe that there is an automatic tension between science and religion. Some are comfortable with the notion that the laws of nature are God's laws. The great scientist and father of modern physics, Newton, certainly believed that by observing nature first-hand, he was seeing the hand of God in action. Thus, many thoroughly modern people with pro-science outlooks can maintain some of their religious beliefs. But new tensions keep arising. The current debates over stem-cells and cloning illustrates the point. Is there a point at which human beings, using science, are playing God? Clearly, due to scientific advances, humans stand on the threshold of achieving great control over the nature and direction of future human development. Once the human genome is mastered and unraveled, great questions will have to be faced. Should the genes associated with certain types of illness and disability be removed from the genome? If you say yes to this question, do you assume that a child with Down's syndrome would live a diminished, unfulfilled, and meaningless life? What about skin color, body type, height and so on? Will we eliminate just cancer or will we tinker with our basic humanity?

People with more liberal leanings, and in particular those with higher education, tend to see the stories in the bible as allegories and parables, meant to spark our thinking on moral and ethical behavior, and not to be accepted as actual events. Fundamentalists, on the other hand, tend to take a more literal approach to the stories in the bible and accept them as the literal truth. This, of course, sets the stage for conflicts between individuals of faith on such issues. For example, most Congregationalists, Methodists, and Episcopalians, cannot accept the stories in the bible at face value. In other Christian denominations, which once accepted traditional beliefs and interpretations regarding the stories, questions have begun to emerge and conflicts have emerged. For example, the African Bishops of the Episcopal Church have threatened to split from the Anglicans over the issue of homosexual marriage.

RELIGION AND GENDER

In hunting and gathering societies, where women produced most of the food, they enjoyed status equal to that of men. However, with the rise of agricultural societies and technological innovations, such as the plow, men became more involved in the production of food and the status of women began to experience a decline. Agricultural societies produce more food, which means surpluses. Food surpluses, in turn, mean people are freed from the production of food to do other things, such as trade, or make handicrafts, and so on, leading to a more complex division of labor. With agriculture and increases in the complexity of the division of labor came private property. Patriarchal societies are interested in passing wealth through the male line, and thus the sexuality of women had to be controlled so that men were certain about their relationship to their children.

As men began to curb women's power and contribution to society, female deities had to be eliminated. Tracing the history of the fall of the feminine side of God clearly demonstrates that religion is a social product. It would be rather hard to keep women in an inferior position in society if God were female. Archeological evidence suggests that, throughout the ancient world, God was, in fact, female. Since only women can bear children, and the whole act of reproduction was rather mysterious to the ancients, especially menstruation, any man who bled in a similar fashion was bound to die; the motherhood status had a special distinction. No man lived except by virtue of being birthed by a mother. Additionally, the exact science of the egg and sperm had not been worked out, so the male contribution to reproduction of the species was not well understood. A logical extension of the motherhood role was the divine feminine, or goddess.

History is replete with goddess. The Egyptians believed that the goddess Nekhebt was the supreme creator. Isis, another Egyptian goddess, was the personification of motherhood. Anat, and her rival Asherah, were both goddesses worshiped in Palestine. Asarte was the Philistine goddess of procreation. These important goddesses were eventually displaced by masculine gods as men began to rise in prominence and importance in agricultural societies such as Egypt, Rome, and Greece. In Egypt, Ra replaced Nekhebt. Yahweh replaces Anat and Asherah. In Greece, Zeus becomes the primary God. As patriarchal social relations began to emerge the divine feminine was pushed out of religion. Around 1000 B.C. in India, where, for example, there where several important female goddess, women enjoyed near equality with men. However, with the rise of Hinduism, women became inferior and it soon became doubtful if women could even gain salvation if she was not reborn as a man. Even today, Orthodox Jews recite a prayer in which they thank the Lord for not being born a woman. In Christianity, it is well known that Saint Paul viewed women as inferior to men, based on his claim that Adam was created first, and that Eve was created from his rib and had deceived him, thus blaming women for "original" sin.

Although there has been significant movement toward greater roles for women in the church in recent years, most of the major religions define women as inferior to men and as dependent on men. The Catholic Church stands out in this respect. Few religious opportunities were available for women until very recently. In Christianity, women's inferior position is based on several themes. Women are seen as temptresses who use their attractiveness and sexuality to beguile men away from celibacy and virginity, which have long been considered as superior to giving in to sexual drives. If a man does yield to his sexuality it should only be within the confines of the institution of marriage, where women should be silent, subordinate, and stay in the background. Muslim women were veiled from all eyes except their husband's. Leadership and decision making are reserved for men. Of course, this contradicts a number of themes in the bible. For example, Jesus treated women and men as equals, to the great displeasure of some of his disciples. He performed miracles on both women and men and singled women out for their strong expressions of faith. Additionally, Jesus had several women among his closest friends and confidants, such as Mary Magdalene.

Many women today adopt the tradition-affirming roles the major religions have circumscribed for them. That is, they tend to keep silent in church and refrain from trying to exercise any religious authority over men. Many women believe that, since their subservient roles are explained in the Bible, Koran, or Torah, female subordination is divinely ordained and they should not go against the "will of God." This view is prevalent among Catholics, Latter Day Saints (Mormons), and many other denominations. Many Islamic women are happy, for example, to cover themselves from head to foot, and to only go about in the company of a father, brother, uncle or husband. The idea of a "traditional family," is largely based on the family structure of patriarchy, in which women and children are subservient to husbands and fathers. Women stay in the home and nurture while husbands make the political, economic, and religious decisions. The Catholic Church provides specialized avenues for women who want to stay in traditional roles but not in the traditional family: female monastic orders. Female novices join monastic orders in large numbers worldwide, although their numbers have declined recently. Nevertheless, in spite of their specialized role in the Catholic Church, they are not allowed to behave like priests. In many denominations, women are usually in charge of kitchen duties during social events going on in the church.

The traditional view of women as emotional, vain, dependent, weak, and as divinely ordained to be caregivers was challenged by feminism. Feminists believe that women who subscribe to the traditional forms of religion, in which they are subservient, suffer from **false consciousness**. In other words, such women are unaware of the history of religious ideas and developments and are unaware that over the course of history men used religion to create and maintain patriarchal social systems. Women who believe in traditional religious values cannot make the connection between religious ideas and discrimination against women in the broader society. In the 19th Century, women who were committed to their religious values began to seek changes that would allow for greater roles for women in religious life, including ordination.

Today, many religious denominations, including Presbyterians, Lutherans, Episcopalians, and Unitarians, to name a few, permit the ordination of women. In recent years there has been a six-fold increase in the number of new female clergy, although this is still far behind other female professions. Most denominations which ordain women have only modest numbers, from four to six percent of all clergy. Nevertheless, about eighty percent of women who are ordained serve as pastors. Even though women have made major gains in the religious profession, most parishioners still prefer male pastors, and women tend to be assigned as "assistant or associate" pastors or to non-parish roles. There is still resistance to the ordination of women. The Catholic Church, Orthodox Judaism, and over one hundred other Christian denominations do not allow women to be ordained.

RELIGIOUS FUNDAMENTALISM

Religious fundamentalism is a religious movement that began in the early 1900s within American Protestantism. Conservative Protestants, informed by the ideas of **Calvinism**, became disturbed by the spread of secularism and liberal theology. **Secularism** refers to humanistic ideas, such as being charitable and equitable to all humans and an interest in social justice, but detached from any religious reference. In other words, secularism is concerned with civil and social service to humanity without the need of organized religion. **Liberation theology** views social justice, human rights, and helping the poor as *the* Christian, and specifically Roman Catholic, mission. Clearly, as previously discussed, feminist attempts to reconsider the role of women in religion through reinterpretation of scripture, known as feminist theology, is also part of liberal theology. **Process theology**, which holds that all experience, included that of women, the poor, homosexuals, and even the experiences of other forms of organic life, are interrelated and part of reality.

Liberal theology deserves an entire text of its own. Here I can only point out that secularism and liberal theology were threatening to organized religions, particularly the Catholic Church and the dominant Protestant denominations. Secularism and liberal theology represented social movements aimed at increasing the power of the poor, women, and the oppressed, at the expense of established religious, economic, and social leaders. Secularism is a threat to organized religion because it maintains that you can be a good, moral, and ethical person outside of the boundaries of religion. Religious leaders tend to see morality as the domain of the church, not civil society. The various forms of liberal theology were threatening because they might undo centuries of established religious doctrine and lead to radical changes, such as the ordination of women. Liberal theology is particularly threatening to patriarchy and the social structures that support it.

Secularism and liberal theology were outgrowths of modernization. Science and the growth of technology displaced previous views about the world. For example, many religious people believe that God made the world about six thousand years ago. This date is based on calculations a Jesuit priest made using data derived from the bible. This belief is hard to maintain in the face of modern science which can handily demonstrate, and conclusively, that the world is much older than six thousand years. In a sense, fundamentalists want to turn the clock back to earlier times when human beings relied on mystical and metaphysical explanations of reality.

Five trends of modernization have been connected to fundamentalism. First, the solidarity of small communities was destroyed by urbanization. Second, modern people, because they live in large communities, feel more anonymous and strongly adhere to a spirit of individualism. Third, modern people, unlike people of the past, are future oriented. They are concerned about education, careers, what is going on in the economy, and so on. This emphasis on the future often leads to uncertainty and anxiety. Modern individuals are simply less connected to the past and tradition. Fourth, modern people have choices and alternatives not available to people in the past. Lots of choice can lead to indecision. And fifth, secularization has displaced the old definitions of reality, which relied on God, with the explanations of science and reason. For these reasons, modern people sometimes feel adrift and disconnected from community, tradition, and the security of black and white explanations of reality provided by religious leaders.

Modernization was not the only process that led to the rise of fundamentalism in the United States. Science advanced the idea of empirical evidence rather than reliance on the Bible. Marxist social philosophy, with its emphasis on social justice is particularly threatening to religion. Calvinist religious doctrine states that only a small number of people will enter heaven. Consequently, one way of knowing whether or not you are among that number is to look for signs that God has favored you. Wealth and status could be construed as signs of such favor. Additionally, there are a number of other themes, such as hard work, thrift, savings, and so on, that would be directly threatened by a philosophy that suggests that wealth should be transferred from the elites to the poor. Of course, some churches are fantastically wealthy so any redistribution of wealth could cost them dearly. Darwinism, with the suggestion that humans may have evolved through natural selection from other primates, was especially objectionable. If humans did evolve over the long haul of history, the creation story would have to be abandoned. A growing emphasis on "civil society" was also perceived as a threat to the religious establishment. Liberals were emphasizing individual involvement in social service as a route to individual fulfillment and finding meaning of life outside of the Christian community. It takes little effort to conclude that many religious denominations would prefer civil government to get out of the business of charity for the poor because it diminishes both the role and power of churches. Lastly, academic scholars were beginning to publish material suggesting that the Bible is a human creation and the modern religions "evolved" out of older religions. Especially disturbing is the suggestion that many Christian beliefs and practices have their origins in paganism.

An early reaction to these developments occurred in 1910. The Christian Evangelicals published a manifesto of the basic Christian beliefs they felt were beyond reproach. Most of the ideas they supported are still around today. The Bible was divinely inspired. Jesus Christ was born of a virgin. Christ atoned for the sins of humanity through his death on the cross. Jesus was bodily resurrected and will come again as the savior of humankind. Jesus was God. Human beings are naturally sinful and can only be saved by the grace of God. Lastly, humans must accept Jesus as their savior or they cannot be resurrected on the last day. Fundamentalists are committed to traditional morality, are opposed to women's rights or abortion rights, are anti-gay rights and oppose gay marriage, are anti-intellectual, tend to favor the Republican political party, favor status-quo with respect to economic or racial discrimination, and tend to view those who do not agree with them as evil. Fundamentalists tend to see social programs to aid the poor as evil, probably due to the belief that all one has to do is accept Jesus as your personal savior and your life will become better. There is a tendency among fundamentalists to see poverty as God's will. Certainly, public welfare programs enable people not to seek out religious solutions to economic problems. In this sense, civil society is in competition with certain churches for "clients," i.e. the poor.

Today, the Fundamentalist Right is extremely active politically. Television, the internet and electronic mail, direct mail technology, and political action groups have given the new right the ability to mobilize large masses of people relatively quickly. **The New Right** is opposed to the legalization of abortion, pornography, and tolerance for homosexuality. They believe that the United States is the chosen instrument of God and that Christians have a moral obligation to use the democratic process to create a social system under their control. Fundamentalists seek to institute prayer and Bible reading in public schools. Additionally, given the opportunity, the New Right would abolish abortion rights and the Equal Rights Amendment. At the top of the fundamentalist agenda is the defeat of the entire liberal social experiment established by the United States Constitution and the political system that evolved from it. Modern fundamentalists seek to establish a **theocracy**. In this sense, the Theocratic Right would replace our democracy with a form of civil government ruled by religious elite, supposedly with God as the head. Civil law would be replaced by "Bible law," and government leaders would be members of a church. The Catholic Church and its Vatican bureaucracy is a prime example of a theocracy.

NEW DIRECTIONS IN RELIGION—ANIMISM REDUX

One of the earliest, if not the earliest, religious belief system was **animism**—the belief the rivers, trees, forests, inanimate objects and even animals possess a soul. Take a flood for example. If your preliterate tribe lives by a river and your entire livelihood depends upon farming the delta next to the river, and each year the river floods and leaves behind the nutrients necessary for your crops to be plentiful, you begin to understand that there is an underlying order to your life. But you know nothing about soil nutrients. You do not have a science of geology, thus you do not know precisely why the river floods each year. You only understand that if it does not flood, your crops are likely to fail, and you are likely to starve. It is no stretch of the imagination to see how a religion might evolve out of the belief that the river has a spirit and that the river spirit may at times be friendly toward you and at other times may be unfriendly. This would give preliterate people an explanation when the river either does not flood or floods too much, destroying the surrounding community.

Like other humans, the river could be seen to possess desire, will, moods, and personality. In order to keep the river spirit happy and cooperative, it might be a good idea to placate it with prayers, tributes, or sacrifices. This is how a spiritual world probably began to develop. People began to believe that rocks, rivers, and other things have spirits. These spirits were given human qualities. Once they had human qualities you could argue with them or try to persuade them to be cooperative. These forms of persuasion became highly ritualized, leading to the establishment of a system of religious beliefs. One of the earliest components of the division of labor in human societies was the development of a priestly caste. With the arrival of priesthood, some people were tasked with the specialization of dealing with the spirits. This, of course, was the beginning of organized religion and religious bureaucracy.

It is but one step from the belief that rivers have human qualities to the belief that human-like gods with great supernatural powers can affect the behavior of a river. It is quite possible in the evolution of religious belief systems that humans made the leap from believing that living things and inanimate objects are possessed by spirits, to the belief that the spirits have human-like qualities and personalities. From there the next step is to believe that human-like gods, with humanistic personalities and supernatural powers, favor or disfavor mortals by influencing inanimate objects, rivers, trees, and living things. Early human societies were organized around the family—soon family relationships among human-like gods emerged.

By the time agricultural societies began to emerge, complete with a division of labor and patriarchy, it is no surprise to find these social realities reflected in religious belief systems, where gods are related to each other and have specialization among them. If there is a tribal chief, there must be a chief god. Since most tribal chiefs were men, the chief god must be male. Since the original division of labor was based on sex, and women were responsible for housekeeping and nurturing, the god of love must be female. Since men were responsible for security and were familiar with weapons due to their hunting responsibly, the god of war must be male. This division of labor is clearly discernible in the religious beliefs of the Egyptians and Greeks. The anthropological explanation claims that people have a cognitive need to explain what is happening around them. Thus, preliterate people tended to rely on supernatural forces and beings to explain events.

Fast-forward to the present. One way of seeing post-modern society is the belief that old ways of thinking, believing, and doing the world are increasingly problematic. Perhaps the most comprehensive approach of questioning contemporary society and its discontents is to focus on the rapidly deteriorating environment that sustains, indeed is, the web of life on Earth. Environmental consciousness includes not just a radical critique of a mindless, consumerist society but also relocates the notion of the sacred as not residing with supernatural beings in some next-world paradise. Rather, environmentalism at least implicitly argues that the sacred exists in the here and now: in clean streams and air; in organic gardens and toxin-free food; and in zero-emission energy-use and sustainable agriculture and commerce. In a very real sense, modern environmental consciousness focuses not on some past mythical Eden but the idea that Eden is the Earth, the whole Earth, and nothing but the Earth itself and we are doing the devil's work by despoiling it. By putting the sacred back into the earth environmentalists are more akin to indigenous peoples who have held animistic beliefs than they are to patriarchal, hierarchical religions that function by facilitating the continuing destruction of the planet. Thus, to many environmentalists that old time religion, by ignoring environmental concerns, performs a latent dysfunction by implicitly endorsing business [and mindless consumption] as usual. In a secularized sense, environmentalism is the new animism: an evolving set of beliefs and practices that returns worship to the great Goddess: Mother Earth.

ಸಾ ೦೮ ಸಾ ೦೮

REFERENCES

Allport, G. W. (1957). *The individual and his religion.* New York: Macmillan.

Barker, E. (1984). *The making of a moonie.* Oxford, England: Basil Blackwell Publisher.

Borhek, J. T., & Curtis, R. F. (1975). *A sociology of belief.* New York: John Wiley.

Brass, P. R. (2003). *The production of Hindu-Muslim violence in contemporary India.* Seattle, WA: University of Washington Press.

Clark, W. H. (1958). *The psychology of religion.* New York: Macmillan.

Condran, J. G., & Tamney, J. B. (1985). Religious 'nones': 1957 to 1982. *Sociological Analysis, 46*(4), 415.

Cornwall, M. (1988). The influence of three agents of religious socialization: Family, church, and peers. In Darwin L. Thomas (Ed.), *The religion and family connection*, (p. 226). Provo, UT: Religious Studies Center, Brigham Young University.

Demerath, N. J., III, (1965). *Social class in American Protestantism.* Chicago: Rand McNally.

DeVinne, D. (1857). *The Methodist Episcopal Church and slavery.* New York: F. Hart.

Eliot, C. (1921). *Hinduism and Buddhism*, (Vol. 2, pp. 176-178). London: Routledge & Kegan Paul.

Elkind, D. (1964). Age changes in the meaning of religious identity. *Review of Religious Research, 6*(1), 36-40.

Engels, F. (1954). *Anti-Dühring.* Quoted in Freedman, *Marxist social thought*, (pp. 438-440). Moscow: Foreign Language Publishing House.

Fichter, J. (1951). *Southern Parish* (Chicago: University of Chicago Press,); idem *Social Relations in the Urban Parish* (Chicago: University of Chicago Press, 1954).

Gallup, G. (1979). *The Gallup Poll: Public opinion 1979.* Wilmington, DE: Scholarly Resources.

Gallup, G. (1984). *Religion in America 1984.* Gallup Report No. 222. Princeton, NJ: Princeton Religion Research Center.

Glock C. Y., & Stark, R. (1965). *Religion and society in tension.* Chicago: Rand Mcnally.

Glock C. Y., & Stark, R. (1966). *Christian beliefs and anti-Semitism.* New York: Harper & Row.

Glock, C. Y. (1959). The religious revival in America. In Jane Zahn (Ed.), *Religion and the face of America*, (pp. 25-42). Berkeley, CA: University of California.

Glock, C. Y. (1962). On the study of religious commitment. *Religious Education, 62*(4), 98-110.

Hadaway, C. K., & Roof, W. C. (1988). Apostasy in American churches: Evidence from national data. In David G. Bromley (Ed.), *Falling from the faith*, (pp. 29-46). Newbury Park, CA: Sage Publications.

Hadaway, C. K., Marler, P. L., & Chaves, M. (1993). What the polls don't show: A closer look at U.S. church attendance. *American Sociological Review, 58*(6), 744.

Hadden, J. K. (1969). *The gathering storm in the churches.* Garden City, NY: Doubleday.

Harrell, D. E., Jr., (1971). *White sects and Black men in the recent south.* Nashville, TN: Vanderbilt University Press.

Haselden, K. (1959). *The racial problem in Christian perspective.* New York: Harper & Row.

Hoffer, E. (1951). *The true believer.* New York: Mentor Books.

Hoge, D. R., & Petrillo, G. H. (1978). Determinants of church participation and attitudes among high school youth. *Journal for the Scientific Study of Religion, 17*(4), 359-379.

Jacobs, J. (1987). Deconversion from religious movements. *Journal for the Scientific Study of Religion, 26*(3), 294-308.

Jacquet, C. H., Jr., (Ed.), (1989). *Yearbook of American churches, 1989.* Nashville: Abingdon Press.

Johnstone, R. L. (1966). *The effectiveness of Lutheran elementary and secondary schools as agencies of Christian education.* St. Louis, MO: Concordia Seminary Research Center.

Juergensmeyer, M. (2000). *Terror in the mind of God.* Berkeley, CA: University of California Press.

Latourette, K. S. (1953). *A history of Christianity.* New York: Harper & Brothers.

Leaf, M. J. (1984). *Song of hope: The green revolution in a Punjab village.* New Brunswick, NJ: Rutgers University Press.

Lenski, G. E. (1961). *The religious factor.* Garden City, NY: Doubleday.

Levine, S. V. (1986). *Radical departures: Desperate detours to growing up.* New York: Harcourt Brace Jovanovich.

Ling, T. (1966). *Buddha, Marx, and God.* London: Macmillan.

Lofland, J. (1966). *Doomsday cult.* Englewood Cliffs, NJ: Prentice Hall.

Lofland, J., & Skonovd, N. (1981). Conversion motifs. *Journal for the Scientific Study of Religion, 20*(4), 373-385.

Marx, K. (1964). Contribution to the critique of Hegel's Philosophy of Right. In Reinhold Niebuhr (Ed.), *Marx and Engels on religion,* (p. 42). New York: Schocken Books.

Marx, K., & Engels, F. (1968). *Toward the criticism of Hegel's Philosophy of right.* (Glen Waas, Trans.) Quoted in Robert Freedman, *Marxist social thought* New York: Harcourt Brace Jovanovich.

Matlack, L. (1849) *History of American slavery and Methodism from 1780 to 1849.* New York: Lucius Matlack.

Mattison, H. (1859). *The impending crisis of 1860.* New York: Mason Brothers.

Moellering, R. (1965). *Christian conscience and Negro emancipation.* Philadelphia, PA: Fortress Press.

Murray, A. E. (1966). *Presbyterians and the Negro—A history.* Philadelphia, PA: Presbyterian Historical Society.

National Opinion Research Center data abstracted from Table 1 of Jenifer Hamil-Luker and Christian Smith, "Religious Authority and Public Opinion on the Right to Die," *Sociology of Religion 59,* no. 4 (1998): 382.

National Opinion Research Center data abstracted from Table 2 of Michael Corbett and Julia Mitchell Corbett, *Politics and Religion in the United States* (New York: Garland Press, 1999), p. 268.

National Opinion Research Center data reported in Wade Clark Roof and William McKinney, *American Mainline Religion* (New Brunswick, NJ: Rutgers University Press, 1987), pp. 211-212.

Noss, J. B. (1949). *Man's religions.* New York: Macmillan.

Pin, E. (1964). Social classes and their religious approaches. In Louis Schneider (Ed.), *Religion, culture, and society.* New York: John Wiley.

Pope, L. (1942). *Millhands and preachers.* New Haven, CT: Yale University Press.

Potvin, R. H., & Sloane, D. M. (1985). Parental control, age, and religious practice. *Review of Religious Research, 27*(1), 10.

Quoted in Charles Swaney (1926). *Episcopal Methodism and slavery.* Boston, MA: R. G. Madger.

Quoted in W. W. Sweet, (1912). *The Methodist Episcopal Church and the Civil War.* Cincinnati, OH: Methodist Book Concerns Press.

Reed, E. (2002). Southern Baptists Blast TNIV. *Christianity Today, 46*(10), 17.

Richardson, J. T., & Stewart, M. (1978). Conversion Process Models and the Jesus Movement. In James T. Richardson (Ed.), *Conversion careers: In and out of the new religions.* Beverly Hills, CA: Sage Publications.

Richardson, J. T., Stewart, M. W., & Simmonds, R. B. (1978). *Organized miracles.* New Brunswick, NJ: Transaction Books.

Risley, H. (1957). The tribes and castes of Bengal. Quoted by N. Presad, *The myth of the caste system.* Petna: Prakashan.

Robins, C. (1979). Conversion, life crises, and stability among women in the East African revival. In Benneta Jules-Rosette (Ed.), *New religions of Africa*, (p. 197). Norwood, NJ: Ablex Publishing Corporation.

Rockford, E. B., Jr., (1958). *Hare krishna in America.* New Brunswick, NJ: Rutgers University Press.

Schroeder, W. W., & Obenhaus, V. (1964). *Religion in American culture.* New York: Free Press.

Sheatsley, P. B. (1966). White attitudes toward the Negro. Quoted in Hadden, *The Gathering Storm. Daedalus, 95*(1), 217-238.

Smith, C., & Faris, R. (2005). Socioeconomic inequality in the American religious system: An update and assessment. *Journal for the Scientific Study of Religion 44*(1), 98.

Snow, D. A., & Machalek, R. (1983). Second thoughts on the presumed fragility of unconventional beliefs. In Eileen Barker (Ed.) *Of gods and men: New religious movements in the West*, (p. 41). Macon, GA: Mercer University Press.

Snow, D. A., & Phillips, C. (1980). The Lofland-Stark Model: A critical reassessment. *Social Problems, 27*(4), 430-447.

Stark R., & Glock, C. Y. (1968) *American piety: The nature of religious commitment.* Berkeley, CA: University of California Press.

Stott, G. N. (1988). Familial influence on religious involvement. In Darvin L. Thomas, (Ed.) *The religion and family connection*, (pp. 258-271). Provo, UT: Religious Studies Center, Brigham Young University.

Texas Baptists End Most of Their Support for 6 Seminaries (2000, November 17). *Chronicle of Higher Education*, p. A53.

Thomas, J. L. (1951). Religious training in the Roman Catholic family. *American Journal of Sociology, 62*(2), 178-183.

Thouless, R. H. (1978). The psychology of conversion. In Walter E. Conn (Ed.) *Conversion*, (p. 143). New York: Alba House.

Vernon, G. M. (1962). *Sociology of religion.* New York: McGraw-Hill.

Wallace, A. F. C. (1966). *Religion: An anthropological view.* New York: Random House.

Weber, M. (1947). *Economy and society.* New York: Oxford University Press. (Originally published in 1922).

Weber, M. (1958). The social psychology of the world religions. In H. Gerth, & C. Wright Mills, (Trans. and Eds.) *From Max Weber.* (p. 276). New York: Oxford University Press.

Wright, S. A. (1984). Post-Involvement attitudes of voluntary defectors from controversial new religious movements. *Journal for the Scientific Study of Religion, 23*(2), 172-182.

Wright, S. A.(1983). Defection from new religious movements. In D. G. Bromley, & J. T. Richardson (Eds.), *The brainwashing/deprogramming controversy*, (pp. 106-121), New York: The Edwin Mellen Press.

Young, R. K., Benson, W. M., & Holtzman, W. H. (1960). Changes in attitudes toward the Negro in a Southern University. *Journal of Abnormal and Social Psychology, 60*(1), 131-133.

Zetterberg, H. (1952). The religious conversion as a change of social roles. *Sociology and Social Research, 36*(1), 159-166.

10 | THE INDIVIDUAL, STEREOTYPES, PREJUDICE, AND DISCRIMINATION
by Frank O. Taylor, Ph.D.

In my life I have never used, nor felt the need to use, the "N" word. I know very few people who even would. I have never referred to any woman as a "bitch" or "whore," or any of the other related slang words that refer to one's sex or gender. I would never dream of using these words but I have heard them used.

When I was a child I lived in the South, Florida to be precise. I recall one day traveling with my mother to have my vision tested. We took the bus into downtown Sarasota. I was pretty young, a 4th grader. I was thirsty and I went to take a drink of water from the fountain, wandering off from my mother. Just as I was about to get a drink an elderly woman grabbed my ear and dragged me away from the fountain, scolding me about drinking after "those people." My mother saved me and was forced to explain about one, never wandering away from the bus stop, and two, segregation.

Segregation was part of my life, as it was every Southerner's. I became aware of segregation early in life, even though I am white. Black folks watched motion pictures from the balcony, when I was a child. If they wanted popcorn or other refreshments while at the theater, they had to go outside and be served out of a window that opened into the alley. There were no black children in my school, neighborhood, or church. We were entirely segregated. Every aspect of life was separate. Black children attended different schools, worshiped in different churches, and lived in different neighborhoods.

Then one day it all changed. A new student came to school. It seems there were not enough black children to go around because only one child was assigned to our class. I have thought about this for decades of my life now. I wonder what it must have been like to be the only black child in an all white school, especially after having been educated, to that time, in an all black environment. I would imagine it was difficult. I remember that she could scrape and fight as good as any boy. Of course, most of the girls could. But even though she went to school with us, almost no one ever played with her or interacted with her in any way. If you did, you risked being alienated from the other children. **Social distance** refers to lack of interaction with people who are literally right next to you.

People often believe that segregation is now a thing of the past and black people should "get over it." Just because segregation is no longer legal does not mean that racism is a thing or the past or that segregation no longer exists. In many cities throughout the

199

nation, black children spend their entire childhood with virtually no interaction of any kind with whites. This is known as **de-facto segregation**. It is a form of economic segregation. When the laws preventing the geographic mobility of blacks were struck down in the 1960s, affluent blacks left the inner cities of the industrial North and the segregated communities of the South. Those who could not leave because they lacked the financial resources remained behind. They are there to this day in cities as varied as Chicago, Cleveland, Detroit, Milwaukee, New York, Washington, D.C., and Philadelphia, to name a few.

I made friends with the little black girl who came to my 4th grade class. Once she called some other boys, who were teasing her, "stupid crackers." I knew what stupid meant and agreed with her that those boys were stupid. But I had never heard of a cracker. I asked her what it meant. She did not know either! I asked my mother. She told me a "cracker" was basically someone who was white, Southern, and racist. Being in the 4th grade, I could not comprehend what a racist was either. I soon learned lots of other words, I will not mention here, related to race and sex. Suffice it to say that my own socialization was chock full of racist and sexist terms, concepts, and language. I no longer hear those words too much, related to either sexism or racism. Does that mean that sexism and racism are artifacts of history? In this section I argue that they are not.

Well, let us be clear – things are better on both fronts. There has been a lot of progress toward equality between the races and sexes in my lifetime. On the other hand, as the recent fracas over the use of the term "ho" by the radio commentator Don Imus demonstrates, there remains work to be done. He was fired from his network for calling Rutgers women's basketball players "nappy-headed ho's and Jigaboos." These are racist slurs. The point Imus was making was that, compared to their opponents, the Rutgers women looked "ghetto." But here is the rub: who is this white person to make judgments like that? How do people feel when racist or sexist slurs are used to describe them?

Things have more or less gone underground in my lifetime. You no longer hear people making the mistake Don Imus did, openly using racist slurs like I heard in my childhood. Society has become more tolerant. Overt discrimination and racism is mostly illegal today. But covert discrimination is not illegal and is widely practiced. Today bigots are more likely to use arguments that are not *manifestly* racist or sexist. In my childhood people would claim in public that blacks were intellectually inferior. Today, people with that sentiment know better than to voice it. Instead they say things like: "affirmative action is 'reverse' discrimination"; or "discrimination is no longer a problem." When it comes to sexism, people no longer claim, as they once did, that women are not capable of being as logical as a man. They say things like: "men and women have equal opportunities in society today." Even a cursory examination of the relevant statistics related to education and income is enough to dispel the notion that equality has been reached.

PREJUDICE AND STEREOTYPES

Prejudice refers to an illogical attitude. It is a *feeling* we get when we encounter a member of a particular group or someone with a particular attribute. Prejudice ranges from mildly negative or positive to extremely negative or positive. Prejudice invokes a range of emotions, including distrust, hate, anger, fear, disgust, and the like. For example, I once saw two young white women walking on their way down the street, undoubtedly returning to work from their lunch break, encounter a young black man in hip-hop apparel. Just before they passed the young man, both women moved their handbags to their left side, as the man passed them on their right. Obviously, this behavior, even if unconscious, indicates some level of fear.

Stereotypes are generalized beliefs people hold about groups. There are lots of stereotypes. Here is a very brief list of some stereotypes associated with a handful of groups:

- Women are unreliable, if you hire them, they will just get pregnant and leave.
- African Americans are loud, lazy, and antagonistic.
- Asian Americans are intelligent, quiet, and industrious.
- European Americans are achievement oriented and egotistical.
- Mexican Americans are family oriented, mostly Catholic, and working or lower class.

Stereotypes, like prejudice, can be positive or negative. Oddly enough, people can hold positive stereotypes about groups they dislike. For example, a lot of people, who basically do not like Asian Americans, nevertheless believe that they are smart at mathematics and computer science.

DISCRIMINATION

Discrimination refers to behaviors, or actions, as opposed to feelings. To discriminate means to take an action – to treat one person differently than another on the basis of group membership. In an experiment my social psychology class completed, the same man appeared in two pictures – in one picture he was smoking a cigarette, and in the other he was not. There was no difference in the two pictures other than in one he had a cigarette in his hand and in the other he did not. He was wearing the same clothes, in the same pose, and the background was exactly the same. Two groups of students were given the pictures and asked to circle the words, listed underneath the picture, which they thought described the man. The students with the picture of the man with a cigarette chose words with negative connotations much more frequently than the students with the non-smoking picture. In sum, the smoker was perceived to have negative attributes and the non-smoker was perceived to have positive attributes, in spite of the fact that it was the same individual in both pictures!

In a study of hiring practices, Black and White job applicants were paired on the basis of similar education, job experience, and work history. The only difference between the two applicants on each team was that one was Black and one was White. White applicants were significantly more likely to advance in the interviewing and hiring process than were Black applicants. In a similar study on renting practices, college students were assigned to one of three experimental groups: White speakers of middle class English, African Americans who spoke with a thick "Black" accent and African Americans who spoke middle class English but with a distinguishable Black accent. The intent of the research was to measure to what extent a caller could be identified racially by their speech and what effect that might have on being shown an apartment to rent. Black students speaking with the thick "Black" accent were least likely to be shown the rental apartment. Such experiments demonstrate that covert racial discrimination is still a problem. In recent Presidential elections, all over the nation, voting problems emerged in largely Black, democratic, districts, suggesting Republican efforts to suppress the voting rights of Black voters, again!

Gender Discrimination: Sexual Harassment

About one-half of women in the United States report that they have experienced sexual harassment in their academic or professional pursuits. Sexual harassment is a fairly common form of discrimination. There are two types of sexual harassment. **Quid pro quo harassment** refers to the attempt to trade sex for various types of favors, such as a letter of recommendation, a promotion, or a good grade. The second type of sexual harassment is **Hostile environment harassment**. In this case the workplace is sexually intimidating or hostile for one gender, usually women.

What qualifies as harassment depends. A lot of behavior can be offensive without necessarily being illegal. In general, if the harassing behavior is performed by someone in power, such as a college professor or employer, it is more likely to be viewed as sexually harassing than if engaged in by someone who is single and attractive. Women are more likely than men to define pressure to date, physical contact and other suggestive behavior as harassment. Overly masculine men and those who view sexual prowess as a sign of power are more likely to engage in sexual harassment, especially if they are in social settings where there is an opportunity to sexually harass women and there is a high level of tolerance for it.

Institutional Discrimination

Students typically are hard pressed to imagine or understand the subject of institutional discrimination. How can an institution discriminate? This type of discrimination is **covert discrimination** because it is so hard to see. **Institutional discrimination** refers to legal, economic, political, and cultural mechanisms that limit opportunities for some groups, while advancing opportunities for others. This type of discrimination is built right into the normative operation of society.

For example, most Colleges and Universities have an entrance examination. On the face of it, this *seems* like a fair and universal way to determine who can avail themselves of the advantages of a higher education. An objective test has the appearance of fairness. Each individual will succeed or fail based on their personal merits – no discrimination, right? Wrong. Some people will do well and some people will do poorly. In part, some people will perform poorly on these examinations due not to their native intelligence or lack of motivation, but due to lack of educational opportunities in their past. For instance, some people attended high quality private boarding schools. Others attended high quality magnate schools. While other students attended extremely poor inner city schools. To a great extent, performance on entrance examinations is correlated with social class and educational resources in neighborhoods. If your school is crumbling in decay and without educational resources you may not be as well prepared for higher education as other children, who attended schools with lots of resources.

There are plenty of examples of institutional racism. The United States Armed Forces are required to discharge anyone who admits that their sexual orientation is homosexual, for example. Whether you agree or disagree with the policy, it is an example of an institution discriminating. In many states, homosexuals do not have the same legal rights as heterosexuals. Many mortgage and insurance companies practice redlining, where they draw a red line around inner city neighborhoods and do not allow their underwriters to give loans or write insurance polices for those who live inside the red line. This virtually means that those who live in the inner city cannot get the loans they need to renovate their properties. Across the nation, in spite of laws to the contrary, women's sports programs are under-funded and under supported. Millions of inner city children are growing up in social environments with high rates of unemployment, crime, and urban decay. This reality will negatively impact their educational and occupational opportunities. These same children will have a difficult time competing economically due to their poor educational background.

Psychological Costs of Prejudice, Stereotyping, and Discrimination

Token Effect

What is the effect of merely knowing that one is the member of a group characterized by negative stereotypes and prejudices? During graduate school a fellow graduate student constantly obsessed over whether or not he was being evaluated by our professors based on his ability or the fact that he was a minority "token." Clearly, he was as intellectually gifted as any student in the doctoral program but he suffered great psychological anguish about being a Mexican American. He became so obsessed over the question he eventually had to seek counseling because he was no longer able to concentrate on the task at hand – writing his dissertation. Research indicates that this is a common experience for women in all male environments and for minorities in predominantly white institutions.

Cognitive Performance

Membership in a negatively stereotyped group has detrimental effects upon cognitive performance. In one interesting experiment, male and female college students were told they were participating in a marketing test. They were asked to try on sweaters or swimsuits and to take a math test while they had the article of clothing on. Each of the subjects had previously performed well on the math test. The women in swimsuits performed more poorly than the men in swimsuits or the women in sweaters. It seems that very few women *think* they have bodies that measure up to cultural standards of beauty. In other words, trying on swimsuits in front of a mirror made the women self conscious about stereotypes of women. Once the negative stereotypes had been invoked related to physical beauty by the swimsuits, negative stereotypes about mathematical ability were invoked by the math test. Their attention was diverted and they performed poorly. Clearly, cultural stereotypes affect cognitive performance.

Stereotype Threats

There are literally thousands of stereotypes about a variety of groups. **Stereotype threat** refers to the fear that one may confirm a negative stereotype held about one's group. In one experiment, White men only performed poorly on a test when they were led to believe they were being compared to Asian men. In another experiment, Black students did not perform up to their known abilities when their race was made salient and they thought there was a danger that their performance would reinforce negative stereotypes about their level of intelligence compared to Whites. On one math test, women in the control group did very well but women in the experimental group, after listening to a lecture on gender differences in mathematical ability did poorly. These are but a few examples of how the *fear* of being turned into a representative for your group hinders performance on a variety of tests.

Coping with Prejudice, Stereotypes, and Discrimination

There are a variety of strategies that help people cope with negative stereotypes and prejudices. Self-handicapping is one strategy. **Self-handicapping** refers to the deliberate sabotage of one's own performance. You put up obstacles to success in order to have a plausible explanation for a poor performance. Anxiety about a poor performance can be relieved if you create a situation in which you can claim to have not had a "fair" chance or that you did not "try." Once, in my research methods course, a student who I knew was finished with his project deliberately "forgot" to bring the disk with the presentation on it. I sent her home to get it and although her dorm room was directly across the parking lot she only managed to get back to class in the last five minutes. She gave her presentation, and then pressured me to take into account that she did not really have the time to do a good job, after she *deliberately* sabotaged herself! As if I did not know what she was up to! When I questioned her about her behavior she revealed that she was afraid of statistics.

Another strategy used to deal with stereotype threat is to **redefine the situation**. In the process of interacting with others we come to have certain definitions about what is going on in different social settings. We respond according to our *definition* of what is happening. If, for example, academic performance is an area where Black students feel they may be negatively stereotyped, they may choose to redefine academic performance as less important or less relevant for them. In other words, you may disidentify with the areas of life susceptible to stereotype threats. The danger of doing this, of course, is to actually perform less well academically, and end up facing economic challenges unnecessarily.

Disidentification and self-handicapping may be effective in the short run but over the long run ignoring academic performance will have negative consequences for economic outcomes in life. A better strategy would be to have programs in place that try to eliminate or diminish negative stereotypes. For example, in one study Black students participated in a program that treated academic performance as something akin to an organ, which if exercised properly, can become stronger. At the end of the program, Black students were achieving more academic success than at the beginning of the program.

THE FUNCTIONS OF PREJUDICE, STEREOTYPING AND DISCRIMINATION

Why do people often feel favorably biased toward their own group and actually *hate* members of other groups? After all, it seems reasonable to assume that one could like members of one's own group without hating others. The answer seems to be that in-group cohesion serves several important functions for human beings.

First, prejudicial assumptions, stereotypical thinking, and discrimination help support and protect one's own group. This may be especially true if the groups *think* they are competing for scarce resources. Research demonstrates that people often have an in-group bias even when the other members of the group are anonymous and group membership is only a label. Also, historically there has never been a time humans did not live in groups. Cooperative group living is necessary for human survival, thus, the behaviors and norms that strengthened group bonds were more likely to be passed on from generation to generation. Additionally, actual conflict with other groups can increase the solidarity one feels for one's own group.

A second function of negative prejudices and stereotypes is that it serves the interests of powerful institutions and individuals. The threat of external conflict is often a powerful force for creating group unity and solidarity. Following the events of 911, if you recall, one could hardly drive a mile in any direction without seeing hundreds of American flags flying from homes and vehicles. Some people think that Hitler encouraged anti-Semitism, for example, as a means for unifying Germany under his control. Thus, Jews were defined as a "threat," in order to unify German citizens. At the end of the cold war, powerful institutions in the United States had to cast about for new enemies in order to maintain their power and social prestige. Without enemies the defense industry would quickly cease to be so powerful.

A third function of prejudice and stereotypes is that it helps individuals feel good about their success in life. It is easy to avoid the guilt that may be associated with proof that one's advantages and successes in life are not really the result of hard work but of social networks, favoritism, nepotism, and other forms of in-group bias. In other words, you can feel better about yourself if you believe that stereotypes about others who have less are accurate. People do not want to view their advantages as systematic. People want to define their advantages as the result of hard work and competition in a social system that is fair and just. Prejudiced people believe that any other person who works as hard as they do can also succeed. If others are unsuccessful, the prejudiced person thinks it is because they are lazy and unmotivated, not because the system is manipulated by power groups to hold them back.

To summarize the functions of prejudicial and stereotypical thinking, and discrimination:

1. In-group bias supports the behaviors and norms associated with group living.

2. Out-group bias creates in-group solidarity.

3. Prejudice, stereotypes, and discrimination can serve the vested interests of powerful institutions and individuals.

4. Prejudice, stereotypes, and discrimination help people avoid the guilt that would otherwise be associated with their affluence.

IN-GROUP BIAS

Social Dominance Orientation

Members of affluent groups often suffer no guilt associated with their advantages in life. In fact, they frequently believe in the negative stereotypes about lower status-groups and feel that the prejudice and discrimination directed at such groups is entirely justified. People with a **social dominance orientation** *want* their group to dominate everyone else. They often feel that it is necessary to step on others to get ahead in life and that those at the top deserve more power and influence. Conversely, they feel that those at the bottom deserve less because they are *worth* less.

Likely this is a mechanism to avoid cognitive dissonance. **Cognitive dissonance** means that if we believe in two conflicting values some form of mental or emotional stress will occur. It is difficult to take unfair advantage of someone, due to your power and position, and feel positive toward them at the same time. To achieve mental harmony or to alleviate cognitive dissonance, dominant individuals must *rationalize* that those they take advantage of *deserve* to lose or have less. Those who are cheated and treated unfairly are defined as *bad* people through the use of negative stereotypes. People with a social dominance orientation are like the wife beater who feels that his wife deserved to be beaten because she provoked him.

Inter-group Competition

When people *expect* to compete economically, for jobs, income, education, housing and other resources we could hypothesize that **inter-group competition** would increase. Research tends to bear out this hypothesis. Economic data gathered between 1882 and 1930 suggests that during economic recessions murder rates of Black people in the

South increased. And the violence was not limited to just the South. In the industrial North, violence against Blacks and immigrants increased during economic hard times and returned to normal levels when the economy recovered.

In the 1960s, the social psychologist Muzafer Sherif designed a famous experiment to test inter-group conflict. He selected 22 fifth grade boys who were extremely similar to each other in terms of social class background, educational achievement, and family and religious background. He wondered if he could create the conditions necessary to get boys from the same group to compete with each other. They boys were sent to a summer camp and divided into two groups, the Rattlers and the Eagles and began to engage in a variety of athletic competitions for which winners received trophies and other rewards. It was not long before the boys in each group began to form negative opinions and stereotypes about the boys in the other group. Finally, after full-scale fist fights began to break out, the experiment had to be terminated. Professor Sherif was successful in demonstrating that even people quite similar to each other could be induced to engage in conflict if divided into groups in which group identity was reinforced.

Self-Fulfilling Prophecy and Inter-Group Competition

Prejudice and negative stereotypes breed discrimination, which reproduces prejudice and negative stereotypes. Here is an example of how the **self-fulfilling prophecy** works. A common negative stereotype about inner city Black children is that they have poor intellectual abilities. This negative stereotype, in turn, influences teacher's and administrator's assumptions about the educational potential of Black inner city students. These negative stereotypes influence what educational track Black students are placed in, which is generally the low ability group, vocational education, or special programs for the learning disabled. Being placed in these low ability groups, of course, is correlated with fewer opportunities to learn, less complex and demanding work, and less homework. Finally, when these children are assessed and tested, they perform less well than their peers placed in the higher ability tracks. Is their poor performance due to lack of intelligence or lack of being taught? In any case, their poor test scores then reinforce the original negative stereotypes and the cycle is perpetuated. A good argument could be made that tracking these inner city children into low ability groups, and then denying them the same educational opportunities as other children is a form of discrimination, and that is the source of poor test performance, rather than intellectual potential.

The self-fulfilling prophecy is a vicious cycle. Groups competing with each other economically come to hold negative stereotypes about each other. It is no mystery why education is a battle field – education is the key to economic success. Your score on an

IQ test will not get you a job. You will need the appropriate credential: a college degree. Powerful people in society are interested in passing on their economic advantages to their children but they do not want to do so in an overtly racist or sexist manner. They rely on the educational system because that way the blame for failure can be shifted to individuals rather than the system. If people who fail educationally can be labeled as less intelligent they can be blamed for their failure and poverty in spite of the fact that they never had the same educational opportunities in the first place.

CONFORMITY, SOCIAL APPROVAL, AND PREJUDICE

Often we want to belong to a certain group – we want to "fit in." One way of fitting in is to adopt the attitudes and behaviors of the group. Sometimes, even though we may privately disagree with the racist or sexist stereotypes and prejudice of the group, we go along for the sake of acceptance. In fact, over time, we may change our attitudes and behaviors because we desire to conform.

There is evidence that people who are extremely racist also score high on scales of conformity and are high **self-monitors**. Self-monitors are people who are aware of their self-presentation in different social settings and who look to the attitudes, beliefs, and behaviors of others to guide them. People who have a strong desire to "fit in," particularly those with lower status in the group or newcomers to the group, are most likely to try to conform to the group's norms. If those norms are sexist or racist, conformists are likely to adopt negative prejudices.

Changing Times

Over the last 40 years social attitudes towards women and minorities has changed for the positive. On issues of interracial marriage, gay and lesbian marriage, racial integration, and female or black presidential candidates, attitudes have become more accepting and tolerant. Today, most people believe that discrimination against people based on sex, ethnicity, or race is not appropriate and should remain illegal. This change in public attitudes is probably related to changing social norms. If the desire for approval leads to the development of racist attitudes, if the group is bigoted, that same desire for approval may lead to egalitarian attitudes as social norms against discrimination become more widely shared. However, the recent legal battles over gay marriage demonstrate that equality has not been reached.

Religiosity and Prejudice

Tolerance is a major theme in all of the great religions. A quick look at the headlines reveals that there is a good deal of religious conflict in the world. Why are people who describe themselves as very religious sometimes also so prejudiced? The answer seems to be that there are different ways to be religious. People have different religious motivations. Some people are characterized by **extrinsic religiosity**, or the desire to make friends, gain status, or receive other forms of social support. For these people, religion is a means to an end and the ideas, concepts, and messages of their religion have little effect on their self-concept. These people are most likely to be prejudiced.

Some people describe religion as a lifelong journey towards the truth. This is **quest religiosity**. The quest oriented individual views religion in complex terms. They do not expect simple answers in life or religion. I once spoke to a person who believed that he was on such a religious journey and he said that "he took the Bible seriously, and therefore could not take it literally." As you may suspect, quest oriented individuals are open-minded and not given to prejudices.

A third type of religiosity is known as **intrinsic religiosity**. Individuals with an intrinsic religious orientation see religion as an end in itself. They try to live their lives by religious principles. Since most religions teach tolerance intrinsically religious people could be expected to be low on prejudice and this seems to be the case.

SELF-IMAGE, PREJUDICE, STEREOTYPES, AND DISCRIMINATION

When I was younger I used to hear my father say something frequently: "I'm free, white, and 21." As a child, I really did not know what that meant. Sometime between the ages of 10 and 15, however, I understood that it was a reference to others who were lower on the social ladder. Truthfully, I do not know why my father used to say it, but I suspect that it was a matter of socialization. He had heard others say it. He grew up in the South in the 1930s so he would have known about segregation. You see, during his childhood, there were others, further down the social ladder that, although legally "free," were not *really* free, and not white.

I suppose my father derived some sense of security from the situation in which someone else would always be below him. In a similar vein, I used to hear my mother exclaim quite frequently that "it's a man's world." Of course, this expression came from those further down the social ladder. More importantly, people derived a sense of belonging through the expression of such sentiments. My father belonged to the "brotherhood" of white guys, who thought they would always be better off than people of color. Likewise, my mother belonged to the "sisterhood" of wives who suffered under the domination of their husbands.

Personal and Social Identity

A wave of anti-immigration sentiment is, again, sweeping the United States. We are constantly bombarded by headlines claiming that "immigrants are invading the nation" or that are "boarders are under attack." This seems like an odd sentiment for a nation comprised of immigrants. Unless you have Native American ancestors, your family emigrated here. What is the source of these feelings? When people are faced with economic hardship they often have a sense of personal failure. When the factory closes it doors, moves to Mexico, and lays-off all of its employees, people often ponder "who" is to blame for their suffering. Actually, the decisions of corporate leaders and governmental economic policies are in fact to blame but they are hard to identify. Ordinary people do not study economic policy. It is much easier to blame immigrants for job loss.

In this situation people often turn to an easily identifiable group. **Scapegoating** refers to the process of blaming members of socially **derogated groups** for one's frustrations and failures. Scapegoating is most effective if society provides easily identified groups for which negative stereotypes already exist. It is interesting too that the most vitriolic accusations are directed toward Mexicans who enter the United States rather than Canadians, who are mostly of white European ancestry. Perhaps the source of the indignation about Mexicans stems from the racism of the indignant.

Social Identity Theory claims that, just like for personal identity, people try to manage their social identities. **Social identity** refers to attributes such as your sex, ethnicity, race, religion, age, social class, social status, occupation, level of education, and the like. In other words, each of us belongs to a variety of groups. Some of these groups have higher social standing than others. One way to manage your social identity is to make *downward social comparisons* – creating positive feelings about your social identity by disparaging members of other groups as "lower" than you. Here we see the psychological effect of the saying mentioned previously: free, white, and 21.

Of course, those who have more prestigious social identities are threatened by groups trying to improve their social standing. A derogated group will try to eliminate the negative stereotypes with which they are associated. Also, they may try to improve their social standing through political, educational, and occupational gains. A quick review of immigration in the United States reveals that many ethnic groups, such as Jews, Germans, Irish, and so on were able, through a variety of means, to improve their social standing to the point where they are today indistinguishable from Anglos. Of course, it helps if the group is white.

Thus, for the dominant social identities, endorsing and perpetuating negative stereotypes of women and other minorities serves several functions. First, labeling minorities as less "intelligent," "unfit," "socially irresponsible," "prone to crime and violence," or "sexually promiscuous," allows members of the dominant groups to feel better about themselves. Second, stereotypes and prejudices obscure the lack of social opportunities, to which advantaged groups have access, and labels failure as an "individualistic" trait. Third, negative stereotypes make discrimination against certain groups seem justified and easier to accomplish. We have discussed how this works with the self-fulfilling prophecy.

In-Group Identification

The more strongly attached one is to their groups, the more likely they will adopt group prejudices, stereotypes, and biases. This is particularly true if they stand to lose if their group's social standing is weakened. In one experiment, college students, who were anonymous, were tested to see how strong they identified with their in-groups. They were given the job of allocating extra-credit points to fellow students in their class. Some of the students allocating points had strong in-group identification and some did not. Some of the students receiving the points were members of their group and some were not. Not surprisingly, students allocating extra credit points, who were strongly attached to their in-groups, gave the most points to other students in their groups. Students who were lower on in-group attachment were egalitarian in their extra credit allocations. This example leads us to conclude that in-group identification is associated with discrimination.

Authoritarian Personality

Social psychologists were troubled by the holocaust. How could ordinary German citizens have participated in such atrocities? For that matter, the same question could be asked about U.S. involvement in Iraq, which has seen nearly a million civilian deaths. In the 1950s the theory of authoritarian personality emerged as an explanation of why some people hold extremely negative prejudices, and are willing to act on them. The **authoritarian personality** describes a person who views social reality in black-and-white terms. They follow the conventions of society and have little tolerance for those who challenge those conventions. They are often described as "kissing ass" above and "kicking ass" below in terms of their position on the social ladder.

For decades social psychologists stressed that the authoritarian personality was a consequence of **authoritarian parenting**, in which children are severely punished, even for minor infractions. Such children become hostile towards parents but, since they are afraid to act against those who provide for them, they *displace* their anger onto weaker members of society.

Recent research indicates that there are other ways to acquire an authoritarian personality. People can become more authoritarian through simple observation, without much punishment. In other words, role-modeled behavior may suffice. To get ahead in some social settings, such as the military, individuals are forced to become more authoritarian. Other social settings inherently stress authoritarianism, such as the Church. The point is that social psychologists now realize that authoritarianism is not necessarily a psychological "flaw." Events can increase the overall level of authoritarianism in society. After September 11th, for example, support for the President increased dramatically and people had little tolerance for those who argued for peace.

To some degree, everyone holds some negative stereotypes and prejudices. Some people are extremely authoritarian while others are not. Decades of research, carried out in a variety of nations, has demonstrated that the theory of an authoritarian personality is valid. People who have authoritarian characteristics are more negatively prejudiced against women and minorities than people who are not authoritarian.

Failure, Prejudice and Discrimination

In our society we are encouraged to view economic success as a *personal* attribute. What this means is that when we get a promotion or a pay raise at work we are likely to refer to all the hard work we put into the effort. We justify economic success by referring to our individual effort. We are unlikely to regard our success as having much to do with seniority systems, cronyism, social networks, or the work of others on our behalf. Since we are usually unaware of the systemic nature of economic life, when we fail economically it can be a blow to our self-esteem.

One effective strategy to deal with personal failure, such as losing your job, is to derogate members of a negatively stereotyped group. In other words, we may heap more abuse upon easily identified groups we presume to be lower down the social ladder, blaming them for our economic and social problems. I think this is happening on a national scale today. As more and more major corporations close their operations in the United States and relocate to other parts of the world, where there are no labor unions, no laws protecting labor or consumers, no environmental legislation, and so on, Americans are casting about for any way to raise their self-esteem. Rather than blame those actually responsible for the decline in our standard of living – CEOs, boards of directors, and politicians – which would require a lot of self-education and awareness of global economic and political policy, many just look for the usual suspects – illegal immigrants. Heaping abuse on Mexicans here illegally will not restore the jobs, for instance, in the steel or automobile industries. Even if every single illegal immigrant could be expelled from the nation our jobs would still be in South Korea, China, Taiwan, Mexico, and anywhere else U.S. corporations think they can exploit labor for profits.

In one experiment individuals took an intelligence test and were randomly given fake feedback, either positive or negative. Students *primed* in this manner then went on to the second part of the experiment were they were asked to take part in evaluating job applicants on personality and job qualifications. Some of the job candidates were members of minority ethnic groups. Subjects who were given false *positive* feedback about their performance on the intelligence test were more accurate and equitable in their evaluation of the job candidates, regardless of the candidate's ethnicity. On the other hand, subjects who were given clues that they did poorly on the intelligence test ranked the minority ethnic job candidates much less favorably. These results support the idea that failure can motivate individuals to behave in prejudicial and discriminatory ways.

Over the last 40 years, we can note that on a variety of fronts, including the economic, political, and cultural, major improvements have occurred for women and minorities. While outright equality has not been achieved, and sexism and racism remain problematic, women and minorities have fought hard to improve their social standing. During the last 20 years, the United States has lost its industrial base as the nation shifted from an industrial to a service and information based economy. Blue collar men have been particularly hard hit and even White collar workers are now seeing the erosion of their standard of living.

The result of the erosion of our nation's standard of living has been a backlash against women and minorities. All over the nation, policies and programs, such as Affirmative Action, are under attack. These programs are often labeled as "reverse discrimination." Thus, we see that as previously subservient groups begin to achieve the American Dream, they are often held up as scapegoats for the failure of established groups that are losing ground. The claim that women and minorities, through affirmative action programs, are "taking jobs away from *qualified* people (code for white men) is largely nonsense. *Globalization* is the culprit. Unfortunately, globalization is not as easy to blame as your next door neighbor, who may happen to be a woman or ethnic minority.

Self Esteem and Prejudice

We have discussed how derogating out-groups can be effective in boosting self-esteem. We might suspect, then, that people with low self-esteem in general, regardless of personal failure, may be more inclined to derogate out-groups than people with high levels of self-esteem. The evidence on this hypothesis is surprising. It turns out that both low self-esteem and high-self esteem individuals favor their in-group. High self-esteem people may even have a greater in-group bias than low self-esteem people. The research does tend to bear out that people with low-self esteem tend to be negatively prejudiced against derogated groups.

In a study of sorority women with high self-esteem researchers discovered that women with high self-esteem who were members of high-status sororities had little bias towards other sorority women. On the other hand, women with high self-esteem who were members of low-status sororities were highly biased against members of other sororities. We can conclude from this discussion that there is probably an interaction between self-esteem and external threats. People with high self esteem, when faced with a loss of their social status are just as likely to derogate out-groups as people with low self esteem.

STEREOTYPES AS MENTAL SHORTCUTS

Functions of Stereotypes

I once conducted a quick experiment in one of my social psychology courses. I took two photographs with my digital camera. One was a photograph of a Black man and one was a Photograph of a White man. Each of these individuals was dressed nondescriptly and holding an object that was very hard to see. The White guy actually was holding a child's small cap-gun. The Black guy was holding his wallet. Below the pictures were groups of descriptive words that students examining the picture were given. Students were asked to circle any particular word if they felt the word described the person in the picture. Most students thought the Black guy was holding a gun and they circled words describing the Black guy as menacing, threatening, and potentially criminal. Although the White guy actually had the gun, few students identified him as threatening. Other research typically finds that in stressful situations people are highly likely to respond to stereotypes and schemas rather than what is *actually* happening.

Cognitive processing is time consuming. Imagine how difficult it would be to *actually* get to know every person we are ever going to meet in our lifetime. Stereotypes provide us with a mental shortcut around cognitive processing. There are four functions of stereotypes:

1. Cognitive shortcuts: stereotypes can be invoked quickly, eliminating the need to expend time and effort getting to know people on an individual basis. If you can categorize people as members of one group or another, you can infer that they have the qualities generally associated with that group.

2. Ready made interpretations: stereotypes help us interpret behavior that is otherwise ambiguous.

3. Ready made explanations: stereotypes often supply explanations for behavior.

4. Provide standards for evaluation: Often, we are in situations where we evaluate members of different groups.

As you may guess, reliance on stereotypes often leads to incorrect conclusions. In New York City, police officers shot a Black man, Amadou Diallo, 19 times and fired over 40 shots because they thought his wallet was a gun. This was the inspiration for my in-class experiment. In other words, Mr. Diallo's behavior was ambiguous and racial stereotypes made the police officers *see* a "gun." Once, during an advising session with a student I glanced casually at my watch, as I often do. I inadvertently sent a signal to her that she should conclude her business because I was busy. She simply misinterpreted the gesture but rushed out without all the information she needed. Some people may conclude that the good grades of a man reflect natural ability whereas the same grades for a woman reflect luck. Although we cannot escape using stereotypes, at least we should try to be more aware of the dangers of relying upon them instead of actual investigation.

Accuracy of Stereotypes

In spite of the fact that many stereotypes are inaccurate and using them often leads to incorrect conclusions, some stereotypes are actually relatively accurate. In as much as a stereotype is an accurate, or nearly so, assessment of a group by using stereotypes is cognitively useful. Let us take for example some stereotypes about College professors. Often people *believe* that professors are "brainy," or "nerdy." A student once gave me a CD of songs she had burned because she felt the songs reflected my "nerd at heart." It is true that college professors spend a lot of time engaged in activities usually associated with intellectual effort, such as reading, writing, and research. So there is some truth to the stereotypes. They are reasonably accurate and serve to describe what members of the group do, at least some of the time. However, anyone who has spent anytime around me when I'm in my part-time musician role would never mistake me for a nerd.

Stereotypes work by exaggerating the differences between groups and the similarities within groups. For example, comparing men to men, in reality, some are more aggressive than others and some are extremely passive. The same is true for women – some are more aggressive than others. Stereotypes ignore these within group differences by emphasizing difference *between* groups. The stereotype holds that men, as a group, are more aggressive than women as a group. At the same time the in-group differences are smoothed out to give the impression of homogeneity. This stereotype about aggression works most of the time because men are slightly more aggressive than women. Researchers have found that people often make quite accurate estimates of sex differences, even if their assessments are based on stereotypes.

Perceived Out-Group Homogeneity

People have a tendency to overestimate the level of similarity members of one group have to each other. This effect is called **perceived out-group homogeneity**. This effect has the function of making cognitive processing easier – it makes it easy to apply the stereotype. For example, if a student believes that all Asian Americans are good at computer science, they may conclude that all Asian Americans they meet share that attribute. They will be able to form an opinion about the next Asian American they meet without the necessity of actually having to take the time to form an impression through social interaction. If the stereotype is reasonably accurate, it is cognitively efficient to use one.

Activation of Stereotypes

Racial and gender stereotypes can often be automatically invoked in individuals even when they are not thinking about racial or gender categories. In one experiment, subjects were asked to identify words as the letters of the word appeared on a computer screen. The words were associated with positive Black stereotypes (musical), negative Black stereotypes (dangerous), positive White stereotypes (educated), and negative White stereotypes (materialistic). Researchers hypothesized that if stereotypes could be applied, subjects would recognize the words being spelled out on the computer more quickly. Additionally, the subjects were subliminally primed with representations of Black or White. The subliminal cues appear to have automatically activated racial stereotypes. The subliminal Black cue caused the subjects to quickly recognize words associated with *negative* Black stereotypes, such as dangerous, but not positive Black stereotypes. Conversely, the subliminal White cue caused subjects to quickly recognize words associated with *positive* White stereotypes but not the negative stereotypes. From this we may conclude that even when people are not trying to form impressions of others, simply knowing what the stereotypes are makes it easier to automatically stimulate them.

Stereotypes, Moods, and Emotions

Our moods and emotions can have a dramatic effect on our ability to think things through closely. In general, people in a good mood are less motivated to expend the cognitive energy to think something through and are consequently, more likely to rely on stereotypes. Oddly, even though people in a good mood rely more on stereotypes they have more favorable impressions of others in general. People in a bad mood are more likely to pay attention to detail and therefore less likely to rely on stereotypes. And they are less likely to have favorable impressions of others. Thus, the impact of mood on stereotypes is complicated. Everybody falls into a number of categories, some positive and some negative. People in a good mood tend to react to people on the basis of membership in positive categories. People in a bad mood do the opposite. Lastly, every category has positive and negative stereotypes. People in a good mood respond to the positive stereotypes for the group, while people in a bad mood tend to respond the group's negative stereotypes.

Cognitively Taxing Situations

Frequently we have to rely on stereotypes because the situation is so complex we cannot avoid it. When we are performing several tasks simultaneously, that each requires some level of cognitive work; we often revert to reliance on stereotypes to form impressions of others. Sometime we are only performing one task, which is especially taxing cognitively, when we have to evaluate someone or form an impression of him or her. Other times, we just do not have a lot of time available. Many of my students who have graduated and gone on to work in the human service fields lament that they can only spend 10 or 15 minutes with "clients." If this is the case it would be hard not to rely upon stereotypes in the process of assessment. The more complex and cognitively taxing the circumstances the more likely we are to rely upon stereotypes. Students who are going to go on to work as professionals in the field of human service should be aware of the proclivity to rely on stereotypes when the situation is cognitively taxing.

ℰᴑ Ꮯᴣ ℰᴑ Ꮯᴣ

REFERENCES

Aberson, C. L., Healy, M., & Romero, V. (2000). Ingroup bias and self-esteem: A meta-analysis. *Personality and Social Psychology Review, 4*, 157-173.
Adorno, T. W., Frenkel-Brunswik, E., Levinson, D. J., & Sanford, R. N. (1950). *The authoritarian*

personality. New York: Harper and Row.

Allport, G. W. (1954). *The nature of prejudice*. Reading, MA: Addison-Wesley.

Allport, G. W., & Kramer, B. M. (1946). Some roots of prejudice. *Journal of Psychology, 22*, 9-39.

Allport, G. W., & Ross, J. M. (1967). Personal religious orientation and prejudice. *Journal of Personality and Social Psychology, 5*, 432-443.

Altemeyer, B. (1988). The other "authoritarian personality." In M. P. Zanna (Ed.), *Advances in Experimental Social Psychology* (Vol. 30, pp. 48-49). New York: Academic Press.

Alvora, E. M., & Crano, W. D. (1997). Indirect minority influence: Evidence for leniency in source evaluation and counterargumentation. *Journal of Personality and Social Psychology, 72*, 949-964.

Aronson, E. (1969). The theory of cognitive dissonance: A current perspective. In L. Berkowitz (Ed.), *Advances in experimental social psychology*. (Vol. 4, pp. 1-34). San Diego, CA: Academic Press.

Aronson, J., Fried, C.B., & Good, C. (2002). Reducing effects of stereotype threat on African American college students by shaping theories of intelligence. *Journal of Experimental Social Psychology, 38*, 113-125.

Aronson, J., Lustina, M. J., Good, C., Keough, K., Steel, C. M., & Brown J. (1999). When white men can't do math: Necessary and sufficient factors in stereotype threat. *Journal of Experimental Social Psychology, 35,* 29-46.

Ashburn-Nardo, L., Voils, C. I., & Monteith, M. J. (2001). Implicit associations as the seeds of ingroup bias: How easily do they take root? *Journal of Personality and Social Psychology, 81*, 789-799.

Axelrod, R. (1984). *The evolution of cooperation*. New York: Basic Books.

Axelrod, R., & Hamilton, W. D. (1981). The evolution of cooperation *Science, 211*, 1390-1396.

Axelrod, R., Riolo, R. L., & Cohen, M. D. (2002). Beyond geography: Cooperation with persistent links in the absence of clustered neighborhoods. *Personality & Social Psychology Review, 6*, 341-346.

Ayers, I., & Siegelman, P. (1995). Race and gender discrimination in bargaining for a new car. *American Economic Review, 85*, 304-321.

Banaji, M. R., & Greenwald, A. G. (1994). Implicit social cognition: Attitudes, self-esteem, and stereotypes. *Psychological Review, 102*, 4-27.

Batson, C. D., & Burris, C. T. (1994). Personal religion: Depressant or stimulant of prejudice and discrimination. In M. P. Zanna, & J. M. Olson (Eds.), *The psychology of prejudice: The Ontario Symposium* (Vol. 7, pp. 149-169). Hillsdale, NJ: Erlbaum.

Batson, C. D., & Ventis, W. L. (1982). *The religious experience: A social-psychological perspective*. New York: Oxford University Press.

Batson, C. D., Flink, C. H., Schoenrade, P. A., Fultz, J., & Pych, V. (1986). Religious orientation and overt versus covert racial prejudice. *Journal of Personality and Social Psychology, 50*, 175-181.

Beal, D. J., O'Neal, E. C., Ong, J., & Ruscher, J. B. (2000). The ways and means of interracial aggression: Modern racists' use of covert retaliation. *Personality and Social psychology Bulletin, 26*, 1225-1238.

Blair, I. V., & Banaji, M. R. (1996). Automatic and controlled processes in stereotype priming. *Journal of Personality and Social Psychology, 70*, 1143-1163.

Blanchard, F. A., Crandall, C. S., Brighman, J. C., & Vaughn, L. A. (1994). Condemning and condoning racism: A social context approach to interracial settings. *Journal of Applied Psychology, 79*, 993-997.

Blanchard, F. A., Lilly, T., & Vaughn, L. A. (1991). Reducing the expression of racial prejudice. *Psychological Science, 2*, 101-105.

Blanchard, F. A., Weigel, R. H., & Cook, S. W. (1975). The effect of relative competence of group members upon interpersonal attraction in cooperating interracial groups. *Journal of Personality and Social Psychology, 32*, 519-530.

Blumenthal, J. A. (1998). The reasonable woman standard: A meta-analytic review of gender differences in perceptions of sexual harassment. *Law and Human Behavior, 22*, 33-57.

Bonacich, E. (1972). A theory of ethnic antagonism: The split labor market. *American Sociological*

Review, 37, 547-559.

Branscombe, N. R., & Wann, D. L. (1992). Physiological arousal and reactions to outgroup members during competitions that implicate an important social identity. *Aggressive Behavior, 18,* 85-93.

Brewer, M. B. (1979). In-group bias in the minimal intergroup situation: A cognitive-motivational analysis. *Psychological Bulletin, 86,* 307-324.

Brewer, M. B., & Alexander, M. G. (2002). Intergroup emotions and images. In D. M. Mackie, & E. R. Smith (Eds.), *From prejudice to intergroup relations: Differentiated reactions to social groups* (pp. 209-225). New York: Psychology Press.

Brewer, M. B., & Campbell, D. T. (1976). *Ethnocentrism and intergroup attitudes: East African evidence.* New York: Sage.

Brewer, M. B., (1997). On the social origins of human nature. In C. McGarty, & S. A. Haslam (Eds.), *The message of social psychology: Perspectives on mind in society.* (pp. 54-62). Oxford, U.K.: Blackwell.

Cialdini, R. B., & Richardson, K. D. (1980). Two indirect tactics of image management: Basking and blasting. *Journal of Personality and Social Psychology, 39,* 406-415.

Cohen, L. L., & Swim, J. K. (1995). The differential impact of gender ratios on women and men: Tokenism, self-confidence, and expectations. *Personality and Social Psychology Bulletin, 21,* 876-884.

Cox, C. L., Smith, S. L., & Insko, C. A. (1996). Categorical race versus individuating belief as determinants of discrimination: A study of southern adolescents in 1966, 1979, and 1993. *Journal of Experimental Social Psychology, 32,* 39-70.

Cox, O. C. (1959). *Caste, class, and race: A study in social dynamics.* New York: Monthly Review Press.

Crandall, C. S., & Eshleman, A. & O'Brien, L. (2002). Social norms and the expression and suppression of prejudice. *Journal of Personality and Social Psychology, 82,* 359-378.

Crandall, C. S., & Eshleman, A. (2003). A justification-suppression of the expression and experience of prejudice. *Psychological Bulletin, 129,* 414-446.

Crocker, J., & Major, B. (1989). Social stigma and self-esteem: The self-protective properties of stigma. *Psychological Review, 96,* 608-630.

Crocker, J., & Schwartz, I. (1985). Prejudice and ingroup favoritism in a minimal intergroup situation: Effects of self-esteem. *Personality and Social Psychology Bulletin, 11,* 379-386.

Crocker, J., Thompson, L. L., McGraw, K. M., & Ingerman, C. (1987). Downward comparison, prejudice, and evaluations of others: Effects of self-esteem and threat. *Journal of Personality and Social Psychology, 52,* 907-916.

Davidson, O. G. (1996). *The best of enemies: Race and redemption in the New South.* New York: Scribner.

Deaux, K., & LaFrance, M. (1998). Gender. In D. T. Gilbert, S. T. Fiske, & G. Lindzey (Eds.), *The handbook of social psychology* (4th ed., Vol. 1, pp. 788-827). New York: McGraw-Hill.

Deaux, K., & Lewis, L. L. (1984). The structure of gender stereotypes: Interrelationships among components and gender label. *Journal of Personality and Social Psychology, 46,* 991-1004.

Devine, P. G. (1989). Stereotypes and prejudice: Their automatic and controlled components. *Journal of personality and Social psychology, 56,* 5-18.

Devos, T., Silver, L. A., Mackie, D. M., & Smith, E. R. (1992). Experiencing intergroup emotions. In D.M. Mackie & E.R. Smith (Eds.), *From prejudice to intergroup emotions: Differential reactions to social groups* (pp. 111-134). New York: Psychology Press.

Donahue, M. J. (1985). Intrinsic and extrinsic religiousness: Review and meta-analysis. *Journal of Personality and Social Psychology, 48,* 400-419.

Dovidio, J. F., & Gaertner, S. L. (2000). Aversive racism and selection decisions: 1989 and 1999. *Psychological Science, 11,* 315-319.

Dovidio, J. F., Kawakami, K., & Gaertner, S. L., (1992). Implicit and explicit prejudice and interracial interaction. *Journal of Personality and Social Psychology, 82,* 62-68.

Faley, R. H., Knapp, D. E., Kustis, G. A., & Dubois, C. L. Z. (1999). Estimating the organizational costs of sexual harassment: The case of the U.S. Army. *Journal of Business and Psychology 13*, 461-484.

Fazio, R. H., & Zanna, M. P. (1981). Direct experience and attitude-behavior consistency. In L. Berkowitz (Ed.), *Advances in experimental social psychology* (Vol. 14, pp. 162-202). New York: Academic Press .

Fazio, R. H., Sherman, S. J., & Herr, P. M. (1982). The feature-positive effect in self-perception process. *Journal of Personality and Social Psychology, 42,* 404-411.

Fazio, R. H., Zanna, M. P., & Cooper, J. (1977). Dissonance and self-perception. *Journal of Experimental Social Psychology, 13,* 464-479.

Feagin, J. R., & Feagin, C. B. (1999). *Racial and ethnic relations* (6th ed.). Upper Saddle River, NJ: Prentice-Hall.

Fiske, S. T. (1993). Controlling other people: The impact of power on stereotyping. *American Psychologist, 48,* 621-628.

Fiske, S. T., & Von Hendy, H. M. (1992). Personality feedback and situational norms can control stereotyping processes. *Journal of Personality and Social Psychology, 62,* 577-596.

Fiske, S. T., Cuddy, A. J., Glick, P., & Xu, J. (2002). A model of (often mixed) stereotype content: Competence and warmth respectively follow from perceived status and competition. *Journal of Personality and Social Psychology, 82,* 878-902.

Ford, T. E. (2000). Effects of sexist humor on tolerance of sexist events. *Personality and Social Psychology Bulletin, 26,* 1094-1107.

Ford, T. E., Wentzel, E. R., & Lorion, F. (2001). Effects of exposure to sexist humor on perceptions of normative tolerance of sexism. *European Journal of Social Psychology, 31,* 677-691.

Frazier, P. A., Cochran, C. C., & Olsen, A. M. (1995). Social science research on lay definitions of sexual harassment. *Journal of Social Issues, 51,* 21-38.

Frieze, I. H., Fisher, J. R., Hanusa, B. H., McHugh, M. C., & Valle, V. H. (1978). Attributions of the causes of success and failure as internal and external barriers to achievement. In J. L. Sherman, & F. I. Denmark (Eds.), *The psychology of women: Future directions in research* (pp. 19-552). New York: Psychological Dimensions.

Gaertner, S. L., & Bickman, L. (1971). Effects of race on the elicitation of helping behavior. *Journal of Personality and Social Psychology,* 20, 218-222.

Gaertner, S. L., & Dovidio, J. F. (1977). The subtlety of white racism, arousal, and helping behavior. *Journal of Personality and Social Psychology,* 35, 691-707.

Gaertner, S. L., & Dovidio, J. F. (1986). The aversive form of racism. In J. F. Dovidio, & S. I. Gaertner (Eds.), *Prejudice, discrimination, and racism* (pp. 61-89). Orlando, FL: Academic Press.

Gaertner, S. L., Mann, J. A., Dovidio, J. F., Murrell, A. J., & Pomare, M. (1990). How does cooperation reduce intergroup bias? *Journal of Personality and Social Psychology, 58,* 692-704.

Gagnon, A., & Bourhis, R. Y. (1996). Discrimination in the minimal group paradigm: Social identity of self-interest. *Personality and Social Psychology Bulletin, 22,* 1289-1301.

Glick, P., & Fiske, S. T. (1996). The Ambivalent Sexism Inventory: Differentiating hostile and benevolent sexism. *Journal of Personality and Social Psychology, 70,* 491-512.

Glick, P., et. al. (2000). Beyond prejudice as simple antipathy: Hostile and benevolent sexism across cultures. *Journal of Personality and Social Psychology, 79,* 763-775.

Gonzales, P. M., Blanton, H., & Williams, K. J. (2002). The effects of stereotypes threat and double-minority status on the test performance of Latino women. *Personality and Social Psychology Bulletin, 28,* 659-670.

Greenwald, A. G., Oakes, M. A., & Hoffman, H. G. (2003) Targets of discrimination: Effects of race on responses to weapons holders. *Journal of Experimental Social Psychology, 39,* 399-405.

Greenwald, A. G., Pickrell, J. E., & Farnham, S. D. (2002). Implicit partisanship: Taking sides for no reason. *Journal of Personality and Social Psychology, 83,* 367-379.

Guimond, S. (2000). Group socialization and prejudice: the social transmission of intergroup attitudes and beliefs. *European Journal of Social Psychology, 30,* 335-354.

Guimond, S., Dambrun, M., Michinov, N., & Duarte, S. (2003). Does social dominance generate prejudice? Integrating individual and contextual determinants of intergroup cognitions. *Journal of Personality and Social Psychology, 84,* 697-721.

Haddock, G., Zanna, M. P., & Esses, V. M. (1993). Assessing the structure of prejudicial attitudes: The case of attitudes toward homosexuals. *Journal of Personality and Social Psychology, 65,* 1105-1118.

Haddock, G., Zanna, M. P., & Esses, V. M. (1994). The (limited) role of trait-laden stereotypes in predicting attitudes toward native peoples. *British Journal of Social Psychology, 33,* 83-106.

Hamilton, D. L. (1981). *Cognitive processes in stereotyping and intergroup behavior.* Hillsdale, NJ: Erlbaum.

Heal, M. R., Foster, J. B., Mannix, L. M., & Dovidio, J. F. (2003). Formal and interpersonal discrimination: A field study of bias toward homosexual applicants. *Personality and Social psychology Bulletin, 28,* 815-825.

Hepworth, J. T., & West, S. G. (1998). Lynchings and the economy: A time-series reanalysis of Hovland and Sears (1940). *Journal of Personality and Social Psychology, 55,* 239-247.

Hertel, G., & Kerr, N. L. (2001). Priming ingroup favoritism: The impact of normative scripts in the minimal group paradigm. *Journal of Experimental Social Psychology, 37,* 316-324.

Hertel, G., & Kerr, N. L., & Messé, L. A. (2000). Motivation gains in performance groups: Paradigmatic and theoretical developments on the Kohler effect. *Journal of Personality and Social Psychology, 79,* 580-601.

Hodson, G., Dovidio, J. F., & Gaertner, S. L. (2002). Processes in racial discrimination: Differential weighting of conflicting information. *Personality and Social Psychology Bulletin, 28,* 460-471.

Hovland, C. I., & Sears, R. (1940). Minor studies in aggression: VI. Correlation of lynching with economic indices. *Journal of Psychology, 9,* 301-310.

Hunter, J. A., Platow, M. J., Howard, M. L., & Stringer, M. (1996). Social identity and intergroup evaluation bias: Realistic categories and domain specific self-esteem in a conflict setting. *European Journal of Social Psychology, 26,* 631-647.

Insko, C. A., Schopler, J., Graetz, K. A., Drigotas, S. M., Currey, D. P., Smith, S. L., Brazil, D., & Bernstein, G. (1994). Individual-intergroup discontinuity in the Prisoner's Dilemma game. *Journal of Conflict Resolution, 38,* 87-116.

Jetten, J., Spears, R., & Manstead, A. S. R. (1997). Strength of identification and intergroup differentiation: The influence of group norms. *Journal of Social Psychology, 27,* 603-609.

Jost, J. T., & Burgess, D. (2000). Attitudinal ambivalence and the conflict between group and system justification motives in low status groups. *Personality and Social Psychology Bulletin, 26,* 293-305.

Katz, I., Wakenhut, J., & Hass, R. G. (1986). Racial ambivalence, value duality, and behavior. In J. H. F. Dovidio, & S. L. Gaertner (Eds.), *Prejudice, Discrimination, and Racism* (pp. 35-59). Orlando, FL: Academic Press.

Kelly, H. H., & Stahelski, A. J. (1970). Social interaction basis of cooperators' and competitors' beliefs about others. *Journal of Personality and Social Psychology, 16,* 66-91.

Major, B., Spencer, S., Schmader, T., Wolfe, C., & Crocker, J. (1998). Coping with negative stereotypes about intellectual performance: The role of psychological disengagement. *Personality and Social Psychology Bulletin, 24,* 34-50.

McCauley, C. R. (1995). Are stereotypes exaggerated? A sampling of racial, gender, academic, occupational, and political stereotypes. In Y. T. Lee, L. J. Jussim, & C. R. McCauley (Eds.), *Stereotype accuracy: Toward appreciating group differences* (pp. 215-243). Washington, DC: American Psychological Association.

McIntyre, R. B., Paulson, R. M., & Lord, C. G. (2003). Alleviating women's mathematics stereotype threat through salience of group achievements. *Journal of Experimental Social Psychology, 39,* 83-90.

Mullen, B., & Hu, L. T. (1989). Perceptions of ingroup and outgroup variability: A meta-analytic integration. *Basic and Applied Social Psychology, 10*, 233-252.

Mullin, C. R., & Linz, D. (1995). Desensitization and resensitization to violence against women: Effects of exposure to sexually violent films on judgments of domestic violence victims. *Journal of Personality and Social Psychology, 69*, 449-459.

Neuberg, S. L., & Cottrell, C. A. (2002). Intergroup emotions: A biocultural approach. In D. M. Mackie, & E. R. Smith (Eds.), *From prejudice to intergroup emotions: Differentiated reactions to social groups* (pp. 265-283). New York: Psychological Press.

Niemann, Y. F., Jennings, L., Rozelle, R. M., Baxter, J.C., & Sullivan, E. (1994). Use of free responses and cluster analysis to determine stereotypes of eight groups. *Personality and Social Psychology Bulletin, 20*, 3790390.

Oakes, P. J., Haslam, S. A., & Turner, J. C. (1994). *Stereotyping and social reality*. Oxford, UK: Blackwell.

Osborne, J. W. (1995). Academics, Self-esteem, and race: A look at the underlying assumptions of the dis-identification hypothesis. *Personality and Social Psychology Bulletin, 21*, 449-455.

Ottai, V., & Lee, Y.-T. (1995). Accuracy: A neglected component of stereotype research. In Y.-T. Lee, L. J. Jussim, & C. R. McCauley (Eds.), *Stereotype accuracy: Toward appreciating group differences* (pp. 29-59). Washington, DC: American Psychological Association.

Otten, S., & Moskowitz, G. B. (2000). Evidence for implicit evaluative ingroup bias: Affect-biased spontaneous trait inference in a minimal group paradigm. *Journal of Experimental Social Psychology, 36*, 77-89.

Park, B., Judd, C. M., & Ryan, C. S. (1991). Social categorization and the representation of variability information. In W. Stroebe, & M. Hewstone (Eds.), *European review of social psychology* (Vol. 2, pp. 211-245). New York: Wiley.

Payne, B. K. (2001). Prejudice and perception: the role of automatic and controlled processes in misperceiving a weapon. *Journal of Personality and Social Psychology, 81*, 181-192.

Payne, B. K., Lambert, A. J., & Jacoby, L. L. (2002). Best laid plans: Effects of goals on accessibility bias and cognitive control in race-based misperceptions of weapons. *Journal of Experimental Social Psychology, 38*, 384-396.

Pettigrew, T. F. (1958). Personality and sociocultural factors in intergroup attitudes: A cross-national comparison. *Conflict Resolution, 2*, 29-42.

Pettigrew, T. F. (1979). The ultimate attribution error: Extending Allport's cognitive analysis of prejudice. *Personality and Social Psychology Bulletin, 5*, 461-476.

Pettigrew, T. F. (1997). Generalized intergroup contact effects on prejudice. *Personality and Social Psychology Bulletin, 23*, 173-185.

Pettigrew, T. F., & Meertens, R. W. (1995). Subtle and blatant prejudice in western Europe. *European Journal of Social Psychology, 25*, 57-75.

Pettigrew, T. F., & Tropp, L. R. (2000). Does intergroup contact reduce prejudice" Recent meta-analytic findings. In S. Oskamp (Ed.), *Reducing prejudice and discrimination*. The Claremont Symposium on Applied Social Psychology (pp. 93-114). Mahwah, NJ: Erlbaum.

Pinel, E. (1999). Stigma consciousness: The psychological legacy of social stereotypes. *Journal of Personality and Social Psychology, 76*, 114-128.

Plant, E. A., & Devine, P. G. (1998). Internal and external motivation to respond without prejudice. *Journal of Personality and Social Psychology, 75*, 811-832.

Plant, E. A., & Devine, P. G. (2001). Responses to other-imposed pro-Black pressure: Acceptance or backlash? *Journal of Experimental Social Psychology, 37*, 468-501.

Pratto, F., Sidanious, J., Stallworth, L. M., & Malle, B. F. (1994). Social dominance orientation: A personality variable predicting social and political attitudes. *Journal of Personality and Social Psychology, 67*, 741-763.

Pryor, J. B., & Day, J. D. (1998). Interpretations of sexual harassment: An attributional analysis. *Sex Roles, 18*, 405-417.

Pryor, J. B., LaVite, C., & Stoler, L. (1993). A social psychological analysis of sexual harassment: the person/situation interaction. *Journal of Experimental Social Psychology, 21*, 362-379.

Reich, M. (1971). The economics of racism. In D. M. Gordon (ed.), *Problems in political economy* (pp. 107-113). Lexington, MA: Heath.

Richeson, J. A., & Shelton, J. N. (2003). When prejudice does not pay: Effects of interracial contact on executive function. *Psychological Science, 14*, 287-290.

Rotundo, M., Nguyen, D. H., & Sackett, P. R. (2001). A meta-analytic review of gender differences in perceptions of sexual harassment. *Journal of Applied Psychology, 86*, 914-922.

Saenz, D. S. (1994). Token status and problem-solving deficits: Detrimental effects of distinctiveness and performance monitoring. *Social Cognition, 12*, 61-74.

Sales, S. M., & Friend, K. E. (1973). Success and failure as determinants of level of authoritarianism. *Behavioral Sciences, 18*, 163-172.

Scarr, S. (1981). The transmission of authoritarian attitudes in families: Genetic resemblance in social-political attitudes? In S. Scarr (Ed.), *Race, social class, and individual differences* (pp. 399-427). Hillsdale, NJ: Erlbaum.

Schopler, J,. et al. (2001). When groups are more competitive than individuals: The domain of the discontinuity effect. *Journal of Personality and Social Psychology, 80*, 632-644.

Schulman, K. A., et al. (1999). The effects of race and sex on physicians' recommendations for cardiac catheterization. *New England Journal of Medicine, 340*, 618-626.

Sherif, M., Harvey, O. J., White, B. J., Hood, W. R., & Sherif, C. W. (1961/1988). *The robbers cave experiment: Intergroup conflict and cooperation.* Middletown, CT: Wesleyan University Press.

Shih, M., Pittinsky, T. L., & Ambady, N. (1999). Stereotype susceptibility: Identity salience and shifts in quantitative performance. *Psychological Science, 10*, 80-83.

Sidanius, J., & Pratto, F. (1993). The inevitability of oppression and the dynamics of social dominance. In P. Sniderman, & P.Tetlock (Eds.), *Prejudice, politics, and the American dilemma* (pp. 173-211). Stanford, CA: Stanford University Press.

Sidanius, J., & Pratto, F. (1999*). Social dominance: An intergroup theory of social hierarchy and oppression.* New York: Cambridge University Press.

Sigelman, C. K., Howell, J. L., Cornell, D. P., Cutright, J. D., & Dewey, J. C. (1991). Courtesy stigma: The social implications of associating with a gay person. *Journal of Social Psychology, 131*, 45-56.

Snyder, C. R., Lassegard, M., & Ford, C. E. (1986). Distancing after group success and failure: Basking in reflected glory and cutting off reflected failure. *Journal of Personality and Social Psychology, 51*, 382-388.

Spencer, S. J., Fein, S., Wolfe, C. T., Fong, C., & Dunn, M. A. (1998). Automatic activation of stereotypes: the role of self-image threat. *Personality and Social Psychology Bulletin, 24*, 1139-1152.

Steele, C. M., & Aronson, J. (1995). Stereotype threat and the intellectual test performance of African Americans. *Journal of Personality and Social Psychology, 69*, 797-811.

Stone, J. (2002). Battling doubt by avoiding practice: the effects of stereotype threat on self-handicapping in white athletes. *Personality and Social Psychology Bulletin, 28*, 1667-1678,

Stone, J., Lynch, C. I., Sjomeling, M., & Darley, J. M. (1999). Stereotype threat effects on black and white athletic performance. *Journal of Personality and Social Psychology, 77*, 1213-1227.

Swim, J. K., & Miller, D. L. (1999). White guilt: Its antecedents and consequences for attitudes toward affirmative action. *Personality and Social Psychology Bulletin, 25*, 500-514.

Swim, J. K., & Sanna, L. J. (1996). He's skilled, she's lucky: A meta-analysis of observers' attributions for women's and men's successes and failures. *Personality and Social Psychology Bulletin, 22*, 507-519.

Swim, J. K., Ferguson, M. J. & Hyers, L. L. (1999). Avoiding stigma by association: Subtle prejudice against lesbians in the form of social distancing. *Basic and Applied Social Psychology, 21*, 61-68.

Tajefel, H., & Turner, J. (1979). An integrative theory of intergroup conflict. In W. G. Austin, & S. Worchel (Eds.), *The social psychology of intergroup relations* (pp. 33-47). Monterey, CA: Brooks-Cole.

Tajefel, H., & Turner, J. (1986). The social identity theory of intergroup behavior. In S. Worchel, & W. G. Austin (Eds.), *Psychology, of intergroup relations* (2nd ed., pp. 7-24). Chicago: Nelson-Hall.

Terkel, S. (1992). *Race: How blacks and whites think and feel about the American obsession.* New York: Anchor.

Von Hippel, W., Sekaquaptewa, D., & Vargas, P. (1997). The linguistic intergroup bias as an implicit indicator of prejudice. *Journal of experimental Social Psychology, 33*, 490-509.

Whitley, B. E., & Lee, S. E. (2000). The relationship of authoritarianism and related constructions to attitudes toward homosexuality. *Journal of Applied Social Psychology, 30*, 144-170.

Wills, T. A. (1981). Downward comparison principles in social psychology. *Psychological Bulletin, 90*, 245-271.

Wittenbrink, B., & Henly, J. R. (1996). Creating social reality: Informational social influence and the content of stereotypic beliefs. *Personality and Social Psychology Bulletin*, 22, 598-610.

Wittenbrink, B., Judd, C. M., & Park, B. (1997). Evidence for racial prejudice at the implicit level and its relationship with questionnaire measures. *Journal of Personality and Social Psychology, 72*, 262-274.

Wylie, R. (1979). *The self-concept* (vol. 2). Lincoln: University of Nebraska Press.

Yinger, J. (1995). *Closed doors, opportunities lost: The continuing costs of housing discrimination.* New York: Russell Sage Foundations.

11 | THE INDIVIDUAL AND GENDER SCRIPTS
by Alexander F. Rice

The sense of identity each of us possesses includes knowing what it is like to be male or female. It is important to differentiate between the biological traits that distinguish males and females (sex) and the social and psychological traits associated with masculinity and femininity (gender). Gender roles are social roles associated with being male or female. Our conception of ourselves as either male or female constitutes our gender identity. Each of us receives an elaborate socialization with regard to gender, regardless of the society into which we are born. There are various cross-cultural variations in gender. Gender-role expectations are taught and reinforced through socialization from the moment of birth onward. Two distinct mechanisms are primarily responsible for gender-role socialization: differential treatment and identification with role models. Gender roles are changing constantly but there are adult gender expectations that apply to men and women in American society. But how do we develop these gender roles?

THEORIES OF SOCIALIZATION

There are many different theories of socialization used to examine how this process is accomplished for children. The theories of socialization utilized in this chapter are symbolic interaction theory concerning the "generalized other" and "looking glass self," social learning theory, and gender schema theory.

SYMBOLIC INTERACTION THEORY

Symbolic interaction theory is influenced by the ideas of two early sociologists, Charles H. Cooley and George Herbert Mead. The basis behind symbolic interaction theory is that the individual develops a personality through interaction with others and by using symbols to define who they are.

The idea of the "looking glass self" is that children determine who they are based on how they imagine others see them and their positive or negative reactions to those reflected appraisals. Symbolic interaction theory asserts that the child does not develop a self-concept until he or she has acquired the concept of others. Similar to the ideas of Cooley are those of Mead, regarding the "generalized other." Mead suggests that socialization occurs through a maturational process. Through interaction with others, children go through four stages of social and personality development. As children move through these stages, they go from being the center of the universe, toward understanding others' rights and expectations. The four stages that Mead refers to are:

> *The Prepatory Stage* (birth to 2 years) – The child is unaware of any other personality and behaves as though he or she is the center of the universe.

> *The Play Stage* (2 to 7 years) – The child moves through rapid emulation of roles he or she perceives. Through the practice of pretending to be others, for example, a doctor, teacher, or rock star, the child begins to understand the concept of "others."

> *The Game Stage* (7 years and up) - The maturing child perceives others' expectations, and self's rights, gradually acquiring the ability to take the role of the generalized other, which is simply a mixture of all the socially approved values and behaviors necessary for social adaptation and interaction.

> *The Reference Stage* (15 to adult) - The person uses knowledge he has acquired from family, school, church, etc. as reference on how to act in certain social settings.

When children interact with a parent, friend, or teacher, they use imagination to put themselves in the other's role. When doing this, children primarily learn to view themselves from the point of view of a particular person. Eventually, as children come to understand how social relationships work, they begin to see themselves from the point of view of the generalized other, and understand the expectations that society has of them. Through role-playing, children learn the give and take, compromise, adjustment, and reciprocity that help lead to a sense of self. As children move through the stages that Mead describes, they come to understand that symbols have specific functions for the individual (Charon, 2001). Children then develop a sense of self, including gender identity, and participate in their own socialization. This theory is closely related to social learning theory.

SOCIAL LEARNING THEORY

Social learning theory considers socialization in terms of rewards and punishments. Specifically, social learning theory is concerned with the way children model behavior they view in others such as cooperation, selfishness, and aggressiveness. The child receives approval for the appropriate behavior or is reprimanded for behavior that is considered inappropriate. These behaviors include personal hygiene, toilet training, and table manners. As with other behaviors, gender roles are learned directly through reprimands and rewards and indirectly through observation and imitation (Bandura and Walters, 1963; Mischel, 1966; Bandura, 1986). Imitation or modeling appears to be spontaneous in children, but through reinforcement, specific patterns of behavior soon develop.

It is really quite simple. Differential reinforcement occurs for doing either "boy" or "girl" things. In anticipation of the consequences of these behaviors, the child learns to get the label applied to him or herself that is associated with rewards. This becomes the basis for gender identity. It becomes apparent that the two sexes behave differently and that two gender roles are proper. As parents, teachers, and peers model gender role behavior during the critical primary socialization years, children, through reinforcement, tend to follow in line with their role models. Gender identity results from this continued reinforcement. Therefore, the assumption is that "knowledge about gender roles either precedes or is acquired at the same time as gendered identity" (Intons-Peterson, 1988). In contrast to many psychoanalytical theories, social learning views gender socialization primarily in terms of environmental influences.

Some of the earliest research on social learning theory and gender socialization was conducted by Lynn (1959, 1969) to account for the difficulty that boys encounter in gender role socialization. Lynn asserts that during the first years of primary socialization, the father is not likely to be available as much as the mother. And when the father is home, the contact is qualitatively different from contact with the mother in terms of intimacy. Stereotypically, fathers are the breadwinners and disciplinarians whereas mothers are the nurturers. Levy (1989) maintains that it is the mother who provides the basis of all subsequent learning in the child. What is generalized is that male role models are often scarce and boys must somehow put together a definition of masculinity based on incomplete information. They are often told what they should not do rather than what they should do. For example, parents often say things like, "big boys don't cry" and "don't be a sissy, take it like a man." Girls tend to have an easier time in this respect due to continuous contact with the mother and the use of her as a role model.

Lynn (1969) further contends that it is the lack of exposure to males at an early age that leads boys to view masculinity in a stereotyped manner. This may explain why the male role is more inflexible and also why males often tend to be insecure about their gender identity. This view of masculinity has many consequences. Male peer groups encourage the belief that aggression and toughness are virtues. Males exhibit hostility toward both females and homosexuals, and cross-gender behavior in boys is viewed more negatively than when it occurs in girls, with women more accepting of cross-gender children than men (Carter and McCloskey, 1983; Fagot, 1985; Martin, 1990). Men's fear of ridicule propels them to exaggerate anti-homosexual and sexist remarks to ensure that others do not get "the wrong idea" concerning their masculinity (Kimmel, 1994). Although the research does not confirm that modeling in itself is responsible for gender role acquisition, it does indicate that gender appropriate behavior is strongly associated with parental and social approval. Boys learn that their role is much more desirable and brings with it more self-esteem.

It would be a mistake to assume that the socialization path for girls is easy because of the availability of the mother as a constant role model. Young children are bombarded with stimuli that suggest that higher worth, prestige, and rewards are given to males. Girls are offered gender roles that are associated with less worth and must model behavior that may be held in lower esteem. These gender expectations lead to a preference for masculine behavior. But, where do these models come from?

REFERENCE GROUPS

Family

The family is the child's first reference group. In addition, friends, teachers, and the media also play a part in acting as role models and reinforcing acceptable behavior (Beal, 1994). Parents begin the process by encouraging sons to be more independent, competitive, and achieving than daughters. They also encourage daughters to be more passive and to seek protection. This would include dressing their daughters more decoratively and their sons in more practical styles. Parents also provide children with sex-typed toys and encourage sex-appropriate play activities while discouraging play activities that are deemed to be more appropriate for the opposite sex, such as boys playing with dolls.

One area in which there was marked difference was the encouragement of sex-typed activities (Lytton & Romney, 1991). When sex-specific toys are provided to children, the result is different play and problem-solving experiences for children. Because boys are given more opportunities to explore their world and engage in more physical activities than girls, girls usually experience a more restrictive world.

The key components of social learning theory are reinforcement and modeling. Children receive social rewards for engaging in the activities and behaviors that parents deem appropriate for their gender. While role models are important for children to imitate, the absence of role models also has an effect on children. When girls see few other girls enrolled in higher math classes or boys see few boys enrolled in home economics or nursing classes, for example, they may be less likely to pursue those activities themselves (Beal, 1994). The nature of children within the social learning framework is as imitators of behavior. This puts children in the role of waiting for reinforcement of a behavior and learning by engaging in behaviors that are observed or reinforced. Research conducted by Bandura (1977) on the relationship between children and aggression has shown that children will engage in aggressive behaviors after observing those behaviors even without direct reinforcement.

There are differences in the reinforcement fathers and mothers give to sons and daughters. A study of parent-toddler interaction found that mothers responded more to daughters and fathers to sons. Fathers gave more emotional responses and mothers gave more instructions (Fagot, Leinbach, and O'Boyle, 1992). Mothers also give more verbal stimulation to sons than to daughters. Even parents who claim to be egalitarian in their dealings with their children have been found to discourage certain non-traditional play behaviors more in one gender than the other. Again, the example of parents discouraging their sons from playing with dolls, or their daughters from playing with trucks comes into effect (Weisner, and Wilson-Mitchell, 1990). This behavior on the part of parents serves to model and reinforce stereotyped behaviors in children.

Children learn through observing their parents how to fit in and manage their environment. According to social learning theory, children are motivated by their strong desire to be like those in their world (Beal, 1994). Children want to identify with their same sex parent; when they imitate role models, it is because they have admiration for those role models (Beal, 1994). When children imitate what they see, they are either reinforced positively for behaving as parental or peer group norms dictate, or negatively if they stray from the norm. For example, a boy who takes a home economics course may feel uncomfortable if he is the only male in the class, whereas, when a young woman tries to go to an all male school, she may be disliked and considered an outsider because she is doing something that her peer group considers inappropriate. Because children are conditioned through social learning to behave in socially approved ways if they want to get along in society, it is easier and more comfortable to simply accept those behaviors which society deems appropriate. The desired outcome for children is that they imitate appropriate behaviors and become suitable members of society. These behaviors are rewarded with praise and encouragement. Behaviors, which are deemed to be inappropriate or unacceptable, are discouraged.

Peer Groups and School

As children age and develop, they are introduced to the world outside of the family. They soon realize that gender role patterns that were established within the family are also true within their peer groups. Parents usually initiate the first relationships for their children. These relationships often develop later into friendships chosen by the children themselves. Toddlers often play with same age children and parents do not feel the need to separate them by gender at this early age. But as school age approaches, the situation changes rapidly. The same-sex peer group becomes a major context for social interaction and socialization.

The best way to view the stereotyped differences is through the games children play. Activities, games, and overall socialization are strongly related to gender. The games of boys are more complex, competitive, rule-governed, and allow for more role differentiation and a larger number of participants than games played by girls (Lever, 1978; Ignico and Mead, 1990; Corsaro and Elder, 1990). Girls are often encouraged to play games like hopscotch and jump rope, which usually involves groups of only two or three, and are less competitive. The stereotype that generally associates competitive behavior with masculinity but not femininity is consistently supported by research (King et al., 1991). This further separates the two genders.

Gender segregation and the influence of peers continue throughout the school years. As suggested by the research on games, boys interact in larger groups and have more extensive peer relationships, with girls having more intensive ones (Corsaro and Elder, 1990; O'Connor, 1992). This is consistent with research demonstrating that self-disclosure, intimacy, and trust are higher for women, especially female best-friend pairs (Buhrke and Fuqua, 1987). Rotenberg (1984) hypothesizes that after children gain a pattern of same-sex relationships, these relationships are reinforced through a same-sex pattern of trust. Gender boundaries are then monitored and enforced by peers and the worlds of male and female are further divided.

GENDER SCHEMA THEORY

Gender schema theory offers an information processing approach to socialization in that the theory describes and explains the child's developing content and organization of gender knowledge (Bem, 1981). A basic assumption of gender schema theory is that gender knowledge is multidimensional, with children believing that there are behaviors, attitudes, characteristics, and occupations which are gender related (Huston, 1983). These beliefs are internalized by children and become a part of their socialization into adult roles. Within gender schema theory children are seen as active participants in the socialization process. As children move through childhood, they increase their knowledge about gender. They also start to show an understanding about gender and recognize that the world is divided into male and female elements as early as two years of age (Fagot, Leinbach, and O'Boyle, 1992). Preschool children in particular, have been shown to rely heavily on gender labeling (Martin, Wood, & Little, 1990). As children grow older, they have more knowledge about gender roles and are more likely to make inferences about gender behavior and attitudes based on little information (Golombok & Fivush, 1994). Some studies have shown that children become more flexible in their gender differentiations as they get older (Signorella, Bigler, & Liben, 1993). For some children gender is an important way of organizing their environment and thinking about the world. These children are very concerned with what behaviors are appropriate or inappropriate based on gender (Levy & Carter, 1989). Gender schema theory also views gender typed behavior as being guided by the child's anticipation of the responses of others (Bussey & Bandura, 1992). Thus, motivation for the child comes through the desire to do what is culturally and socially correct.

Gender schema theory also has elements of social learning because children are observing gender related behaviors and imitating them. Symbolic interaction theory focuses on the learning of language and other symbols commonly used in society and developing a sense of self and a sense of how to get along in society based on these symbols. Children determine their self-concept by accepting the view of others, or looking glass self, and also by taking the role of others, or generalized other. Socially approved behaviors come from family, friends, the media, and school. Whether or not those socially approved behaviors and attitudes are acceptable for both males and females throughout life is sometimes raised as a question of concern, and leads to the question of whether a neutral gender role orientation might be more salient for individuals in today's society. Influences on gender role socialization include parents, friends, the media (mainly television), and school.

Gender role socialization, which almost always includes some degree of gender role stereotyping, begins at birth. As children grow and develop, the gender stereotypes they are exposed to at home are reinforced by other things in their environment and are thus perpetuated throughout childhood (Martin, Wood, & Little, 1990). As children move into the larger world of friends and school, those around them reinforce many of their ideas and beliefs. A further reinforcement of acceptable and appropriate behavior is shown to children through the media. Through all these socialization agents, children learn gender-stereotyped behavior. As children develop, these gender stereotypes become firmly fixed beliefs. It has been suggested that children develop gender stereotypes in three stages:

1. Learning what types of things are associated with each sex (i.e., boys play with cars, girls play with dolls).

2. Learning associations for what is relevant to their own sex but not the opposite sex.

3. Learning the associations relevant to the opposite sex. (Martin, Wood, & Little, 1990).

Parental Influence

A child's earliest exposure to what it means to be male or female comes from parents. From the time their children are babies, parents treat sons and daughters differently, dressing infants in gender specific colors, giving gender-differentiated toys and expecting different behavior from boys and girls (Thorne, 1993). Parents have different expectations of sons and daughters as early as 24 hours after birth. Children internalize parental messages regarding gender at an early age, with awareness of adult sex role differences being found in two-year-old children (Weinraub et al., 1984). One study found that children at two and a half years of age use gender stereotypes in negotiating their world and are likely to generalize gender stereotypes to a variety of activities, objects, and occupations (Fagot, Leinbach, and O'Boyle, 1992). Parents encourage their sons and daughters to participate in sex-typed activities, including doll playing and engaging in housekeeping activities for girls and playing with trucks and engaging in sports activities for boys (Eccles, Jacobs & Harold, 1990). Children's toy preferences have been related to parental sex typing (Etaugh and Liss, 1992). Parents provide gender-differentiated toys and reward the child for behavior that is gender stereotyped. While both mothers and fathers contribute to the gender stereotyping of their children, fathers have been found to reinforce gender stereotypes more often than mothers. Even children's rooms are gender stereotyped. Girls' rooms have more pink, dolls, and manipulative toys, and boys' rooms have more blue, sports equipment, tools and toy trucks. Boys are more likely to have maintenance chores around the house, such as taking out the trash and mowing the lawn, while girls are more likely to have domestic chores such as washing the dishes and doing the laundry. This assignment of household tasks by gender leads children to link certain types of work with gender. Some studies have suggested that parent-shaping as a socializing factor has little impact on a child's sex role development (Lytton & Romney, 1991). Other research suggests that parents are the primary influence on gender role development during the early years of life (Kaplan, 1991). Parental attitudes towards their children have a strong impact on the child's developing sense of self and self-esteem, with parental warmth and support being key factors for the child. Often, parents give subtle messages regarding gender and what is acceptable for each gender. Sex role stereotypes are well established in early childhood. Messages about what is appropriate based on gender are so strong that even when children are exposed to different attitudes and experiences, they will revert to stereotyped choices. Children who have parents with strong egalitarian values tend to be more informed about non sex-typed objects and occupations than other children (Weisner and Wilson-Mitchell, 1990). Children whose mothers work outside the home are not as traditional in sex role orientation as children whose mothers stay home (Weinraub, Jaeger, and Hoffman, 1988). In fact, preschool children whose mothers work outside the home experience the world with a sense that everyone in the family gets to become a member of the outside world, and their sense of self includes the knowledge that they have the ability to make choices which are not hindered by gender (Davies & Banks, 1992).

Boys and girls also have different styles of play and interaction from one another. Boys choose more rough and tumble play and competitive activities than girls. Often, girls and their activities are seen as inferior to boys and their activities. The skills and abilities children learn from friends are different for boys and girls. In peer interactions, boys learn to negotiate conflict and be one of the guys. Girls are more likely to communicate one-on-one and learn the skill of listening. Boys and girls also use language in different ways, with boys using language to maintain independence and girls using language to establish a relationship with their friends. Boys initiate more conflicts than girls and are more likely to solve those conflicts with physical aggression. Children tend to not like aggressive girls, and girls are likely to be shunned when acting aggressively (Fagot, Leinbach, and O'Boyle 1992). Feedback from friends on gender appropriate behaviors and attitudes is important to children, and children seek out same sex friends because of their need to establish gender identity (Beal, 1994).

There also appears to be differences in the ways that boys and girls approach friendships. Boys seem to need to establish status with a group of buddies; girls are more likely to create intimate friendships with one or two close friends (Beal, 1994). Boys also appear to be more sensitive than females to peer feedback on what constitutes appropriate masculine activities (Fagot, Leinbach, and O'Brien 1992). Within their same sex playgroups, children punish those who deviate from gender appropriate activities, by making critical remarks or ignoring the friend (Beal, 1994). It is more acceptable among children's peer groups for girls to be "tomboys" than it is for boys to be "sissies" (Kaplan, 1991). This seems to indicate that masculine behaviors are valued more highly by children. Because masculine behaviors are indicators of higher self-esteem in children than feminine behaviors, this may indicate that the cultivation of an androgynous orientation may be particularly beneficial for girls (Bem, 1981). Because peer groups have a strong influence on the gender role socialization of children, and because gender stereotypes are reinforced by parents, school and the media, children often grow up with a sense of self that is based on outdated or unrealistic ideas of what it is to be male or female. Parents who wish to raise their children in a non-gender stereotyped way face difficulties because so many aspects of society are gender stereotyped with behaviors and attitudes differentiated by sex (Bem, 1981). Non-gender stereotyped behavior takes longer to develop in children than stereotypic behavior because the child has to learn, and then unlearn, traditional behaviors (Sedney, 1987). Stereotypic behavior leads to gender inequality throughout the life process.

PATRIARCHY AND SEXISM

The concept of gender varies from culture to culture, and to some degree, patriarchy is universal in the world. **Patriarchy** literally means "the rule of fathers," but more generally it refers to a social situation where men are dominant over women in wealth, status, and power. Patriarchy is associated with a set of ideas, a "patriarchal ideology" that acts to explain and justify this dominance and attributes it to inherent natural differences between men and women. Sociologists tend to see patriarchy as a social product and not as an outcome of innate differences between the sexes and they focus attention on the way that gender roles in a society affect power differentials between men and women. Despite mythical tales of societies dominated by female "Amazons," **matriarchy**, a form of social organization in which females dominate, has never been documented in human history (Gough 1971). Although patriarchy may be universal, there is a difference in the amount of power that is given to women worldwide. For example, women in the United States have much more power than those in Africa or Pakistan. But that power is much less than that of males.

Sexism is the belief that one sex is innately superior to the other. This is the ideological basis of patriarchy. Sexism is perpetuated by systems of patriarchy where male-dominated structures and social arrangements reinforce the oppression of women. Patriarchy almost by definition also exhibits androcentrism, meaning male centered. Coupled with patriarchy, androcentrism assumes that male norms operate throughout all social institutions and becomes the standard to which all persons adhere. Males become the unit of analysis and this is extremely detrimental to women.

Patriarchy and sexism create social systems that oppress women. The costs of patriarchy and sexism are staggering. It limits the talents and ambitions of women. Marilyn French (1985) argues that patriarchy causes men to relentlessly seek control not only over women, but also of themselves and their own world. As the oldest social institution, the family is seen as the place where patriarchy originated and eventually reproduced throughout society. Violence against women is a prime example. Violence in the home includes spousal battering, marital rape, and incest. With the possible exception of the military, the home may be the most violent setting where men and women interact. Government estimates indicate that around 2 million women are assaulted each year in a variety of settings.

Rape is a form of violence that many women fear. According to the Bureau of Justice Statistics, persons age 12 or older experienced an average annual 140,990 completed rapes, 109,230 attempted rapes, and 152,680 completed and attempted sexual assaults between 1992 and 2000, according to the National Crime Victimization Survey (NCVS). Most rapes and sexual assaults were committed against females: Female victims accounted for 94% of all completed rapes, 91% of all attempted rapes, and 89% of all completed and attempted sexual assaults, (*BJS* 1992-2000). Added to the number of physical assaults suffered by women each year, these numbers are pretty grim. Most women who are assaulted or raped know their assailant, as is the case in date or **acquaintance rape**. Researchers have concluded that most female students, and even some male students, have experienced forced or coerced sex. Sadly, date rapes go largely unreported because the victims often feel that they are partially to blame because they know the person and went on the date voluntarily.

The abuse of women tends to be built into our culture. Most rapes involve someone who was trusted by the victim. The forms of violence against women constitute a culture of rape, from the attempts to control female sexuality through patriarchy to whistles directed at women on city streets. Even language is used to control the sexuality of women. When men refer to each other as dogs or studs they are rarely offended. However, referring to women as dogs or bitches equate women with animals. Animals are considered property. Men also use female pronouns when referring to property, such as their cars or boats, saying, "She sure is a beauty." There are a number of sexual norms related to patriarchy. For example, it is generally accepted that men should be older than their spouse and more sexually experienced. Men often initiate sex, decide what position to engage in, and how long it lasts. Clearly, such norms help men control the sexuality of women.

When we examine power in personal relationships, we find that women are systematically disadvantaged. Power is an important source of prestige. Regardless of the social institution, be it the family, church, or work place, most women occupy positions subordinate to men. This is very apparent when it comes to work around the home.

FIRST AND SECOND SHIFT

In sociologist Arlie Hochschild's landmark 1989 book, The Second Shift, the author summarized more than a decade of research showing that in 80 percent of two-parent American families, women are responsible for the majority of household and child-rearing tasks regardless of their demographic circumstances. It makes no difference whether they are in their 20s, 30s, or 40s, rich or poor, well-educated or not, married or not, Caucasian, Asian, Latino or African-American. The common thread among women in all of these groups is that they do most of the shopping, cleaning, cooking, laundry, doctor appointments, birthday parties, and many other tasks involved in rearing children and running a household. Even women who work for eight hours (or more) a day at paying jobs outside the home still assume the brunt of the domestic work that is required to keep a family going. In essence, they come home to a "second shift" from which their male partners are largely exempt.

Hochschild (1989) has well documented the phenomenon she terms the second shift. Even women who work the same full-time hours as their husbands spend more time than men on housekeeping and childcare.

> Most women without children spend much more time than men on housework; with children, they devote more time to both housework and child care. Just as there is a wage gap between men and women in the workplace, there is a "leisure gap" between them at home. Most women work one shift at the office or factory and a "second shift" at home. (Hochschild, 1989, p. 4)

Despite national findings that 78% of husbands believe that if both spouses work full time, they should share housework equally (Huber & Spitze, 1978), numerous studies have found that the burden of housework and childcare is still shouldered by wives. Compiling the findings of several studies, Bergmann (1986) and Blau and Ferber (1986) estimated that depending on the definition of housework, full-time homemakers spent an average of 40 to 48 hours per week on housework, and working wives spent 22 to 23 hours per week, while husbands spent only 8.5 to 12 hours per week on household tasks.

Even when men's contributions to housework increased, this did not necessarily signify an increase in their overall labor contribution. For example, while one study found that husbands housework time had increased by about an hour per week, their time spent at paid employment had decreased by about the same amount (Juster & Stafford, 1984). Comparisons of the amount of hours of women and men's paid and unpaid labor have consistently yielded Hochschild's (1989) leisure gap. One study of white working couples found women worked a total of 87 hours compared to 76 hours for their husbands, resulting in an 11 hours-per-week leisure gap (Coverman, 1983). Married mothers were observed to average 85 hours a week on paid employment, housework, and child care, while married fathers averaged only 66 hours, making a weekly leisure gap of 19 hours (Googins, 1987). Professional women with children were found to spend 30 hours a week more on paid and unpaid work than their husbands (Yogev, 1981). This does not even cover what single mothers face.

237

FEMINISM

Feminism is the advocacy of social equality for men and women, in opposition to patriarchy and sexism. This is the view of personal experiences through the lens of gender. Liberal feminists believe that people should be free to develop their own talents and pursue their own interests. They also endorse reproductive freedom for all women. Most feminists agree on five general principles:

1. **The importance of change.** Feminism is critical of the status quo, advocating change toward social equality for both sexes.

2. **Expanding human choice.** Feminists maintain that cultural conceptions of gender divide the full range of human qualities into two opposing and limited spheres: the female world of emotions and cooperation and the male world of rationality and competition. As an alternative, feminists propose a "reintegration of humanity" by which each human can develop all human traits (French, 1985).

3. **Eliminating gender stratification.** Feminism opposes laws and cultural norms that limit the education, income, and job opportunities for women.

4. **Ending sexual violence.** Feminists argue that patriarchy distorts the relationships between women and men, encouraging violence against women in the form of rape, domestic abuse, sexual harassment, and pornography (Millet, 1970; J. Bernard, 1973; Dworkin, 1987).

5. **Promoting sexual autonomy.** Feminists support the rights of women to control their own sexuality and reproduction. In other words, the right to control your own body, whether it is choosing to bear children or terminate a pregnancy.

There are many who oppose feminism, both men and women. These people hold conventional views about gender. They have been socialized to believe that women are the weaker of the two sexes. This opposition is similar to the reasons that many white people have about the social equality of people of color. They want to keep the status quo, or, in other words, preserve their own privileges. Men also believe that feminism threatens their masculinity. Men who have been socialized to value strength and dominance feel uneasy about feminist ideals of men as gentle and warm (Doyle, 1983). Similarly, women whose lives center on their husbands and children may see feminism as trying to deprive them of cherished roles that give meaning to their lives (Marshall, 1985).

ഈ ഇ ഈ ഇ

REFERENCES

Bandura, A. (1977). *Social learning theory.* Englewood Cliffs, NJ: Prentice-Hall Inc.

Bandura, A. (1986). *Social foundations of thought and action: A social cognitive.* Englewood Cliffs, NJ: Prentice Hall.

Bandura A., & Walters, R. H. (1963). *Social learning and personality development.* New York: Holt, Rinehart, and Winston, Inc.

Beal, C. (1994). *Boys and girls: The development of gender roles.* New York: McGraw-Hill.

Beere, C. A. (1990). *Gender roles: A handbook of tests and measures.* New York: Greenwood.

Bem, S. L. (1981). Gender schema theory: A cognitive account of sex typing. *Psychological Review,88*(4), 354-364.

Bergmann, B. R. (1986). *The economic emergence of women.* New York: Basic Books.

Bernard, J. (1973). *The future of marriage.* New Haven, CN: Yale University Press.

Blau, F. D, & Ferber, M. A. (1986). *The economics of women, men, and work.* Englewood Cliffs, NJ: Prentice-Hall.

Buhrke, R. A., & Fuqua, D. R. (1987). Sex differences in same- and cross-sex supportive relationships. *Sex Roles, 17,* 339-352.

Bureau of Justice Statistics. Retrieved May 22, (2007) from (http://www.ojp.usdoj.gov/bjs/pub/pdf/rsarp00.pdf).

Bussey, K., & Bandura, A. (1992). Self-regulatory mechanisms governing gender development. *Child Development, 63*(5), 1236.

Carter, B. D., & McCloskey, L. A. (1984). Peers and the maintenance of sex-typed behavior: The development of children's conceptions of cross-gender behavior in their peers. *Social Cognition, 2(14),* 294-314.

Charon, J. M. (2001). *Symbolic Interactionism.* Upper Saddle River, NJ: Prentiss Hall.

Cohen, L. R. (1991). Sexual harassment and the law. *Society, 28(4),* 8-13.

Corsaro, W. A, & Elder, D. (1990). Children's peer cultures. *Annual Review of Sociology, 16,* 197-220.

Coverman, S. (1983). Gender, domestic labor time, and wage inequality. *American Sociological Review, 48,* 623-636.

Davies, B., & Banks, C. (1992). The Gender Trap: A feminist poststructuralist analysis of primary school children's talk about gender. *Journal of Curriculum Studies, 24,* 1-25.

Doyle, J. A. (1983). *The Male Experience.* Dubuque, IA: Wm C. Brown.

Dworkin, A. (1987). *Intercourse.* New York: Free Press.

Eccles, J. S., Jacobs, J. E., & Harold, R. D. (1990). Gender role stereotypes, expectancy effects, and parents' socialization of gender differences. *Journal of Social Issues, 46,* 186-201.

Etaugh, C., & Liss, M.B. (1992). Home, school, and playroom: Training grounds for adult Gender roles. *Sex Roles, 26,* 129-147.

Fagot, B. I. (1985). Beyond the reinforcement principle: Another step toward understanding sex roles. *Developmental Psychology, 21,* 1097-1104.

Fagot, B. I., Leinbach, M.D., & O'Boyle, C. (1992). Gender labeling, gender stereotyping, and parenting behaviors. *Developmental Psychology, 28,* 225-230.

French, M. (1985). *Beyond Power: On women, men, and morals.* New York: Summit Books.

Golombok, S., & Fivush, R. (1994). *Gender development.* New York: Cambridge University Press.

Googins, B. (with D. Burden). (1987). *Balancing job and homelife study: Managing work and stress in corporations.* Unpublished manuscript, School of Social Work, Boston University.

Gough, K. (1971). The Origin of the family. *Journal of Marriage and the Family, 33*(4), 760-71.

Hochschild, A. (with A. Machung) (1989). *The second shift: Working parents and the revolution at home.* New York: Viking.

Huber, J., & Spitze, G. (1978). *Sex stratification: Children, housework and jobs.* New York: Academic Press.

Huston, A. C., O'Brien, M., & Risley, T. R. (1983). Sex-typed play of toddlers in a day care center. *Journal of Applied Developmental Psychology, 4*(1), 1-9.

Ignico, A. A., & Mead, B. J. (1990). Children's perceptions of the gender-appropriateness of physical activities. *Perceptual and Motor Skills, 71*, 1275-81.

Intons-Peterson, M. J. (1988). *Children's concepts of gender.* Norwood, NJ: Ablex.

Juster, F. T., & Stafford, F. T. (Eds.) (1985). *Time, goods, and well-being.* Ann Arbor, MI: Institute for Social Research, University of Michigan.

Kaplan, P. (1991). *A child's odyssey.* St. Paul, MN: West Publishing Company.

Kessler, R. C., & McLeod, J. (1984). Sex differences in vulnerability to undesirable life events. American Sociological Review, 49, 620-631.

Kimmel, M. S. (1994). Masculinity as homophobia: Fear, shame and silence in the construction of gender identity in Theorizing Masculinities. Thousand Oaks, CA: Sage Publications

Landers, R. M. (1990). Gender, race, and the state courts. Radcliffe Quarterly, 76(4), 6-9.

Lever, J. (1978). Sex differences in the complexity of children's games. American Sociological Review 43(4), 471-483.

Levy, G. D., & Carter, B. D. (1989). Gender schema, gender constancy, and gender-role knowledge: The roles of cognitive factors in preschoolers' gender-role stereotype attributions. *Developmental Psychology, 25*, 444-449.

Lynn, D. B. (1959). A note on sex differences in the development of masculine and feminine identification. Psychological Review, 66, 126-35.

Lynn, D. B. (1969). *Parental and sex-role identification: A theoretical formulation.* Berkeley, CA: McCutchan.

Lytton, H., & Romney, D. M. (1991). Parents' differential socialization of boys and girls: A meta-analysis." *Psychological Bulletin, 109*, 267-296.

Marshall, S. E. (1985). Ladies against women: Mobilization dilemmas of antifeminist movements. *Social Problems, 32*(4), 348-62.

Martin, C. L., Wood, C. H., & Little, J. K. (1990). The development of gender stereotype components. *Child Development, 61*, 1891-1904.

Millet, K. (1970). *Sexual Politics.* Garden City, NY: Doubleday.

Mischel, W. A. (1966). Social-learning view of sex differences in behavior. In E. E. Maccoby, (Ed.). *The Development of Sex Differences* Stanford, CA: Stanford University.

National Organization for Women. (2002). Watch out, listen up! 2002 *Feminist Primetime Report.* Washington, DC: National Organization for Women.

O'Connor, P. (1992). Friendships between women: A critical review. New York: Guilford.

Rotenberg, K. J. (1984). Sex differences in children's trust in peers. Sex Roles, 11, 953-957.

Sedney, M. A. (1987). Development of androgyny: Parental influences. *Psychology of Women Quarterly, 11*, 311-326.

Signorella, M. L., Bigler, R. S., & Liben, L. S. (1993). Early gender-role development. *Developmental Review, 3*, 147-183.

Thorne, B. (1993). *Gender play: Girls and boys in school.* New Brunswick, NJ: Rutgers University Press.

Valian, V. (1999). *Why so slow?: The advancement of women.* Cambridge, MA: MIT Press.

Weinraub, M., Clemens, L. P., Sachloff, A., Ethridge, T., Gracely, E., & Myers, B. (1984). The development of sex role stereotypes in the third year: Relationships to gender labeling, gender identity, sex-typed toy preferences, and family characteristics. *Child Development, 55*, 1493-1504.

Weinraub, M., Jaeger, E., & Hoffman, L.W. (1988). Predicting infant outcomes in families of employed and nonemployed mothers. *Early Childhood Research Quarterly, 3*, 361-378.

Weisner, T. S., & Wilson-Mitchell, J. E. (1990). Nonconventional family life-styles and sex typing in six-year-olds. *Child Development, 61*(6), 1915.

Yogev, S. (1981). Do professional women have egalitarian marital relationships? *Journal of Marriage and the Family, 43,* 865-871.

12 | THE INDIVIDUAL AND MENTAL HEALTH
by Valerie R. Matteson

According to the National Alliance on Mental Illness (NAMI), there are almost 30 million Americans (about 1 in 10) diagnosed with mental illness. The stereotypes of mental illness often include seeing the mentally ill as violent, disheveled in appearance, poor. The reality of mental illness is that it doesn't discriminate: it affects all social classes, ethnic groups, and regions of the country.

In American society, mental illness is generally attributed to a character flaw but a controllable aspect of personality. A community that is educated about mental illness, treatment, and recovery options is generally more accepting of a person with a mental illness. A community that is not well informed is more likely to discriminate against the person. They will socially distance themselves from the affected individual.

Be that as it may, among the most commonly rendered diagnoses are the **psychoses** which include: major or (unipolar} depression, bipolar disorder, and schizophrenia.

Depression is can be managed with medication and cognitive therapy. The most prescribed medication for depression is antidepressants. As with any medication there may be side effects. Negative side effects can range from weight gain to more serious side effects including seizures. Side effects are one of the reasons that many people stop taking medications. There are many antidepressants on the market and new ones are entering the market each year. Drug companies have capitalized on depression by bombarding viewers' with advertisements for different medications and by encouraging those suffering to seek treatment and utilize the effects of medications. Optimally, this function of corporate self-interest may facilitate symptom-control of those who are accurately diagnosed.

MAJOR DEPRESSIVE DISORDER

According to the National Institute of Mental Health (NIMH) major (or unipolar) depression is a medical illness that affects over 15 million Americans. Major depressive disorder (MDD) affects a person emotionally, physically, and cognitively. A person may not want to get out of bed, take a shower, or be able to take care of their family.

According to the DSM-IV-TR (2000) the criteria for diagnosis of Major Depressive Disorder are:

- Depressed mood most of the day

- Markedly disinterest or pleasure in all, or almost all, activities most of the day

- Significant weight loss when not dieting or weight gain, or decrease or increase in appetite

- Insomnia or hypersomnia

- Psychomotor agitation or retardation

- Fatigue or loss of energy

- Feelings of worthlessness or excessive or inappropriate guilt nearly every day

- Diminished ability to think or concentrate, indecisiveness

- Recurrent thoughts of death, recurrent suicidal ideation without a specific plan, or a suicide attempt, a suicide plan for committing suicide

Statistically, women are more affected by major depression than men. Gender roles may have an impact on why women are more affected than men. Women are socialized to take care of the family and home, which are often overwhelming duties with little or no encouragement. Men are more likely to be diagnosed with "male" characteristics, such as violence, anger, or controlling behaviors.

Depression increases the difficulties the person has interacting with or attending functions for family, school, or work. An alteration of identity occurs with the illness, with some incorporating the illness into their identity. Others experience role confusion. They are not sure who they are, what others expect of them, or how they should treat others. Depression is one of the most well known mental illnesses; there are commercials, advertisements in magazines, and billboards telling people to seek treatment.

BI-POLAR/MANIC DEPRESSIVE

Bi-polar affects over 10 million Americans. It disrupts work, leisure activities, home, and family. Bi-polar can cause a great amount of conflict in relationships with family and friends.

According to the DSM-IV-TR (2000) the criteria for Bi-Polar Disorder (Manic Depressive):

Manic Symptoms:

- Inflated self-esteem

- Decreased need for sleep

- More talkative than usual or pressure to keep talking

- Flight of ideas or subjective experience that thoughts are racing

- Distractibility

- Increase in goal-directed activity (socially, work, or school, sexually) or psychomotor agitation

- Excessive involvement in pleasurable activities that have a high potential for painful consequences (buying sprees, sexual indiscretions, or foolish business investments)

The Depressive Symptoms associated with Bi-Polar Disorder are the same as listed for Major Depression. Bi-Polar I is the reoccurrence of mania and depression. Bi-Polar II disorder has less intense mania known as hypomania with episodes of depression. A person that experiences four or more episodes a year has what is called rapid cycling bipolar disorder.

Medication is often the key for optimal living. As with other mental illnesses, the medications have many different side effects. Those on bi-polar medication are more likely to take different medications for different symptoms. Many will take antidepressants, anti-anxiety, or anti-psychotic medication. Different medications may also be prescribed to help with some of the side effects.

SCHIZOPHRENIA

Schizophrenia affects about two million Americans and it is often chronic, chaotic, with recovery being difficult.

According to the DSM-IV-TR (2000) the criterion for Schizophrenia is:
- Delusions

- Hallucinations

- Disorganized Speech

- Grossly disorganized or catatonic behavior

- Negative symptoms (affective flattening, alogia, or avolition)

Schizophrenia is the diagnostic category that includes the most severe mental illnesses. This term is used to describe people who are extremely withdrawn from their surroundings or who act like they are living in another world. There are subtypes of schizophrenia. These include paranoid, disorganized, catatonic, undifferentiated, and residual.

- The Paranoid Type is a form of schizophrenia that is characterized by a preoccupation of bizarre delusions of being persecuted or harassed. Auditory hallucinations that are related to the delusions' theme are also prevalent.

- The Disorganized Type, or Hebephrenic, is a form of schizophrenia that is characterized by a disorganized behavior, disorganized speech, and flat affect. Involving a disturbance in behavior, communication, and thought, there is a lacking of any consistent theme.

- The Undifferentiated Type is a form of schizophrenia that is characterized by a number of schizophrenic symptoms such as delusions, disorganized behavior, disorganized speech, flat affect, or hallucinations but does not meet the criteria for any other type of schizophrenia.

- The Residual Type is a form of schizophrenia that is characterized by a previous diagnosis of schizophrenia, but no longer having any of the prominent psychotic symptoms. There are some remaining symptoms of the disorder however, such as eccentric behavior, emotional blunting, illogical thinking, or social withdrawal.

Medication is typically prescribed and it can mean the difference between institutionalization and surviving in the community. Medication to treat schizophrenia is often necessary and encouraged by professionals.

A man this author knows was in a state mental institution for about twenty years. He is a paranoid schizophrenic. He was admitted as a sixteen-year-old boy and discharged as thirty six year old man. Peers are important to the socialization of a sixteen year old. Considering that he was in an institution at that time the institution became his socialization agent. While institutionalized he endured electric shock treatments, restraints, and overmedication. He was restrained and imprisoned for so long that he had to be comprehensively re-integrated into society. Imagine, for a moment, being removed from society for twenty years, then attempting to fit back in. Currently, he is in his fifties, goes to work, and maintains an apartment. He is fortunate that he survived with enough of his core identity intact. Re-entering society would necessitate role negotiations and learning how to adjust these roles accordingly.

No one would know that he has a mental illness. How do you think others would treat him if they knew he was a diagnosed paranoid schizophrenic? Would people treat him differently? It is quite likely that this is an instance that ignorance by others, if not bliss for person in question, is certainly preferable to disclosure.

INDIVIDUAL

Individuals diagnosed with mental illness encounter stigma whether it be real or perceived. Fear of stigma is a major reason why many don't seek treatment but instead suffer through their lives. Feelings of being socially distanced by their peers, family, and other groups are some of the reasons why many don't seek treatment. Upon the diagnosis, the person feels more intense negative emotions such as anger, sadness, loss of self, loss of purpose, and loss of self-esteem among other things. They also develop a fear of being institutionalized because of delusions, hallucinations, or other abnormal behaviors. Since deviance is generally frowned upon, and those with a mental illness are many times considered deviant, social distance is increased. Symptoms of their illness can also be hard to manage, so they often decide to socially isolate themselves, decreasing outside contact with family, friends, and co-workers.

Individuals of lower socio-economic status (SES) are more likely to be diagnosed mentally ill compared to the middle or upper class counterparts. One major reason is that lower socio-economic people generally have to endure the problems and stresses associated with chronic poverty. The struggle to survive and meet their everyday needs thus increases the likelihood of being diagnosed with a mental illness. In turn, the mentally ill face obstacles because they are not able to hold down a job, qualify for any state or federal programs, or afford their medications. They often end up on the street trying to survive. Without effective resources a mentally ill person from the middle or high-income status can slide/drift into the lower class status. (Link, Lennon, & Dohrenwend, 1993; Rodgers & Mann, 1993).

Regardless of social class, the mentally ill person is informally and formally sanctioned. The in-group or other groups in which the person has membership conduct informal sanctions. The closer the ties are to the members of the in-group, the less severe the sanctions may be. Regardless, exclusion will occur. There may be one or two people within the group that will maintain friendship ties. An acquaintance of mine entered an inpatient unit to get help with medications. Friends discovered the admission and instantly became judgmental and began excluding him from social gatherings. When questioned, the response was, "I am uncomfortable around "those" people." Needless to say he suffered greater symptoms because what he considered to be his support network was now shrinking.

The formal sanctions by the government or institutions such as the police or mental health agencies include arrest and/or involuntary commitment. Involuntary commitment is a form of social control. A person that is considered unsafe or has made threats about others is likely to find themselves inside of a police car on the way to an inpatient unit.

Many of the mentally ill become fearful of the police and the mental health system. Involuntary commitment generally is due to being seen as a threat to oneself, to others, or to property. That certainly covers a lot of ground.

Involuntary commitment has various consequences other than just being labeled mentally ill. There is a public record since this is a court proceeding. A judge listens to the evidence presented and then makes a decision. A mental health worker, a psychiatrist, or a psychologist can present the evidence. If the judge decides to commit the person, the person is picked up and taken to the inpatient unit. In Pennsylvania, an involuntary commitment of five days is known as a 302. Once an inpatient and the five days are up, the psychiatrist can petition the court for a twenty-day involuntary commitment, known as a 303. If a person enters into a facility voluntarily and decides to leave after two days, they can sign themselves out, but must wait seventy-two hours before being released.

While in Pennsylvania, a person that has been involuntarily committed to a mental institution is no longer able to own or register a firearm. However, as with much of the general population mentally ill individuals are more likely to harm themselves than others with a firearm. When one considers how much control the individual loses when diagnosed with a mental illness, maybe the reluctance to seek treatment can be understood.

FAMILY

Historically, mentally ill persons were either institutionalized or hidden away by family. As education and deinstitutionalization took place, the mentally ill were slowly incorporated back into communities with or without support from the family. Professionals that work with the mentally ill, try to incorporate the family throughout the process of treatment and recovery.

The stigma that families associate with mental illness can alter how they interact with the person. Family beliefs about mental illness can be a powerful predictor of how the person will be treated within the family. If family beliefs about mental illness are negative, they will usually treat the person negatively. A family that is educated and willing to be involved in the recovery process can be a positive support network. The more positive a family is, the better the chances are that the outcome for the diagnosed person will be positive.

During a visit to a mental institution it was apparent that patients were treated differently by visiting family and friends. The visitors were talking down to the person, in low tones and treating them like they were infants. Condescending questions like, "Do you think you will be going to work tomorrow?" "Are you ever going to get better?" And statements such as "Get a grip," "Move on, this is just a phase, tomorrow you will wake up and feel like yourself." These are dehumanizing and demoralizing to the individual. This type of attitude and demeanor imposed throughout the day demotes a mentally ill person from normal roles and statuses.

This illustrates a larger theme of family dynamics in relation to mental illness: role strain and role conflict, while a pervasive aspect of all families, are endemic to ones in which a member is mentally ill.

There are other considerations as well. A mother diagnosed with a severe mental illness is fearful of losing parental rights. Although there are cases in which the removal of the children from the parent is warranted, custody of children have been lost over, because of a mental illness diagnosis. Alternatively, keeping the family intact can be a powerful incentive for the mentally ill person to stay in therapy and recover. Generally, if the parent, significant other, and child stay supportive then the probability of recovery is promising.

Families can be great resources for the affected person. They can help them recover more quickly and feel better about the decisions that they are making. Instead of criticizing, they can reassure, encourage, and offer general support. Those families that are negative hinder the recovery process because the person feels ashamed and guilty, and blames him or herself for causing strife within the family and an already stressed family system can be broken.

NAVIGATION OF THE MENTAL HEALTH SYSTEM

The mental health system is a maze without a map. One's socioeconomic status (SES) can be the difference between treatment and recovery. The rich can afford services and the poor are dependent upon the local mental health clinic. In the public sector of mental health services, the client/patient is known as a consumer. The rich seek posh private institutions, expensive psychiatrists, and therapists, which is often covered by insurance. The poor generally have no health insurance, may apply for Medicaid and be denied. Thus they have no services available. Even if they go to the local mental health clinic, the medications that are prescribed cannot be filled because they cannot afford them.

The bureaucracy of the mental health system makes it nearly impossible to receive many needed services. New patients encounter many obstacles trying to utilize services. The first obstacle is insurance or lack thereof. A person without coverage cannot be seen. Insurance companies usually only cover ten sessions with a therapist and limited contact with a psychiatrist. Mental health clinic appointments are also hard to come by in a timely manner, as the clinics are generally understaffed. Emergencies are generally directed toward hospital emergency rooms or a crisis center.

An example of medicines that a person needs to take each month and the cost associated with them might explain why many are not medicine compliant. Risperdal, an anti-psychotic medication, is about $700 for a thirty-day supply. Ativan, an anti-anxiety medication, is $52 for a thirty-day supply. Lamictal, an anti-seizure medication that is used for mania and as a mood stabilizer, is $135 for a thirty-day supply. Wellbutrin XL, an antidepressant, is $102.50 for a thirty-day supply. The total is almost $1000 for a one-month supply of medication to help with the quality of life for those with mental illnesses. No wonder the pharmaceutical companies are making such large profits. Without medical coverage how does one pay for these medications.

Interestingly enough the programs that are shown on TV that advertise free or low-cost prescriptions are usually complicated and cumbersome. The ads make it seem very easy with no hassle and all will be accepted. I know an individual that needs medication to maintain his bipolar disorder and has been rejected by Medicaid because he makes "too much" money. He works at a factory barely making eight dollars an hour. He called a program that was advertised and his medication was not on the list. How does he get his medications? Not taking his medication can lead to him losing his job, which may not be a bad thing, because he will then qualify for Medicaid. But this is a blow to his self-esteem, self-respect, and how others view him. This is a problem within the system. If this is an ongoing struggle, how many can continue to fight?

Psychiatrists and therapists want clients to take their medication, but if there is no insurance or programs to help with the cost, the client is unlikely to be med-compliant. Many of the medicines that help with hallucinations and delusions are costly. There are also indirect costs to the individual related to the symptoms. Indirect costs can be defined in different ways, but mostly they refer to lost productivity at home, school, and the workplace.

There are other types of mental illnesses with whom others would prefer not to deal. One of these includes people that self-injure. The author has seen how differently "cutters" are treated in an emergency room situation. If a person that cuts enters the ER for treatment and the doctor decides that stitches are needed, most often the decision will be to "teach" the person a lesson. Most often this is done by not giving the patient a numbing agent. This is unfair treatment. Where are the patient's rights? If this were to happen to anyone else under different circumstances, a lawsuit would probably be filed.

A person with mental illness has to adjust to the negative impact on their personal identity. Salience of roles disappear and there is conflict about which role should be played. Should they play the role of mentally ill individual or should one be the noncompliant patient? Belief and value systems are now in conflict with each other. If they were taught that the mentally ill were deviant, does that make them deviant as well? This is a vicious cycle.

SOCIETAL VIEW

We are socialized to like and dislike certain groups. The mentally ill are included in these groups. A family walking down the street sees an individual that is behaving outside of the norm and the parent will automatically move the child to the other side for "protection" from the "crazy" person. Although words may or may not be spoken to the child, an unspoken socialization occurred. The unspoken message is that of disregard, fear, and shame toward others abnormal behavior.

Social exclusion from work, education, or rewards that others receive is often withheld. Mental illness does not mean a person isn't capable of working, getting an education, or starting a family. Working can increase the well-being for the person, encouraging involvement in the community. Discrimination can occur when the person discloses or others find out. Although there are laws to protect those with disabilities, many are still discriminated against within the workforce. This is covert discrimination and as with all other forms of discrimination difficult to prove.

Common misconceptions regarding mental illness that they are: dangerous, worthless, violent, and unpredictable (Link and Phelan, 1985; Trad, 1991; Bissland and Munger, 1985). These beliefs perpetuate stigma. However, many people I know that have a diagnosed mental illness are fun, loving, and trusting of those within their group. They are emphatic, encouraging, and often available when you need them. I enjoy that they laugh at themselves, share their experiences, and make me laugh. Just because someone is different does not mean that they are not interesting, funny, or a good person.

Still for every individual to assert the contrary the mass media encourages both the stereotypes and thus the associated stigma. For example, when a person deviates from the norms, such as murder-suicide, school shootings, and other violent actions, there is generally a mental health implication. Contrary to common stereotypes of violence, mentally ill are more likely to become victims of homicide (Cuvelier, 2002; Monahan, 1992; Teplin, 1985) than is the general population.

Society has a perverse need of categorizing and labeling people by class, culture, and race and ethnicity and this social force is examined in this context via labeling theory. Sociologist Thomas Scheff (1966) has argued that mental illness is myth, that labeling a person mentally ill actually caused the person to maintain the mental illness identity: an incorporation of the negative stigma if you will. When a mentally ill patient enters the hospital, they are encouraged to accept their illness. If they do not, they are in denial. A person in denial cannot accept treatment therefore cannot enter recovery.

According to Scheff (1996), families do not consider other family members "crazy" until the label is attached. This makes a lot of sense. A person that is acting out side of the norms, but not committing a crime, is often labeled a deviant, crazy, or mentally ill in order to explain their behavior. A label is attached to a person and the person becomes attached to the label. The label becomes the identity and all behaviors attached to that identity become incorporated into values and beliefs. A person that has been "labeled" mentally ill, that is hospitalized, will begin to contribute to the symptoms in order to live up to the expectations of the illness.

STIGMA

The person, the family, and society perceive the stigma attached to mental illness in many ways. One type is **social distancing**. According to Feldman and Crandall (2007) social distancing has three major categories: personal responsibility, dangerousness, and rarity. Personal responsibility perceived by others as the reason for the mental illness increases social distancing. Social exclusion takes place and the person is no longer deemed worthy of sympathy, understanding, or encouragement and is instead punished.

The more a person is perceived as dangerous, the more social distance and exclusion from society occurs though ironically we have seen that mentally ill persons are less likely to be violent, but instead are more likely to be victims of crime. In addition, the more society views the illness as not responding to treatment or poor prognosis, the greater the social distance.

Rarity is the last aspect that perpetuates stigma. Feldman and Crandall (2007) explained that this last point needs further research and studies done in order to get a better understanding of how rarity and social distancing interact. If all three are present the social distance can be increased. If education and exposure to mental illness are increased, social distancing can be decreased. Overt stigma is becoming less, but the covert stigma is very prevalent in society.

The concept of the definition of the situation has already been introduced and its application here is obvious: if one perceives another as dangerous, that person is [potentially] dangerous and will be reacted to accordingly. It does not matter if the person is actually dangerous because the final perception is "danger." Stigma is perpetuated by the definition of the situation. This could be applied in all aspects of mental illness. If people perceive themselves as mentally ill, they will take on the role. Perception plays a very large role in the stigmatization process.

Once in the system, it is very difficult to get out. Many mental illnesses are manageable with medications, therapists, and psychiatrists. It is important to mention that some professionals that work the mental health field also help perpetuate mental illness and slow recovery. As with every profession there are those that encourage recovery. Even a person that has become self-sufficient once again is going to have to redefine their role within the system.

MENTAL ILLNESS AS A MYTH

Is mental illness just a myth, or is there some legitimacy to the claim that people can be afflicted with a life-altering handicap developed in the brain and mind? Pursuing the theme of stigma there is at least one psychiatrist that is a critic of the modern day diagnosis of mental illness: Thomas Szasz. Szasz's critique of psychiatry argues that diagnoses of mental illness are ultimately arbitrary. A psychiatrist could, if he were so inclined, diagnose as mentally ill someone with whose worldview he disagreed. This is essentially what it means to say that a person is "suffering from delusions." If the psychiatrist could make a case that the "patient" might harm him or herself or others he could have the person confined and forcibly "treated."

In Szasz's view, this should not be possible. For decades, what he calls his "passion against coercion" has driven him to denounce involuntary mental hospitalization, while his insistence on individual responsibility has made him a dedicated opponent of the insanity defense. If someone commits a crime, Szasz says, he should be punished, not "treated." But if they have not violated anyone's rights, they should be left alone, no matter how bizarre their behavior. Szasz's attack on a concept that most people took for granted (and still do), bolstered by the efforts of civil libertarians and other social critics, encouraged skepticism about the justification for coercive psychiatry. That uneasiness led to legal reforms in the 1960s and '70s that made it harder to lock up people deemed to be crazy. Szasz wrote,

> "Mental illness is a myth whose function is to disguise and thus render more palatable the bitter pill of moral conflicts in human relations," "In asserting that there is no such thing as mental illness, I do not deny that people have problems coping with life and each other" (Szasz, 1984).

Likewise, Szasz (1984) has never denied that organic conditions such as Alzheimer's disease or untreated syphilis can have an impact on thought and behavior. But he insists on evidence of an underlying physical defect, and he emphasizes that behavior itself is never a disease. "Classifying thoughts, feelings, and behaviors as diseases is a logical and semantic error, like classifying the whale as a fish," he writes on his Web site (www.szasz.com). This error has serious consequences, Szasz argues: "The classification of misbehavior as illness provides an ideological justification for state-sponsored social control." As he put forth in his 1990 book "The Untamed Tongue," "What people nowadays call mental illness, especially in a legal context, is not a fact, but a strategy; not a condition, but a policy; in short it is not a disease that the alleged patient has, but a decision which those who call him mentally ill make about how to act toward him, whether he likes it or not."

The collaboration between government and psychiatry results in what Szasz calls the "therapeutic state," a system in which disapproved thoughts, emotions, and actions are repressed ("cured") through pseudomedical interventions. Thus illegal drug use, smoking, overeating, gambling, shoplifting, sexual promiscuity, shyness, anxiety, unhappiness, racial bigotry, unconventional religious beliefs, and suicide are all considered diseases or symptoms of diseases, things that happen to people against their will. Szasz believes this sort of thinking undermines individual responsibility and invites coercive paternalism.

By referring to people with life problems as ill, we imply that something is wrong with them and they must change. According to Szasz (1997), this is why troubled people are encouraged to become patients and to become dependent on professional care. Something to think about, don't you agree?

CONCLUSION

It is not hard to conceive that mentally ill individuals encounter many obstacles outside of normal everyday conflicts. Discrimination, prejudice, and stigma make it difficult, but with determination, healthy support networks, and learned coping skills, many can reenter society and contribute successfully. Mental illness is not a death sentence; it is something that is manageable with a lot of hard work. Overcoming the stigma and managing the symptoms can help a person be an asset to society. Being accepted is important to people and the same applies to those with mental illness. People with mental illness tend to create their own groups and maintain their own norms. You never really know who has a mental illness. There isn't a sticker or tattoo that one wears. People that you wouldn't even consider could have mental illness, such as a family doctor, psychiatrist, college professor, college student, judge, or anyone from the different walks of life, could actually be under treatment for a mental illness.

ഇ ഌ ഇ ഌ

REFERENCES

American Psychiatric Association, (2000). Test revision: *Diagnostic and statistical manual of mental disorders*, (4th ed), Text Revision. Washington, DC: Author.
Bissland, J. H., & Munger, R. (1985). Implications of changing attitudes toward mental illness. *Journal of Social Psychology, 125*, 515-517.

Christenson, R., & Dowrick, P. W. (1983). Myths of mid-winter depression. *Community Mental Health Journal, 19,* 177-186.

Cuverlier, M. (2002, May/June). Victim, not villain. *Psychology Today.* p.23.

Feldman, D. B., & Crandall, C. S. (2007). Dimensions of mental illness stigma: What about mental illness causes social rejection? *Journal of Social and Clinical Psychology, 26,* 137-154.

Link, B. G., & Phelan J. C. (1999). Public conceptions of mental illness: Labels, cause, dangerousness, and social distance. *American Journal of Public Health, 89,* 1328-1333.

Link, B. G., Dohrenwend, B. P., & Skodol, A. E. (1986). Socioeconomic status and schizophrenia: Noisome occupational characteristics as a risk factor. *American Sociological Review, 51,* 242-258.

Monahan, J. (1992, April). Mental disorder and violent behavior. *American Psychologist,* pp. 511-521.

National Alliance on Mental Illness [NAMI]. *Major depression.* Reviewed by Dr. Ken Duckworth, NAMI Medical Director, September 2006. Retrieved on May 15, 2006 from www.nami.org.

Rodgers, B., & Mann, S. L. (1993). Re-thinking the analysis of intergenerational social mobility: A comment on John W. Fox's' social class, mental illness, and social mobility. *Journal of Health and Social Behavior, 34,* 165-172.

Scheff, T. J. (1966). *Being mentally ill.* Chicago: Aldine.

Smyth, A., & Thompson, C. (1990). *SAD: Seasonal affective disorder.* New York: Unwin.

Strock, M. (2000) *Plain talk about depression.* Public Information and Communication Branch, National Institute of Mental Health (NIMH). NIH Publication No. 00-3561. Retrieved on May 15, 2006 from http://www.nimh.nih.gov/publicat/depression.cfm#ptdep1.

Szasz, T. S. (1984). *The myth of mental illness.* Rev. ed. New York: Perennial.

Szasz, T. S. (1997). *Insanity: The idea and its consequences.* Syracuse, NY: Syracuse University Press.

Szasz, T. S. Summary statement and manifesto. *Myth of mental illness.* Retrieved May 29, 2007 from http://www.szasz.com/manifesto.html.

Teplin, L. A. (1985). The criminality of the mentally ill: A dangerous misconception. *American Journal of Psychiatry, 142,* 593-598.

Thio, A. (2004). *Deviant behavior.* (7th Ed.). Boston: Allyn and Bacon.

Trad, P. V. (1991). The ultimate stigma of mental illness. *American Journal of Psychotherapy, 45,* 463-466.

13 | THE INDIVIDUAL AND THE MASS MEDIA
by Frank O. Taylor, Ph.D.

Prior to the advent of the mass media people entertained themselves with stories told by word of mouth. The oral tradition, historically, was fundamental to passing the values, beliefs, morals, and history of a group or society from one generation to the next. Oral stories had a socialization function as well, as children learned that stories were not just for entertainment but also had a moral. The oral tradition, in our culture, has largely been replaced by the mass media. By **mass media** we refer to print media, such as books and magazines, visual media, such as television and movies, and aural media, such as music. The function of the modern mass media is clearly an orientation towards making a profit.

Sociologically, we are interested in manifest and latent functions of the media. First, what is meant by the term function? The function of an automobile, for example, is first and foremost transportation from one place to another. **Manifest functions** are those that are easy to discern or intended. Clearly, transportation, and perhaps safety, is the manifest functions of automobiles. **Latent functions** are either unintended functions or unrecognized by most people. A latent function of automobiles may be related to social status. Automobiles were not specifically invented for the purpose of helping some individuals demonstrate their wealth. Nevertheless, that is easily accomplished by the purchase of a rather expensive automobile. We may ask the same questions of the media.

Are there manifest and latent messages in the media? Are negative stereotypes about the poor, women, and minorities present in the mass media? Does the mass media encourage passive or active engagement? Are there consequences if engagement with the media is mostly passive? Do the media encourage or inhibit critical thinking? We will consider all of these questions in this chapter.

THE MASS MEDIA AND SOCIALIZATION

There are three reasons why we should be concerned about the mass media. First, research demonstrates that the media can influence culture. When you read a book, your engagement with that artifact of print media involves your imagination as you recreate in your mind the scenery and the mannerisms and appearance of the characters involved. We may say that such engagement involves critical thinking, on some level. On the other hand, when you watch a movie, others have already made decisions about these issues, removing the ability of the audience to think creatively or use their imagination.

A lot of editing goes into the modern mass media. This kind of editing influences the interpretations reached by the consumers. For instance, if there is a peace protest or march in Washington D.C., and many thousands of people are marching, if editors want to create the impression that only a handful of people were involved, they will use pictures taken with a tight-angle, so that the viewer can see only a dozen or so faces. Conversely, if the editor wants to create the impression that many people were involved, they will use pictures taken from a wide-angle, in which a sea of marchers can be seen by the viewer. The same principles are involved in letters to the editor in popular newspapers and in the production of motion pictures and virtually all of modern mass media. The point is that the modern mass media turns the viewer into a passive consumer of media messages.

My father was a huge fan of science fiction and monster movies when I was a child. Consequently, I spent a lot of my childhood terrified, particularly at night, that the monster under the bed or in the closet was going to get me. Many children end up being afraid of non-existent monsters. Once I was in the movie theater to watch an extremely violent movie called Robocop, which indicates that what your parents let you watch as a child influences what you choose to watch as an adult. In any case, there was a guy in there with his young daughter, who was no more than five or six years old. Ten minutes into the movie he was saying over and over to his petrified daughter, "it's just make believe, it isn't real." We see in this example one of the major problems with the modern mass media, it can expose young children to inappropriate sexual and violent content. One wonders if six-year-old kids should see a human being dissolved in a vat of acid.

Secondly, the mass media can spread culture. Modern technology, including computers, cell-phones, the Internet, and satellite communication have spread US style consumerism all over the world. You can now eat Big Mac's in Europe or Asia. Europeans can now vacation at Disney World. Indeed, many of our jobs can be exported to Third World nations today based on the technology created by the entertainment industry. Now, thanks to the Internet and satellite communication, corporate owners and managers in the U.S. can stay in constant contact with their low-paid workers anywhere in the world.

Thirdly, the media is influenced by culture. What determines what we see on the television, for example? Some television shows seem to last for years and years, while others last only a season or two. We must remember that in the final analysis, shows that make a profit stay on the air and those that do not, regardless of their quality, fall by the wayside. What determines whether or not a television show earns a profit? In a word: advertising. If lots of people tune in to the show, advertisers will pay huge sums of money to have their products highlighted on the broadcast. When only a few people watch a given television show, advertisers are less willing to pay for commercials.

On the bright side, recent developments have given parents some control over the content of what their children can be exposed to by the mass media. The Children's Television Act of 1990 mandated that each hour of children's programming contain only 10.5 minutes of commercials during the week and 12 minutes of commercials per hour during the weekend. The new V-chip technology lets parents block certain programming if they deem it inappropriate for their children. Lastly, the television and movie ratings systems are designed to help prevent underage children from viewing certain content based on their age.

TELEVISION AND MOVIES

This chapter will primarily be concerned with two types of modern mass media, television and movies, and print media. There are, obviously, many other important types of mass media, but it would be beyond the scope of this chapter to deal with every aspect of the media. What we attempt to do here is make the case for the importance of media analysis as an academic exercise. When adults think about media analysis they approach the subject from the point of view of adults. In other words, adults realize that commercials are trying to sell products, monsters are not real, and that glorification of sex and violence is meant to get people into the movie theaters. Adults have their full-cognitive capacities in play when considering what effect the mass media has on their values, beliefs, and behaviors. However, the same is not true for children. Children develop their cognitive capacities through the process of socialization. If the mass media is part of the socialization of children, we must ask ourselves what, exactly, children are being exposed to. In the first half of this chapter we will consider television and the movies. Children's books will be analyzed in the second half of the chapter.

TV, the Movies, and Childhood Socialization

Since children have not reached cognitive maturity when they begin to consume the manifest and latent messages contained within the mass media, they are more vulnerable to those messages. For example, children do not realize that make-believe images and characters, such as cartoons, are not real. When a child less than five years old sees the cartoon character Sponge Bob, for instance, they think they are seeing a real person who lives in the television. Children interact with toys and other objects, such as stuffed animals, as if those objects are real. Kids often kiss and hug their favorite stuffed animal or even a blanket. The point is that children are not able to distinguish reality from fantasy.

When young children see gender stereotypes on television they may accept them as natural and attempt to model those behaviors. Children, of course, do not understand that most of the behaviors of men and women on television and the movies, and particularly in commercials, are stereotypical and not based on actual behavior. What stereotypes are children being exposed to? Men are portrayed as the ones having adventures, going to work, making decisions, being out-of-doors, and in active roles. On the other hand, women are mostly associated with domesticity, being passive, afraid, victimized, nurturing, and family-oriented. Clearly, these stereotypes do not reflect the entire range of behaviors men and women engage in.

It is extremely problematic that children are not capable of distinguishing commercials as attempts to sell products. Kids do not realize that advertisers are trying to exploit them. In general, advertisers are trying to instill in children the desire to obtain, largely through their parents, products that are not healthy for them, such as cereal laced with sugar and other chemicals. From birth, we are bombarded with commercials with this message: all of your problems can be solved quickly if your purchase the right product. Unfortunately, many, if not all, of life's problems cannot be solved with a new car, a new home, different clothes, new toys, or prescription medication. It boils down to this: children are being taught, at the very point in their lives when they do not have the critical thinking skills to reject the message, that every problem can be solved through consumerism.

The male hero, who also happens to be a violent sociopath, has invaded our televisions and movie screens. A sociopath is a person without a social consciousness who is unconcerned about inflicting violence and suffering on others. In one episode of *The Shield*, a corrupt police officer is shot directly in the face by a fellow officer. The primary character in *House*, a physician, is addicted to drugs and seems to be completely devoid of basic human feelings and emotions in the treatment of his patients, which he approaches as a mere intellectual exercise. In the popular television show *24*, people in police custody are often tortured and brutalized. These are but a handful of examples from thousands to choose from. These characters are not just people with flaws, like any human being. These characters are completely unapologetic about their use of violence and harming others. Of course, we do not want children seeing these programs. But these programs reflect the values and beliefs of the entertainment industry as an industry. The message of such programs is clear: violence works, it is often justified, and it is basically harmless. The effects of violence on both the perpetrators and the victims are largely overlooked.

Some Important Concerns

A lot of the debate about the impact of television and the movies centers about aggression and violence. However, there are a variety of issues that should also be considered when we think about the impact the mass media has had on our lives.

Our Daily Lives

Television and the movies have changed the way we live our daily lives. Even though my grandfather had to commute at least one hour to work every morning, which meant he had to get up early, every weekday evening he stayed up late to watch Johnny Carson on *The Late Show*. Millions of television viewers arrange their daily lives around their favorite television shows. We must assume that if this were not the case, other popular family rituals would be engaged in, such as playing games or talking with each other. I distinctly remember when my father came home with the family's first television. Many of the things we used to do almost ceased entirely. Such family interaction included playing outdoors, playing games, singing, telling stories, and the like. It would be hard to gauge the impact television has had on meal arrangements, sleeping patterns, conversations, and leisure time. Because television is a passive activity, each hour we watch it is an hour less to spend with our children in some type of productive, parent/child bond-enhancing, activity.

How I used to love Halloween when I was a child. And *not* because of the candy either. My brother and I were very competitive when it came to dreaming up our costumes. It was a big production in the household. We would draw pictures of costumes and eventually we would go to the store with our Mother to buy the material necessary to construct them. Today, most children get their costumes off the rack at the retail store. What was a common exercise in creative thinking and imagination and an opportunity for families to bond together, has been reduced to one trip to the store and an exercise in obtaining candy for the sake of candy.

Halloween, and Christmas too, has become commercialized. Very few people take any time to ponder what is lost when commercial entities begin to take over activities that were once entirely the domain of families. In our family, we wrote our own stories and read them to each other. We made our own music with actual musical instruments. Today, most children rely on the mass media for fashion tips, hairstyles, music, and sports. Being poor, for example, forced us to make-up our own outdoors games, complete with goals, objectives, and rules. Today, a short trip to the retail store suffices for much of what once was creative activity. Why make Barbie clothes with Mom when you can just buy them at the toy store? I suspect that very few of us have stopped to consider just how extensive consumerism has intervened in out daily lives. Why make

Christmas decorations with the children when you can simply purchase them, leaving you more time to spend in front of the television?

Social and Physical Activities

Obviously, for each minute a child spends in front of the television, regardless of the quality of the programming, they spend one minute less engaged in any other activity – such as playing with other children. It is funny that we worry more about the influence of television on our children's behavior than we do about the behavior television prevents! On average, children spend about 3 – 5 hours a day watching television with little parental supervision. Of course, one concern is associated with what they are watching especially if they are being exposed to the male sociopath discussed above. On the other hand, time spent in front of the television takes time away from other important activities. Interactions with family and peers are important for the Play and Game Stages of self-development. Children could be developing important social skills, such as those associated with communication, cooperation, manners, and so on, if they were interacting with their peers instead of watching television. Reading, playing games with friends and peers, or pursuing hobbies are all probably more important activities than viewing television, even if it is quality programming.

Family Interactions

Family identity and a sense of togetherness are derived from the rituals that are regularly engaged in. These types of activities include eating meals together, perhaps attending church together, talking to each other, playing games, other activities which typically include adults and children interacting together, such as drawing, coloring, or reading books. Many of these family interactions that are essential to the socialization process of children can be interrupted in a negative way by television. Most homes have at least one television and increasingly several. In some sense, watching television together could be considered a family ritual. However, it is bound to stifle conversation and it is essentially passive. On the positive side, when parents discuss with their children what is viewed on television children may learn good problem solving strategies, and other skills associated with language and social development. In sum, homes with multiple television sets probably experience a decline in family interaction if individual members of the family view programs in private.

Television and Children's Perceptions of Reality

As noted previously, preschool children cannot distinguish reality from fantasy. Consequently, they do not understand that what is occurring on television is "acting." It seems real to them. Preschoolers cannot tell the difference between the programs and the commercials nor can they tell the difference between cartoon characters and real people. For preschoolers, television has as much validity as reality. This leaves preschoolers especially susceptible to commercial messages. For example, children may believe that they cannot be hurt if they fall a great distance, like a cartoon character or that they really will be stronger if they eat a certain brand of cereal. Unfortunately, for preschool children the television seems like an accurate reflection of the broader world.

Around age seven children begin to be able to figure out that everything on television is not real. By age five most children understand that commercials are not part of the program, even if they are not fully capable of understanding that commercials are trying to sell them something. Children eventually learn to distinguish fact from fiction. By age ten kids are generally able to tell the difference between what is real, as in the evening news, and what is make believe, as in cartoons. However, even adolescents are susceptible to television advertising.

Effects of Television on Imagination and Aggressive Behavior

Does watching television stifle the imagination and creative potential of children? Research indicates that children with lower levels of imagination are more likely to act out at school aggressively if they tend to watch a lot of violence on television. Conversely, children with higher levels of imagination are less likely to engage in aggression or impulsive acts. It seems that the type of program viewed has important effects:

- Nonviolent programming does not increase play which relies upon children's imagination.

- Violent programming, on the other hand, tends to lean against the type of play that involves children's imagination.

- Educational programs can increase children's imaginative play.

We can conclude from these results that nonviolent programming is at least neutral, regarding imaginative play, while violent programming has negative effects on imaginative play.

Television can introduce children to situations they would not usually experience in ordinary life. They may witness rape, murder, violent beatings, war, assassination, and terrifying monsters, such as vampires, werewolves, and zombies! I remember seeing a particularly terrifying movie as a young adult, *The Texas Chainsaw Massacre*. This movie dealt with cannibalism but it was almost entirely implied. Nevertheless, I was so freaked out that I had nightmares for weeks. Over the years, in order to keep audiences scared out of their wits, movies have become more graphic. Today, audiences actually see the horrible mutilations that were only implied in the 1950s and 1960s. When I was a child people killed in war movies just dropped to the ground. Today their brains explode or parts of their bodies are blown off.

The hypothesis that there is a correlation between televised aggression and violence and aggressive behavior is one of the most widely researched in all of social science. In spite of what many would have us believe, the link between viewing violence in the media and aggression is confirmed and accepted by social scientists. Compared to children who are not allowed to view violence on television, children who view high levels of violent programming are more likely to become aggressive and violent. Television and movies are like role models in that children learn *how* to be violent by watching. If children are exposed to a lot of media violence they may become desensitized to violence or believe, unrealistically, that they could be the victims of violent crime by a stranger.

In one television documentary, which, by the way, could never be replicated in an academic setting, children were allowed to discover a handgun hidden among their usual toys. All of the children in the experiment had been regularly warned not to play with guns by their parents and teachers and told that if they found a gun to get an adult but never touch it. Additionally, none of the children in the experiment had any actual experience with firearms. Nevertheless, when they discovered the gun they began to look around for bullets and took turns aiming the gun at their friends. None of the children made any attempt to inform an adult about the gun. Although not conclusive, we might certainly infer that these children could only have learned about handguns from the media, since guns were not part of their home environment.

According to Social Learning Theory, children learn from observation of others. In general, attractive role models who are rewarded for their behavior are more likely to be imitated by children than role models who are punished for their behavior. Researchers have found that observational learning does happen regarding television and aggression. And no wonder why when you consider the type and amount of violence on television that is rewarded. The media is chock-full of sociopathic heroes who are rewarded for their violent behavior: Arnold Schwarzenegger, Clint Eastwood, Kevin Costner, and Mel Gibson, come to mind but there are literally dozens of others. Violent sports, such as football, hockey, and professional wrestling all show violent individuals being rewarded for aggression that would be illegal under any other circumstances.

Does viewing violent television affect people's attitudes? Here again the research suggests that it does. People who consume a lot of violence as entertainment tend to be more suspicious of others and more distrustful of others motives, compared to people who do not enjoy watching violence. Children who see a lot of televised violence and aggression are more accepting of others who are aggressive or who use aggression as a strategy to solve problems. However, when adults discuss what children see on television with them, television may change children's attitudes toward violence as an appropriate strategy. Parents might point out, for example, that people are not only harmed but also damaged by violence, and that violence is rarely justified as a means to solve problems.

It seems that media violence has a disinhibiting effect. In other words, televised aggression and violence tends to reduce the social constraints on violent and aggressive behavior. Individuals who view a lot of violent programming tend to have higher levels of aggression and violent behavior as young adults, compared to children who did not view such programming. Also, children who identify with aggressive television characters are likely to experience higher levels of aggression.

Television and the Effects of Advertising

There is little question concerning the amount of advertising children are exposed to. Television networks generate profits through selling airtime to commercial advertisers. Children see about 40,000 commercial annually and this figure is rising. Preschool children are easy targets for advertisers. On a given Sunday morning, children may see as many as one hundred commercials specifically oriented to kids. The advertisers see children as an appropriate target audience for a number of reasons. First, children will eventually become consumers so the earlier they become loyal to a brand the better, as far as the advertisers are concerned. Additionally, children are pretty good beggars and can persuade parents to buy the advertised products.

The more important issue is the messages that televised advertising send to children. The essential message of advertising is that people have problems and the products advertised on television will solve them. Children under eight cannot understand the claims of advertising. Since children do not understand the persuasive messages, they are vulnerable to internalizing them. The prescription drug advertisements are revealing. According to the advertisers all problems can be solved by one drug or the other. All that is necessary to solve your problem quickly is a pill.

Television and the Perpetuation of Values

In spite of the fact that children do not have the cognitive capacities of adults, they spend a lot of time watching adult programming. Unfortunately, they do not have the education, experience, or cognitive skills to interpret what they are seeing. Television communicates the same message regardless of whether an adult or child is the audience. When I was a child the *Dick Van Dyke* and the *Lucille Ball* shows were popular. In these situation comedies married couples were never shown sleeping in the same bed and sex was basically relegated to kissing and hugs. Today, in the mass media the act of sex is closely approximated. Violence, crime, corruption, and other social problems and situations are rampant. For example, in one episode of *Rescue Me*, a firefighter is shown raping his estranged wife. Children and youngsters who view these situations do not understand that the actors are not harmed. As adults, the danger is that children who viewed these programs may see violence as an acceptable solution to their problems. In the same television series, the firefighter who raped his wife helps plan a revenge murder. Can you imagine a society in which revenge killings, spousal rape, and murder were as common as they are in the media?

GENDER STEREOTYPES IN CHILDREN'S BOOKS

One of the most difficult tasks we face when teaching introductory courses in sociology is convincing students that society plays a large role in directing their behavior and shaping their lives. Children steeped in the ideologies of individualism and meritocracy much prefer to view their behavior as a matter of choice, and outcomes in life as congruent with their unique talents and skills. When it comes to gendered behavior, for instance, many people are inclined to believe that differential outcomes in life for women and men are due to natural or innate differences, particularly differences related to biology, rather than the processes of socialization and social forces.

Thus, children must learn to identify themselves as members of various social categories, including categories related to gender, social class, or race and ethnicity, and to think about the ways in which their lives have been shaped and influenced by their membership in those groups. Perhaps the most basic social status is that related to gender. Society has a different set of normative roles for women and men, as well as different responsibilities and kinds of work. What opportunities and outcomes in life one can expect are highly correlated with gender.

Qualitative analysis of children's books reveals that they are full of common stereotypes related to gender. These stereotypes can be found in many popular children's books.

Theoretical Background

Language sets the stage for the development of self-conscious behavior and thought. Through language and interaction, children acquire a social self. Language allows humans to make sense of objects, events, and other people in our environment.

Indeed, it is the mechanism through which humans perceive the world. As children learn how to read, they are exposed to the cultural symbols contained in books. If language shapes and conditions reality then it might be useful to ask what children might be learning about gender when they learn how to read.

Children's books present a microcosm of ideologies, values, and beliefs from the dominant culture. When children learn how to read they are exposed to gender ideologies and scripts. In other words, when children learn how to read they are also learning about culture. Learning to read is part of the process of socialization and an important mechanism through which culture is transmitted from one generation to the next. It is possible that children may use the gender scripts and ideologies in these books when they are role playing and forming an impression of the generalized other, and hence of femaleness and maleness. And it is not just gender that children learn about when they learn how to read, there are cultural scripts and stereotypes about race, social class, and the ideologies of meritocracy, individualism, and the Protestant ethic.

By age seven, and perhaps as early as age four, children begin to understand gender as a basic component of self. Many masculine and feminine characteristics are not biological at all—they are acquired. Gender Schema theory, for instance, suggests that youngsters develop a sense of femaleness and maleness based on gender stereotypes and organize their behavior around them. Children's books, along with other components of the mass media, may be an important source of gender stereotypes that children use to help organize gendered behavior.

An interesting aspect of ideology, and gender ideology in particular, is that people *practice* it. For example, when trying to emulate cultural standards of beauty, women may use cosmetics, certain styles of dress, and even certain colors in order to alter their appearance. The same may be said for men. People may not even be aware that their perceptions about reality and their place in it are constantly structured in an ideological manner. Ideological messages about gender are embedded throughout our culture and when women and men use these stereotypes as standards of comparison to make judgments about themselves or about others, we may say that they are "practicing" gender ideology. Gender ideology is internalized as a system of signs, or in other words, a code. When we uncover the gender code we can think about the ways in which our lives have been structured by it.

A Review of the Findings

Children's pre-school books are an important cultural mechanism for teaching children gender roles. A 1972 study of award-winning children's books discovered that women and girls were almost invisible; boys were portrayed as active and outdoors oriented, while girls were located indoors and more passive, and that men were leaders and women followers (Weitzman et al. 1972). This research was replicated in 1987 and the researchers concluded that although some improvements in roles for women had taken place, the characters in the books were portrayed in traditional gender roles (Williams et al. 1987).

The 1987 research found a majority of the female characters shared no particular behavior; the girls in the books failed to express any career goals, female role models were lacking, and the male characters are still portrayed as more independent. More recent research, based on the same Caldecott Award-winning children's books, found that women were still portrayed in traditional gender-roles usually associated with the household and tools used during housework, whereas males were non-domestic and associated with production-oriented tools and artifacts (Crabb and Bielawski 1994). However, other research conducted in the 1990s suggests that the traditional portrayal of women in children's books is giving way to a more egalitarian depiction for both women and men (Clark, Lennon, and Morris 1993). This certainly suggests that the issues are far from settled and require more research.

Students from EUP Speak Up

Over several years, when discussing the effects of the mass media on childhood socialization, students have brought up some interesting points that should be addressed. I have discovered that the discussion tends to gravitate towards some fairly predictable issues and themes, three of which seem to come up repeatedly:

1. It is only a book and we are reading too much into it—children are not affected by the ideologies in the books,

2. Things have changed and the books no longer reflect attitudes about gender, especially for women, and

3. The books simply reflect reality.

Regarding the claim that the analysis reads too much into the books, it's important to point out that children are just beginning to acquire self and personality at the very time they are reading these books. In other words, they are beginning to learn how the patriarchal gender code embedded in them helps to organize behavior along gendered lines. It can also be pointed out that children will face similar messages from the broader cultural milieu.

The books are themselves, aside from the messages they contain, social artifacts which exist in relationship to other artifacts and social relations—they do not exist in a vacuum. The gender ideologies apparent in the books are also embedded in children's toys, the mass media, and even clothing. It is therefore important that students learn to see these books as only one component of the socialization experience. If language does shape and condition our perceptions of reality, then parents who desire equality for their daughters or egalitarianism for their sons ought to look more closely at what their children are reading. Students who expect to be parents, or perhaps already are, can gain a great deal of insight from simply examining the media their children are exposed to for negative content.

With a little training, anyone can learn to subject the mass media to critical analysis. For several years I had students examine popular children's books for latent messages in relation to gender stereotypes. I present here some of the more interesting observations. In relation to whether or not gender ideologies and stereotypes are present in the books, two women make the following comments:

> I have never thought of these ideas as I have read these books to my children, I am quite offended by the messages that are so craftily hidden by the authors.

> I never realized how children's books could have such stereotypical views within them. However, now that I am aware of these underlying views, I will be more observant.

From these observations it seems clear that students are able to understand that the books can actually influence children's perspectives about gender, as gender schema theory suggests. Moreover, it is apparent that these women had not previously given much thought to the gender roles actually portrayed in the books.

This woman's reflection handily demonstrates her ability to find gender scripts and themes in children's books:

> There was a part in the book where a female dog asked a male dog if he liked her hat. Every time he said no, until in the end he finally said yes when she had on the most fancy hat. The last picture showed them going off together. This was a symbol of power of looks. Showing how the male dog wouldn't take her until he liked her hat, and that the girl dog got a new hat each time to impress him.

Her observation certainly illustrates the connection between gender scripts in the media and the continuing importance of personal attractiveness for women. Thus, women in the classroom begin to understand that they may have internalized certain behaviors and attitudes with respect to their appearance when they were very young. Conversely, the same is true of the men, who begin to see that they have learned to see women, partly, as sexual objects.

Another common theme that tends to surface during the discussion is the claim that gender inequality is a thing of the past. While it is true that significant social, educational, and occupational gains have been made by women, there is still a long way to go before gender equality is reached. Gender stratification remains apparent in the family, in education, in the mass media, in the labor force, in housework, in income and wealth, and even in religion. Even when women are in the work force they often encounter a **glass ceiling**, which prevents their being promoted much beyond middle level management. Women still face a considerable amount of violence in the home. You should try to think about the ways certain children's books support and help reproduce gender stratification and just how early in life you began to be exposed to these realities.

While considering whether or not negative gender stereotypes for women are a thing of the past, these men contributed the following comments:

> Until someone actually sits down and reads a book and analyzes every picture and word, you don't see the hidden messages or problems with inequality that kids are being exposed to. It wasn't just in one or two of the books. There were cases of inequality and different cultural messages in every book.

> Gender plays a large role in these books. For instance, in these books it is very rare that you will see the male being shorter than the female, or the female protecting the male in a dangerous situation. The female is almost always portrayed as the follower and the leader is more likely the male. The mothers in these books are usually housewives who stay home cleaning and cooking all day, while the father goes to a job everyday and comes home and roughhouses with the children, or relaxes after a hard day's work. Some of these things may have been true at the time, but in today's society most women work everyday to help earn a living.

Both men admitted that they had, as a matter of fact, read the books when they were children. Thus, students are able to understand that when the books were actually published is a moot point if parents are still buying them for their children. A striking observation is brought out in the first of these two observations—regarding the extent of the problem, negative gender stereotypes were present in all of the books examined. The second student appropriately points out that women are increasingly part of the work force and that stereotypes relegating them only to the household are an ongoing problem.

A third interpretation often voiced during discussion is that the books simply reflect reality. With a little effort, students can be spurred into thinking of lots of women and men they have known or know who do not fall into the traditional definitions of "feminine" and "masculine." In other words, not all men are dominant and independent, nor are all women submissive, passive, and dependent. If the books do not accurately reflect reality for boys, they do a worse job of reflecting reality for girls, who are nearly invisible in them. Moreover, research suggests that most children do not develop consistently feminine or masculine personalities.

These women made the following comment regarding how accurately the books reflect reality:

> Not all boys are bad, not all girls are prissy. Not all mothers are housewives, not all fathers are doing all the work. There were just a lot of wrong messages in the books.

> Living in the world as a female I would like to believe that none of that was true, but from all the facts and learning everything that we have in class I believe otherwise.

These comments clearly draw attention to the lack of accuracy, let alone diversity, in some children's books. One of the advantages of the exercise is that students are clearly able, with a little prodding, to realize that these children's books do not accurately reflect the actual behavior of either gender. All in all, I think most instructors who decide to try the exercise will be pleasantly surprised by the level of sophistication students are able to achieve using content analysis. It is a very student-friendly methodology.

One of the central issues this research raises is the question of whether or not the gender stereotypes embedded in children's books are simply reflecting innate differences between the sexes, or whether they are, in fact, reproducing and reinforcing culturally-based gender stereotypes. Although this research can not directly determine the extent to which any particular student's gender identity was influenced by children's books, it is an issue students should consider.

How can parents become more aware of the cultural scripts contained in the mass media? One good strategy is to reexamine media you were familiar with as children. In this case, you are trying to recall your childhood and to identify your favorite children's books, cartoons, storybooks, textbooks, and even games. Locate the particular media you remember and conduct a latent analysis for gender stereotypes. Look at the pictures, the colors used, what the characters are doing, and the text of the books.

A second strategy would be to conduct a broader latent analysis using current media. This analysis can focus on advertisements, commercials, magazines, television programs—such as situation comedies, or movies. For example, certain, if not all Disney movies, including *The Lion King*, *The Little Mermaid*, and *Aladdin*, lend themselves quite well to a latent analysis of gender stereotypes. You can find these movies in any video rental establishment. Sit down for as little as an hour and take a look at these videos from a new point of view. Instead of becoming engrossed by the story, as you have been trained to do, try to pay attention to manifest and latent messages in the story. Ask yourself what little girls and boys would pick up about culture, race, social class, or gender by watching these videos.

The next time you consume any type of media look for the following:

- Identifiable gender stereotypes

- Similarity to gender stereotypes found in other media

- What role the media plays in transmitting gender stereotypes to future generations

- How accurately the gender stereotypes describe you or other women and men you know

- To what extent you have incorporated gender stereotypes, presented in the mass media, as part of your gender identity

- To what extent your gender role-performances approximate the gender stereotypes you see in the media

- How your identity changes in different social settings and how that is reflected in the media

These types of analysis are fun and interesting, but also help students address and think about the extent to which the media perpetuates stereotypes.

Gender is perhaps the basic dimension through which individuals perceive the social world and their place in it. Gender shapes social organization and influences how we interact with each other and even how we evaluate ourselves. Additionally, gender shapes our feelings, thoughts, and behaviors from birth to death. Children learn early on that society has different expectations and standards for girls and boys. However, before children can learn what the standards are, and thereby apply gendered standards to themselves, they must learn the gender code. This code is clearly embedded in the children's books used in the exercise. Since children begin to understand gender and apply gender stereotypes at an early age we can reasonably ask what such books, and the mass media in general, are teaching children about gender, race, ethnicity, social class, and a variety of other issues related to social inequality.

This woman's reflection, I think, aptly summarizes the hypothesis that we are shaped by the mass media:

> To see how these books were meant to encourage little boys and degrade little girls was just shocking. During the class discussion, it seemed that most of the books had almost all male characters doing everything important and female characters, if any, were always in secondary roles. Male characters were strong and showed lots of imagination. While female characters were weaker and usually more subdued, with their pink bows and clothing. If a mother figure appeared in a book she was always cleaning or cooking. Father figures worked hard and were more of the authority figure. All the characters seemed white and middle to upper class. All the trouble-makers or everything that was evil or bad was colored in black, while everything good and happy were colored in primary colors. Thinking about all these messages reminded me of how when I was younger my father once said to me "you hammer like a girl," to which I replied "what the hell does that mean?" He had no answer.

From these remarks it seems clear that very few people can fail to recognize gender stereotypes in popular children's books. I conclude with a comment from one of the men, who had a somewhat broader view:

> I realized that children are introduced to racism, social class, and sexual roles at a very young age and they don't even know it. I think the reason we did this exercise was to prove the point that we, as children, are unable to avoid these biases we grow up with. They are everywhere, even in children's books.

ॐ ॐ ॐ ॐ

REFERENCES

Abrahamson, M. (1983). *Social research methods.* Englewood Cliffs, NJ: Prentice Hall.

Andreasen, M. (2001). Evolution in the family's use of television: An overview. In J. Bryant, & J. A. Bryant (Eds.), *Television and the American Family* (2nd ed.). Mahwah, NJ: Erlbaum.

Atkin, C., & Gibson, W. (1978). *Children's nutrition learning from television advertising.* Unpublished Manuscript, Michigan State University, East Lansing.

Bandura, A. (1974). Behavior theory and the models of man. *American Psychologist, 29,* 859-869.

Bandura, A. (1989). Social cognitive theory. In R. Vasta (Ed.), *Annals of Child Development: Vol. 6. Six Theories of Child Development: Revised Formulations and Current Issues.* Greenwich, CT: JAI Press.

Barclay, K., Benelli, C., & Curtis, A. (1995). Literacy begins at birth: What caregivers can learn from parents of children who read early. *Young Children, 50*(4), 24-28.

Begley, S. (1997, Spring/Summer). How to build a baby's brain. *Newsweek,* 28-32.

Bem, S. L. (1981). Gender schema theory: A cognitive account of sex typing. *Psychological Review 88*: 354-64.

Bem, S. L. (1983). Gender schema theory and its implications for child development: raising gender-schematic children in a gender-schematic society. *Signs: Journal of Women in Culture and Society 8*: 598-616.

Bem, S. L. (1984). *Androgyny and gender-schema theory: A conceptual and empirical integration. Nebraska symposium on motivation*: Psychology and Gender 32, 179-226.

Bem, S. L. (1993). *The lenses of gender: Transforming the debate on sexual inequality.* New Haven, CT: Yale University Press.

Bennett, W. J. (1993). *The book of virtues: A treasury of great moral stories.* New York: Simon & Schuster.

Benokraitis, N., & Feagin, J. (1995). *Modern sexism: Blatant, subtle, and overt discrimination.* (2nd ed.) Englewood Cliffs, NJ: Prentice Hall.

Berg, B. L. (2001). *Qualitative research methods for the social sciences.* (4th ed.) Boston, MA: Allyn and Bacon.

Berger, P. L. (1963). *Invitation to sociology: A humanistic perspective.* New York: Doubleday.

Bernard, J. (1981). *The female world.* New York: Free Press.

Bettelheim, B. (1976). *The uses of enchantment: The meaning and importance of fairy tales.* New York: Random House.

Bianchi, S. M., & Spain, D. (1996). Women, work, and family in America. *Population Bulletin, 51*(3), 1-47.

Bronfenbrenner, U. (1970b, November), *Who cares for American's children?* Paper Presented at the National Association of Educators of Young Children Conference, Boston.

Bryant, J., & Rockwell, S. C. (1994). Effects of massive exposure to sexually oriented prime-time television programming on adolescents' moral judgment. In D. Zillman, J. Bryant, & A. C. Huston (Eds.), *Media, Children, and the Family: Social Scientific, Psychodynamic, and Clinical Perspectives.* Hillsdale, NJ: Erlbaum.

Campbell, J. (1968). *The hero with a thousand faces* (2nd ed.). Princeton, NJ: Princeton University Press.

Cantor, J. (1998). *"Mommy, I'm scared": How TV and movies frighten children and what we can do to protect them.* San Diego, CA: Harcourt Brace.

Cashdan, S. (1999). *The witch must die: How fairy tales shape our lives.* New York: Basic Books.

Center for Communication and Social Policy. (1998). *National Television Violence Study* (Vol. 3).

Thousand Oaks, CA: Sage.

Char, C. A., & Meringoff, L. K. (1981, January). The role of story illustrations: Children's story comprehension in three different media. *Harvard Project Zero Technical Report* (No. 22).

Charles, M. (1992). Cross-national variation in occupational segregation. *American Sociological Review, 57*(4), 483-502.

Chomsky, N. (1972). Stages in language development and reading exposure. *Harvard Educational Review, 42*, 1-33.

Christenson, P. G., Henriksen, L., & Roberts, D. F. (2000). *Substance use in popular prime-time television*. Washington, DC: Office of National Drug Control Policy.

Clark, R., Lennon, R., & Morris, L. (1993). Of Caldecotts and Kings: Gendered images in recent children's books by black and non-black illustrators. *Gender and Society, 7*(2), 227-45.

Comstock, G., & Paik, H. (1991). *Television and the American child*. San Diego, CA: Academic Press.

Comstock, G., & Scharrer, E. (1999). *Television: What's on, who's watching and what it means*. San Diego, CA: Academic Press.

Comstock, G., & Scharrer, E. (2001). The use of television and other film-related media. In D. G. Singer, & J. L. Singer (Eds.), *Handbook of Children and the Media*. Thousand Oaks, CA: Sage.

Condry, J. (1989). *The psychology of television*. Hillsdale, NJ: Erlbaum.

Condry, J., Bence, P., & Scheibe, C. (1988). Non-Program content of children's television. *Journal of Broadcasting and Electronic Media, 32*(3), 255-270.

Crespo, C. J., Smit, E., Troiano, R. P., Bartlett, S. J., Macera, C. A., & Anderson, R. E. (2001). Television watching, energy intake, and obesity in U.S. children. *Archives of Pediatric and Adolescent Medicine, 155*, 360-365.

Davis, D. M. (1993). Cited in "T.V. Is a Blonde, Blonde World." *American Demographics, Special Issue: Women Change Places*. Ithaca, New York.

Dennison, B. A., Erb, T. A., & Jenkins, P. L. (2002). Television viewing and television in bedroom associated with overweight risk among low-income preschool children. *Pediatrics, 109*, 1028-1035.

Desmond, R. (2001). Free reading: Implication for child development. In D. G. Singer, & J. L. Singer (Eds.), *Handbook of Children and the Media*. Thousand Oaks, CA: Sage.

Dorr, A., & Rabin, B. E. (1995). Parents, children, and television. In M. H. Bornstein (Eds.), *Handbook of Parenting* (Vol. 4). Mahwah, NJ: Erlbaum.

Dougherty, W. H., & Engle, R. E. (1987). An '80s look for sex equality in Caldecott Winners and Honor Books. *Reading Teacher, 40*(4), 394-398.

Eagly, A. H., & Wood, W. (1999). The origins of sex differences in human behavior: Evolved dispositions verses social roles. *American Psychologist, 54*, 408-23.

Esslin, M. (1982). *The age of television*. San Francisco: Freeman.

Evans, E. D., Rutberg, J., Sather, C., & Turner, C. (1991). Content analysis of contemporary teen magazines for adolescent teen females. *Youth Society, 23*(1), 99-120.

Fiske, E. B. (1980). School vs. television. *Parents, 55*(1), 54-59.

Flavell, J. (1986). The development of children's knowledge about the appearance-reality distinction. *American Psychologist, 41*, 418-425.

Flavell, J. H., Miller, P. H., & Miller, S. A. (2001). *Cognitive development* (4th ed.). Englewood Cliffs, NJ: Prentice-Hall.

Fuller, R., & Schoenberger, R. (1991). The gender salary gap: Do academic achievements, intern experience, and college major make a difference? *Social Science Quarterly 72* (4): 715-26.

Gatz, I. L. (1975). On children and television. *Elementary School Journal, 75*(7), 415-418.

Geen, R. G. (1994). Television and aggression: Recent development in research and theory. In D. Zillman, J. Bryant, & A. C. Huston (Eds.), *Media, children and the family: Social scientific, psychodynamic and clinical perspectives*. Hillsdale, NJ: Erlbaum.

Gelles, R. J., & Cornell, C. P. (1990). *Intimate violence in families*. (2nd ed). Newbury Park, CA: Sage.

Gerbner, G., Gross, L., Morgan, M., & Signorielli, N. (2002). Growing up with television: Cultivation process. In J. Bryant, & D. Zillman (Eds.), *Media effects: Advances in theory and research* (2nd ed.). Mahwah, NJ: Erlbaum.

Gollnick, D. M., & Chinn, P. C. (2005). *Multicultural education in a pluralistic society* (7th ed.). Upper Saddle River, NJ: Merrill/Prentice-Hall.

Greenberg, B. S. (1994). Content trends in media sex. In D. Zillman, J. Bryant, & A. C. Houston (Eds.), *Media, children and the family: Social scientific, psychodynamic, and clinical perspectives.* Hillsdale, NJ: Erlbaum.

Greenfield, P. M. (1984). *Mind and media: The effects of television, video games and computers.* Cambridge, MA: Harvard University Press.

Healy, J. (1990). *Endangered minds: Why children don't think and what to do about it.* New York: Touchstone Books.

Healy, J. (1998). *Failure to connect: How computers affect our children's minds and what we can do about it.* New York: Touchstone.

Heck, M. C. (1980). The ideological dimensions of media messages. In *Culture, Media, Language: Working Papers in Cultural Studies*, 1972-1979. New York: Hutchinson and Co., Ltd.

Holsti, O. R. (1968). Content Analysis. In G. Lindzey, & E. Aaronson (Eds.), *The Handbook of Social Psychology.* Reading, MA: Addison-Wesley.

Holsti, O. R. (1969). *Content analysis for the social sciences and humanities.* Reading, MA: Addison-Wesley.

Huck, C. S., & Helper, S. (Eds.). (1996). *Children's literature in the elementary school* (6th ed.). New York: WCB/McGraw-Hill.

Huesmann, L. R, Moise-Titus, J., Podolski, C., & Eron, L. D. (2003). Longitudinal relations between children's exposure to TV violence and their aggressive and violent behavior in young adulthood: 1977-1992. *Developmental Psychology, 39*(2), 201-221.

Huesmann, L. R., Eron, L. D., Klein, R., Brice, P., & Fisher, P. (1983). Mitigating the imitation of aggressive behavior by changing children's attitudes about media violence. *Journal of Personality and Social Psychology, 44*, 899-910.

Huston, A. C., & Wright, J. C. (1998). Mass media and children's development. In W. Damon (Ed.), *Handbook of Child Psychology.* (5th ed., Vol. 4). New York: Wiley.

Huston, A. C., Zillman, D., & Bryandt, J. (1994). Media influence, public policy, and the family. In D. Zillman, J. Bryant, & A. C. Huston (Eds.), *Media, children, and the family: Social scientific, psychodynamic, and clinical perspectives.* Hillsdale, NJ: Erlbaum.

Kaiser Family Foundation. (2005a). *Generation M: Media in the lives of 8 – 18-year olds.* Menlo Park, CA: Author.

Kunkel, D. (2001). Children and television advertising. In D. G. Singer, & J. L. Singer (Eds.), *Handbook of children and the media.* Thousand Oaks, CA: Sage.

Kunkel, D., Wilcox, B. L., Cantor, J., Palmer, E., Linn, S., & Dowrick, P. (2004). *Report of the APA Task Force on Advertising and Children.* Washington, DC: American Psychological Association.

Leibert, R. M., Neil, M., & Davidson, E. S. (1973). *The early window: Effects of television on children and youth.* New York: Pergamon Press.

Levin, D. E. (1998). *Remote control childhood? Combating the hazards of media culture.* Washington, DC: National Association for Education of Young Children.

Lonigan, C. J., Burgess, S. R., & Anthony, J. L. (2000). Development of emergent literacy and early reading skills in preschool children: Evidence from a latent-variable longitudinal study. *Developmental Psychology, 36*, 596-613.

Loy, P. H., & Stewart, L. P. (1984). The extent and effects of sexual harassment of working women. *Sociological Focus, 17*(1): 31-43.

Macionis, J. J. (2001). *Sociology.* (8th ed). Upper Saddle River, NJ: Prentice Hall.

Malamuth, N. M., & Impett, E. A. (2001). Research on sex in the media. In D. G. Singer, & J. L. Singer

(Eds.). *Handbook of children and the media*. Thousand Oaks, CA: Sage.

Mann, J. (1982). *What Is TV doing to America? U.S. News & World Report, 93*(5), 27-30.

McLane, J. B., & McNamee, G. D. (1990). *Early literacy*. Cambridge, MA: Harvard University Press.

McLuhan, M. (1964). *Understanding media: The extension of man*. New York: McGraw-Hill.

McLuhan, M. (1989). A McLuhan Mosaic. In G. Sanderson, & F. Macdonald (Eds.), *Marshall McLuhan: The man and his message*. Golden, CO: Fulcrum.

McNeal, J. (1987). *Children as consumers*. Lexington, MA: Lexington Books.

Mead, G. H. (1934). *Mind, self, and society*. Chicago: University of Chicago Press.

Mediascope. (1997). *National television violence study* (Vol. 2). Studio City, CA: Author.

Mills, C. W. (1956). *The sociological imagination*. New York: Oxford University Press.

Neuman, S. G. (1991). *Literacy in the television age: The myth of the TV effect*. Norwood, NJ: Ablex.

Norton, D. E., & Norton, S. E. (2002). *Through the eyes of a child: An introduction to children's literature* (6th ed.). Upper Saddle River, NJ: Merrill.

Ollenburger, J. C., & Moore, H. A. (1992). *A sociology of women: The intersection of patriarchy, capitalism and colonization*. Englewood Cliffs, NJ: Prentice Hall.

Paul, E. F. (1991). Bared buttocks and federal cases. *Society, 28*(4), 4-7.

Pear, R. (1987, September 4). Women reduce lag in earnings, but disparities with men remain. *New York Times*, pp. 1, 7.

Pearl, D. (1984). Violence and aggression. *Society, 21*(6), 17-22.

Perse, E. M. (2001). *Media effects and society*. Mahwah, NJ: Erlbaum.

Piaget, J. (1962). *Play, dreams, and imitation in childhood* (C. Gattegno, & F. M. Hodgson, Trans.). New York: Norton.

Postman, N. (1982). *The disappearance of childhood*. New York: Dell.

Roberts, D. F., & Foehr, U. G. (2004). *Kids and the media in America*. New York: Cambridge University Press.

Rovenger, J. (2000). Fostering emotional intelligence. *School Library Journal, 46*(2), 40-43.

Sadker, D., & Sadker, M. (2003). *Teacher, schools, and society* (6th ed.). New York: McGraw-Hill.

Sadker, M., Sadker, D., & Klein, S. (1991). The issue of gender in elementary and secondary Education. *Review of Research in Education, 17*, 269-334.

Sapir, E. (1929). *The status of linguistics as a science*. Language 5 (September-October 1994), 5-8.

Sapir, E. (1949). *Selected writings of Edward Sapir in language, culture, and personality*. David G. Mandelbaum, (Ed.) Berkeley, CA: University of California Press.

Scheibe, C. (1989). *Character portrayal and values in network TV commercials*. Unpublished Master's Thesis, Cornell University, Ithaca, NY. Cited in J. Condry, The Psychology of Television (Hillsdale, NJ: Erlbaum, 1989).

Schickedanz, J. (1986). *More than the ABCs: The early stages of reading and writing*. Washington, DC: National Association for the Education of Young Children.

Schwartz, M. D. (1987). Gender and injury in spousal assault. *Sociological Focus, 20*(1), 61-75.

Sellitz, C., Jahoda, M., Deutsch, M., & Cook S. W. (1967). *Research methods in social relations*. (2nd ed). New York: Holt, Rienhart, & Winston.

Signorella, M. L., Bigler, R. S., & Liben, L. S. (1993). Developmental difference in children's gender schemata about others: A meta-analytic review. *Developmental Review, 13*, 147-183.

Signorielli, N. (2001). Television's gender role images and contribution to stereotyping: Past, present, future. In D. G. Singer, & J. L. Singer (Eds.), *Handbook of Children and the Media*. Thousand Oaks, CA: Sage.

Singer, D. G., & Singer, J. L. (1990). *House of make-believe*. Cambridge, MA: Harvard University Press.

Singer, D. G., Singer, J. L., & Zuckerman, D. M. (1990). *The parent's guide: Use TV to your child's advantage*. Reston, VA: Acropolis Books.

Smolowe, J. (1994, July 4). When violence hits home. *Time*, (Vol. 144, No. 1), pp. 18-25.

Sprafkin, J. M., Liebert, R. M., & Poulos, R. W. (1975). Effects of a prosocial example on children's helping. *Journal of Experimental Child Psychology, 20,* 119-126.

Stabiner, K. (1993, August 15). Get 'em while they're young. *Los Angeles Times Magazine,* pp. 12, 14, 15, 16, 38.

Stalp, M. C., & Grant, L. (2001). Teaching qualitative coding in undergraduate field methods classes: An exercise based on personal ads. *Teaching Sociology, 29,* 209-18.

Strasburger, V. C. (2001). Children, adolescents, drugs, and the media. In D. G. Singer, & J. L. Singer (Eds.), *Handbook of children and the media.* Thousand Oaks, CA: Sage.

Strasburger, V. C., & Wilson, B. J. (2002). *Children, adolescents, and the media.* Thousand Oaks, CA: Sage.

Straus, M. A., & Gelles, R. J. (1986). Social change and change in family violence from 1975 to 1985 as revealed by two national surveys. *Journal of Marriage and Family, 48*(4), 465-79.

Strauss, A. L. (1987). *Qualitative analysis for social scientists.* New York: Cambridge University Press.

Taylor, F. O. (1998). The continuing significance of Structural Marxism for Feminist social theory. *Current Perspectives in Social Theory, 18,* 101-29.

Teale, W. H. (1984). Reading to young children: Its significance for literary development. In H. Coleman, A. Oberg, & F. Smith (Eds.), *Awakening and literacy.* Portsmouth, NH: Heinemann.

Valkenburg, P. M. (2001). Television and the child's developing imagination. In D. G. Singer, & J. L. Singer (Eds.), *Handbook of children and the media.* Thousand Oaks, CA: Sage.

Waldfogel, J. (1997). The effect of children on women's wages. *American Sociological Review, 62*(2), 209-17.

Walzer, S. (2001). Developing sociologists through qualitative study of college life. *Teaching Sociology, 29,* 88-94.

Wartella, E. A., & Jennings, N. (2000). Children and computers: New technology—old concerns. *The Future of Children, 10*(2), 31-43.

Weitzman, L. J. (1979). Sex role socialization. In *Woman: a Feminist Perspective,* (2nd ed.), edited by Jo Freeman. Palo Alto, CA: Mayfield.

Whorf, B. L. (1956). The relation of habitual thought and behavior to language. In *Language, Thought and Reality.* (pp. 134-59). Cambridge, MA: The Technology Press of MIT/New York.

Williams, A. J., Vernon, J. A., Williams, M. C., & Malecha, K. (1987). Sex-role socialization in picture books: An update. *Social Science Quarterly, 68*(3), 148-56.

Winn, M. (1977). *The plug-in drug.* New York: Bantam.

Wright, J. C., Huston, A. C., Reitz, A. L., & Piemymat, S. (1994). Young children's perceptions of television reality. Determinants and developmental differences. *Developmental Psychology, 30*(2), 229-239.

Wright, J. C., St. Peters, M., & Huston, A. C. (1990). Family television use and its relation to children's cognitive skills and social behavior. In J. Bryant (Ed.), *Television and the American Family.* Hillsdale, NJ: Erlbaum.

Yamagata, H., Yeh, K. S., Stewaman, S., & Dodge, H. (1997). Sex segregation and glass ceilings: A comparative static model of women's career opportunities in the federal government over a quarter century. *American Journal of Sociology, 103* (3), 566-632.

TERMS AND DEFINITIONS

A Priori. Society exists prior to us, and it continues to exist after we are gone.

Achieved Status. A status entered after birth and usually due at least in part to individual behavior.

Acquaintance Rape. Acquaintance rape occurs when someone is raped by a perpetrator they are familiar with or know.

Additive Task. The supervisor or professor just assigns the task to the entire group and group activity is the sum of effort from each member.

Affiliation Motive. An emotional drive identified by William James about our desire to have close relationships with friends, family, and lovers.

Alienation. Alienation is the feeling that you are not in control of your life. It is a feeling of powerlessness, normlessness, and of being cut off from the product of one's labor, from other people, and from oneself.

Animism. Animism is the belief the rivers, trees, forests, inanimate objects and even animals possess a soul, or otherwise can act like a human being, with motive.

Anxious/Ambivalent. In this category of attachment people desire closer relationships but have high levels of anxiety about themselves. Anxious people are preoccupied with their faults and shortcomings and fear that those they are close to will discover their negative traits.

Asceticism. The doctrine that through renunciation of worldly pleasures it is possible to achieve a high spiritual or intellectual state.

Ascribed Status. A status assigned at birth.

Authoritarian Parenting. Authoritarian parenting is a type of parenting in which children are severely punished, even for minor infractions. This style of parenting is associated with authoritarianism later in life.

Authoritarian Personality. Authoritarian personality describes a person who views social reality in black-and-white terms. They follow the conventions of society and have little tolerance for those who challenge those conventions.

Beliefs. Beliefs are statements about what is thought to be real.

Biological Determinism. The belief that genetic factors explain differences in human behavior is called biological determinism.

Bureaucracy. A bureaucracy is a formal organization designed to achieve maximum efficiency

Castes. Castes are social status or position conferred by a system based on ascription.

Coalition. A coalition is an alliance forged to meet a common goal.

Cognitive Dissonance. Cognitive dissonance is a psychological term which describes the uncomfortable tension that comes from holding two conflicting thoughts at the same time, or from engaging in behavior that conflicts with one's beliefs.

Commitment. Commitment refers to the conscious decision to stay together through thick-and-thin.

Companionate Love. Companionate love is a more practical type of love. Couples who experience companionate love emphasize trust, caring, and friendship. Their lives are deeply intertwined and their activities are highly coordinated.

Compassionate Love. Compassionate love involves high levels of intimacy and commitment, but very little passion.

Competitive Interdependence. If rewards are structured in such a way as to make one person's loss another's gain people will compete. The outcomes for individuals are independent of each other.

Competitors. Competitors are people that have a value system that stresses individual gains relative to the group.

Complex Task. In the complex task group assignment, a division of labor, such that each group member is given a critical task to complete and an equal, or nearly so, amount of work, is created.

Conformity. Conformity refers to the tendency to change our behavior to be consistent with the group.

Conjunctive Task. In this type of group process each member has individual expertise.

Conspicuous Consumption. This refers to the open display of wastefulness designed to impress others. Also, the purchasing of products intended to affirm or enhance an individual's prestige.

Constraint Commitment. In this type of commitment, the partners lack other choices. This type of commitment is really based on external forces, such as lack of time, energy, emotion, or money. The partners are stuck with each other and make the best of it.

Consummate Love. Consummate love has nearly equal parts of intimacy, passion, and commitment. In our society, consummate love is often seen as the ideal type for which all couples should strive.

Cooperative Interdependence. In this group the outcomes of group members are all linked to each other. In order for a single individual to succeed, everyone in the group must succeed.

Cooperators. Cooperators are people that have internalized a value system in which maximization of group rewards is the most desirable.

Correspondent Outcomes. When both partners are receiving similar rewards from the relationship outcomes are said to be correspondent.

Covert Discrimination. A type of discrimination that is hidden or disguised in context is covert, rather than overt.

Cultural Assimilation. Cultural assimilation is a process by which a racial or ethnic minority loses its distinctive identity and lifeways and conforms to cultural patterns of the dominant group.

Cultural Determinism. Cultural determinism is the belief that individual differences are caused by socialization and are, therefore, changeable.

Culture. Culture is a learned set of practices, beliefs, values, rules for proper conduct, and material objects shared by members of a society.

De Facto Segregation. De facto segregation is a form of segregation that is an unintended consequence of social or ecological arrangements.

Decision Rules. Decision rules are rules that groups use in arriving at a decision.

Definition of the Situation. Definition of the situation conveys who is present in terms of roles, and thus, how a situation is organized. For symbolic interactionists, the concept of role provides a key link between the perspective and behavior of individuals and the social situations in which they find themselves.

Deindividuation. The temporary loss of your individual identity and social self is called deindividuation.

Derogated Groups. Derogated groups are devalued groups, such as prisoners or homeless persons.

Deviant. Deviance refers to personal behavior that violates any social norm.

Discrimination. Discrimination refers to behaviors, or actions, as opposed to feelings. To discriminate means to take an action – to treat one person differently than another on the basis of group membership. Positive or negative behavior based on stereotyped beliefs about the occupants of a status.

Disjunctive Task. In this group process, only one person needs to be successful in order for the entire group to succeed.

Dismissing/Avoidant Attachment. People characterized by this type of attachment can seem aloof and distant. They are slow to disclose personal feelings and ideas because they are distrustful of others.

Dormant Catholic. Those who are not members of any particular church but were baptized and confirmed as Catholics and will probably want to be married by a Catholic priest and have the priest administer their last rites.

Downward Social Comparisons. A psychological mechanism for creating positive feelings about your social identity by disparaging members of other groups as "lower" than you is a downward social comparison.

Dyad. A Dyad is a two-member group.

Ego. Ego is a concept in Freud's personality system. Your ego is the part of your personality that attempts to balance the impulses and drives of the id against the directives of society, represented in the personality by the superego. The ego emerges as the basis of personality as each individual strikes the balance between impulsive behavior and social norms in a variety of ways.

Emergent. The self emerges (or develops) from social interactions with others.

Empty Love. Empty love is mostly commitment but little passion or intimacy.

Equity Rule. The Equity rule is frequently applied by partners to see if their relationship is fair. No personal relationship is entirely equitable; some inequality is bound to exist.

Ethnocentrism. Ethnocentrism refers to the fact that the dominant group tends to record history from their point of view, paying little attention to the point of view of other groups or their accomplishments. Judging other cultures by your own cultural standards and since, of course, other cultures are different, they are therefore inferior. Ethnocentrism means an inability to appreciate others whose culture may include a different racial group, ethnic group, religion, morality, language, political system, economic system, etc. It also means an inability to see a common humanity and human condition facing all women and men in all cultures and societies beneath the surface variations in social and cultural traditions.

Evaluation Apprehension. Evaluation apprehension refers to the anxious expectations you may feel when you know you are going to be assessed. For simple tasks, awareness of being evaluated often leads to greater effort. But for more complex tasks, the pressure of evaluation may harm performance.

Exit. Exit refers to the ultimate destruction of the relationship with the partners ending it.

Expressive Goals. Expressive goals are related to meeting emotional needs, such as a sense of belonging, a sense of togetherness, and a sense of personal worth that are fulfilled by being involved with a particular group.

Extrinsic Religiosity. Extrinsic religiosity refers to the desire to make friends, gain status, or receive other forms of social support. For these people, religion is a means to an end and the ideas, concepts, and messages of their religion have little effect on their self-concept. These people are most likely to be prejudiced.

False Consciousness. False consciousness is a sociological concept usually associated with misunderstanding your social class position in society. However, false consciousness can also operate in relationships. You may be unaware that you are, in fact, the dependent partner or the partner receiving fewer rewards and positive outcomes. False consciousness, on a broader scale, occurs whenever you fail to recognize the exploitative nature of any social relationship you participle in.

Fearful Avoidant Attachment. Individuals who have fearful or avoidant attachments score high on both anxiety and avoidance. These people not only have negative attitudes about themselves they view others as untrustworthy and uncaring. These individuals worry that they are unlovable and try to keep others at a distance.

Femininity. Femininity is a set of beliefs describing the ideal female.

Feminism. Feminism is a theoretical and ideological framework that directly opposes sexism by supporting gender equality.

Formal Sanctions. Formal sanctions refer to sanctions associated with the official agents of social control. A clearly defined reward or punishment with specific people authorized to deliver it.

Free Rider. A free rider is someone who enjoys group membership but either did not make the initial sacrifices the other members of the group did or is unwilling to do so if called upon.

Gender Ideology. A belief system that stereotypes one into specific occupations, roles, etc, because of their gender is known as a gender ideology.

Gender Schema Theory. Gender Schema Theory refers to an information processing approach to socialization in that the theory describes and explains the child's developing content and organization of gender knowledge (Bem, 1981). A basic assumption of gender schema theory is that gender knowledge is multidimensional, with children believing that there are behaviors, attitudes, characteristics, and occupations which are gender related (Huston, 1983).

Gender Stereotype. A gender stereotype is a rigid, oversimplified belief that is applied to all members of a specific gender.

Generalized Other. The self's organization of the roles of others is called the generalized other. It means the self is taking the related roles of all others in a social situation rather than the role of just on other person. The term generalized other does not refer to an actual group of people, but rather to an idea or conception a person derives from his or her experiences. The person then regulates behavior in terms of the supposed opinions and attitudes of others.

Glass Ceiling. The glass ceiling is an invisible barrier, or covert set of social relationships, that tends to keep women in the bottom rungs of the corporate ladder.

Group Superiority. Group superiority refers to the tendency to see one's own group and culture as superior to others.

Group. A group is at least two people who interact with each other based on shared norms, values, and beliefs. The smallest group is a dyad.

Halo Effect. The halo effect is the belief that a person who has one positive attribute, such as good looks, has other positive attributes.

Heretic. A heretic is a person who holds religious beliefs in conflict with the dogma of the church (especially the Roman Catholic Church), or any other institution. Also, a heretic could be a person who holds unorthodox opinions in any field (not merely religion).

Hostile Environment Harassment. In the hostile workplace sexual harassment is sexually intimidating or hostile for one gender, usually women.

Id. The Id is a reflection of primitive drives within the individual.

Ideal Self. The ideal self is your personal idea of the perfect person.

Identity Salience. Identity salience represents one of the ways, and a theoretically most important way, that the identities making up the self can be organized (p. 206 Stryker & Serpe, 1982). Importantly, it influences how much effort we put into each role and how well we perform in each role.

Ideologies. Ideologies refers to clusters of values that tend to hang together to form a cohesive belief system. Ideologies are often invoked to explain inequalities.

Individualism. Individualism is an ideological doctrine that holds that the rights and interests of the individual are, or ought to be, equal if not greater than those of the group.

Individualists. Individualists are people concerned with their own gains period, and are not concerned about the group.

Infatuation. Infatuation is mostly passion, but little intimacy and commitment.

Informal Sanction. A loosely defined reward or punishment with no specific people authorized to impose it is an informal sanction. Getting a reprimand, in the form of a glare or stare is an informal sanction.

In-Group Bias. The preferential treatment people give to whom they perceive to be members of their own groups is in-group bias.

In-Group Cohesion. In-group cohesion refers to the process of sticking together within the group.

In-Group. An exclusive circle of people with a common purpose is an in-group. In-groups can also refer to a group you desire to become of member of or a group you already belong to.

Institutional Discrimination. Institutional discrimination refers to legal, economic, political, and cultural mechanisms that limit opportunities for some groups, while advancing opportunities for others. This type of discrimination is built right into the normative operation of society.

Institutions. Institutions are complex social structures that meet basic human needs. Also, sets of roles graded in authority that have been embodied in consistent patterns of actions that have been legitimated and sanctioned by society or segments of that society; whose purpose is to carry out certain activities or prescribed needs of that society or segments of that society. - C. Wright Mills, *The Sociological Imagination* (New York: Oxford University Press, 1959), p. 30.

Interdependence. Interdependence refers to a reciprocal relation between interdependent entities (objects or individuals or groups).

Inter-Group Competition. Inter-group competition refers to a conflict between groups.

Internalization. Internalization is the processes through which children learn to identify and use the appropriate set of norms in different social settings.

Intimacy. Intimacy refers to the close feelings people develop for each other. Intimate couples know each other very well and care deeply about each other's welfare,

Intrinsic Religiosity. Individuals with an intrinsic religious orientation see religion as an end in itself. They try to live their lives by religious principles. Since most religions teach tolerance intrinsically religious people could be expected to be low on prejudice and this seems to be the case.

Labeling Theory. Labeling theory is a theory that holds that societies often reinforce their boundaries by labeling people as well as their acts as deviant.

Language. Language refers to a system of symbols that allows communication between people to take place. Language is the medium through which culture is transmitted from one generation to the next.

Latent Functions. Latent functions are unintended and unrecognized operations of a social institution with generally positive outcomes.

Legitimate Authority. Legitimate authority refers to power that is associated with one's position in the authority hierarchy.

Looking-Glass Self. Cooley's concept that individuals use others like mirrors and base their conceptions of self on what is reflected to them during social interaction is known as the looking-glass self.

Loyalty. Loyalty refers to the behavior of committed partners wait for negative situations in their relationships to improve and attempt to maintain the relationship through effective communication.

Majority-Wins Rule. Majority-wins is a rule that holds that a simple majority (51%) of group members is needed for a particular course of action.

Manifest Function. Manifest function refers to the anticipated and intended outcome of the operation of a social institution.

Marginal Catholic. Marginal Catholics are those who almost never attend church beyond weddings, funerals, and occasionally at Christmas.

Master Status. A master status is the status we most often activate and use.

Matching Principle. According to the matching principle, we tend to prefer people who have similar attitudes, likes and dislikes, and similar experiences.

Material Culture. Material culture refers to the tangible things we create as a culture. Material culture can refer to homes, automobiles, highways, roads, and interstates, buildings, boats, books, computers, or anything else that society produces.

Matriarchy. Matriarchy is a form of social organization in which a female is the family head and title is traced through the female line.

Mental Illness. Mental illness refers to a disease of the mind; the psychological state of someone who has emotional or behavioral problems serious enough to require psychiatric intervention.

Meritocracy. Meritocracy is a system in which the talented are chosen and moved ahead on the basis of their achievements. Can also be described as a society where status is achieved on the basis of merit; this might involve the possession of attributes, which are valued in a society.

Meso-Level. A meso-level analysis is focused at the institutional level such as local governments and universities.

Micro-Level. A micro-level analysis refers to face-to-face interactions in small groups of people.

Mind. Mind refers to the ability to think, particularly about the self. Mind depends upon language and symbols, in turn generated by culture.

Model Catholic. The Model Catholic refers to those who generally observe the rituals, such as not eating meat on Fridays and Lent, and attend mass most of the time.

Morals. Morals are conceptions of right and wrong.

Naturalistic View. People who take the naturalistic view feel that there must be an underlying order or purpose in life because they can observe that order in nature.

Neglect. Neglect in a relationship is destructive. Less committed partners often passively let the relationship deteriorate, ignoring, or refusing to discuss the issue.

Negotiated Order. In a negotiated order one is able to function due to understanding in a broad sense what your role is in relationship to your superiors and other peers.

Norm of Reciprocity. According to the norm of reciprocity, which all human children learn early in life, if you ask someone for a favor, you must be willing to return the favor for the person who helped you. If someone helps you on a project; the ethical thing to do is to return the favor and help him or her, which has the function of reducing competition.

Norms. Norms are rules of society that attaches sanctions to the behavior or appearance of status occupants.

Nuclear Catholic. Nuclear Catholics are those highly involved in parish life.

Out-Group. An out-group is a devalued group. Out-groups often are opposed to your in-group.

Overt Discrimination. Overt discrimination is a type of discrimination that is used openly.

Partial Birth Abortion. Partial birth abortion is the killing of an unborn baby of at least 20 weeks by pulling it out of the birth canal with forceps, but leaving the head inside. An incision is made in the back of the baby's neck and the brain tissue is suctioned out. The head is then removed from the uterus.

Passion. Passion refers to the desire the individuals feel for each other. The emotional state characterized by arousal, sexual desire, and excitement.

Passionate Love. Passionate love is highly emotional. In this type of love the focus is on the "chemistry" the couple experiences.

Patriarchy. Patriarchy is a form of social organization in which a male is the family head and title is traced through the male line.

Peer Groups. Peer groups are a collection of people who share a level of social standing, especially in terms of age.

Perceived Out-Group Homogeneity. When people have a tendency to overestimate the level of similarity members of one group have to each other, it is called perceived out-group homogeneity. This effect has the function of making cognitive processing easier – it makes it easy to apply the stereotype.

Personal Dedication. Personal dedication happens when a couple has a "we" identity. Their personal sense of self includes the other person. They prefer not to do something if the other cannot for some reason.

Play Stage (2 to 7 years). The play stage is the stage in which the child moves through rapid emulation of roles he or she perceives. Through the practice of pretending to be others, for example, a doctor, teacher, or rock star, the child begins to understand the concept of "others."

Political Socialization. Political socialization refers to the influences and experiences that lead people to define their political orientation as liberal or conservative.

Possible-Self. Possible-self is based on self-conceptions about oneself in the future.

Prejudice. Prejudice refers to an illogical attitude. It is a *feeling* we get when we encounter a member of a particular group or someone with a particular attribute.

Presentation of Self. Presentation of self refers to the process through which we try to convince others that we have the personal qualities and characteristics we believe we do.

Primary Group. A primary group is a small group characterized by face-to-face interaction.

Primary Socialization. Primary socialization is the learning of culture that occurs in the family.

Principle of Least Interest. The principle of least interest posits that the partner that is less interested in continuing the relationship generally has greater power. The partner that is more dependent upon the other is usually the one more interested in continuing in the relationship.

Private Self-Consciousness. Private self-consciousness refers to our actual goals and beliefs. Actors with high levels of private self-consciousness are more concerned with their internal goals and try harder to achieve personal standards.

Propinquity Principle. The propinquity principle refers to nearness of time and place. We tend to care most for those with whom we spend the most time.

Protestant Ethic. The Protestant ethic is an ascetic orientation that encourages hard work, thrift, and righteous forms of godliness.

Psychoses. Any severe mental disorder in which contact with reality is lost or highly distorted may be referred to as psychoses.

Public Self-Consciousness. Public self-consciousness refers to the concerns we often have with what others think of us.

Quest Religiosity. Quest religiosity refers to people that describe religion as a lifelong journey towards the truth.

Quid Pro Quo Harassment. Quid pro quo harassment refers to the attempt to trade sex for various types of favors, such as a letter of recommendation, a promotion, or a good grade.

Racism. Racism refers to the illogical belief that one race is superior to all others. Racism is a negative attitude toward certain races.

Racist Slurs. Racist slurs are words and phrases used to derogate another individual, race, culture, or group outside of your own.

Rationality. Rationality refers to a reliance on reason and the scientific method as the basis of decision making.

Reciprocal Interaction Network. Reciprocal networks are complementary relationships influenced by variables such as social class, race or ethnicity, gender and community. The existential security of any individual is dependent upon the location of the local world within the existing social structure.

Redefine the Situation. Redefining the situation is a strategy used to deal with stereotype threat. In the process of interacting with others we come to have certain definitions about what is going on in different social settings and we respond according to our *definition* of what is happening.

Reference Group. A reference group is used as a standard of desirable or undesirable appearance or behavior.

Reflected Appraisals. Messages we get about ourselves from others are referred to as reflected appraisals. Reflected appraisals are part of the Looking-Glass self.

Reinforcement-Affect Model. The reinforcement-affect model stresses that the major goal in affiliation is the desire to feel good. Consequently, we tend to like people we associate with warm feelings or positive rewards and tend to dislike people we associate with negative feelings.

Relationship Monitors. Relationship monitors have an awareness of the emotional state of family members and the health of the relationships. Often a role expectation held by wives and mothers.

Religiosity. Religiosity refers to the range of behaviors associated with religion and the intensity with which religious convictions are felt.

Risky Shift. The risky shift occurs when groups make decisions collectively which the individuals involved would consider too risky.

Role Strain. Role-strain refers to a situation where fulfilling a certain role has a conflict with fulfilling another role. While role conflict takes place across different role sets, role strain happens within the same role set.

Role Taking. Role-taking consists of imagining oneself in the role of the other and appraising, from the standpoint of that role, or social position, "the situation, oneself in the situation and possible lines of action" (Matsueda, 1992).

Role Theory. Role theory refers to the idea that an actor's social identity is largely a function of the validated social positions, which they occupy.

Role. A role is the expected behavior associated with a particular status position - what the individual or group occupying a particular status position is supposed to do.

Role-Conflict. Role conflict refers to the incompatibility of enactment of two or more different roles that one person can enact at a certain time or place.

Role-Enactments. Role enactments are the normative behaviors we engage in when carrying out the rights, duties, and obligations of a status.

Role-Expectations. Role expectations refer to those roles society generally expects people to perform, or anticipated behaviors of people who occupy a status.

Role-Identity. Role identity refers to a description of yourself based on the position you occupy.

Role-Performance. Role performance refers to the actual behavior of people who occupy a status, such as flair, style, or personality.

Romantic Love. Romantic love is a type of love that is often described as an all-consuming emotional experience. When the lover is absence, a nearly physical experience of loss or separation is felt.

Scapegoating. Scapegoating refers to the process of blaming members of socially derogated groups for one's frustrations and failures.

Secondary Group. A secondary group that is large and impersonal with a formal organization.

Secondary Socialization. Secondary socialization is that which occurs outside of the family.

Secure Attachment. Secure attachment refers to adults who are low on both anxiety and avoidance. These adults are more open and easy to get along with.

Self-Concept. Self-concept refers to how we think and feel about ourselves. Our sense of self comes from our communication and interaction with others.

Self. That aspect of the personality consisting of the individual's conception of himself or herself is called the self. The way a person perceives himself or herself is a result of his or her experiences with other people, the way they act toward him or her. The self develops during the process of socialization through social interaction.

Self-Complexity. Self-complexity is a buffer against stressful events in life. Actors with high levels of self-complexity, think about themselves from a variety of standpoints. The world is not black and white to them. They are generally more creative than people with less self-complexity.

Self-Disclosure. Self-disclosure refers to conversations with significant others in which we share intimate details about our hopes and dreams, fears, personal experiences, attitudes, and expectations.

Self-Esteem. Self-esteem refers to an overall evaluation we make of ourselves – either high or low.

Self-Fulfilling Prophecy. The prediction of events that do in fact come about, because of one's belief in the prediction and enactment or lack of enactment on that belief, thus reinforcing the belief, i.e., if a person or group predicts and deeply believes that certain events will come about, that person or group will (sometimes unconsciously) modify behaviors or engage in those behaviors that will create those situations that will cause the predicted events to come about.

Self-Handicapping. Self-handicapping refers to the deliberate sabotage of one's own performance. You put up obstacles to success in order to have a plausible explanation for a poor performance.

Self-Knowledge. Self-knowledge is the understanding of one's self, or of one's own character, powers, limitations, etc.

Self-Monitors. Self-monitors are people who are aware of their self-presentation in different social settings and who look to the attitudes, beliefs, and behaviors of others to guide them.

Self-Presentation. Self-presentation refers to our efforts to control the impression we make on others. It involves our dress, mannerisms, symbols, language, behavior, body language, and so on that we rely upon during interactions with each other.

Self-Schema. Self-schemas are highly organized set of beliefs about oneself. A self-schema refers to the usual ways in which we think about ourselves.

Self-Verification. Self-verification is the motivation to maintain a consistent sense of self.

Sexism. Sexism is the belief that women and men have different capacities and potentials as the result of innate biological differences. Sexism results in discriminatory or abusive behavior towards members of the opposite sex.

Significant Others. Significant others are parents, siblings, close friends, teachers, bosses, lovers, spouses, and our own children from whom we seek reflected appraisal. Because most of us choose friends and social locations staffed with similar others, and because significant others tend to be in our lives for a long time, continuity in these "reflected_appraisals" contributes to a feeling of self-stability.

Social Competence. People who are socially competent understand how to behave in almost any social setting and make good role models for others in the group.

Social Contagion. Social contagion refers to a given behavior that spreads automatically and easily, and often decays as quickly as it spreads.

Social Control. Social control refers the means and processes by which a group secures its members' conformity to its expectations - to its values, its ideology, its norms, and to the appropriate roles that are attached to the various status positions in the group.

Social Dilemma. Social dilemma refers to a situation where an outcome desirable for you is undesirable for the group.

Social Distance. Social distance refers to the gulf between the experiences of the affluent and the poor. Also refers to the self-imposed boundaries people often maintain.

Social Dominance Orientation. People with a social dominance orientation *want* his or her group to dominate everyone else. They often feel that it is necessary to step on others to get ahead in life and that those at the top deserve more power and influence. Conversely, they feel that those at the bottom deserve less because they are *worth* less.

Social Exchange Theory. Social exchange theory suggests that affiliation and friendship are motivated by the desire to maximize rewards and minimize costs. From this perspective, people are rational beings who calculate the costs and benefits of affiliation, much like a financial transaction.

Social Exclusion. Social exclusion relates to the alienation or disenfranchisement of certain people within a society. It is often connected to some degree to the disabled, racial minorities, women, and the elderly.

Social Facilitation. Social facilitation refers to performance that is improved by the presence of others.

Social Identity. Social identity refers to attributes such as your sex, ethnicity, race, religion, age, social class, social status, occupation, level of education, and the like.

Social Inhibition. Social inhibition refers to performance that is hindered by the presence of others

Social Integration. The bringing together of people from diverse backgrounds so that they share common social experiences and develop commonly held norms, attitudes, and beliefs.

Social Learning Theory. Social learning theory is a theory of socialization that focuses on learning through the imitation of models.

Social Loafers. Social loafers are those in the group who rely on others to get things done.

Social Network. A social network is a social structure made up of individuals or organizations that are tied by one or more specific types of relations.

Social Norms. Social norms are shared rules and expectations about how members of certain groups, such as families, should behave.

Social Organization. Social organization refers to human society in which we are directly engaged in the production of, and constitution of, the social environments in which we live.

Social Penetration. Social penetration refers to trying to get to know our partner's inner self. The depth of the disclosure may increase, and personal information about our inner most thoughts and emotions are shared.

Social Psychology. Social psychology refers to the study of the effects of social environments on the psychological functioning of individuals.

Social Roles. Social roles are clusters of norms that apply to anyone in a particular position in a group, such as the family.

Social Structure. Social structure is the institutional framework that makes for order in daily, weekly, and yearly interaction between people. It is social institutions that promote the necessary order to make social structure possible. Societies are "divided" generally into two components - social structure and social processes - that interpenetrate each other; i.e., are dialectically interrelated. Social structure is the institutional framework that makes for order in daily, weekly, and yearly interaction between people. It is social institutions that promote the necessary order to make social structure possible.

Socialization. Socialization is a lifelong process whereby we learn and internalize the attitudes, values, beliefs, and norms of our culture and develop a sense of self.

Sociation. Sociation is a predisposition toward interaction with other humans, possibly an instinct or drive to create and acquire language. The nature of the interaction will be socially conditioned by whatever group the individual happens to be born into.

Spoiled Identity. Spoiled identity refers to groups of people often ridiculed by society or held up as examples of bad behavior

Status Set. Status set refers to the entire collection of social statuses occupied by an individual or group.

Status. Status is a socially defined position in a social structure. It is a position that an individual occupies in a group, such as leader or follower; doctor or nurse; mother or son; student or professor, etc. A status can also be a specific position of one group in relation to another group, such as executives and secretaries in a large office.

Stereotype Threat. Stereotype threat refers to the fear that one may confirm a negative stereotype held about one's group.

Stereotype. A stereotype is a rigid, oversimplified, and illogical belief that is applied to all members of a group or social category.

Super Ego. Super ego refers to the reflection of values, beliefs, morals, rules, and norms of behavior internalized by the individual during socialization. The superego functions as conscience and is the root cause of feelings of guilt and anxiety within individuals.

Symbolic Interaction Theory. Symbolic interaction theory is a theory influenced by the ideas of two early sociologists, Charles H. Cooley and George Herbert Mead. The basis behind symbolic interaction theory is that the individual develops a personality through interaction with others and by using symbols to define who they are.

Symbols. Symbols are objects, sounds, names, or shared meanings created by a group that stands for something else, especially a material thing that stands for something that is not material. The bald eagle is a symbol of the United States of America.

Take the Self-as-Other. Taking the self-as-other refers to inferring your personal characteristics from observing and evaluating your own behavior.

Taking the Role-of-the-Other. Taking the role-of-the-other refers to examining yourself from the point of view of others.

Theocracy. A theocracy is a state dominated by religious leaders and religious institutions.

Triad. A triad is a group of three people, with more varied and complex role possibilities than a dyad.

Truth-Wins Rule. In this truth-wins situation, there is likely an obvious or correct proposal that makes more sense than other proposals that are flawed. The Truth-Wins rule is likely to be agreed upon for extremely important decisions where the costs of making a mistake would be very negative.

Unanimity Rule. Under the unanimity rule no course of action can be decided upon and no decision made unless all the members of the group agree without dissent.

Values. Values refer to the standards by which our culture defines what is good or bad, desirable or undesirable, beautiful or ugly. Values serve as broad guidelines that define how things ought to be.

Voice. Voice refers to raising an issue for discussion. When a problem is voiced, committed partners try to rescue the relationship by talking about the problem.

Working Self-Concept. Working self-concept is the part of the self that is relevant to the particular situation in which you are involved.

SUBJECT INDEX